MAYA EXODUS

Maya Exodus

Indigenous Struggle for Citizenship in Chiapas

HEIDI MOKSNES

University of Oklahoma Press : Norman

Publication of this book is made possible through the generosity of Edith Kinney Gaylord.

Library of Congress Cataloging-in-Publication Data

Moksnes, Heidi.
  Maya exodus : indigenous struggle for citizenship in Chiapas / Heidi Moksnes.
    p. cm.
  Includes bibliographical references and index.
  ISBN 978-0-8061-4292-0 (pbk. : alk. paper)   1. Tzotzil Indians—Mexico—Chenalhó—Politics and government.   2. Tzotzil Indians—Mexico—Chenalhó—Government relations.   3. Tzotzil Indians—Mexico—Chenalhó—Religion.
4. Liberation theology—Mexico—Chenalhó.   5. Indian Catholics—Mexico—Chenalhó.   6. Self-determination, National—Mexico—Chenalhó.   7. Citizenship—Mexico—Chenalhó.   8. Chenalhó (Mexico)—Social conditions.
9. Chenalhó (Mexico)—Economic conditions.   10. Chenalhó (Mexico)—Politics and government.   I. Title.
  F1221.T9M64 2012
  323.1197'428707275–dc23
                                                                2012017572

To Ivana and Alvin

Contents

Illustrations

FIGURES

MAPS

Preface and Acknowledgments

This book is in several ways the result of the way my life has become intertwined with the lives of Catholic villagers of San Pedro Chenalhó in the highlands of Chiapas. At the time of my first and main fieldwork in Chenalhó in the mid-1990s, this interconnection was already apparent. We occupied distinct sites in an interrelated but unequal world, where Pedrano Catholics sought international support for their political struggle against marginalization and poverty, and where I, as a privileged foreigner, was allowed to take part in their lives as a witness. We also increasingly expressed ourselves in the same sphere of discourse, with concepts such as indigenous peoples, human rights, and citizenship.

This interconnection became even more pronounced in 1997, the year after I finished fieldwork, when Pedrano Catholics and their political association, Las Abejas, became international headline news when they fell victim to paramilitary violence culminating in the massacre of forty-five unarmed members in the village of Acteal. In my own country of Sweden, as in many other countries, politicians under pressure from Chiapas support groups demanded an investigation into the protection of human rights in Mexico. These support groups also collected money for the displaced families of Chenalhó and invited Las Abejas representatives to their countries to speak. For some years, my host family and I exchanged greetings and letters back and forth via Swedish journalists and activists who, like thousands of other foreigners, visited Chenalhó. Ever since, I have seen the familiar faces of friends and acquaintances in Chenalhó appear in television documentaries, newspapers, and websites.

Over the years, I have followed the news of developments in Chenalhó and the situation of Pedrano Catholics, and I have watched Las Abejas become a symbol, for the global pro-Zapatista movement, of pacifist indigenous resistance in Chiapas. I have tried to comply with my responsibilities as a witness, writing in Swedish journals and speaking on Swedish radio and in public lectures, and striving, with other activists, to influence Swedish and European politicians to put pressure on the Mexican government to change its politics toward Maya people in Chiapas. For many years now, I seem to have lived partly turned toward a distant Chenalhó and the people I came to know there, and to feel a continual yearning to be there.

I am forever grateful to Pedrano Catholics in Chenalhó for allowing and enabling me to write this book. My particular thanks go to the members of the chapel group of Yibeljoj, most of whom now live in Nuevo Yibeljoj, who graciously let me participate in their chapel services throughout my stay, and the many women and men in the group who shared their life stories and reflections with me in interviews. I am also indebted to the municipal group of catechists in Chenalhó, who, like the leaders of Las Abejas, kindly agreed to my presence in their meetings, many also offering individual interviews on various issues.

Above all, I am indebted to my host family during my year in Chenalhó. Mariano Pérez Sántiz and Antonia Ruiz Pérez and their three children at the time, Patricia, Manuel de Jesús, and Lilia, opened their home and hearts for me. Mariano's mother, Apolonia Sántiz Jiménez, widow and head of the lineage compound, took special care to make sure I felt welcome as their guest, and we quickly found ways to make jokes across language barriers. Her other adult children—Martha, Marcela, Rosa, Felipe, Juan, Vicente, Roberto, and Juan—and their families also treated me affectionately. With all of them, I have come to share a cherished friendship that still continues.

Sebastián Gómez Pérez, Vicente Pérez Sántiz, José Vázquez, and the only non-Pedrano, Merit Ichin Santiesteban, helped me as interpreters in the interviews I conducted in Tzotzil. Special thanks go to the Pedranos who did the tedious work of transcribing and translating many hours of recordings: Sebastián Gómez Pérez, Gustavo Jiménez, José Alfredo Jiménez Pérez, Mariano Pérez Sántiz, Alonzo Vázquez, and José Vázquez.

Sebastián also assisted me after I left Mexico, making sure the transla-
tions were sent to me.

In 2006, four of these Pedranos—Gustavo, José Alfredo, Mariano, and
Sebastián—became my collaborators in a second research project among
Tzotzil migrants to San Cristóbal. They conducted interviews of exceptional quality that highlighted what came to be central issues also for the
present book. In 2008, they all came to Sweden to discuss the results, and
I was happy to finally be able to reciprocate some of the hospitality I had
been shown. Over the years, the same four men have also responded to
various questions I have sent them by fax, and increasingly, e-mail. I am
fortunate to be able to illustrate this book with pictures taken by José
Alfredo Jiménez Pérez, today a skilled videographer, to complement my
own photos from the 1990s.

I am certain many Pedrano Catholics would disagree with much of
what I describe, and I want to stress that I here present only my own, and
partial, understanding. However, my hope is that most would not greatly
disapprove of the broader picture I am trying to paint of their lives, concerns, and struggles.

Throughout the years in San Cristóbal de Las Casas, from the time I
first arrived in 1985 as a young, inquisitive, and rather unfocused student,
and up until my later visits, I have benefited from the competence, assistance, and kindness of many people, of whom I will here just mention
a few: the late Andrés Aubry, Araceli Burguete, Inés Castro, Yolanda Castro, Patricia Figueroa Fuentes, Gustavo García, Judith Herrera Jácome,
Julieta Hernández, Stan Malinowitz, Toni Martell, Mari Carmen Mar-
tínez, the late Nancy Modiano, Georgina Molina, Gaspar Morquecho,
June Nash, Margarito Ruiz, Diane and Jan Rus, Vern Sterk, and Miguel
Vargas. With their different experiences and perspectives on Maya communities and Chiapas, whether as activists, scholars, or otherwise, they
have furthered my own understanding and made me feel at home, many
becoming longtime friends.

I am indebted to Esther Lorenzana, a pastoral worker in Chenalhó,
whose remarkable generosity made me feel welcome and cared for during my fieldwork. I am also grateful to Padre Miguel Chanteau for his
kindness toward me. Thanks are due also to the other pastoral workers

of Las Hermanas del Divino Pastor and to the indigenous lay nuns of Comunidad de Indígenas Misioneras.

This book covers a development unfolding over many years, and the process of writing has been long; it draws on my PhD dissertation from 2003 as well as later research and has benefited from the support of more people than I can give credit to here. My thanks go to researchers and fellow PhD students in the Department of Social Anthropology, University of Gothenburg, Sweden, for inspirational discussions throughout the years and for helpful comments on papers I presented at seminars. Special thanks to Kaj Århem, tireless and supportive tutor of my dissertation. Bruce Kapferer read excerpts from earlier chapters, and I am grateful for his thoughtful comments. I was delighted to have George Collier as the external opponent at my PhD defense, and this book is to a significant degree influenced by his insight that "human rights" can be a double-edged political tool.

I want to thank my current colleagues at the Uppsala Centre for Sustainable Development at Uppsala University for supporting me through the various stages of completing this book, even when I set aside other tasks in order to write. Special thanks go to Lars Rudebeck, and at Stockholm University, Beppe Karlsson, for helpful and encouraging comments on parts of the text. I also wish to thank the anonymous reviewers for the University of Oklahoma Press for their highly valuable comments, and Alessandra Jacobi Tamulevich, acquisitions editor at the press, for her continuous encouragement during the long revision process. The research for this book was made possible by a grant for my dissertation project from Sida, the Swedish International Development Cooperation Agency, and support from the Department of Social Anthropology, University of Gothenburg, as well as a second grant from Sida for research focusing on the Maya organization of urban neighborhoods in San Cristóbal.

Several parts of this work have been published elsewhere, and I wish to thank the publishers for granting me permission to reproduce portions here. Parts of the introduction and chapter 8 first appeared in *Social Analysis* (2004), also published in *State, Sovereignty, War: Civil Violence in Emerging Global Realities,* edited by Bruce Kapferer (2004). Parts of chapters 1 and 6 appeared in *Journal of Peasant Studies* (2005), also published in *Rural Chiapas Ten Years after the Zapatista Uprising*, edited by Sarah Washbrook (2006). Parts of chapter 7 appeared in *European Review of Latin American and Caribbean Studies (Revista Europea de Estudios Latino-americanos y del Caribe)* (2004).

Throughout the years, Jan Rus, longtime scholar of Tzotzil peoples, has been a special mentor and has encouraged and challenged my learning process about the Maya highlands. He and Christine Eber, with whom I am very proud to share Chenalhó as a field, have brought their expertise to reading and commenting either on chapters or on the entire manuscript. Through our e-mail exchange over the years, they have also generously shared everything from knowledge and data to reflections on various issues that I have wrestled with.

Furthermore, I am grateful to Kaj Århem, Jan Rus, and Nancy Modiano for their encouragement when I first worried about the wisdom of doing fieldwork in a remote rural community in a wheelchair, each giving arguments that made me go ahead. I owe special thanks to the activists of various Chiapas support groups that existed in Sweden for some years, as well as to the students of the Chiapas courses at Färnebo Folkhögskola, with whom I could share my concerns for what was going on in faraway Chiapas, and the (vain) efforts to influence international politics.

Special gratitude goes to my parents Kjell and Astrid Moksnes, who taught me to trust my own abilities and choices, and to not take limitations for granted. My brother Per-Olav, his wife, Claudia Cabrera, and their children, Anton and Clara, have been encouraging through the years, and made both the United States and Guatemala part of my extended family–thereby further interconnecting my different worlds. I also want to thank my friends, especially Agneta Sjöberg and Jasenka Trtak, for being so patient with my unsocial behavior for repeated periods now over many years, first, with the dissertation, later, the book manuscript.

Last, I want thank my partner and fellow anthropologist Ivana Maček and our son, Alvin, who, very longed-for, was born in 2004. Their love, Alvin's spirited humor, and Ivana's unending and multifaceted support and companionship ever since my initial fieldwork, made it possible for me to complete this book. I am happy to have been able to share Chiapas with both, and hope to continue doing so.

Notes on Orthography

This book uses the orthography for Tzotzil employed by the Centro Estatal de Lenguas, Arte y Literatura Indígenas (Center for Indigenous Languages, Art, and Literature, or CELALI) and most of the newer generations of literate Tzotzil speakers. It spells the [k] sound with "k" instead of earlier orthography using "c" or "q," and "ts" instead of "tz." However, I continue, like most, to write "Tzotzil" with a "z." Tzotzil uses glottal stops after certain consonants and vowels. These are marked with an apostrophe.

Pronunciation: "ch" is pronounced like "change" in English, "j" is pronounced like the "j" in Spanish "justo," and "x" is pronounced "sh," so that "mixa" (a type of ceremony) is pronounced "misha."

Spanish words will appear in quotation marks at first mention; thereafter they will be in regular typeface. Tzotzil words will be italicized throughout.

Glossary and List of Acronyms

(Tzotzil terms are in italics)

AEDPCH Asamblea Estatal Democrática del Pueblo Chiapaneco (Democratic State Assembly of the People of Chiapas)

ANIPA Asamblea Nacional Indígena Plural por la Autonomía (National Pluralistic Indigenous Assembly for Autonomy)

anjel Pedrano mountain deity

calpul customary subdivision of the municipality of Chenalhó

catechist lay leader serving in a Catholic chapel or church

cargo position in the Maya municipal politico-religious leadership (also other positions taken in service of the community)

CCRI Comité Clandestino Revolucionario Indígena (Clandestine Revolutionary Indigenous Committee), the highest leadership of EZLN

CENAMI Centro Nacional de Ayuda a las Misiones Indígenas (National Center for Assistance to the Indigenous Missions)

CEOIC Consejo Estatal de Organizaciones Indígenas y Campesinas (State Council of Indigenous and Peasant Organizations)

Ch'ul Banamil Holy Earth, Pedrano feminine deity

CIOAC Central Independiente de Obreros Agrícolas y Campesinos (Independent Confederation of Agricultural Workers and Peasants)

CNPA Coordinadora Nacional Plan de Ayala (National Coordinating Committee of Plan de Ayala)

COCOPA Comisión de Concordia y Pacificación (Commission for Conciliation and Pacification)

CODIMUJ Coordinadora Diocesana de Mujeres (Diocesan Coordination of Women)

CONAI Comisión Nacional de Intermediación (National Mediation Commission)

CONASUPO Compañía Nacional de Subsistencias Populares (National Company of Subsidized Basic Products)

conjunto musical band used in Catholic chapel groups

costumbre term used in Chenalhó to refer to "traditional" religion, contrasted with Catholic or Protestant religion

creyente "believer," commonly used in the diocese to designate ordinary church members (cf. **catechists**)

CRIACH Consejo de Representantes Indígenas de los Altos de Chiapas (Council of Indigenous Representatives of the Chiapas Highlands)

ejido agricultural cooperative created by agrarian reform, its members holding individual land titles for usufruct

EZLN Ejército Zapatista de Liberación Nacional (Zapatista Army of National Liberation)

finca large farm or plantation

FIPI Frente Independiente de Pueblos Indios (Independent Front of Indigenous Peoples)

Frente Cardenista Partido del Frente Cardenista de Reconstrucción Nacional (Party of the Cardenist Front for National Reconstruction, PFCRN), no longer in existence

FZLN Frente Zapatista de Liberación Nacional (Zapatista Front for National Liberation)

j-ilol traditional Pedrano healer

INMECAFE Instituto Mexicano del Café (Mexican Coffee Institute)

k'ajal one of two geographic-political sections of Chenalhó (cf. *olon*)

kabildo vinik ceremonial leader, responsible for carrying out *mixa*

kuxlejal life

mantal order or directive

mats' drink made of ground corn mixed with water

mestizo term commonly used in Mexico to designate the population that does not identify itself as indigenous; descendants of indigenous-white parentage *mixa*   ceremonial procession to the holy sites of a community; "mass"

NAFTA   North American Free Trade Agreement

NGO   nongovernmental organization

OCEZ   Organización Campesina Emiliano Zapata (Emiliano Zapata Peasant Organization)

olon   one of two geographic-political sections of Chenalhó (cf. *k'ajal*)

PAN   Partido Acción Nacional (National Action Party)

paraje   common term in Chiapas for rural village

pasado   a person who has held a **cargo**

Pedrano   indigenous inhabitant of San Pedro Chenalhó

PRD   Partido de la Revolución Democrática (Party of the Democratic Revolution)

PRI   Partido Revolucionario Institucional (Institutional Revolutionary Party)

PROCAMPO   Programa de Apoyo Directo al Campo (National Program for Direct Rural Support), a state subsidy to peasants for the production of basic grains

PROGRESA   Programa de Educación, Salud y Alimentación (Education, Health, and Nutrition Program)

PST   Partido Socialista de los Trabajadores (Socialist Workers Party), no longer in existence

SOCAMA   Solidaridad Campesina-Magisterial (Peasant-Teacher Solidarity)

totil-me'il   ("father-mother") the historical ancestors, political leaders of the past, as well as a deity

Tzotzil   second-largest Mayan language in Chiapas

Xi'Nich   Coordinadora de Organizaciones Sociales Indígenas (Coalition of Indigenous Social Organizations)

Chronology
Key Events for Pedrano Catholics

1960   Samuel Ruiz is installed as bishop of the Diocese of San Cristóbal de Las Casas, Chiapas.

1974   Ruiz hosts First Indigenous Congress in San Cristóbal.

1975   First Diocesan Assembly held with pastoral workers. The bishop declares the diocese's "preferential option for the poor."

1992   Large indigenous demonstration in San Cristóbal manifests 500 years of resistance.

       Catholics in San Pedro Chenalhó form Las Abejas.

1994   The Zapatista Army of National Liberation (EZLN) occupies municipal buildings throughout Chiapas on January 1, initiating a rebellion.

       Catholic Pedranos create Sociedad Civil in Chenalhó as part of a "Peace Process" instigated by Bishop Ruiz to halt the conflict between EZLN and the government. Sociedad Civil soon merges with Las Abejas.

1996   EZLN and the Mexican government sign Peace Accords on Indigenous Rights and Culture, known as the San Andrés Accords, on February 16.

1997   The Acteal massacre on December 22 is the culmination of paramilitary terror against members of Las Abejas and Zapatista base groups in Chenalhó.

1998   Las Abejas denounces the massacre before the United Nations in Geneva and writes a letter to a Secretary General Kofi Annan asking for UN intervention to establish justice and peace in Chiapas.

The first Pedranos are sentenced for involvement in the Acteal massacre. In subsequent years, a total of 80 Pedrano men are sentenced, as well as 15 lower-level officials, one of whom is Pedrano, the former municipal president.

2000   Partido Revolucionario Institucional (PRI) suffers historic defeat by Partido Acción Nacional (PAN) in federal elections.

Samuel Ruiz retires as bishop of the diocese and is replaced by Felipe Arizmendi.

Displaced members of Las Abejas from Yibeljoj leave their refugee camp in X'oyep and establish Nuevo Yibeljoj, adjacent to Yibeljoj.

2001   Remaining displaced members of Las Abejas leave their refugee camps in Chenalhó to return to their home villages.

2006   PAN wins the federal elections.

2008   Las Abejas is divided into two separate organizations: Sociedad Civil Las Abejas ("Las Abejas de Acteal") and Asociación Civil Las Abejas ("Las Abejas A.C.").

2009   Mexican Supreme Court decides on August 12 that serious irregularities during the trials require the release of 29 Pedrano men sentenced for involvement in the Acteal massacre, and the retrial of another 16 men.

Maps

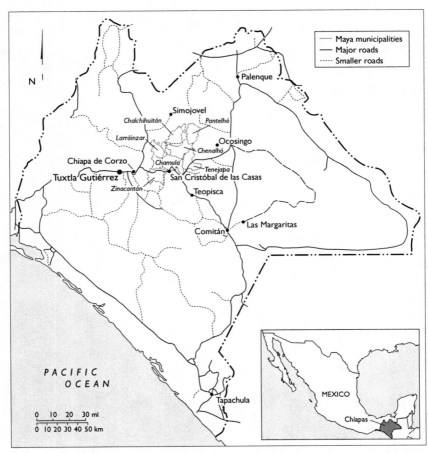

Map 1. State of Chiapas, showing the borders of major highland Maya municipalities. Cartography by Bill Nelson.

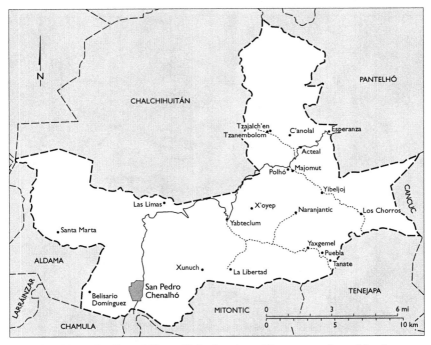

Map 2.   Municipality of Chenalhó, showing villages mentioned in the text.
The municipal capital is called San Pedro Chenalhó. Cartography by Bill
Nelson.

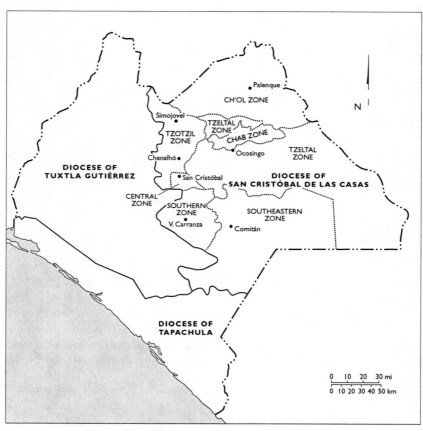

Map 3.   Catholic Diocese of San Cristóbal de Las Casas, showing the zones of the diocese's seven pastoral teams. ("CHAB" is an acronym for Chilón, Arena, Bajachón.) Cartography by Bill Nelson.

Introduction

One of the first nights with my host family in Chenalhó, as we sat around the fire in the kitchen hut after the evening meal, my host, Mariano Pérez Sántiz, asked if I knew the story of Exodus. He told me about the people of Israel who had lived under slavery and the oppressive pharaoh, and their flight from Egypt under the leadership of Moses. Their own bishop, Samuel Ruiz, he said, was the present-day Moses who would lead them, the indigenous peasants, toward liberation from oppression and injustice. In contrast to the Israelites, he added, they would not have to travel physically and leave their homes. Their Exodus would be a spiritual and political one.[1]

Over and over during my yearlong stay in San Pedro Chenalhó, Chiapas, I heard Catholic villagers talk of their hope for Exodus and about the poverty and suffering they wished to escape. Poverty is what most highland Mayas describe as the principal burden of their lives and as something that sharply distinguishes them from others, the non-indigenous. In various ways, they strive to control the degree and impact of this poverty, and many hope that someday they, or their grandchildren, will finally see it end.

For most of the twentieth century, one such strategy, besides their own hard labor, was to create a relationship of clientelism with the Mexican state; that is, to petition for land and development programs in exchange for their political loyalty. This approach offered certain results, such as land titles, support for cultivation, and improved infrastructure. From the 1970s on, however, as poverty continued, a growing number of Mayas began to define the government as the root of the problem. Its policies were seen as exploiting and discriminating against indigenous peoples economically, politically, and socially. Many rejected the bonds of loyalty and dependency they had developed with the state. Since the 1990s, Mayas have increasingly demanded to be fully recognized as citizens democratically participating in the nation-state. Employing a global discourse on human rights, many Mayas now claim the "right to have rights" (Arendt, e.g., 1968:296–98) and refer to universally acknowledged entitlements defined and established in international conventions as well as in the Mexican constitution. They further demand the right to "difference" in relation to the dominant mestizo population—the right to affirm and rearticulate their identity as indigenous people.

Mayas thus participate in a global transformation in the nature of local struggles, in which contemporary rights discourses and identity politics have become widespread means to attempt to accomplish substantial improvement in people's lives. By sharing with me and other outsiders their story of poverty and the struggle to escape it, Mayas in Chiapas are not only denouncing their marginalization, they are also seeking recognition that their living conditions violate shared notions of rights-based justice, and claiming their place in a global civil society that protests such conditions.

This book is about the longed-for liberation of a group of Mayas from oppression and poverty—their Exodus. To achieve this liberation, they have appropriated a rights-focused political discourse to demand better living conditions and an improved position in the Mexican nation-state. I describe the various consequences of this struggle, the most notorious of which was the paramilitary persecution they suffered in 1997, culminating in a massacre in the village of Acteal, where forty-five persons, the majority women and children, were killed. The experience of this terror, and the enormous international attention it drew, has spurred them to press their claims and increase their participation in a global arena of political struggle.

This book focuses on a group of Catholic believers in the Tzotzil-speaking municipality of San Pedro Chenalhó in highland Chiapas, and their political association, Las Abejas.[2] In villages throughout Chenalhó, they have formed chapel groups aligned with the Catholic Diocese of

San Cristóbal de Las Casas. Like Catholic Mayas elsewhere in the diocese, they describe themselves as followers of "the Word of God," "la Palabra de Dios," referring to the Bible. They differentiate themselves from Protestants and from practitioners of the "traditional" religion, called "costumbre" in Chenalhó.[3]

Catholic "Pedranos"—as Maya inhabitants of the municipality of San Pedro Chenalhó are known—attribute their striving for societal transformation to their religious devotion, which encourages them to endure patiently the efforts and sacrifices demanded by their struggle. With a perspective influenced by the formerly explicit leanings of the Catholic Diocese toward liberation theology, as well as by politicized indigenous discourses, they explain their present predicament and their hope for change. Catholic villagers commonly hold that the poverty of indigenous peoples in Mexico originated with Spanish colonial rule, was perpetuated by subsequent national governments through centuries of exploitation, and continues today under low-intensity warfare waged by military and paramilitary groups against Mayas who oppose this oppression. They say their suffering is contrary to the will of God, who will help set them free.

Their notion of a universal God, who cares for a humanity where all are created equal and condemns the injustice wrought against the poor, has also laid the ground for their embrace of universal rights and the conventions and laws where these are articulated. Catholic Pedranos often emphasize that the treatment to which they are subject violates rights established both in the Mexican constitution and in the United Nations regulations concerning general human rights, the rights of indigenous peoples, and for example, the rights of civil populations in warfare. Thereby, God and the notion of universal rights constitute for Catholic villagers absolute verification of their mistreatment.

While Pedrano Catholics engage in political and theological discourses formed largely in global arenas, their interpretations and motivations are situated in a specific, local context. In this book, I am concerned with how these global, "modernist" notions of society, identity, and rights in their localized usage are made to speak about particular life-worlds and experiences, and about a possible different state of affairs. I look at how Pedrano Catholics, through claiming a rights-based citizenship, endeavor to renegotiate their position in the Mexican nation-state, but also how they are restructuring local Maya life.

A central concern is how the Mexican state has responded to Pedrano Catholics' claims with measures ranging from passive avoidance to violent repression. This leads me to discuss, in the last chapter, what possibilities Pedrano Catholics have to achieve the citizenship they demand. Stressing principled demands for collective rights to social justice, they refuse to accept limited federal programs aimed at individual families, which they regard as a continuation of earlier divisive and co-optive government strategies. However, since social equality is not on the government's agenda, they find few alternative paths to redress their poverty in any concrete way.

This catch-22 stems from the contradictions produced by neoliberal governance. As Jon Shefner (2008:200) puts it, the aim of democratization—the flagship of neoliberalism—is to "enhance citizens' influence over the state," while the aim of neoliberal politics is to remove the realm of economics from the state, instead leaving it to market forces. This is what John Comaroff and Jean Comaroff (1997:126) have described as democracy becoming a "small idea," no longer able to improve life conditions. They suggest that with the parallel spread of market economy and democratization, "'the people' are being empowered in the politics of the state at the very moment when the state is becoming irrelevant and the politics that count are moving elsewhere," and they further ask: "Is democracy rising because it has become politically beside the point?" The experiences of Pedrano Catholics and Las Abejas thus elucidate, I suggest, the limits of rights-based citizenship claims within the neoliberal state.

SOCIAL PROTEST AND CLAIMS FOR RIGHTS

The notion of universal human rights has become one of the most dominant political values worldwide, acknowledged—in theory—by governments and intergovernmental bodies, corporations, nongovernmental organizations (NGOs), and advocacy networks. Actors with diverse, often colliding interests invoke "human rights" and struggle over definitions and implementation in various political arenas. Rights discourse is used increasingly by the marginalized poor, including indigenous peoples, when organizing social protest and presenting claims to decision makers, whether governments, corporations, or international bodies such as the World Bank. They frequently turn to international networks of NGOs and activists to mobilize support for their claims, often using ratification by governments or other parties to official rights conventions as a tool to exert pressure, with, at times, at least partially successful results (Brysk 2002; Wilson and Mitchell 2003; Shafir and Brysk 2006; Goodale and Merry 2007). Thus, human rights discourse has offered local actors a new tool to contest different forms of oppression.

The spreading use of rights discourse is part of the increasing connection between local and global struggles for social change. A significant number of rural and urban poor today have gained access to new transnational arenas in which to act and draw support for local struggles. Finding themselves increasingly exposed to global economic and political decisions affecting their livelihoods, but over which they have little control, they use these arenas to gain leverage in their claims. The emergence of transnational civil societies—temporary convergences of disparate actors defining at least partially shared political agendas—has made it possible to mobilize international backing for local causes as well as define jointly held objectives on more global scales (Keck and Sikkink 1998; Brysk 2000; Khagram, Riker, and Sikkink 2002; Naidoo 2010). The Zapatista uprising in Chiapas beginning in 1994, and the international support network that quickly evolved, united by a joint criticism of neoliberal politics, is one of the more salient examples of this development (Castells 1997; Nash 2001). To a significant degree, the increasing interconnection between local struggles and transnational networks and NGOs has strengthened local agency, and sometimes, as in the case of Chiapas, has eased dependence on state institutions and resources.

In this collaboration, the use of shared discourses has been of great importance. By framing local grievances in globally translatable idioms, complaints and demands not only make sense, but can be seen as significant to a wide range of people, thus enabling a broad mobilization of support (Keck and Sikkink 1998). It should be noted, however, that this sharing is possible through implicit agreements made between parties with unequal access to power and resources, for marginalized groups are highly dependent on the agendas of others. Local struggles have significantly more chance to gain attention and support when presented in terms that reflect the discourses and issues that enjoy high global currency at the moment (Bob 2005). While some groups will be able to mobilize massive transnational campaigns, others may never reach outside the immediate region.

Furthermore, the appropriation of globalized discourses influences to some extent the way politics on the ground are conducted (Merry 2006). The use of rights discourse, it should be emphasized, constitutes "one historically specific way of conceptualizing the relations of entitlement and obligation," in which marginalized groups present claims referring to "rights" instead of "needs" (Cowan, Dembour, and Wilson 2001:1, 12). Some authors stress the continuing influence of Western law on rights discourse, especially concerning the perception of civil and political rights, which structure and delimit the entailed notions of political agency (J. Collier, Maurer, and Suárez-Navaz 1995; Woodiwiss 2002).

When local actors use these discourses for their own purposes, however, they also "distort" established usage, becoming part of the continuous contestation of how to define and apply rights, or how society should be formed. Thus, these struggles in the global margins are both constituted by the hegemonies to which they are subject, and at the same time, resistant to and disruptive of dominant conceptions and hierarchies (Holston 2008; Pitarch, Speed, and Leyva-Solano 2008; Dagnino 2010).

To a great extent, the claims that local actors present through rights discourse—for land, social services, or influence—are age-old. Demands for dignity and autonomy have likewise long been integral to resistance to different forms of exploitation (Scott 1990). Backing these demands by an invocation of "rights," however, the claimants intend to alter their relation to the broader society and remake ascribed identities that have defined them as politically subordinate and socially inferior subjects. They often link their rights-based claims to demands for an effective realization of citizenship, where their integration as members of the nation-state implies access to rights articulated in the constitution and laws. Marginalized people, who in practice have been without rights, thus begin to define themselves as subjects with the rights of citizens

(Dagnino 2003; 2007; Jelin 2003; Yashar 2005). This, of course, corresponds with a classical liberal notion of citizenship as entailing "a juridical status of legal personhood" that grants rights (Marshall 1964; Cohen 1999:248). But, similar to the historic process Thomas Marshall (1964) describes, the demands raised often attempt to contest and extend the conventional limits of citizenship.

The claim for rights often includes the liberal notion of basic civil and political rights, known as the "first generation of rights," as held by the individual citizen and defined in the UN International Covenant on Civil and Political Rights of 1966. But the main focus among the new actors is often the claim for the "collective enjoyment of social justice" (Harvey 1998:27). This involves what is known as the "second generation of rights," as defined in the UN International Covenant on Economic, Social and Cultural Rights of 1976. When the United Nations had articulated the preceding Universal Declaration of Human Rights of 1948, significant tensions had arisen between different nations regarding the priority of these two generations of rights, resulting in the authoring of the two separate covenants of 1966 and 1976. Among the radical left in Latin America, for example, this distinction of rights and the common emphasis by successive U.S. governments on the first generation of rights, with its explicit protection of private property, caused a deep suspicion of rights claims for many years and a preference for other forms for struggle (Engler 2000). Increasingly, however, Latin American activists began to employ rights discourse in their mobilization against authoritarian regimes during the 1970s, both to protest political oppression and persecution and to demand economic and social change. In Latin America and elsewhere, especially after the end of the Cold War and the drastic decline of socialist discourses, "'rights' became the terrain on which virtually all movements for social justice and equality were waged" (Speed 2008:25).[4]

The rights demands have been further broadened to include the right to difference, whether defined by ethnicity, gender, or sexuality; differences that have been marginalized and stigmatized by dominant social groups. This development is reflected in the changing character of social movements in Latin America since the 1980s. The emergence of identity politics through ethnic, women's, and gay movements has, together with ecological and human rights movements, been intrinsic to diversifying and reconstituting the political sphere, creating new democratic spaces all through the continent (Eckstein 1989; Jelin 1996; Jelin and Hershberg 1996; Alvarez, Dagnino, and Escobar 1998; Harvey 1998).[5]

The growth of a global indigenous movement came about as part of these identity-based movements, which presented rights claims based on "difference" and self-determination. In Latin America, where organized indigenous rebellion has a history as long as colonialism, "indigenous peoples" emerged as a publicly recognized political category and collective identity during the last decades of the twentieth century (Fischer and Brown 1996; Diaz-Polanco 1997; Warren and Jackson 2002). Transforming previous class-based demands into a discourse centering on ethnic identity, indigenous organizations critique the present structure of nation-states and the nationalist projects of cultural homogenization. Instead, they demand collective rights for indigenous peoples for local self-determination, and frequently, ethnically based representation in political bodies on a regional and national level (Burguete Cal y Mayor 2000; Sieder 2002; Yashar 2005, 2007).

The indigenous struggle in Latin America is highly interrelated with the growth of indigenous politicization internationally. Through their representatives, indigenous peoples since the 1970s have participated in regional, national, and global networks, forming an international community of indigenous organizations that, in spite of its heterogeneous character, has developed a shared political discourse and a largely shared political agenda (Sanders 1977; Stavenhagen 1992; Charters, Malezer, and Tauli-Corpuz 2011). The indigenous demands have gradually gained a degree of legitimacy and the support of international actors such as human rights NGOs, various activist organizations, and bodies such as the United Nations and the World Bank. This is also manifested in different international agreements, of which the most important are considered to be the International Labour Organization (ILO) Convention 169, the UN Declaration on the Rights of Indigenous Peoples, and that establishing the UN Permanent Forum on Indigenous Issues. Such broad international discourse on universally human and specifically indigenous rights has, in turn, influenced and strengthened local and national indigenous struggles (Ivison, Patton, and Sanders 2000).

Poor and marginalized groups' claims for rights and citizenship employ as well as broaden the classic notions of citizenship. These claims reveal that severe social inequalities deny large numbers of people access to the rights they supposedly have as citizens. Such groups are demanding what has been called "social citizenship"—one that is inclusive and substantive and that ensures all citizens the full exercise of their rights, including the "social rights" to welfare, to be granted by the state (Paoli and Telles 1998; de la Peña 2002; cf. Marshall 1964). Furthermore, these groups demand an expansion of the political agency entailed with the notion of *demos*, the self-ruling political community where principles of political equality and participation of all members are central (Cohen 1999; Benhabib 2004). Neil Harvey (1998:33) describes how citizenship among marginalized groups in Latin America is "a collective enterprise rather than an individual prerogative" and how "the people" is constituted as a political actor. This claim is especially developed by indigenous organizations, which commonly posit an indigenous collectivity both as the holder of rights and as political agent, and which request that constitutions recognize collective rights and collective citizenship (Stavenhagen 2002; de la Peña 2002:46; see also Dagnino 1998). And last, through their insistence on recognition, stigmatized groups demand to be acknowledged, despite their "difference," as part of an *ethnos*, "a community of shared fate, memories, and moral sympathies" (Cohen 1999; Benhabib 2004:211). This is the implication of the Zapatista slogan "Never again a Mexico without us!" Thus, the notion of citizenship is imbued with a sense of a fundamental, universal right to equality, democratic participation, and dignity through what June Nash (2001:3) describes as an "appeal to morality."

HUMAN RIGHTS AND NEOLIBERALISM

Of course, human rights are not only invoked by social movements and other groups exerting social criticism "from below." States and international institutions of the present day themselves often portray rights-based citizenship as one of the building blocks of a democratic society. In the dominant neoliberal mode of governance—albeit shaken by economic crises—as well as in classical liberal views of the state, civil and political rights are considered essential to a well-functioning civil society as a counterforce to the authoritarian drive of the state. A similar perception is established through the notion of "good governance," which emphasizes accountability, openness, and transparency as well as popular participation through decentralized state structures. The concept of "good governance" is promoted by, for example, the World Bank and the International Monetary Fund (IMF) as well as the Organisation for Economic Co-operation and Development (OECD). In neoliberalism, this mode of governance is regarded as codependent with a freely operating market economy and associated with the assurance of individual autonomy, where people can act without any undue restrictions either on the market or on civil society. In the neoliberal ideal, the role of the (downsized) state should be primarily to ensure basic institutional structures, the rule of law, and the elimination of market impediments, with many of its former functions transferred either to the market or civil society actors (Schild 1998; Mendez 2002; Turner 2003).

States following the neoliberal model are therefore withdrawing from formerly expected duties of assuring even the poor at least limited access to welfare and "common goods." Now the open market is relied upon to provide such services. In various countries in Latin America, the shift to neoliberal governance in the last decades of the twentieth century led to the end of earlier implicit "social contracts" between corporatist states—that is, states that strove to incorporate large sectors of society as allies—and their national populations. The abandonment of the social contracts commonly resulted in worsened economic conditions for the poor (Eckstein and Wickham-Crowley 2003:12–13; Yashar 2005:68).[6] In Mexico, the transformation of the political and economic system was initiated after the economic crises that began with the oil crises in the 1970s and culminated in 1982. Saved from economic collapse by huge emergency loans, the Mexican government became dependent on explicit or implied directives from the IMF, the U.S. government, and a series of private financial corporations, all of which imposed significant restrictions on its governance (Sassen 2003:75–76). The successive presidencies of Miguel de la Madrid, Carlos Salinas, and Ernesto Zedillo in the 1980s and 1990s gradually dismantled most of the previous subsidies and price controls that were aimed at supporting the impoverished Mexican peasant population, and removed agrarian reform from the national agenda. In 1992, Article 27 of the constitution was revised to open up ejidal and communal land for privatization. Federal supports to the meager peasant agricultural production were no longer seen as viable for national economic development (Smith 1991; G. Collier and Quaratiello 1999; Gledhill 2000, 2008). Mexico aimed to compete on the world market with labor and produce, and to attract national and international corporations and investors, from which all citizens were supposed to benefit.

All that remained of the former large-scale, universal social policies were strict "emergency efforts directed toward certain specific sectors of society whose survival is at risk" (Dagnino 2003:216). In Mexico, such policies have consisted of a series of highly reduced and selective programs for the most impoverished families, such as Programa Nacional de Solidaridad (PRONASOL), launched by Salinas; Programa de Educación, Salud y Alimentación (PROGRESA) of Zedillo; and its successor, the Oportunidades program of presidents Vicente Fox and Felipe Calderón, both of the PAN party. The Mexican government, as well as outside observers, has described the Oportunidades program in particular as an attempt to move away from former paternalistic bonds tying people to the ruling party and instead to strengthen citizen participation and rights (Rocha Menocal 2005:347). Some critics, however, hold that such policies tend to "emphasize the responsibility of the poor and other disadvantaged groups to secure their own well-being," while doing little to improve their actual rights as citizens (Basok and Ilcan 2006:310). Evelina Dagnino (2003:217) argues that "the targets of these policies are seen not as citizens entitled to rights but as 'needy' human beings to be dealt with by public or private charity."

On the other hand, neoliberal governance and diminishing government patronage have in many cases opened up more room for social movements and other civil society actors and allowed greater political pluralism (Holzner 2006:77). With the move toward market liberalization and in response to increasing domestic pressure as well as the demands of foreign creditors, each successive Mexican government undertook a process of democratization. This process, focusing on electoral reform, eventually led to the defeat of the Partido Revolucionario Institucional (PRI) in the presidential elections of 2000. Each administration has also manifested its concern for the protection of human rights of citizens by instituting formal instruments for oversight, including the National Human Rights Commission in 1990, followed by the formation of state commissions (Keck and Sikkink 1998:114).

Neoliberal governments thus emphasize the first-generation civil and political rights of citizenship while frequently downplaying any state responsibility to ensure second-generation rights, especially economic rights. This greatly influences the political space made accessible for citizens. While many social actors have benefited from the increased independence of civil society and the heightened demands for the rights of citizenship, they also find their political agency highly circumscribed by the broader political and legal framework. Neoliberal governance offers, and even encourages, the judicial assessment of human rights claims posed against the state, whereby states are held accountable in court for possible breaches of human rights regulations. Court rulings, however, tend to privilege the protection of civil and political rights, not economic, social, and cultural rights. Thus, for example, the property rights of landowners or corporations are commonly given priority over the economic and social rights to employment, a decent salary, housing, or collective bargaining by unions (see, e.g., Hirshl 2000; Baxi 2002; Eklund 2008). Similarly, local communities claiming the right to environmental protection or a common good such as water, for example, have found themselves on the losing end against transnational corporations' demands that commercial contracts be followed (see, e.g., Gledhill 2003n1; Spronk and Webber 2007). In a study by Ran Hirschl (2000) of three different countries, demands for economic and social rights were found to receive few or no positive court rulings, because the required interference with state regulations was regarded as a threat to human liberty and equality.[7]

Furthermore, the orientation toward courts of law implies what has been called a judicialization of politics, whereby political agency is directed toward judiciary bodies instead of bodies of political governance (Jacobson and Ruffer 2003; Sieder, Schjolden, and Angell 2005; Hirschl 2008; Couso, Huneeus, and Sieder 2010). While the possibility to achieve positive court rulings gives social movements a means to exert pressure on states, these strategies have problematic aspects. By taking issues to court instead of the streets, so to speak, traditional democratic practices of political mobilization, civic participation, and even voting are often bypassed, which reduces their role in people's political engagement. Judicialization thus diminishes popular political influence on societal governance, instead favoring the "rule of rules"—the rules the states themselves set up, nationally or internationally. Furthermore, judicial agency requires knowledge of legal texts and procedures, thus increasing the dependency of local movements on professionalized NGOs as mediators with the state (Speed and Reyes 2005). As a result, the choice to focus social protest on demands for rights, while contesting state dominance, reaffirms and strengthens the same.

The demands by indigenous organizations for *collective* rights have achieved a certain resonance, in spite of colliding with the liberal emphasis on *individual* rights. Neoliberal multiculturalism, which recognizes the right to cultural difference and has opened up spheres for a degree of local self-determination in various countries, corresponds with the decentering of the state and its diminished role in governance. In 1990, Mexico was one of the first countries to ratify ILO Convention 169 on the rights of indigenous peoples, and in 1991, Article 4 of the Mexican constitution was changed to define Mexico as a multiethnic country, granting certain cultural rights to its indigenous population, but without real implementation in government policies.[8] The Mexican government signed the Peace Accords on Indigenous Rights and Culture, known as the San Andrés Accords, in 1996, after negotiations with the Ejército Zapatista de Liberación Nacional (Zapatista Army of National Liberation, EZLN). (The San Andrés Accords were eventually transformed to a watered-down version approved by the Mexican Congress in 2001.)[9] However, as has been argued by several critics, these formal concessions do not accede to indigenous demands for control of land and natural resources, nor for broader social rights (Hale 2002, 2005; Gledhill 2008). This is a politics of the "indio permitido" (the permitted Indian), as Charles Hale (2005:24) puts it, while more costly indigenous demands continue to be rejected.

In sum, states' response to popular demands for rights has generally been to contain them within spheres that do not challenge the political and economic form of governance. Nevertheless, broad protests, of which the Zapatista uprising is the most famous Mexican example, have been mounted directly against neoliberal policies. Such protests imply a threat to the economic predictability necessary to attract and maintain investors. With decreasing resources and redistributive capacity, the Mexican government today is less able to manage opposition through state clientelism, instead resorting to overt—and less overt—repression and the "militarization of internal security" (Gledhill 2000:115–16; Collier and Collier 2005; Speed and Reyes 2005:54). One expression of this growing militarization is that the armed forces have begun to participate directly with the local and federal police with greater use of force, in Mexico as well as other Latin American countries (Ferreyra and Segura 2000; López-Montiel 2000; Pereira and Davis 2000). Militarization has escalated dramatically in Mexico with the government's attempt to control the drug cartels in a declared "war on drugs."

Contrary to the Mexican government's ostensible concern for human rights, expressed in, for example, the various official human rights commissions, human rights violations have not decreased in Mexico but continue elevated. Although these violations are due in significant part to the drug cartels' skyrocketing use of violence, the government is responsible for a high number of violations, many of which are committed by the military (see, e.g., Amnesty International 1997, 2010; Human Rights Watch 2004).[10] In 2009, a report by the Office of the UN High Commissioner for Human Rights in Mexico "documented threats and attacks against human rights defenders by both state officials and private individuals. It also highlighted the lack of effective action to investigate and prevent attacks. Human rights defenders, particularly those working on economic, cultural and social rights, faced fabricated criminal charges and unfair trial proceedings" (Amnesty International 2010:225). Amnesty International found in its annual report for 2009 that "Indigenous Peoples and members of marginalized communities were frequently subjected to unfair judicial proceedings. The rights of communities to their land and homes were overlooked or challenged in several cases in order to exploit local resources" (2010:225). As Alison Brysk (2000:265) concludes, there is "a mixed picture of increasing human rights violations combined with increased state accountability."

INDIGENOUS RIGHTS CLAIMS IN CHIAPAS

Among Mayas in Chiapas, it appears that Protestant villagers were the first to use the language of human rights in the 1970s to protest their expulsion in large numbers from their communities after their conversion, when indigenous municipal leaders saw them as a threat to their political and economic control (see Kovic 2005). Invoking Article 24 of the Mexican constitution, the expelled Protestants began to claim their right as Mexican citizens to choose their own religion.[11] The broader indigenous movement, in contrast, influenced by various socialist ideologies, continued to frame its demands in class terms for several more years. In the 1970s, such protests focused on access to land and credit and were raised by the new, indigenous-based, peasant organizations such as the Central Independiente de Obreros Agrícolas y Campesinos (CIOAC), Coordinadora Nacional Plan de Ayala (CNPA), and Organización Campesina Emiliano Zapata (OCEZ) (Harvey 1998; G. Collier and Quaratiello 1999; Hernández Castillo 2006a:120–21). These groups arose in the volatile region of the northern, eastern, and southern slopes of the Chiapas highlands, where the majority of Mayas lived in plantation quarters or in ethnically mixed communities, often subjugated to mestizo political control (see map 1, state of Chiapas). In the central highlands of the state, in contrast, where Mayas lived in largely self-governed municipalities, the state had co-opted the indigenous leadership, minimizing political unrest for decades (J. Rus 1994; J. Rus, Hernández Castillo, and Mattiace 2001). However, with the federal governments' switch to neoliberal policies in the 1980s and the ensuing cuts in subsidies and government spending in the rural areas, indigenous discontent grew, and indigenous organizations mounted a series of protests, including land invasions, roadblocks, and other actions (J. Rus, Hernández Castillo, and Mattiace 2003).[12]

It was not until the early 1990s, however, that indigenous organizations began to assert an indigenous ethnic identity and to claim rights as indigenous peoples. The indigenous demonstration in San Cristóbal on Columbus Day, October 12, 1992, manifesting "500 years of resistance," was one of the largest coordinated political demonstrations in the country, rallying ten thousand Mayas from about twenty different organizations throughout the state and presenting claims for recognition as indigenous peoples within the Mexican nation.[13]

When the EZLN, the Zapatistas, entered the political scene on January 1, 1994, the concepts of democracy, human rights, and the rights of indigenous peoples eventually came to the fore in the contestation of indigenous economic and political marginalization. From the outset, the Zapatistas presented a broad set of demands for improved living conditions, equality, and justice, many of them formulated as demands for rights.[14] These included the so-called Women's Revolutionary Law, which articulated ten fundamental rights of women. The EZLN also severely criticized the lack of political democracy in Mexico, demanded democratic reforms to benefit all citizens, and advocated rewriting the Mexican constitution (Collier and Collier 2005:455). Although EZLN presented demands for indigenous rights and autonomy from the start, they did not give them special priority. The Zapatista leadership was, nevertheless, influenced by the indigenous-rights focus that had been developed by indigenous organizations both in Chiapas and nationwide by organizations such as the Frente Independiente de Pueblos Indios (FIPI) and the Asamblea Nacional Indígena Plural por la Autonomía (ANIPA) (Mattiace 1997; Stephen 1997; Ruiz Hernández 2000).[15] The issue of indigenous rights and self-determination consequently became the topic of the first and only accords between the EZLN and the Mexican government, the San Andrés Accords, signed in 1996. The broad indigenous movement in Chiapas largely supported the demands of the Zapatistas, and for several years, the Zapatistas, civil indigenous organizations, and the many thousands of Mayas affiliated with the Catholic Diocese formed a broad political mobilization, perhaps including the majority of the Maya population in the state. Demands were increasingly presented in terms of rights (Speed and Leyva-Solano 2008).

Other Mayas, however, regarded this polemical position vis-à-vis the government as disruptive, counterproductive, and potentially dangerous. They favored instead a continued loyal attitude toward the ruling party, PRI, loyalty which in subsequent years was rewarded with a great increase in resources allocated. These diverging choices have contributed to the drastic polarization of political and religious positions in Maya villages and urban neighborhoods in recent decades, creating rifts that Nash (1995) describes as "the explosion of communities" and that divide not only communities but also families in Chiapas.

The political and social unrest in the highland Maya communities has been accompanied by an increased interest in the indigenous poor among various groups in the broader mestizo society. Protestant churches and the Catholic Diocese intensified their missionizing in Maya communities in the 1960s and 70s, partly in response to the growing interest in their teachings on the part of the villagers (Pérez Pérez 1992; G. Collier and Quaratiello 1999:56–57). The Catholic Diocese, which under Bishop Samuel Ruiz was guided by liberation theology and an explicit priority to the needs of the indigenous poor, became closely associated with the political mobilization of indigenous communities. A growing number of urban mestizos on the left also began to assist in the peasant organizing that was emerging in the 1970s (Harvey 1998; G. Collier and Quaratiello 1999:66–69). The number of NGOs instigating various projects in support of indigenous peasant communities was also increasing. After the Zapatista rebellion, such interest escalated drastically, including many international organizations as well as activist networks, which often established offices in San Cristóbal, the central town in the highlands (Tavanti 2005:6). Many of the NGOs focused their work on human rights issues. According to Shannon Speed and Álvaro Reyes (2005:53), by the late 1990s there were "ten independent human rights NGOs, four national human rights NGOs, and at least nine international human rights organizations with a permanent or periodic presence in Chiapas." Additional human rights agencies were set up by the state and federal governments. As noted by George Collier and Jean Collier (2005:455–56), these organizations have focused on the area of civil and political rights, for example, illegal detentions and torture by state security forces. These various organizations and churches have constituted important ways for Mayas to connect with broader national and transnational networks and take part in discourses on human and indigenous rights, gender equality, or ethnicity.

GOVERNMENT RESPONSE

The oppositional stance against the Mexican government has been met with violent repression, especially, but not only, directed at the Zapatistas.

The government initially responded to the EZLN uprising with a massive military attack. But the Zapatistas, most of them impoverished, poorly armed peasants, gained broad national and international sympathy with their demands for improved living conditions and increased democracy. The government therefore halted the attack after only ten days. The uprising, however, caused unrest in the financial community since it was regarded as "a litmus test for Mexico's stability" (Silverstein and Cockburn 1995). This added to an already emerging economic crisis that resulted in a devaluation of the peso at the end of 1994. The difficult task for the Mexican government was to achieve political control without using overt state violence. Since 1995, each successive administration appears to have opted for a heavy military presence combined with paramilitary violence to control political protest and marginalize the Zapatistas; the paramilitaries are recruited among indigenous villagers loyal to the government.

Chiapas was for several years the most militarized state in Mexico, to the detriment of its indigenous communities (Nash 2001). Indigenous and human rights organizations hold that as many as 70 thousand soldiers were stationed in the state at one time, amounting to one third of the Mexican armed forces, with a military presence in 58 of a total of 110 municipalities (SIPAZ 2001).[16] As late as 2008, there were 74 military camps and various military checkpoints in the state, as well as repeated reports of threats and harassment against civilian and Zapatista populations, including in Chenalhó (CDHFBC 2009a).

The militarization of Chiapas has occurred partly through the support of the United States, which since 1994 has "granted unprecedented amounts of military aid . . . more than $60 million in equipment and at least 700 U.S.-trained Mexican officers" (Brysk 2000:110). Paramilitary groups have also emerged throughout the state. There have been reports of at least twelve paramilitary groups with varying degrees of governmental and military support, persecuting villagers and activists who oppose the government (CDHFBC 1998a, 2009a). This line of counterinsurgency is said to have commenced in 1995 when Mario Renán Castillo was made head of military operations in Chiapas; he is also thought to be the author of the "Manual of Irregular Warfare" of the Mexican army, in which the deployment of militarized civilians is described as essential for destroying guerilla forces (CDHFBC 1999, 2009a; Belling-hausen 2004).[17] The series of Mexican administrations has continually denied any official involvement in the paramilitary activities in Chiapas, but in 2009, declassified documents from the U.S. Defense Intelligence Agency (DIA) attested to the support of the Mexican military, under orders from President Salinas, in the creation and training of anti-Zapatista armed groups in Chiapas.[18]

The escalating paramilitary violence in Chiapas reached a peak in 1997 in the Maya municipality of San Pedro Chenalhó, when months of persecution by paramilitaries recruited within the municipality culminated in some ten thousand villagers fleeing their homes, most taking refuge in rapidly formed camps inside Chenalhó. On December 22, 1997, in the village of Acteal, a group of paramilitaries killed forty-five unarmed members of Las Abejas, said to have gathered to pray near the village chapel. The massacre, and the predicament of the displaced, received massive international attention and led to a severe crisis for the Mexican government. Las Abejas, in turn, has become a symbol of indigenous resistance nationally as well as internationally. Since the Zapatista rebellion in 1994, Las Abejas members describe themselves as part of the indigenous struggle for social justice and rights and emphasize their use of pacifist means. In subsequent chapters, I will describe how the members of Las Abejas, the majority of them Pedrano Catholics, attempt to reconstitute their position within the Mexican state and how they, before and after the massacre, have developed demands for substantive citizenship and rights necessary to achieve such a change.

DOING FIELDWORK IN CHIAPAS

Most of the fieldwork on which this book is based on was conducted after the Zapatista uprising but before the paramilitary persecution started in Chenalhó. I spent a total of fourteen months in the field from March to November 1995 and from February to July 1996, of which about eight months were spent in Chenalhó. I conducted complementary work during month-long visits in May 1998 and July 2006. In October 2008, when four Pedrano friends came to Sweden for two weeks to collaborate on another research project, they further updated me on developments in

Chenalhó, and I greatly benefited from our discussions on some of the central issues addressed in this book. During my absence from Chiapas, I have followed political events in Chenalhó and Chiapas closely through the Internet and e-mail news bulletins, as well as by phone and e-mail exchange with Pedrano friends.

I first visited Chiapas as an undergraduate student in 1985, staying for seven months until July 1986 while collecting material for my BA thesis, with additional visits during fall 1990 and fall 1992. I focused on the evolution of the indigenous movement in the highlands and interviewed leaders and members of various indigenous organizations, including expelled Protestants, and became acquainted with a few Maya families with whom I still have contact. Having this long historical perspective on the Chiapas highlands and knowing people from different groups have helped me to better understand some of the changes that have taken place in the last decades.

During 1995–96, the period when I did most of the fieldwork for this book, the political situation in Chiapas was precarious, developing into what local human rights NGOs described as low-intensity warfare. At the time of my arrival in 1995, the Mexican army, responding to inter-national pressure, had recently halted its second attempt to crush the Zapatistas by military force, and the military checkpoints had just been removed from the highways. Many people, both those working in NGOs in town and indigenous people in the rural communities, feared repres-sion for their political opposition and suffered various forms of intimida-tion. This included the Catholic Diocese, which during this period had become the target of a campaign by local citizens and national interest groups that accused it of direct involvement with the Zapatista upris-ing. To be allowed to do fieldwork among members of a group opposed to the government, aligned with the diocese, depended on their trust in me. After some careful orientation among longtime friends in sev-eral local NGOs, I was introduced to the nun working with the Word of God Catholics in Chenalhó, and through her, to the catechist leaders in Chenalhó at their monthly meeting in the village of Yabteclum. At this meeting, I presented my request to do fieldwork with their group, the catechists approved, and they suggested that I live in the village of Yibel-joj with the family of the leading catechist there. The following Sunday, I went to Yibeljoj to present the same petition at the Sunday service of the Catholic group, and again, the assembled men and women approved it. At the time, in contrast to many other municipalities, Chenalhó had no military or paramilitary presence. Nevertheless, whenever I was in San Cristóbal, where I kept a rented house for overnight errands, I tried to keep as low a profile as possible and never disclosed information about events in Chenalhó. Eventually, I grew as careful and secretive as many of my Mexican activist friends, and like them, I sometimes did not know when my suspicions of dangerous situations were pure paranoia or valid judgments.[19]

It was quite clear that the main reason the Pedrano catechists permitted my work was that they identified me as part of a broad international community that they had learned was in support of indigenous demands for justice and dignity. Because of the highly polarized political climate, it was not possible to be "neutral"; both catechists and regular church members in Chenalhó demanded that I show I was not on the side of the PRI government (cf. Kovic 2005; Speed 2008). I myself confirmed this identity, since it was part of how I saw myself in relation to the indigenous struggle in Chiapas. I explained that I wanted to write a book about their work in the Catholic community for my doctoral degree at my university, but also that I wanted to write about their lives and struggle so other people would learn about it, not only through my dissertation but also from newspaper articles in Sweden. This was approved. Frequently during the following year, people talked to me with the explicit purpose of making known to others the circumstances they grappled with in their lives. Thus, I came to serve as witness, and I have continued to be aware of the responsibility such a role carries.

While Pedrano Catholics demanded to know whether I was "on their side" in the conflict and that I would disseminate their testimonies outside Mexico, they never expected me to take active part in their political work in Chenalhó or in the broader state of Chiapas. To the contrary, I sensed that they would have found it preposterous if I had. I was not identified with their mestizo allies in San Cristóbal, whom they did expect to be involved, but as an outside witness. Also, I felt it important, as a temporarily visiting foreigner, not to engage in political activity or influence people to make choices for which I would not have to bear any real consequences, except the risk of being expelled from the country. Only those having to bear the costs should make such choices. Therefore, I have limited my activist work concerning Chiapas to Sweden and the transnational arena. In Chenalhó I felt that my role was to try to bracket out my own opinions and preconceptions in order to understand what motivations and reasons drive people there to make the choices they make; I was there to listen and learn. Much that has been written about Chiapas after the Zapatista uprising has been highly politicized, the region sometimes becoming the projection screen for various revolutionary visions. In some writings, it is difficult to distinguish the political agenda of the author from that of the people described. In order to avoid this as far as possible, I have made a constant effort to have my inquiries be guided by the actual concerns I sensed were central for Catholic Pedranos and other villagers. However, my own political inclinations as well as the unspoken "moral contract" I entered into with Pedrano Catholics, and the kindness and hospitality I was shown, have undeniably influenced my perception of what happened in Chenalhó. I have tried, both during fieldwork and in writing, to consciously restrain my "positive bias" toward the Catholic group and to be open to villagers of different positions and choices, both religious and political. Since I am not a Catholic but rather an agnostic, this has possibly helped this approach, while it certainly has also limited my understanding of the faith of the villagers.

A significant part of my fieldwork consisted of attending meetings. First there was the Sunday service of the Catholic chapel group in Yibeljoj, the village where I was staying, where the group met to pray and reflect on the Bible in the chapel they had built. There were monthly catechist meetings and other Catholic encounters at the municipal level in the village of Yabteclum. I also attended village- and municipal-level meetings of Las Abejas, the political adjunct to the Pedrano Catholics. After some months I asked for permission to tape the meetings I attended, which was granted. I was also allowed to tape the interviews I made with leaders of Las Abejas, catechists from various chapel groups, and men and women of the Yibeljoj chapel group, all of whom also were members of Las Abejas. In addition, I interviewed a few villagers of other affiliations. I held few interviews during the first months; the majority took place in the last couple of months of my stay since I wanted villagers to have some confidence in me and my work. All interviews were held in Chenalhó, except those made during my return visit in 1998, which were held in San Cristóbal, since foreigners at the time were not allowed to enter Chenalhó. Most of the interviews with catechists and Las Abejas leaders were conducted in Spanish and were unstructured but addressed specific issues. The interviews with chapel members in Yibeljoj were semi-structured, almost all taking place in the grassy yard of the Catholic chapel during times when no other people were around.

Most of these interviews were conducted in Tzotzil with a Pedrano interpreter. My knowledge of Tzotzil regrettably advanced only to a rudimentary level, giving me only a general idea of what people were talking about. I usually discussed the issues to be addressed beforehand with the interpreter and kept my interventions during the interviews to a minimum. The format of guided conversations relied much on the skills of my interpreters and whether they were able to make people feel at ease. Certainly, my use of a tape recorder and interpreter influenced the information I was given in interviews. I was rarely told things that would question the leadership of the catechists or disclose present controversies within the group. I had to notice such tensions myself at the meetings, or understand by indirect comments. Most people I interviewed, however, showed a great willingness to talk, and I was frequently surprised by the openness I was shown on personal topics as well. I often felt that my attention and interest, including the presence of the tape recorder, gave a value and weight to the life stories and experiences of the persons who shared them with me, and that it was appreciated (cf. Kovic 2005). Because of the sensitive political situation, I took care to choose interpreters who came from the same politico-religious groups as those interviewed, the majority, of course, Pedrano Catholics. Notes and tapes were coded so as not to disclose names and places. All my tapes were transcribed in Tzotzil and then translated to Spanish, mostly by a few Pedrano Catholic men who had proved to be excellent at the trade.

During fieldwork, I wondered whether there were possible precedents for the factional divisions of the community. Oddly, there have been few attempts by anthropologists to relate the present politico-religious factions in highland Maya communities to earlier forms of loyalties between villagers. Thus, I asked a Pedrano villager I trusted to make a "politico-religious map" of the factions in Yibeljoj with the help of the village census made by the local schoolteachers. This map depicted all sections of the village and the approximate location of each house, which was given a number. The names of the members of each house were listed separately. This list also noted—in code—the past and present political and religious affiliation of family members above fifteen years of age. Upon my return in 1998, we also noted the Tzotzil lineage name of all adults; these names are not used today in formal registration and thus were absent from the census.[20]

In this book, I use the real names of villages and factions in Chenalhó. After the outbreak in 1997 of paramilitary violence in Chenalhó, the political position and actions of Pedrano Catholics have become widely known, and various villages, including the community where I lived during fieldwork—Yibeljoj—have become historical sites mentioned in various publications. I also use people's real names—with their permission—because, since they have already suffered persecution for their political position, their opinions are well known. Following a tradition of several scholars on Chiapas, perhaps most importantly Jan Rus, I find it important to acknowledge the contribution and authority of individual Mayas in my writing, and to place their statements in specific time. Such information is given in footnotes after all direct quotes in the text.

One of my hesitations when first planning to do fieldwork in Chiapas was the limitations it would pose to be there in a wheelchair. After a traffic accident when I was a child, I am paralyzed from my waist down and use a wheelchair to move. Although my disability had been no impediment to my previous work in Chiapas, it had been conducted primarily in urban settings. Being in the hilly countryside was something different. However, doing fieldwork on wheels proved to both open and close doors. At the initial meeting with the catechists in Chenalhó, I sensed that one of the reasons they allowed my stay was my disability; a definite weakness that in some sense made me more human and thus more similar to them. Although I was a rich foreigner, I also had suffered and was struggling. Thus, although my disability often made me more strange and "other" in relation to Pedranos, it simultaneously lessened the distance between us, sometimes quite physically when clusters of children leaned on my wheelchair during Sunday chapel meetings or men poked at different parts of the chair to inquire about its technical construction and function.

Because of my use of a wheelchair, certain practical arrangements had to be made. When the catechists decided which village I was to stay in, one of the criteria was that it be accessible by car—I had bought a car with a sturdy suspension that could master difficult terrain. Yibeljoj fit that criterion, though during the rainy season, only barely. I was invited to live with the family of the principal catechist, whose house lay just off the road and only a hundred meters down the road from the Catholic chapel. Since their latrine lay down a hill I could not navigate, my host organized the construction of a separate latrine for me, large enough to serve also as the place for my baths, with a water tap nearby to fill my bucket. When the family saw me struggle the first week with the mud in the yard—the rains had begun—my host told me to bring bags of cement from San Cristóbal, and he swiftly constructed two paved ramps: one from the house to the kitchen hut, and another from the kitchen

My host's mother, *left*, with a grandchild, my host family, and me outside their home in Yibeljoj, 1995.

across the backyard to my latrine. Although I first tried to protest this intervention in their home, I was told it was an advantage for them to have these mud-free paths. During my yearlong stay, members of my extended host family continually gave me a hand when I needed one: to get from the house out to the road, to carry things to or from my car, or to help me up the rugged slope to the church. To reciprocate somewhat, I offered rides with my car or did errands in town for them.[21]

Obviously, my work suffered certain limitations because of my restricted mobility. I had no access to houses or chapels that lay any distance from a dirt road, and thus I could only visit a few homes. This also meant my interactions were confined to my host family and the Catholic group since I could not wander around much to make contact with other villagers. In spite of several attempts, I was unable to borrow a horse that could take me to the Presbyterian chapel in Yibeljoj to participate in some of their gatherings.

I attempted to share some of the living conditions and work of my host family and other Pedranos, but in this I was much hindered by my disability. While in urban settings I am used to being totally self-sufficient, here I had to rely on frequent help and could perform only a few of the daily tasks of the household. I often felt confined to a role as a rich and spoiled gringa. Although, as a city person, I have no illusions that I could have contributed much anyway, I was now unable to share the experience of walking the dwindling paths, working in the field, carrying firewood, washing clothes in the river, or carrying children on my back. I only hope I got a sense of these practices through what I learned indirectly, and that I showed in other ways a willingness to take part in people's lives. I knew my hosts appreciated that I learned to make and enjoy my own *mats'*, or "pozol" in Spanish, corn masa mixed with water in a bowl that Pedranos drink daily and that both fills you up and quenches thirst, and is astoundingly revitalizing.[22] The small tasks I could perform in the household were met with good grace and some initial amusement—the first times I swept the yard, family members called enthusiastically to each other to come look at the performance of their unusual guest. With the happy assistance of five-year-old Jesús, the young son in my family, I was able to do dishes down by the water tap. Jesús often insisted that I take a rest on my bed during the day so he could wheel around in my wheelchair in the room, something he enjoyed immensely.

The most difficult aspect of my fieldwork, and of readjusting to life in Sweden afterward, was beyond all that, however. It consisted of learning to know, like, and largely identify with people who lived in circumstances of severe poverty. I could not conceptually fit both their and my own type of lives into my head; they seemed not part of the same world. I have not been able to reconcile my feelings, and I do not think it is possible.

During my stay, Pedranos talked to me about their poverty, how hard it is to live under such conditions, and how much they want to find ways to a better way of life. I also sensed that it was this frustration over their poverty and inability to offer their children secure access to food, and if sick, a cure, which propelled Pedranos' engagement in the various religious and political groups. For these reasons it became important for me to understand Pedranos' perceptions of themselves as poor and exposed to circumstances beyond their control. Poverty, suffering, and the longing for change are therefore the central themes of this book.

OUTLINE OF THE BOOK

Although this book addresses transnational discourses and politics, it is in many senses a classic monograph, where I strive to offer a "thick description" of the local appropriation of such discourses. Two central lines of inquiry are developed throughout the book. One addresses how Pedrano Catholics are reinterpreting what their poverty and suffering signifies and creating a moral discourse on rights, thereby validating their claims to recognition and a changed position in the broader Mexican society. The second focus is on how this endeavor is shaped by what I suggest has been an ongoing concern among Pedranos: the construction of cohesive social collectivities to uphold alliances with patron deities for protection. It should be emphasized that this book focuses solely on the "official" Catholic group in Chenalhó, affiliated with the Catholic Diocese of San Cristóbal de Las Casas, and not those Catholics who, after joining the Zapatistas in 1994, broke away from the diocese.[23]

The book is divided into three parts. Part I addresses the patron-client form of relationship that Pedranos came to develop with the corporatist Mexican state and how they eventually broke this bond. First, in chapter 1, I describe how notions of poverty, community, and state subordination have come to affect Pedranos' orientation to the state. I suggest that Pedranos, like Mayas throughout the highlands, have long structured their society in a system that groups villages into overarching subdivisions—in Chenalhó called "calpuls"—and through which people seek the protection of guardian deities. The subdivisions, in turn, are joined in a confederate-like structure. This form of political organization has gradually disintegrated with increasing government interference, the municipal government becoming monopolized by a few Pedrano families and controlled by a powerful, patron-like state. A large number of Pedranos, excluded from access to municipal power and resources, I argue, have formed politico-religious factions with separate structures and links to sources of support outside the municipality. The Catholic community in Chenalhó is one of those factions, and chapter 2 describes how their alliance with the Catholic Diocese was formed. This alliance, I will argue throughout the book, has had a profound impact on how Pedrano Catholics orient themselves not only theologically but also politically.

In part II, chapters 3 through 6, I look at how Pedrano Catholics have restructured their relationship with the divine, their community, their gendering of political agency, and their collective identity. Chapter 3 explores how Catholic men and women through their chapel groups are creating a new form of alliance with God. This alliance, I hold, bears significant similarities to that of traditional villagers, but demands new expressions of veneration. I describe the different roles of "creyentes"—the regular chapel members—and the catechists—the lay leaders—in this endeavor. To be a Word of God Catholic is a highly collective enterprise in Chenalhó, and chapter 4 describes how this collectivity is shaped. While the Pedrano Catholic community may appear at first glance to be structured along lines provided by the diocese, it is also based on long-standing Maya forms of community and leadership, especially those found in traditional calpul organization. It has integrated these with newer forms of communal organization such as assembly-based popular participation. This is also the case for their political association, Las Abejas, described in chapter 4. The most far-reaching change, perhaps, concerns the relation between gender and participation in the public, political sphere, addressed in chapter 5. In chapter 6, I describe how Catholic Pedranos have formed a new collective identity, where their experiences of suffering and vulnerability define them as especially dear to God among a vast, global humanity. This identity lays the ground for their claims for universal human rights, and how they relate such claims to their experiences of paramilitary persecution and the massacre in Acteal.

In part III, I focus on how the changed identity of Pedrano Catholics is reflected in their political activism in opposition to the Mexican state. Chapter 7 describes how Pedrano Catholics, through Las Abejas, decided to side openly with the Zapatistas, albeit in the role of peacemakers, and how the increasing political tensions in Chiapas heightened the antagonism between factions in Chenalhó. Las Abejas, along with the Zapatista support bases, eventually became the target of paramilitary violence. This violence, described in chapter 8, has come to further the position of Pedrano Catholics as rights-claimers, now also calling for an international community to enforce justice. Invoking Christian ethics and international human rights regulations, they struggle to press the Mexican government to recognize their demands for a new position in the nation-state. In the last chapter, I discuss the construction of a Pedrano Catholic citizenship and its collective character, with the communal base for political agency strengthening their enactment of citizenship claims. But I also discuss the various roadblocks that Pedrano Catholics encounter in their claim for improved living conditions through a rights-based citizenship. This leads me to ask to what extent viable room exists in present-day Mexican society for the citizen-claims of Pedrano Catholics, and thus, their possibilities of finding the Exodus—the liberation—they strive for.

PART I

Pedranos and the Patron State

CHAPTER 1

Poverty, Maya Community, and the State

The experiences of poverty and subordination have long been central to the way Pedranos, like other Mayas, define themselves in relation to the broader Mexican society and interact with its authorities. Since the founding of Chenalhó in colonial times, Pedranos have been exposed to hostile, non-indigenous governments—first that of the Spanish crown and, since 1821, that of the Mexican nation-state. Through political and military control, these governments have benefited from indigenous land, labor, and taxes, keeping Pedranos and other highland Mayas in abject poverty. When Lázaro Cárdenas became president in 1934, however, the Mexican state initiated a new type of relationship with Mayas, aiming to integrate indigenous communities into the modernist project of national development and cultural assimilation. This created a patron-client relationship between Pedranos and the state and profoundly influenced the internal political organization of Chenalhó as well as other Maya municipalities. The former system of calpuls, or subdivisions of the municipality, which had a long trajectory in the Maya highlands, gradually dissolved, partly to be replaced by new structures for decision making, including the use of communal assemblies for village-level political participation. Eventually, however, an increasing number of Pedranos began to turn against both the municipal leaders, whom they considered to have been co-opted by the state, and the federal government, which they held responsible for the continued poverty of indigenous peasants. In this chapter I outline this development and how it relates to Pedranos' perceptions of poverty, community, and the Mexican state.

POVERTY AND SUFFERING

San Pedro Chenalhó lies in the midst of several Tzotzil- and Tzeltal-speaking municipalities in the highlands of Chiapas, about seventy kilometers north of the central town of the region, San Cristóbal de Las Casas (see map 2). Like other Maya municipalities, Chenalhó is composed of many small villages scattered among hills covered with cultivated fields. Lying near the southern border of the municipality is the municipal seat, the town of Chenalhó, where the main parish church is located, and which for many years has been the political and religious center of the municipality. The vast majority of the thirty-two thousand inhabitants of the municipality of Chenalhó speak Tzotzil and define themselves as Pedranos (or Sanpedranos) (INEGI 2005). They describe themselves as an ethnically distinct people with their own traditions, identified by the special dress that almost all women wear, though its color composition changes with local fashion trends.[1] The majority of men today wear retail-purchased mestizo clothes. Mestizos now constitute only 0.5 percent of the inhabitants (Torres Burguete 2000); the majority of them reside in the municipal center, where they make a living from commerce.

For most Pedranos, to be peasant is an integral part of their identity. Yet their access to land has for centuries been limited and challenged by mestizo interests; thus many, perhaps most, families rely on supplementary sources of income. An increasing number of women produce handicrafts for the tourist market in San Cristóbal and abroad. From the late 1800s to the 1990s, many men worked seasonally on coffee plantations in the Sierra Madre region of southwestern Chiapas, an option that disappeared when the plantation economy stagnated in the 1990s. Particularly since the beginning of the twenty-first century, Pedranos, like other Mayas, emigrate instead for short or longer periods to other states in Mexico as well as the United States to find employment as unskilled labor in, for example, construction. This trend is rapidly escalating. It is primarily young men who leave, many of them with families to support, but increasingly, young women and couples also emigrate. The remittances these migrants send home are becoming an important source of income for a growing number of Pedrano and other Maya families (Eber 2008; Rus and Rus 2008).

However, even families who support themselves largely through such means try to cultivate at least a small piece of land, whether their own or rented, so as to retain access to a supply of corn and beans, the staple foods. Corn is food and life, and the primary concern of each family is to get enough corn, either from their own fields or purchased, to last them through the year. Many villagers told me how their families, in times of hardship, had survived long periods on only tortillas and a little salt.

Almost 80 percent of the houses in Chenalhó lack electricity, and about 55 percent have no access to running water (CDHFBC 1998a:5). Most houses have walls of wooden boards, a roof of corrugated metal sheets, and a dirt floor where food is cooked on an open hearth. Some wealthier families are able to build high-status concrete houses with roofs of tile, and if money allows, two stories.

For most Pedranos, life is a constant struggle to gather adequate means to support their family, and most have few or no reserves to respond to sickness or other unforeseen expenses. Pedranos highly value the ability to work hard and long, and they take pride in being strong and resilient workers. From an early age, girls and boys learn to endure physical duress and discomfort. I was often struck by this capacity, both in adults and children. Like most other Mayas in Chiapas, Pedranos suffer from malnutrition, especially mothers and children, and the municipality's level of malnutrition ranks as the fourth highest in the state (CDHFBC 1998a:5). Intestinal and respiratory diseases are common and cause 40 percent of all deaths (Freyermuth 2003b:31). As throughout Maya Chiapas, the infant mortality rate is high in Chenalhó: 42.34 deaths per 1,000 live births (INEGI 2000). Almost all middle-aged couples I knew had lost one or two children at a young age.

Poverty in Chenalhó is not only palpable to outsiders, it constitutes an intrinsic part of Pedrano identity. Pedranos commonly describe themselves as a suffering people. The suffering, I was told, is caused by hard work, the resulting body-aches, meager food, poor housing, mud during the rains, and lack of infrastructure. Suffering is associated with disease and the death of infants, children, and adults. In short, Pedranos regard their suffering as a consequence of poverty. The term commonly used in Tzotzil to describe this suffering is *vokol* or *jvokolil*, literally "difficulty," "hardship," or "anguish," usually translated as "sufrimiento" when villagers speak Spanish. Several Pedranos I spoke with, however, emphasized that villagers differ significantly in their level of poverty. Some can build good houses, eat well, and perhaps even invest in a truck or minibus for commercial transport. Others, in contrast, live in abject misery. The economic differences between Pedranos are growing with the present migration, which brings increased access to money for some families, particularly those who lend start-up money to the emigrants at high interest rates (see Rus and Rus 2008 on neighboring Chamula).

Most, if not all, Pedranos integrate poverty and suffering into their discourse on ethnicity and regard these experiences as part of Pedrano and indigenous identity. One man, a middle-aged Pedrano Catholic catechist, told me that poverty is a central characteristic of indigenous peasant life:

"That's why it's called 'indigenous.' That's what 'peasant' means. Because we don't have anything. It's not like in the cities, no, it's not."

I asked: "To be indigenous is to be poor?"

My host's mother, Apolonia Sántiz Jiménez, prepares the soil in her coffee and corn garden by her house in Nuevo Yibeljoj, 2011. Photo by José A. Jiménez Pérez.

He replied: "Yes, to be a peasant, to be working with corn. Working."[2]

Villagers contrast their living conditions with those of mestizos, the opposite "others," who are identified as "the rich," people living a comfortable life in town with no cares for food or shelter. I never heard a Pedrano speak about poor mestizo peasants, who would constitute an anomaly in this sharply dichotomized conflation of people and class. I was often told that mestizos earn their money sitting down, implying without real work, and that they eat by the labor of others. Mestizos are sometimes even referred to as "the fat ones," while Pedranos are "the skinny ones"; class and ethnicity as literally embodied in people's physical makeup (cf. Scheper-Hughes 1992). A Catholic woman in Yibeljoj said: "The mestizos don't feel any burden on them to look for food. They don't go to work with bodies that ache or are sick, they don't have to sacrifice. They support themselves sitting down. We, in contrast, have to make many sacrifices to find our food."[3]

Two other Catholic women in Yibeljoj who were sisters-in-law gave me a clear-cut characterization of the differences between mestizo and Pedrano life. The younger of the two said in her calm, quiet voice:

There is no resemblance [between how we and they live]. We suffer in the mire, we have no adequate house, no good road, not even a good place to sleep. We have no good food, while they in contrast eat well. That's why there is no resemblance. Do you think they'd like to come and live here? No, especially not with the fleas and bedbugs we have! No, there's no resemblance. [Both women laughed, and the more energetic sister-in-law continued:] The mestizos would never get used to living here in the village, here in the municipality. They are accustomed to their own life. They eat well, they walk in the streets and have good houses. They don't suffer. We, in contrast, suffer. A mestizo person could not get used to living here in our house, they wouldn't even enter. Instead, they make fun of us who walk in the mud. That's why we suffer a lot here. . . . The mestizos don't like us because they say we are dirty. If we so much as touch their things they start to tell us stuff, that we are dirty. They despise us.[4]

The moral connotation that the women make of the differences between indigenous peasants and mestizos is widespread. Most Pedranos seem to regard mestizos as exploitative and disrespectful to the Mayas and therefore contributing to their undue suffering. Again and again, Pedranos have experienced patronizing and humiliating treatment by mestizos referring to their indigenousness, on "fincas" (large farms or plantations) and construction sites, in towns, at hospitals, and in offices. Several villagers in the community of Yibeljoj told me in dismay how their parents or other villagers only some decades ago had been made to carry the village mestizo schoolteacher or his wife on a chair on their backs all the way to San Cristóbal. This image of indigenous men carrying mestizos on their backs appears for many Mayas almost to emblemize the history of exploitation by mestizos.

The sense of subjugation extends to the relationship with Mexico as a nation, likewise associated with mestizo rule and domination. Pedranos, like other Mayas, identify themselves as Mexicans. However, the notion of being "Mexican" has not implied full membership in the nation-state. In their interactions with Mexican society outside indigenous communities, Pedranos have been marginalized socially, economically, and politically. Their generalized identity as "Indians" or "indigenous" has ordinarily embodied this sense of exclusion. It is an identity stigmatized by a broader society that defines indigenous Mexicans as "others" outside the sphere of ordinary citizens. I often heard Pedranos express this sense of being excluded from the national society and being considered a backward category of people. A Catholic villager told me he heard that the Mexican government says of the indigenous people in Chiapas: "It said that there are no people in Chiapas. The government said: 'There are no peasants in Chiapas, there are only animals there.' Do you know why they say there are only animals in Chiapas? It's because we don't have much schooling. That's why they say it, since they are all mestizo there, in Mexico [City]."[5]

THE MAKING OF A PATRON GOVERNMENT

The sense of being subject to marginalization and exploitation that the Pedranos expressed contrasts with the hope their parents or grandparents probably felt when the government of President Lázaro Cárdenas initiated drastic reforms in Chiapas in the 1930s. Then, and for several decades thereafter, many Pedranos saw notable improvements. Through land reform, various subsidies, and a series of development projects, the Mexican state presented itself as a benefactor offering the means to better living conditions, to whom indigenous peasants could petition with the hope of a positive response (Hernández Castillo 1994:87–88; J. Rus 1994; G. Collier and Quaratiello 1999:15). Like other Mayas, Pedranos found themselves engaged with state authorities in "what was proclaimed their common struggle against exploitation" (J. Rus 1994:278).

Although Mayas had litigated for land or presented legal protests against mestizo expropriations during the preceding centuries, they had been acutely aware that the legal system and the manner of its application were not designed to benefit their interests (Wasserstrom 1983; Favre 1984). With the new regime, the state demonstrated a radical shift in priorities, redistributing large tracts of land to peasants; in 1949, 45 percent of the nation's cultivable land had become peasant-controlled ejidos, the agricultural cooperatives that were a fruit of the revolutionary agrarian reform from 1927 on (Knight 1991:258). Agrarian reform granted laborers on the former plantations the right to membership in the ejidos and title to land which could be inherited or sold only to other ejido members.[6] In Chiapas, which was tightly controlled by a landowning mestizo elite, Cárdenas sought to push through the belated revolutionary reforms via his local point man Erasto Urbina (J. Rus 1994). With Urbina, Pedranos drove the finca owners out of Chenalhó, and the land was redistributed to the former practically enslaved workers through ejidos.[7] Other parts of the fincas were given in restitution to Pedranos as agrarian communities, "comunidades agrarias," a less regulated form of communal landownership with ancestral claims that formed part of the larger landholding of the municipality (Garza Caligaris 2002:81–82). In a significant move, Pedranos also gained control of the municipal government, which since 1896 had been led by mestizos (J. Rus 2004). In 1944, Urbina installed a Pedrano municipal president—the already influential Manuel Arias Sojom—who was not subordinated to the mestizo municipal secretary (Arias 1994:385).

However, the advent of a benevolent corporatist state brought with it the creation of significant dependency. The hope of receiving more land ended up tying highland Maya communities to the ruling party and government. The local committees of the ejidos and agrarian communities

through which villagers could gain access and entitlement to land were
all enrolled in district and state committees of the national party (J. Rus
2004:15, cf. Knight 1991:263–64).

The dependence on the state and the ruling party was further reinforced by the evolution of federal and regional institutions directed at
indigenous and peasant communities. The institutions provided some
access to resources and transformed Pedrano municipal leaders into
intermediaries for obtaining such assets. The foremost of these institutions was perhaps the National Indigenist Institute (INI), which, newly
founded, established the Tzotzil-Tzeltal Coordinating Center in San
Cristóbal in 1951. Its aim was to promote the economic development
of the indigenous communities and their assimilation into Mexican society. Slowly, some Pedrano villages began to see running water, electricity, health clinics, schools, cooperative stores, and some legal protection
against mestizo exploitation and abuse. With improved infrastructure,
Pedranos also had better access to markets, surrounding cities, and the
lowland plantations (J. Rus 1994:285–88). Under federal presidents Luis
Echeverría and José López Portillo in the economically prosperous 1970s,
a range of new institutions and policies were created, directed toward
rural development (Smith 1991). In Chenalhó, institutions such as the
Mexican Coffee Institute (INMECAFE), National Council of Fruit Cultivation (CONAFRUT), and National Company of Subsidized Basic Products (CONASUPO) made it possible for villagers to receive cheap loans
and sell their produce at regulated prices. They also offered instruction
in agricultural techniques and gave jobs to local men. The Development
Program for the State of Chiapas (PRODESCH) offered projects and the
chance for villagers to become local promoters of the program.[8]

The Mexican state also provided a means for social mobilization and
demands, but through corporatist structures controlled by the government. Through the National Peasant Confederation (CNC), directly tied
to the ruling party, Maya peasants were incorporated into the state apparatus. Membership in CNC opened access to credits and crop subsidies as well as land claims under the agrarian reform. In exchange, the
affiliated peasants provided political loyalty to the ruling party (Harvey
1998:54; G. Collier and Quaratiello 1999:52; J. Rus, Hernández Castillo,
and Mattiace 2003:8–9).

Maya peasants thus became ever more engaged in a continuous process of petitioning for land titles, credits, and other resources. Like other Mayas, Pedranos learned that it was necessary to maintain a good relationship with the state if they wanted access to these resources. One of the central expressions of their loyalty was to vote for the ruling party. Through the introduction of popular elections, the party became known in the most remote of Pedrano villages and was associated with the land reforms that President Cárdenas had implemented as well as with subsequent development programs.[9] The late Vicente Vázquez, an elder from Los Chorros ejido, who had been one of the key persons when the ejido was newly formed, described the arrival of the party: "Don Lázaro Cárdenas was PRI, yes, he was PRI. The PRI positioned itself among the peasants and tried to give them their land. . . . That is why there are many 'colonias' [ejidos] today. . . . Now we began to vote. We began to vote for the government, for the president of the republic, the senate, we voted for all that. We went all the way to San Cristóbal, to Tuxtla, to vote."[10]

A younger Pedrano recounted to me how the legendary Manuel Arias would talk in a similar vein about the arrival of the national party and how it gave out land and liberated the slaves, granting them freedom. But it demanded that people vote for the party, he emphasized.[11] The late Vicente Vázquez described the obligatory participation in the elections: "Anyone who didn't want to go vote, to him they said, 'Why don't you want to vote, why don't you obey? Are you an animal, don't you have a government? Aren't you attached to someone?' That's it, that's the obligation. . . . If we don't obey, they say we're almost like animals, but he who obeys is a person of the government." Thus, to vote for PRI became in Chenalhó an expression of obligatory gratitude toward the national government that had assisted Pedranos in their "liberation," and a repeated affirmation of affiliation and loyalty.

Consequently, a patron-client relationship evolved between Pedranos and the Mexican state. The state became perceived as a mighty "giver of gifts" to the marginalized and poor. Pedranos, in turn, would appeal to official authorities with requests while assuring them of their allegiance and dependability. In this relationship, the experience of suffering and hardship, associated with being indigenous, became the basis of the petitioning role taken on by Pedranos, their poverty legitimizing the demand for resources. It even seems possible that Pedranos created a sense of allegiance to the PRI-ruled state apparatus that was similar to that extended to Pedrano deities, showing veneration in hope of protection. In this way, Pedranos gradually became included in the Mexican nation-state, but still as an economically and politically marginalized group (cf. Hernández Castillo 1994:88). Although the notion of the Mexican nation appears to have been rather vague for most Pedranos, its central power in Mexico City acquired a palpable force, as did the Chiapas state government in Tuxtla Gutiérrez.

CHENALHÓ AND HIGHLAND MAYA CALPULS

The presence of the new, "involved" state would seriously alter the socio-political structure of Chenalhó society, although Pedranos now for the first time in many years could enjoy self-rule with only indigenous men in the municipal government. The form of political organization found in Chenalhó in the early twentieth century has been called a calpul system: an organization into geographic subdivisions that also structured the political, social, and religious life of the community. A central concern of these subdivisions, it appears, has been to uphold alliances with deities for protection and well-being. Because of the profound influence the calpul system had and continues to have on Pedranos' thinking about and organization of their society and their relation to the divine, I will here offer a detailed description. In subsequent chapters on the Catholic community in Chenalhó, I will discuss how Catholic Pedranos continue to draw on certain calpul traits, while rejecting or transforming others.

In Chiapas, ethnographers have reported the existence of customary subdivisions in most highland Maya societies. Called calpuls or barrios, they structure political and religious organization, each subdivision consisting of various rural villages. In an overview of the Tzotzil region, Robert Laughlin (1969:170) writes that, except for the municipality of Venustiano Carranza, "the barrio or calpul is a major unit that serves to group the many parajes or hamlets in the municipality."[12] One of the strongest calpul systems was found in San Pablo Chalchihuitán, Chenalhó's neighboring municipality, which had five geographically bounded calpuls. Each calpul was an endogamous religious unit that performed rituals focused on health and good harvests to ensure the well-being of its members, and that owned land assigned to its patrilines, each of which was in turn associated with a hill or a tree (Guiteras Holmes 1952:105; Pérez López and Ramírez Méndez 1985:6–7; Köhler 1995:3–17).

The subdivision form of organization appears to be historically enduring and related to "a distinctively Mesoamerican pattern of segmentary social organization" (Mulhare 1996a:102).[13] It is most prevalent among the highland Mayas in Chiapas and Guatemala and the Nahuas in Central Mexico, and it builds to a certain extent on pre-colonial forms of social organization (Hill and Monaghan 1987; Mulhare 1996a:98).[14] In its fullest expression, Eileen Mulhare argues, "the customary subdivision system is a true confederacy. Each subdivision has its own sanctuary, patron saint(s) or titular deities, ceremonials and festivals, lands to support civic and/or religious expenditures, cash assessments on the membership, public works and recognized civil and religious officers or leaders" (1996a:97, with reference to Thomas 1979:49; see also Hunt and Nash 1967:268).

In the municipality of Chenalhó, the subdivision system during the last century was composed of a number of village-sized units, grouped under a few overarching, endogamous subdivisions that were linked in a confederate-like structure, each equally represented in the political and religious center of the municipality.[15] In apparent contrast to the neighboring Maya societies, both the large subdivisions and the smaller corporate groups in Chenalhó were called "calpul." However, by the time of Calixta Guiteras Holmes's (1961) fieldwork in 1944 and the mid-1950s, the period of increasing state intervention described above, calpuls had only limited formal recognition and appeared to be in a process of disintegration. Today villages (sometimes called hamlets) have assumed many of the religious and political functions of the former calpuls and in Chenalhó are referred to only as either "parajes" or ejidos. At present there are about eighty parajes and six ejidos in the municipality of Chenalhó.[16] However, Sebastián Gómez and Antonio Vázquez, both Pedranos, could still in the late 1990s tell me about the former calpul organization. As the population increased, new villages were formed from the former calpuls, according to Vázquez.

The small calpuls in Chenalhó were localized corporate groups that held specific religious and political functions. Pedranos told Guiteras in the 1950s that at the time there were thirty small calpuls.[17] Each calpul consisted of several landholding patrilines and seems to have been governed by the local elite of male elders and "pasados" (*pasaroetic* in Tzotzil), men who have held cargos in the municipal ruling body.[18] Of special importance was the "principal" (*kirinsipal* in Tzotzil), who served as the link to the municipal capital.[19] Gómez told me that when problems arose, these principales would summon the pasados and elders of the calpul to meet and decide how to resolve the issue at hand. The principales were also responsible for the extraction of money and collective labor from their community, a classic feature of Mesoamerican subdivisions, and this role continues today.

The village-sized calpuls were earlier organized in a dual barrio system similar to that reported all through Mesoamerica, wherein the subdivisions are grouped in two sets (Hunt and Nash 1967:262). In Chenalhó, as in several other places, one section was called *k'ajal*, "up," "highland," denoting the southwestern half of the municipality, and the other *olon*, "down," "lowland," denoting the northeastern half (Guiteras Holmes 1961:64).[20] Each section was endogamous, Guiteras states, and villagers told her that there had been a certain antagonism between members of the two halves (1961:64–65).[21] People are still categorized by their section, either *olon* or *k'ajal*, Gómez told me. At the time of Guiteras's fieldwork in the 1950s, Chenalhó was organized into three overarching calpuls. Besides *k'ajal* and *olon*, there was a third section called *yutil lum*, denoting a region around the former capital, Yabteclum, which is located in the geographic center of Chenalhó. In the 1950s, each of the three large calpuls held communal lands for the use of its members (Guiteras Holmes 1961:66).

The central political and religious leadership of Chenalhó, as in other highland Maya municipalities, was organized in a confederate-like structure, where all the calpuls were represented (see, e.g., Laughlin 1969:170). The municipal ruling body of Chenalhó is similar to those found in most highland Maya municipalities in Chiapas the last century: a civil-religious hierarchy that outsiders commonly call a "cargo system," and which includes both the constitutionally required municipal government and positions related to more "traditional" and religious tasks, such as the celebration of the saints.[22] During the early twentieth century, the municipal ruling body of Chenalhó was composed of representatives of the two sections, *k'ajal* and *olon*, who used two organizational principles to ensure that both subdivisions were equally represented in the civil-religious hierarchy: rotation, where each subdivision took turns holding civil or religious offices; and parallelism, where each subdivision held an equal number of a certain position every term (Guiteras Holmes 1961:65; Hunt and Nash 1967:264; Arias 1985:119, cf. Thomas 1979:50). These principles are common to many Mesoamerican subdivision systems, Norman Thomas (1979:50) argues, and allow the relative autonomy of each subdivision while simultaneously assuring cooperation and social interaction and counteracting subdivision competition and factionalism. In the 1950s, when there were three municipal sections, or overarching calpuls—*olon, k'ajal,* and *yutil lum*—Guiteras (1961:66) says the rules for equal representation were less formal. However, she adds, "there are always members of the three calpuls in the governmental and religious bodies which represent the entire group." Guiteras (1961:66) describes how villagers coming to the capital would direct themselves to the officeholder from their own calpul, who would take a leading role in solving the matter at hand. There appears to have been a continuing effort among Pedranos to balance the total number of cargos between the *k'ajal, olon,* and *yutil lum* calpuls, and also to divide the cargos somewhat evenly between the villages.[23]

Of central importance for calpul members has been to uphold an alliance with the guardian deities. In their overview of the region, Eva Hunt and June Nash (1967:266) note that each of the calpuls, or barrios, may be identified with animal spirits or specific hills that they say "'belong' to the souls of particular barrios." The various ethnographies of the highlands show how the different units—from family level to the entire municipality—must perform rituals to these deities to ensure the well-being of their members, the most important of these rituals commonly called *mixa.*[24]

Also in Chenalhó, each calpul appears to have been tied in an intimate relationship to deities of the nearby landscape. Gómez and Vázquez said that each calpul was associated with certain hills, springs, and caves surrounding the community. The same holds for present-day villages. A central concern on both local and municipal levels has been to uphold alliances with these guardian deities, who "own" and control the landscape and the natural forces. In exchange for reverence and offerings to the deities, humans are assured of protection and well-being (Guiteras Holmes 1961:287–88; Eber 2000:60). For the local communities in Chenalhó, as in other highland municipalities, the principal guardians are the masculine mountain deities called *anjels*. Each Pedrano village has a personalized relationship to the *anjels* of the surrounding mountains and often bears the name of the senior *anjel* of the largest hill. The various barrios (the term today used to denote village sections) of a village are in turn linked to, and may be named after, the major *anjel* of the smaller hills nearby.[25] Accordingly, every paraje and ejido, and sometimes every barrio, petitions the deities of specific hills for protection, just as calpuls did in former times. Every community in Chenalhó is also dependent on the mighty, feminine Ch'ul Banamil, Holy Earth, the land that humans cultivate and inhabit, who also controls the waters. She is sometimes also called Jme'tik Banamil (Our Mother the Earth) (see Guiteras Holmes 1961:289–90; Eber 2000:60–61).[26]

The dependence on the deities of the surrounding landscape is so significant that a community ought never to be formed without creating an alliance to them. Thus in the 1990s, when a group of three lineages in a barrio of the Xunuch paraje decided to form an independent paraje, Linda Vista, the barrio agreed to "give" them two hills and one cave to be their particular guardians and places for veneration. With their own *anjels*, the families of the new community were able to maintain a relationship with the deities of their immediate landscape and thus ensure the basis for communal life.[27]

The bond between villagers and the *anjels* and the Holy Earth is acknowledged and affirmed in the special ceremonial prayer procession called *mixa*, performed three times a year, following the old Maya agricultural calendar.[28] The *mixa* is performed on behalf of all villagers by the ceremonial leader of the village, the *kabildo vinik* (man of the cabildo), who with an entourage of musicians and assistants visits and prays at the sacred spots at the village springs, caves, and the surrounding mountains, considered entrances for communication with the *anjel* and the Holy Earth (Guiteras Holmes 1961:287–88; Arias 1985:189). All

households in the village are expected to participate indirectly in the
mixa by contributing money, which is collected by the principales. The
mixa ceremony was still performed during my stay in Chenalhó, but because of different religious allegiances, not all villagers agreed to contribute money. Formerly, my host told me, all families also fasted during
the ceremony, and the pasados of the village came together to oversee
the money that had been collected.

The entire municipality of Chenalhó upholds an alliance with protec-
tive deities as well. The most important protectors of the Pedrano people
as a totality are the saintly deities, especially the patron saint San Pedro.
The saints, housed in the municipal church, are honored with individual
yearly festivals involving an elaborate set of rituals led by the cargo-holding
couples, who function as mediators between the whole municipality
and the sacred realm.[29] The municipality, like the local communities,
also has bonds to the Holy Earth and the *anjels* of the four mountains
surrounding the capital town; the *kompixon*, the highest Pedrano ceremonial leader, accompanied by the members of the entire municipal

San Pedro being carried in costumbre procession during Carnival in the
municipal capital of Chenalhó, 1995. Photo by author.

government, performs a *mixa* three times a year, preceding the local
ones (Arias 1985:179). In both the *mixa* and the festivals to the saints,
the municipality acts as one body composed of all individual communities and households. The unified veneration of the Pedrano people is
manifested through the cash contributions of all households, which the
principal of each village collects and brings to the center, but again, with
the increase in religious diversity, not all Pedranos take part. In the past,
the representation of the different levels of calpuls in the municipal *mixa*
and other religious municipal ceremonies was important, and the *k'ajal*
and *olon* sections were mentioned in prayers for the whole municipality
(Arias 1985:181; see also Guiteras Holmes 1961:64).

By tradition, leadership in Chenalhó appears to have been largely
based on seniority and the authority gained from holding prestigious
offices. The cargo holders on the municipal level—the persons holding positions in the civil-religious hierarchy—and the principales and
pasados on the local level, especially the men, formed a body of authorities which Pedranos have relied on for a broad range of concerns, from
religious expertise to moral guidance to political leadership. Villagers
have turned to these authorities to resolve conflicts that could not be
settled on a family level, from land disputes to divorce settlements, their
decision—ideally—being binding (see Guiteras Holmes 1961:73; Garza
Caligaris 2002; cf. J. Collier 1973 on Zinacantán). The authorities, including the municipal president, tended to be elder, monolingual men
with proven moral authority and great knowledge of what were considered "traditional ways," including specialist knowledge of traditional
prayers and ceremonies (Arias 1994:385). Pasados were regarded as
holding special power and insight, depending on how high a cargo they
had held, and they played an important role in influencing social and
political life in the communities. It was from among the male pasados of
a village that the principales were chosen (Guiteras Holmes 1961:73).
Elderly persons in general, of both sexes, were looked to for advice and
guidance. A person's aging was seen as intimately related to a maturation
process whereby a person's soul and level of spiritual "heat" increased,
enhancing his or her knowledge and capacity to reason (Guiteras
Holmes 1961:306; Eber 2000). Pasados and lineage elders could also be
asked to perform ritually demanding petitions on behalf of villagers who

felt they lacked the necessary competence themselves; for example, the complex, formal marriage petitioning made to the parents of the girl a boy wishes to marry. The use of ritualized language is prescribed in various contexts in Chenalhó, and the ability to speak eloquently and with authority is greatly esteemed; this knowledge is particularly expected of ritual experts and pasados (cf. Gossen 1983 on Chamula). During the twentieth century, however, this form of authority was increasingly challenged. This development is related to the broader changes in highland Maya societies during the last century.

STATE EROSION OF THE CALPUL SYSTEM

With the patron-client ties that developed between Pedranos and the Mexican state from the 1930s on and the new structures of governance imposed by the state, the power balance in Chenalhó was altered, as it was in neighboring Maya municipalities. The basis for confederate rule—the equal representation of all the subdivisions—gradually eroded, along with the former leadership system. Instead, a new cadre of young, bilingual men backed by the PRI and state institutions was able to gain increasing influence, legitimizing its authority by also taking on prestigious cargos (see, e.g., J. Rus and Wasserstrom 1980; J. Rus 2010).

The municipal government came to be controlled by those Pedranos who could most successfully maneuver both local politics and relations with the national party. The position of municipal president commanded political and economic resources that greatly overshadowed those of the other positions of leadership in the civil-religious hierarchy. Through his alignment with the official party, the municipal president was the main conduit to higher levels in the party hierarchy as well as to state authorities and various official institutions. In turn, these authorities relied on the municipal president to control the communities and to promote the various development projects that were now being fomented. Outside authorities also influenced the election of subsequent municipal presidents through the installation of municipal PRI committees (Arias 1985:121). The families—and villages or calpuls—excluded from political influence have had few means to counter this hegemony. With the external support the municipal president received from state and party

institutions, his need for the support of his fellow Pedranos was under-
mined (cf. G. Collier and Quaratiello 1999:121).

The municipal presidency became a highly attractive and potentially
lucrative post. In some highland municipalities the presidents enjoyed
"unprecedented accumulation of power and wealth" (J. Rus 1994:294).
In Chenalhó, as in other highland municipalities, certain families came
to monopolize or continuously influence the municipal presidency.
While the abuse and corruption of municipal leaders became extreme
in municipalities such as Chamula (see, e.g., J. Rus 2010), it appears to
have been less so in Chenalhó. However, the Arias family has to a large
extent controlled the government since the 1930s, when the legendary
Manuel Arias Sojom ruled as a bilingual and well-connected scribe in
the municipality before becoming president in 1944. Between 1944 and
2004, sixteen of the twenty-five or so municipal presidents have been
Ariases, many of them teachers.[30]

As a consequence of these changes, it became increasingly difficult
for many villagers to use the presidency as an intermediary in seeking
aid, such as agricultural credits or improved infrastructure, from external agencies and authorities. During my fieldwork in 1995–96, many villagers claimed that the municipal PRI presidency did not represent their
interests and felt alienated from it. In a meeting of Las Abejas, one of the
leaders described the municipal government as corrupt:

> We have elected our municipal president many times, [going to the
> municipal capital] carrying our *mats'* drink in the rain and the cold.
> But when the president begins to work, he works with the [federal]
> government; he lets himself be caught up by the money and leaves
> the people by the wayside. He stops respecting the people, even
> though at the time of the [election] campaign he respected every-
> body and gave us whatever we asked for. The same thing happens
> with the [federal] government. It only gives when it hasn't yet be-
> gun to work. Once it begins, it stops taking us into account.[31]

Pedranos I talked to often described the behavior of the municipal
authorities as arbitrary and unpredictable and not following common
standards of justice and morality. When factionalism increased in the municipality, the municipal authorities frequently refused to offer Pedranos
who were not affiliated with the PRI the assistance municipal authorities

ought to offer, including efforts to solve economic and marital disputes (see G. Collier and Quaratiello 1999:135–39 on similar exclusion in Zinacantán). A family known to me was refused transportation of the body of their dead child from the municipal center to their home village, something that is commonly provided on such occasions. The authorities, who all belonged to the PRI, asked the rhetorical question of which group the family belonged to, aware that they were Catholics and members of Las Abejas, and thus, the authorities implied, not their responsibility.[32]

Village leadership also shifted, controlled increasingly by PRI and state structures. The authority of the former elites—elders, principales, and pasados—was challenged by various new positions of leadership introduced by national legislation. New, important posts were the heads of ejidos and agrarian communities formed in the 1930s and 40s—such as the ejido committee, "comisario ejidal," elected by each ejido, and the centrally seated "comisariado" for the communal land within the parajes. Later, municipal agents became leaders of the villages that acquired the status of municipal agencies (Köhler 1990:33).[33] The local school committees also became influential in villages that had acquired a primary school, consisting of parents (fathers) elected for one year.[34] In most villages, the municipal agent and the school committee have come to function as the governing body, together with the ejido committee in ejidos, and their word weighs heavily in village affairs. Teachers at the new schools and the men holding the various positions created by state development bureaus, such as health and development promoters, also exerted influence on village politics.[35] The municipal and ejido agents took over the role of "messengers" previously held by the principales, bringing reports into the municipal center and orders out to the local units (Arias 1985:183).

Characteristic of all these new positions was that they favored merits such as bilingualism, literacy, and other skills useful for mediating with the broader Mexican society, further diminishing the authority of the, by and large, monolingual older elite. Some of the men belonging to this new generation of young bilingual Pedrano professionals, especially the teachers, also chose to compete as candidates in the elections for the municipal presidency, as happened in many other highland municipalities (Pineda 1993, 1995; Arias 1994).

The authority of seniors is being challenged also in general village and family life. The young are today increasingly prone to question the directives of their older paternal kin, a situation that is further reinforced by the increasing economic independence of young men who, when their fathers cannot give them land for cultivation, seek incomes outside the municipality (see, e.g., Eber 2011).

MAKING DECISIONS IN ASSEMBLIES

The basis for authority in Pedrano communities was altered even further by the increasing use of assembly-based, participatory decision making. The role of assemblies in both ejidos and agrarian communities was introduced by the agrarian reform and is established by the federal Agrarian Law (Appendini 2001:13–14). In both types of landholding, a general assembly of all landowners is supposed to be the basis for major decisions concerning land. The assemblies also must elect the annual members of the ejido or communal committees. While the ejidos in Chenalhó appear to have used assemblies early on, it is unclear when the parajes initiated the use of communal assemblies. There, it may have been teachers and the school committees that began employing village-level meetings to coordinate joint activities, using the ejido assembly as a model (J. Rus, personal communication 2001 and 2009; see also Viqueira in Ruiz Mondragón 2003).

In those indigenous regions in Chiapas where most communities are ejido-based, such as Las Cañadas in the Lacandon forest (Leyva-Solano 1995, 2003) or the Tojolabal highlands (Van der Haar 2001), the assembly model has become the central institution for local governance, handling far more issues than what the Agrarian Law requires, including economic, political, and moral issues, and frequently allowing men holding no ejido land to participate. Although there often are a variety of ejido leadership positions, all chosen yearly by the assembly, ordinary participants in the assembly gatherings appear to have a say in decision making. This horizontal assembly structure may be related to the history of these areas, where most indigenous people lived as plantation workers before land reform and the creation of ejidos. There was less of indigenous civil-religious cargo systems and calpul organization, in contrast to the relatively autonomous Tzotzil and Tzeltal municipalities of the central highlands. And the participatory and horizontal forms of decision making have perhaps been further strengthened by the heavy influence of the Catholic Diocese, as well as Protestant churches and certain political organizations, in these regions since the 1960s (Leyva-Solano 1995:384–95; Harvey 1998:61–65; Van der Haar 2001:138–39; see also chapter 2).

Eventually, however, Maya communities all through Chiapas, including the more hierarchical communities of the central highlands, have appropriated the use of communal assemblies as the primary base for decision making for all matters of shared village life. Generally, only adult men are allowed to participate. The communal assembly is frequently described, both by Mayas and others, as a traditional form of governance, commonly referred to as "usos y costumbre" (habits and custom). It has also served as the model for decision making in most religious and political Maya associations, including the EZLN—which allows women to participate also.

In Chenalhó today, all major decisions at the village level are supposed to be made by communal assemblies in which all men of working age in the village participate; women are not allowed to take part.[36] These assemblies elect the members of the school committee as well as the members of the various temporary commissions that are formed for different tasks. Sometimes the assemblies also elect the municipal agent, although technically he should be chosen by the municipal president.[37]

For some time, it appears, pasados and elders in Chenalhó have been able to influence the decision making of the assemblies, but their role has diminished.[38] However, they continue to hold a certain informal role, in some communities forming part of the group that prepares each assembly meeting. The major actors in the preparatory meetings are the municipal agent, the members of the school committee, and as a rule, the leaders of the respective politico-religious factions of the village. These meetings, I learned during fieldwork, are highly influential not only in setting the agenda for each assembly meeting but also in directing the outcome. When the leaders of the preparatory meetings have been able to find common ground on important issues to be addressed, their presentation of the matter at the assembly greatly influences the decisions the assembly participants eventually make. Thus, although communal decision making in Chenalhó today rests on participatory principles, the authority of leaders continues to be important.

BREAKING THE TIES OF STATE PATRONAGE

While the Mexican state came to exert far-reaching influence and control over Chenalhó and other highland Maya municipalities during the twentieth century, parallel processes emerged that destabilized this control. When local people no longer saw their municipal leaders as representative and legitimate, they developed alliances that sought other roads to gain influence and build community. Gradually, too, people's expectations of the Mexican state and its willingness to improve indigenous life conditions withered, giving way to open criticism of the government and organized political opposition. Eventually, Chenalhó became a mosaic of politico-religious factions.

One of the factors leading to this fracturing was the changing power structure of the communities and the waning influence of former senior authorities, which created room for political pluralism. With the introduction of village assemblies and growing demand for voicing individual opinion in the election of candidates and various other issues, the political became increasingly constructed as a public arena of alliance building—and eventually factionalism—while remaining an utterly male domain of decision making. Furthermore, an increasing number of Pedranos, primarily men, were gaining experience and skills in dealing directly with authorities and institutions of the broader Mexican society, making them less dependent on the official routes of municipal governance. Moreover, the surrounding world became more accessible through the improved roads, as well as increasingly present in daily village life through the lessons taught in the new schools and the growing number of radios in people's homes (cf. Arias 1994). From the 1950s on, and especially with the oil-induced economic boom in the 1970s, there were more possibilities for Maya men to find temporary jobs outside the municipalities (Cancian 1992; G. Collier and Rus 2002). More than the work on the lowland plantations, to which many Pedranos have periodically resorted, these jobs gave increased knowledge about Mexican

society and practice in speaking Spanish. The new generations of Pedranos thus gained tools and confidence to defend themselves against denigrating treatment by mestizos. A politically non-affiliated man in Yibeljoj
described this change to me: "It was always like that, that the mestizos
didn't take us into account. They said whatever they wanted and they
could call us whatever name since we had no education or just a little.
But now, when we have finished primary school, if they speak to us in
Spanish, then we can answer a little, it seems. It's not like the time of the
elders, when even if they were scolded [they could not respond]. Now we
can understand and know how to answer. We can't be afraid of them."[39]

Nonconformist organizations first emerged in the form of Pedranos seeking alternatives to "traditional" religion, locally referred to as
"costumbre," and opposing the conventional structures of authority. By
1953–54, the first small Presbyterian group was formed in the village of
Chimtic by villagers who had learned about the new religion outside
the municipality (Pérez Pérez 1992:105–107). The number of followers
slowly grew and new groups sprang up in other villages. They were paralleled in the 1960s by the first Catholic prayer groups, affiliated directly
with the Catholic Diocese. Other Protestant groups, such as the Pentecostals, emerged as well. The number of Protestants has grown considerably, today accounting for some 35 percent of the population.[40]

At times, Pedrano municipal authorities have persecuted and sometimes expelled converts, especially Presbyterians (Pérez Pérez 1992;
Pérez Enríquez 1994). Still, until 1996, persecutions in Chenalhó were
significantly fewer than in several other highland municipalities, where
religious conversion was seen as a more direct challenge to the municipal government's control (see, e.g., Kovic 2005 on Chamula). The Protestant and Catholic groups in Chenalhó did not initially present real
political opposition to the PRI or the municipal government. But by
1974, a large group of Pedranos, led by Catholic villagers, contested the
teachers' domination of the municipal presidency and put forth their
own campesino candidate, although still under the banner of PRI (Arias
1994:390–91).[41] The same year, Pedranos took part in a broad upsurge
of political discussion and organization among highland Mayas that followed the First Indigenous Congress in San Cristóbal, arranged by the
Catholic Diocese (Arias 1994:391).

In the late 1970s, the first opposition party appeared in Chenalhó. Partido Socialista de los Trabajadores (PST) presented a socialist program and promised land to its followers, attracting many villagers who had little or no land and scant hope of obtaining it through the interminable processing of land claims. During its first years, the party gained the bulk of its followers in the Los Chorros and Puebla ejidos in the northeastern *olon* part of the municipality. Tensions arose between the PST followers and the established PRI authorities at both village and municipal levels, especially when PST followers demanded representation in the municipal government. In 1979, during the Day of the Dead, the first of November, armed PRI villagers backed by the municipal government ambushed PST followers in Yibeljoj, Los Chorros, and La Libertad, resulting in five or six dead and several injured.[42] Support for PST weakened for some time, but the party continued to gather followers, later under the name Frente Cardenista.[43]

Pedranos increasingly questioned their continued poverty and the subjugation they experienced in mestizo society. By now, many had become disillusioned with the government's unfilled promises of substantive economic and other improvements in their life situation, and they began to criticize its politics. Political opposition was further spurred by a series of circumstances that made it increasingly harder for Pedranos and other Mayas to support their families. One was the nationwide economic crisis that began in the early 1980s and struck highland Mayas hard. With the world market prices for oil and coffee plummeting in 1982 and 1989 respectively, the jobs previously found at different construction sites and coffee plantations were significantly reduced in number. The low coffee prices also affected the incomes of Pedranos who cultivated coffee in their own fields. Furthermore, from the early 1980s, Mayas in Chiapas were losing most of the coffee jobs to Maya refugees who had fled the violence in Guatemala, who by 1982 numbered about two hundred thousand in southern Chiapas, and who accepted even less pay than the Mexican Mayas (G. Collier and Rus 2002). The difficulty in finding work as agricultural laborers was increased by the general decline of the agricultural economy in Chiapas, leading many large landowners to abandon plantation cultivation, some instead going into cattle ranching, where there was little need for laborers (J. Rus, Hernández Castillo, and Mattiace 2003). In addition, there was a dramatic increase in the size of the Maya population all over Chiapas in this period. In Chenalhó, the population more than doubled between 1970 and 1990, from some fourteen thousand to thirty-one thousand, further increasing the pressure for land and income.[44] Some of the young, landless Pedrano men and couples joined the large groups of highland Mayas who, especially from the 1970s on, were migrating in search of a livelihood to other regions, especially the Lacandon jungle in eastern Chiapas where state-held land was made available to landless peasants (J. Rus, Hernández Castillo, and Mattiace 2003).

This was the landscape when the federal government, in the early 1980s, began to abandon its former corporative and peasant-oriented policies and move toward a market liberalization of the Mexican economy. Subsequent administrations drastically reduced the support to peasant cultivation and the subsidies directed at the poor sections of the urban and rural population. This included cuts in expenditures on rural schools, health clinics, and housing (J. Rus, Hernández Castillo, and Mattiace 2003). State-run bureaus such as INMECAFE and CONASUPO were dismantled. Although new programs, such as the National Solidarity Program (PRONASOL), were meant to buffer some of these effects, on the whole, the Mayas of Chiapas faced decreasing incomes or means to ensure subsistence (G. Collier and Quaratiello 1999:139–46).

For many Mayas, this meant an end to the patron-client relationship with the Mexican government. More and more Pedranos, like Mayas throughout Chiapas, broke their bonds of loyalty with a state they perceived as failing in its promises and even as the cause of their continued poverty (J. Rus, Hernández Castillo, and Mattiace 2003). While Pedranos still recognized the PRI government as powerful and in control of most resources, they began to think of it as a power you are either for or against. After the Zapatista uprising in 1994, the majority of Pedranos even thought of the PRI government as an adversary and no longer voted for the party.[45] They sought alternatives in political organizations and parties of opposition or in the visions of the Protestant and Catholic prayer groups, who increasingly positioned themselves politically. Two major groups in Chenalhó were outspoken in their opposition to the PRI: the Zapatista support bases, whose members included Catholics who had left the diocese, assorted Protestants, and those who practiced costumbre religion; and Las Abejas, whose members were mainly Catholics affiliated with the diocese. Followers of the Frente Cardenista party were also in opposition until 1996, when they created an alliance with the municipal PRI authorities. This municipal fragmenting reflected the diverging political standpoints of Pedranos, but also the broader political conflict in Chiapas, where the PRI was losing most of its formerly solid support in Maya communities.[46]

In 1997, this factionalism developed into conditions approaching civil warfare in Chenalhó. Paramilitary groups, recruited among PRI and Cardenista villagers, began to attack members of Las Abejas and the Zapatistas, driving almost a third of the total population in Chenalhó from their homes, and culminating in the now-infamous massacre of unarmed Las Abejas members in Acteal, a village in the municipality.[47] For several years afterward, there was an intense military presence in Chenalhó, reportedly to prevent further paramilitary violence. Today, the three major factions in Chenalhó—PRI, the Zapatista autonomous municipality, and Las Abejas—have found nonviolent ways to coexist, although the fear of renewed paramilitary attacks still exists among government oppositional villagers. The PRI, however, continues to control the official municipal government, despite its defeat in the historic national elections in 2000 and 2006.

As a result, Chenalhó has now ceased to be a functioning confederacy or an integrated social and political unit. Political and religious factions not allied with the ruling party have no voice in the municipal government and thus no direct or formal influence. Pedranos may still refer to themselves as being one people, but there are no longer any communal activities, religious or political, that represent all inhabitants. Instead, each of the factions has been consolidated as a distinct and cohesive community of interest to which the members express loyalty and belonging. The new groups are also forming separate power structures. Although these sometimes challenge the power of the municipal government, they often sidestep it altogether. Today, a villager told me, everyone has their own group with their own leaders, and they only obey them, he said. Each of these factions appears to reconstitute many of the calpul characteristics of Pedrano society. Furthermore, the factions are all connected with "mother organizations" or allies outside Chenalhó, which often provide help to their members in approaching Mexican authorities and sometimes in receiving funding for projects—thus to some extent replacing the municipal leaders as intermediaries with the surrounding society.

During my fieldwork in 1995–96, before the violence and terror of 1997, Pedranos were already describing the rifts in their municipality as a source of sadness and unease and as a loss of former unity and solidarity. People talked of the emergence of factions as the period when "the parties arrived," or "the organizations arrived," and with them, "the problems." Pedranos who still supported the government often blamed the Zapatistas and the Catholic Diocese for bringing division and conflict into the municipality. Other villagers, even those who had joined the new groups, were wont to describe the development of factionalism as a government-orchestrated strategy of divide and rule. Many Pedranos were ambivalent, disturbed by the rupture of social bonds but happy with the perspectives and possibilities the new groups offered, and glad to have broken the ties of government patronage. Rosa Pérez Sántiz, a Catholic in Yibeljoj, described these mixed feelings:

> RPS: Before the organizations, life was better. No one was in opposition. With the organizations, the enemies appeared. Those who agree on something become enemies of those who don't agree with them. Those who don't want an organization see themselves as enemies of those who do. Before the organizations, we all had the same opinions, there were no disagreements. That's why we don't want some of the organizations. Before, there was only one organization and there were not many problems.
>
> HM: Does that mean that you were all in favor of the government before, that everyone agreed on that?
>
> RPS: That's how it was. We all liked the government. It was the PRI who favored us, we liked the government very much. It sent us things, it sent us money. Truly, we all liked the government. But now we have awakened.[48]

CHAPTER 2

Building Alliance with the Catholic Diocese

With the dissidence emerging in Chenalhó in the latter half of the twentieth century, a growing number of Pedranos chose to join prayer groups affiliated with the Catholic Diocese. Men, women, and their children began to meet once a week in their own or a neighboring village to pray and listen to what they referred to as the Word of God, led by village men who had received training from the diocese to become catechists. Through this affiliation, they contested, explicitly or implicitly, both conventional Pedrano religiosity and municipal and federal government politics. The growing discontent that spurred such choices among Pedranos as well as other Mayas coincided with the Catholic Diocese's new interest, from the early 1960s on, in strengthening its work in the rural Maya communities, a work that increasingly followed an explicit liberation theology line. Focusing on the experiences of suffering and marginalization among the poor, the liberation theology perspective provided an interpretive framework by which Pedranos could give such experiences new meaning and explain them as the result of unjust societal structures. Increasingly, the diocese also employed the globally expanding rights discourse when describing and denouncing this state of affairs. With these new perspectives, Pedranos found hope for change.

The village chapel groups formed by the Catholic Diocese offered a new, participatory form of communal worship influenced both by the liberation theology notions of an indigenous church—which allowed indigenous lay preachers to direct local worship—and the popularity of village-level services held by the rapidly growing Protestant churches in the region, with which the diocese was under pressure to compete. Like the Protestant churches, the diocese also provided membership in a community that extended beyond the local region. The translocal Catholic community gave Pedrano members a new sense of belonging and fellowship in both local and global arenas, where membership was defined not by class or ethnicity but by faith. This Catholic community has provided a forum for support and resources that, to some extent, bypasses official regional and state structures.

Over time, Catholic Pedranos and the diocese have thus formed an alliance that ensures support for Pedranos within a broader society seen as hostile. In this chapter, I outline how the mutual relationship between Pedranos and the Catholic Diocese developed. As we will see in subsequent chapters, this relationship has been the basis for far-reaching changes undertaken by Pedranos, concerning both their daily life in Chenalhó and their relation to the Mexican nation-state and to international society.

DIOCESAN WORK IN CHENALHÓ

The first Catholic prayer groups in Chenalhó were formed in the 1960s, when the Diocese of San Cristóbal de Las Casas, led by its new bishop, Samuel Ruiz García, initiated an active strategy of missionizing in the Maya region. The diocese had previously acted only through a small number of priests in the Maya area, who limited their services to offering mass and certain sacraments in the municipal capitals.[1] Chenalhó had been served by a priest living in the neighboring Tzotzil municipality of San Andrés Larráinzar. The priest would come to Chenalhó only a few times a year, mainly to celebrate the mass—in Spanish—for the mestizo population in the municipal capital. He also performed group baptisms in connection with important fiestas for saints, to which Pedrano parents from all over the municipality would bring their infants and the prospective godparents. Baptism was the only Catholic sacrament in demand by Pedranos. The ceremony was not perceived as a marker of a different faith but as an integrated ritual of the "traditional" religion, through which the infant's soul would be more firmly tied to the body (Arias

1975:55).[2] Indigenous authorities performed all other religious ceremonies in Chenalhó. Pedranos call this "traditional" religion "costumbre" and distinguish it from Protestantism and Catholicism.

Now, however, the Catholic Church made an effort to reinforce its clerical presence and teachings in Maya communities, since religious practices were considered still to contain many pagan elements (cf. Early 2012). Chenalhó received its first resident parish priest, Miguel Chanteau, of French origin, in 1965. Mass became a weekly event, though attended mainly by mestizos. Chanteau began to visit the communities and gained increasing recognition from Pedrano villagers for his many hours on foot traversing the winding paths. Still, the municipality was large and the villages remote for a sole person to attend to. The number of active followers did not begin to rise in any dramatic way until Chanteau, or Padre Miguel, as he was called, was assisted by local catechists.

The use of catechists was related to an effort by the diocese to accomplish a more active Catholicization of the indigenous population by training lay preachers in the villages to conduct local instruction in the Catholic dogma (Harvey 1998:71–72).[3] In 1961, the diocese decided to establish schools based in San Cristóbal, to which villagers from the Maya communities would come to receive training as lay preachers, or catechists (Fazio 1994:78). One school was founded by the Mexican order Hermanas del Divino Pastor (Sisters of the Good Shepherd), which had begun to work in several highland Maya municipalities. Among these municipalities was Chenalhó, where their pastoral labor complemented that of Padre Miguel. Together they initiated the training of Pedrano catechists.[4]

One of the first catechists in Chenalhó was Pedro Girón López in the Los Chorros ejido. When I met Girón in 1996, he was in his sixties and still full of vigor. Girón explained that his interest in the catechism was triggered by a priest who was visiting the ejido when Girón was a young man. After attending a catechist course for several months in San Cristóbal, Girón began teaching villagers about the Catholic creed and led growing prayer groups in seven villages besides his own ejido: Puebla, Yaxjemel, Taquiuc'um, La Libertad, Yibeljoj, Tzajalucum, and Yabteclum, all located in the northeastern *olon* part of Chenalhó. Every Sunday, he said, he went to visit one of the increasingly larger groups:

Well, people came guided by their interest—those who sought the Word of God. One, two, three people came. After one year there would be four, five people in each village. They began to reflect, since I was not dividing the people, only guiding them on how to live better. I told them not to steal, not to fight, not to kill, not to threaten women; that this is no good, since people need to live contentedly. In this way, I guided the people in every village. Not directly from the Bible, because that is hard, no one knew how to do that, just guidance.[5]

A growing number of Pedranos elsewhere in the municipality began to meet to pray and receive Catholic guidance in weekly encounters. When still only a handful, they would meet in someone's home or go to a neighboring village chapel. When a group was sufficiently large, members built their own chapel, usually a simple wooden structure with a dirt floor.

During this period, catechists were given a more active role in their interpretation of the scripture. In 1968, diocese pastoral workers evaluated the education of catechists and found it to be far too top-down, the courses indoctrinating catechists in Catholic dogma rather than stimulating their own reflection.[6] To enhance catechist involvement, catechist training was decentralized to the respective diocesan pastoral teams, "equipos pastorales," which had been formed in 1965. Each team was responsible for a region, or "zone," of the diocese, usually based on the major Mayan language of the area (see map 3 for the present zone division).[7] The training of catechists was now transferred to localities in the various municipalities and better adapted to local conditions. Similarly, the clergy moved much of their work to the communities, where they began to take part in the experiences and concerns of the catechists and members of the Catholic village chapels.

In Chenalhó, the catechist courses were eventually headquartered in the village of Yabteclum, where a Catholic center was constructed as an adjunct to the old church. This Catholic center became the locus for Pedrano Catholic activities, housing the courses for catechists as well as their monthly meetings and other Catholic gatherings in the municipality. Here a growing number of catechists developed the foundation and structure of the Pedrano Catholic community together with Padre Miguel and nuns from the Hermanas del Divino Pastor.

Creating an Indigenous Church

The reorganization of the diocese was part of the effort to "indigenize" the church, whereby Catholic villagers in the Maya communities would be given a stronger role in parish work. Bishop Ruiz had been increasingly influenced by liberation theological ideas on cultural pluralism that had come out of the Second Vatican Council, 1962–65, and the Second General Conference of CELAM, the Latin American Episcopal Conference, held in Medellín, Colombia, in 1968, where he had been one of the speakers. In line with the discussions at these encounters, Ruiz wanted to promote the recognition of indigenous religiosity. He argued that the diocese should not condemn practices that formerly had been seen as idolatrous, but instead aim for enculturation, whereby the diverse indigenous forms of spirituality would be incorporated into the theological concepts of the Catholic Church (Kovic 2005:50; Early 2012). Local catechists and chapel group members were given more autonomy to determine the manner of their religious expressions, based on their reflection upon scripture and their own lives.[8] The chapel groups were regarded as Christian base communities, "comunidades eclesiales de base," or CEBs, where members, with the guidance of the catechists, prayed and studied the Bible and eventually began to address their broader life situation.

The aim of training indigenous catechists was to increase the indigenous role in and influence over the evangelization of Maya communities, creating an "autochthonous church" (CENAMI 2000). This work was quite successful. By 1998, eight thousand catechists were in the diocese (Kovic 2005:186), making it the most catechist-dense diocese in the global Catholic Church. In order to advance indigenous church leadership, the diocese also nominated a high number of indigenous deacons (*tuneletik* in Tzotzil), who were able to perform certain sacraments.[9] In 2008, there were 344 deacons in the diocese.[10] In contrast to the broader Catholic Church, where the position of deacon is but a step in training to become a full-fledged priest, the Diocese of San Cristóbal regards the deaconship as a permanent position that married indigenous men can hold.

Since unmarried men are not considered socially mature in Maya communities, the Catholic demand of priestly celibacy leads to very few Maya men aspiring to be priests (interview with Toussaint Loera, in Bonner 1999:137–38). The diocese further grants the wives of deacons defined status and roles that are in many ways similar to those of traditional cargoholders in Maya communities.

The diocese does not allow women to be deacons but welcomes women as catechists. Two groups of indigenous women based in San Cristóbal also work as a type of lay nuns.[11] They are unmarried women who have left their home communities to dedicate themselves to the work, usually in collaboration with the Hermanas del Divino Pastor. Some of the lay nuns also work specifically with women in the village chapel groups to discuss and strengthen their role in their communities, and they have been important facilitators in the meetings of the Diocesan Coordination of Women (CODIMUJ).

This local-level organization of church work significantly resembles that of the Protestant churches working in Maya communities. Protestants have been increasingly successful since the 1950s in gaining adherents, a fact that probably has propelled the Catholic Diocese to change (Bonner 1999:135–39; G. Collier and Quaratiello 1999:55–61). Both the Protestant churches and the Catholic Diocese use the "assembly," a form of village-level collective participation practiced in many villages since the introduction of ejidal and communal assemblies (described in chapter 1), as the base where the local group of followers can worship and study the Bible. However, in contrast with the regular ejidal and communal assemblies, chapel group assemblies allow the participation of women and children, thus drastically broadening communal participation. This new openness has been well received; women have rapidly become the majority of participants in the weekly meetings of both Protestant and Catholic churches.

Protestant churches had introduced the use of indigenous lay leaders in the 1940s and granted considerable authority to local chapel groups over their form of worship, as well as offering new positions of influence for villagers (G. Collier and Quaratiello 1999:58). In both Protestant and Catholic chapel groups, lay leaders must be approved by the chapel group assembly before starting their posts. With the use of indigenous lay leaders, services were now for the first time held in the local Mayan language. Influenced by the various Protestant churches and the Summer Institute of Linguistics, the Catholic Diocese gradually began to use Mayan-language written materials also, and to translate the Bible, beginning with a Tzeltal version (Hernández Castillo 1995:420). Another important phenomenon borrowed from the Protestant churches has been the use of the highly popular music bands, "conjuntos," in the worship meetings of Catholic chapel groups. The conjunto songs are almost always in indigenous languages, most with tunes borrowed from popular Mexican music, and the chapel members quickly learn them. Catholic catechists and deacons commonly regard the conjuntos as an important aid in their work, as the music enlivens and animates the chapel meetings.

But unlike Protestant churches, the Catholic chapel groups and the diocese are subordinate to a highly hierarchical worldwide Catholic Church, and ultimately, the authority of the Vatican. The Vatican has repeatedly criticized the high number of indigenous catechists and deacons over the years, expressing concern over their numbers relative to the low number of priests in the diocese, and over the role, albeit informal, granted the wives of the Maya deacons, which contests church conventions. Critics in the diocese argue that the Vatican wants to stop the development of an autochthonous church because it threatens the Vatican's control over the clergy.

Tools for Political Reflection

The results of Vatican II and the CELAM conference of bishops not only led the diocese to strengthen its indigenous participation but also impacted its political orientation. Previously aspiring toward modernist development, Bishop Ruiz had become more and more concerned with the economic and political marginalization of Maya villagers. He now began devoting attention to the political demands emerging in the Maya population throughout the state (Harvey 1998:69; Kovic 2005:49). In 1974, Ruiz hosted the First Indigenous Congress in San Cristóbal de Las Casas, a meeting that is commonly seen as the catalyst for indigenous political mobilization in Chiapas.[12] The congress would also have a great impact on the work of the diocese. The more than one thousand Maya delegates included Catholics from the diocese's four largest language groups, but also non-Catholic representatives of villages and ejidos that had chosen to participate. Discussions focused on the issues of land, health, education, and the commercialization of agricultural products. After this first assembly, the congress continued to meet for the next few years, eventually dissolving but giving rise to other political initiatives and also influencing the work of the diocese (Morales Bermúdez 1992; Hernández Castillo 2001:105–10).

In 1975, in the First Diocesan Assembly, held with the pastoral workers, the liberation theology orientation of the diocese was made explicit when the bishop and clergy declared that the diocese should work with a "preferential option for the poor," who should be helped to become "subjects of their own history."[13] The assembly defined the issue of social justice as a central dimension of diocesan responsibilities. The diocese assigned thematic "work areas" for all the pastoral teams, focusing, for example, on health, production cooperatives, and popular education (CENAMI 2000). The teams also introduced a new method of approaching scripture in the village chapel groups, intended to stimulate reflection not only on the Gospels, but also on how the texts could be used to interpret and define the conditions in which the villagers themselves lived. This method included discussing a few questions at every chapel group meeting. In these questions, chapel members were encouraged to compare the selected Gospel text with their own lives. The method, called *tijwanej* in Tzeltal, was an attempt to improve the didactic format of the village chapel meetings, where the followers were too often the passive recipients of catechist teachings. Instead, the diocese wanted to stimulate communal participation in the analysis of the scripture. The reflection and analysis that arose from the discussions were seen as important also in promoting participatory decision making in the chapel assemblies, as well as broader agreements and political mobilization among Catholic Maya villagers (Leyva-Solano 1995; interview with Toussaint Loera, in Bonner 1999:137).

In the years that followed, local pastoral workers gradually introduced this method to the individual parishes. In Las Cañadas in eastern Chiapas, where Maya peasants emigrated in search of land, the Catholic

Diocese had a considerable influence on the construction of many of the new communities. The *tijwanej* method here constituted the basis for shared, leader-guided reflection and decision making not confined to the chapel service but extending to the broader communal assemblies (Leyva-Solano 1995). In the 1990s, the combined influence of communal assemblies and participatory chapel methods formed the organizational basis for EZLN, which originated in Las Cañadas (Harvey 1998:74).

In Chenalhó, as in other Maya areas, the *tijwanej* method tended to encourage political analysis, and eventually, communitarian actions.[14] Both catechists and regular chapel members in Chenalhó described this period to me as a political awakening, when they began to reflect on the meaning of the Word of God and of the suffering they endured. Several Pedrano catechists had participated in the First Indigenous Congress in 1974, where they had presented testimony about the problems in their municipality and had returned with accounts from other municipalities to share with the chapel members, further strengthening the process of politicization (Arias 1994:391).

The diocese offered increasingly specialized means to meet the concerns that arose in the chapel groups and to strengthen the political agency of the members vis-à-vis the broader Mexican society. Some were tangible projects focused on economic improvements. Pastoral workers in Chenalhó helped create cooperative village stores and small agricultural cooperatives, where a number of Catholics in a given village would cultivate a crop to be sold for shared benefit. The diocese also promoted the formation of loan cooperatives, where Catholics contributed money to a "caja popular," a collective bank offering interest-free loans. These projects were regarded as organized in a spirit of mutual help and communion, similar to the work of the first apostles.[15]

Political networking and activism were another field of activity in which Pedrano Catholics became gradually engaged. Perhaps the most important network is Pueblo Creyente (People of Faith), created in 1991, which draws representatives from all the parishes of the Diocese of San Cristóbal de Las Casas. Through the delegates that Pedrano Catholic communities send to Pueblo Creyente meetings, they participate in a diocese-wide discussion of shared concerns and are able to coordinate political actions, principally in the form of mass demonstrations, known as pilgrimages, directed at particular issues.[16] A similar network is CODIMUJ, which involves women from all the zones of the diocese, the majority of them indigenous catechists. The delegates discuss shared political concerns and plan their work, aimed at strengthening the active participation of women in the chapel groups and communities.

Perhaps most important, political analysis and discussions have for many years been integral to the ongoing training of catechists, guided by the priests, nuns, and other pastoral workers. The yearly courses for catechists in Chenalhó often include descriptions and analyses of historical processes both in the Catholic Church and in Mexican society, which are then related to the present-day situation of the participants. During my fieldwork, the nun from Hermanas del Divino Pastor supplied the data and general focus for the various sessions of the course, which the Pedrano catechist coordinators then developed and adapted for their presentations to the course participants. The municipal-level monthly catechist meetings likewise involve political information and discussions, where the pastoral workers often have an important role both in providing political news and, through their occasional interventions, in influencing the direction of the discussions, although these are always led by catechists. Through the catechists, this political guidance is then conveyed to the members of each village chapel group as part of its weekly Sunday services.

Introducing Human Rights

The diocese introduced the concept of human rights to indigenous communities as a tool to evaluate the conduct of authorities and denounce abuse. Through the Fray Bartolomé de Las Casas Center for Human Rights (known locally as FrayBa), founded in 1989 by Bishop Ruiz, the diocese provided the means for villagers to monitor the conduct of authorities, both indigenous municipal officials and powerful members of the broader Mexican society. For Ruiz, as for many other Catholics who espouse liberation theology, the "preferential option for the poor" guided their appropriation of the broader human rights discourse, which had been dominated by an emphasis on civil and political rights (Engler 2000). By focusing on "the rights of the poor" and "human dignity," Ruiz and others included and sometimes foregrounded social, political, and economic rights and their relation to broader societal structures of inequality and exploitation (Engler 2000; Kovic 2005, 2008).[17] The purpose of the Center for Human Rights, then, was to promote and defend the rights of the poor through the legal protection offered by national and international laws and regulations (Kovic 2005:63; Speed 2008:41). The services of the center, which people associate with the diocese and with a position critical of the government, are principally sought out by Catholic Mayas.[18]

The Center for Human Rights has taken an integrated stance regarding human rights, embracing civil, political, economic, social, and cultural rights (e.g., CDHFBC 2005:3). According to one of the center's publications, some of these rights consist of "sufficient food, adequate housing and clothing, education adapted to specific cultures, work or permanent employment with a fair salary as well as an ecologically, politically, and socially healthy environment" (CDHFBC 2005:1, my translation). It posits liberty, justice, and peace as prerequisites for the fulfillment of these human rights (CDHFBC 2005:3). However, the center focuses its work on two areas in particular. The first concerns violations against civil and political rights in the matter of "executions, torture, arbitrary detentions, disappearances and forced displacement."[19] The second addresses the right to indigenous self-determination, which includes the right of "indigenous villages . . . to land and territory" and "their own systems of justice and exercise of government" (CDHFBC 2005:3.

The Center for Human Rights provides legal assistance to the Maya communities and promotes the formation of local human rights committees (CDHFBC 2000; Kovic 2005:103). In Chenalhó in the early 1990s, Pedranos attending the catechist meetings in Yabteclum chose a few Catholic men to serve as local members of the human rights committees organized by the center. Their task was to collect complaints among villagers on human right abuses or other legal or political matters. They would then report the complaints to the office of the Center for Human Rights in San Cristóbal, which would decide if and how to proceed.[20]

The center also offers education on human rights, the Mexican constitution, and the Mexican federal system and has developed teaching materials especially adapted for workshops with Maya peasants (e.g., CDHFBC 2005). One 1992 example was a series of workshops that the center, along with human rights committee members in Chenalhó, organized for Catholic villagers concerning the changes to Article 27 of the constitution, whereby ejidal and communal land was no longer protected against privatization. This change was regarded as risking the loss of land to outsiders, and ultimately, the survival of indigenous communities (cf. Harvey 1998:186–90). I took part in a human rights workshop in 1996 directed primarily at local representatives of Las Abejas—the political association of the Catholic community in Chenalhó—held in the Catholic center in the village of Yabteclum. Workshop participants were introduced to the notion of human rights and discussed what they should consist of (see also Kovic 2005:107–13).[21]

In its teaching materials, the Center for Human Rights presents human rights as "natural" rights that every person acquires simply by being born: "it's inside us, like our spirit" (CDHFBC 2005:17; see also Kovic 2005:109). The teaching materials define behavior that constitute violations of rights and emphasize that one's human rights should be respected within the family, the community, and the various political organizations. Center literature refers to the social regulations establishing these rights, such as the UN declaration and covenants on rights and the Mexican constitution, described as the fruit of peoples' striving to fight suffering and injustice (CDHFBC 2005:18–20; cf. Speed 2008:41–42). It also provides detailed information about how to process accusations and appeals through the Mexican judiciary system. The violations discussed in the material, however, all concern civil and political rights, rather than economic, social and cultural rights (CDHFBC 2005, pt. 2). As will be discussed in later chapters, the focus on human rights has become a central dimension of the political demands presented by Catholic Pedranos, and of their claims as citizens of the Mexican nation-state. Catholic Pedranos also, it appears, emphasize particularly their demands for civil and political rights.

The Changing Diocese

The composition of clergy working in Chenalhó has changed over the years. In 1998, the Mexican government arrested Miguel Chanteau and expelled him from the country after thirty-three years as parish priest in Chenalhó. The government accused him of "having engaged in unauthorized activities" and of blaming the government for the Acteal massacre in December 1997 (Paulson 1998).[22] The new parish priest was the Jesuit Pedro Arriaga, who from 1998 on, together with two other Jesuits and various novices, supplemented the work being done by the Hermanas del Divino Pastor. An important part of the Jesuits' work was to advise the political association Las Abejas, which is part of the Pedrano Catholic community, and which the diocese regarded as needing guidance with its increasing political and administrative responsibilities after the massacre. The Jesuits also began to minister to the Zapatista Catholics in the municipality. The PRI-led municipal authorities of Chenalhó, however, rejecting the choice of Arriaga and deploring the influence of the diocese in political affairs, sought out the service of Luis Beltrán Mijangos, a priest who despite having being officially suspended by the bishop, administered services anyway for PRI followers in several other indigenous municipalities as well as a conservative anti-diocese faction of San Cristóbal. In 2002, the diocese ordained Marcelo Pérez Pérez as parochial vicar to assist Pastor Arriaga in his leadership of the congregation. Originally from neighboring San Andrés Larráinzar, he was the first Tzotzil priest, and only the second Maya priest, in the diocese. In 2007, Pérez became the Chenalhó parish's pastor, replacing Pedro Arriaga, who was transferred to neighboring Chamula. But in 2011, the diocese moved Pérez to another municipality after he received repeated threats and attacks by unknown persons, probably because of his closeness to Las Abejas. He was replaced by Manuel Pérez Gómez, formerly parish pastor in Simojovel. Nuns from the Hermanas del Divino Pastor continue to work in the parish.

The diocese also has a new bishop. In 2000, Samuel Ruiz retired as planned, replaced by Felipe Arizmendi.[23] Contrary to expectations, Raúl Vera López, auxiliary bishop in the diocese since 1995, was passed over for Bishop Ruiz's post. It was well known that the Vatican considered the work of Ruiz far too radical, and the installation of Vera as auxiliary bishop had been recognized as an attempt by the Vatican to counter Ruiz's influence. But Vera became radicalized during his service in the diocese and eventually became even more outspoken than Ruiz. The choice of Arizmendi was therefore generally interpreted as an attempt by the Vatican, possibly in agreement with the Mexican government, to finally end the liberation theology work of the San Cristóbal diocese. Arizmendi, who formerly had been bishop in the Diocese of Tapachula, Chiapas, was known to be of a conservative bent. Las Abejas leaders responded to the announcement of these changes in a communiqué of January 3, 2000, in which they expressed the shock of now "becoming orphans." They continued: "We need a bishop of the diocese who loves the poor and those in greatest need, may it be a bishop who respects our indigenous culture as the foundation of our lives, with the strength of the Word of God." The schism with the Vatican deepened with the Vatican's ban in 2002 on further ordinations of indigenous deacons in the diocese. In 2002, around eighteen thousand Catholic Mayas participated in the first pilgrimage in San Cristóbal since Ruiz retired, to protest against the Vatican ban on the ordinations.[24]

Under the leadership of Bishop Arizmendi, certain changes in the political work of the diocese have taken place. Arizmendi, as well as Enrique Díaz, who became auxiliary bishop in 2003, has expressed a commitment both to the preferential option for the poor and the constitution of an autochthonous indigenous church, which they believe cannot be a reality without indigenous priests. Arizmendi has ordained the first indigenous priests ever of the diocese, reaching the number of seven in 2009.[25] Some Maya Catholics question the new bishops' dedication to these issues, however (Sánchez Franco 2004). Nevertheless, large pilgrimages with thousands of participants from Maya chapel groups continue to take place in San Cristóbal protesting various political issues.

CATHOLIC PEDRANOS AND THE DIOCESE

Through their long and committed involvement with Catholic villagers in Chenalhó, both the Diocese of San Cristóbal and the Fray Bartolomé de Las Casas Center for Human Rights have become allies of the villagers, I suggest, in a Mexican society in which Pedranos are otherwise marginalized. They recognize the clergy as "walking with" indigenous people, not only on the literal, meandering paths between distant communities, but also on the path the indigenous poor hope will lead to a better life (see Kovic 2005). In the highly politicized climate of Chiapas, the diocese is considered to be on the side of the poor, and not aligned with a government that most Catholic villagers have come to define as oppressive.

The authority of the diocese leadership stems from religious leadership, above all. To uphold their new relationship with God, Pedrano Catholics are dependent on the diocese. They rely on the clergy's expertise to teach them how to interpret the Bible and realize God's will in their own lives, and to perform most of the sacraments. This hierarchy is also manifest in the Pedrano Catholic community's place in the formal structure of the diocese. It is the bishop and the diocesan assembly that set the conditions for being recognized as part of the diocese.

Because the relation between Pedrano Catholics and the clergy aims toward the converts' gradual assimilation of skills in interpreting the Bible, many converts find strength in their interactions. I often heard chapel members express pride in their increasing competence in reflecting upon biblical texts and metaphors, and some of the catechists have

The parish priest, Marcelo Pérez Pérez, celebrates Catholic mass for San Pedro Apóstol in Acteal, June 2011. Photo by José A. Jiménez Pérez.

confidently mastered the interpretation and explication of theological concepts. While Pedranos do not expect to reach the level of theological sophistication of the bishop or pastoral workers, both catechists and regular chapel members appear to value the commitment of the diocese clergy to share knowledge, and they regard their own learning as a process of empowerment.

Pedrano Catholics also rely on the diocese for political guidance. Before making important decisions about how to act as a political collectivity both inside and outside of Chenalhó, they often send a commission of representatives to key persons in the diocese or the Center for Human Rights to seek advice. Especially since the Zapatista uprising, by their support of EZLN demands, Pedrano Catholics—principally through their association, Las Abejas—have come to act on a political scene far broader than that of the municipality, and they often seek counsel from their allies to better survey the whole political panorama. During my stay, the catechist and Las Abejas leaders would generally refrain from taking a position that was not recommended by these advisors.

Pedrano Catholics also turn to the Center for Human Rights when they need legal counsel and assistance in navigating the legal system. After the formation of a human rights committee in Chenalhó in the early 1990s, Pedrano Catholics recur to the Center for Human Rights to give testimony about incidents of human rights abuse, and in serious cases, they may receive help to denounce the abuse and institute legal proceedings. The center also assists when villagers have relatives who have been arrested, to ensure that their human rights are respected in the judicial process, often mediated through the special "indigenous lawyer" of Las Abejas, a Pedrano man with certain skills in official procedures. After the Acteal massacre in 1997, the center has consistently offered advice to Las Abejas on legal proceedings for indemnities and help in processing and publicizing denunciations of paramilitary activities, and it has coordinated the involvement of national and international peace observers.

Personnel at the center also offer informal guidance for dealing with other official institutions and give advice on how to follow bureaucratic procedures for various petitions. Before addressing an application for bringing water or electricity to their village to the corresponding government commission, for example, Pedrano Catholics often go to the Center for Human Rights first.

At times, Pedrano Catholics turn to other civil associations for consultation or assistance, such as Alianza Cívica, a national association that promotes the development of a democratic election process. Alianza Cívica is not related to the Catholic Church but is viewed favorably by the diocese in San Cristóbal, and Pedrano Catholics have probably not received any negative signals from the diocese concerning their collaboration. The Catholic association Caritas has also become important, because it administered much of the aid to the camps for villagers displaced after the violence in 1997.

Villagers turn to the diocese for help in approaching mestizo health institutions, since they anticipate being exposed to denigrating attitudes by the staff. Many Catholic Pedranos ask pastoral clergy to accompany them to try to ensure they receive proper and timely treatment. Sometimes the Pedrano health promoter of a village chapel group will accompany chapel group members to serve as interpreter and facilitator. Pedranos also ask their allies for advice in finding a trustworthy clinic. Thus, when I drove my hostess to San Cristóbal when she had a serious toothache, her husband, who accompanied her, first went to the diocese office to find out what dentist they recommended.

The knowledge that Pedrano Catholics have gained through their Catholic allies drastically strengthens their ability to defend their interests before Mexican authorities and institutions. In lessons taught by clergy and workshops arranged by the Center for Human Rights, Pedrano Catholics are presented with descriptions of Mexican society, its history and institutions, its constitution and laws. They also are provided with information about international law and rights conventions, which is a further advantage when presenting claims to authorities. With such tools, Pedrano Catholics can judge the extent to which the execution of power by authorities corresponds with or violates objective regulations. Both catechists and Las Abejas representatives are greatly improving their literacy and fluency in Spanish; several have acquired the skills to write formal documents and interact with institutions and other authorities. Some of the younger Las Abejas leaders are adept at using cell phones, the Internet, and new social media, thereby sustaining a broad international web of contacts. Many have become familiar with the NGO scene in town and feel less constrained in their interactions with mestizos, especially with the intense presence of Mexican and international observers and visitors after the Acteal massacre in 1997.

Pedrano Catholics are thus developing the means to defend what they have come to define as their constitutionally recognized rights and interests, both in municipal matters and as members of the broader Mexican society. Admittedly, those who have developed these skills are mainly men who hold special positions such as catechists, Las Abejas board members, or various committee heads, but they act on behalf of the larger group, whether the village chapel group or the whole Catholic community, and their accomplishments are regarded as beneficial to all.

Through the support of the diocese, Pedrano Catholics have gained routes to leadership, influence, and urban know-how without being part of the official municipal and village leadership in Chenalhó. Sebastián Gómez, a Catholic Pedrano and former human rights committee member, described the resignation that previously had colored many villagers' interaction with the municipal presidency:

> Before, anything the municipal government decided, whether what people had done was right or wrong, there it ended—there the case ended! If someone is accused of being guilty [of some crime], "Whatever," is all he'd say. "May God help me, since I didn't do anything." That's their way of handling it. . . . But really, they didn't know! They didn't know, they were afraid when they were told, "You're going to the Ministerio Público [the police authority in San Cristóbal]!" Shit, that scared them! And with such rumors, people were really anxious and didn't know what to do. If they were put in jail and stayed there some days, they just withstood it. "What will happen, will happen," they say. . . . They don't know where to make complaints and how to defend themselves by going to a lawyer, speak to a lawyer. . . . Before, only those with education [had such knowledge].[26]

Gómez described how this sense of vulnerability when faced with corrupt municipal authorities began to change when they gained new conceptual and legal tools (see also Kovic 2003a:60):

People learned that you could go to a place, to the Center [for
Human Rights] and also to Asuntos Indígenas [the Department
of Indigenous Affairs]; that with them you could be rescued, that
you had to present yourself to them and give them all the information. People found this out, and they began to practice it all by
themselves since in Asuntos Indígenas there are also interpreters.
. . . Not until then did people begin to defend themselves. . . .
When people learned that it was possible to defend yourself, that
you couldn't punish someone if he wasn't guilty, well, now they
knew. They themselves got organized, like those of the church.
. . . They attended many courses and learned how to defend themselves. Just like Jesus helped the Indians before.[27]

THE DYNAMICS OF SUBORDINATION

The relationship that Pedrano Catholics have with the diocese and their
NGO allies is complex, simultaneously empowering and subordinating.
The interactions that I witnessed were frequently structured as that of
pupils and teachers, where Pedrano Catholics were supposed to gain
knowledge and insights from the teachings offered by their mestizo advisors. The clergy, as well as NGO workers, frequently had little knowledge
of Maya society, institutions, or norms. Because the focus of training was
mestizo society and its institutions, this contributed even further to make
Pedrano spheres of knowledge invisible, or implicitly invalid. These interactions reinforced a historically embedded hierarchy between indigenous peasants and mestizos, and between indigenous knowledge and
mestizo knowledge. The pastoral workers certainly aimed to train the
converts and create autochthonous church-groups. During my fieldwork, the nun, a mestizo, made sure Pedrano Catholics took charge of
all meetings and courses of the Catholic community in Chenalhó, and
all communication was in Tzotzil. Nevertheless, through the authority of
her position, she exerted considerable influence over the direction of
discussions and decisions.

This imbalance was even more accentuated in the interaction with
mestizo NGO workers. In contrast to most pastoral workers, NGO workers usually have little experience of living in indigenous communities
and limited knowledge of Mayan languages. They rely on interpreters in

the meetings and workshops, and the burden of translating concepts and terms lies principally on the interpreter and the indigenous participants. In the various NGO-led workshops and encounters I took part in, Pedranos often showed great respect for the mestizo teachings. They often explained the difficulties they had in grasping the concepts and structures they were presented with as deriving from their own ignorance and slowness. The mestizos, too, often appeared to regard problems in transmitting their teachings as due to limitations on the part of the participants and seemed to underestimate the difficulties posed by any linguistic and cultural translation. Thus, while in one respect empowering the participants, these encounters often conveyed a message to the converts, understood and commonly accepted by Pedrano Catholics, of intellectual inferiority (cf. Hernández Castillo 2003:68–69).

This unequal relationship is to some extent furthered by Pedrano Catholics themselves. In contrast to Pedrano costumbre religion, Pedrano Catholic liberation theology gives ontological relevance, and to some degree, epistemological primacy to the non-Pedrano world outside Chenalhó. It is in this world that the Bible and biblical competence originate, as well as the Mexican constitution and laws, the international conventions on human rights, and the interpretation of their meaning and application. Consequently, Pedrano Catholics seek the expertise of non-indigenous authorities. They rely heavily on their allies—diocesan clergy and selected civil associations—for theological and political guidance. The situation could be described as a voluntary relinquishment to the "other" of the power to define "us" and the way the world really is. A catechist in Yibeljoj, Juan Sántiz, told me of the subordination he felt in relation to the mestizo clergy, and he blamed it on Pedrano Catholics' lack of knowledge and power to end their poverty.

> JS: We who live in the woods, well, obviously we don't know the truth. But as in that time [of the first prophets], it is the great ones who have dedicated themselves to looking at our situation, like Samuel [Ruiz, the bishop]. They put themselves out there so someone will see them, they say it straight to the face of the government that it isn't providing for the poor. That's how they are alike, our Father [Samuel] and the apostles. We who are truly simple are being pulled along by them, because we don't

know or we don't know how to solve it. And they are fulfilling
what is written about what the apostles did.

HM: What is it that you don't know?

JS: Well, what we don't know is. . . . It's because we don't know, we
don't know how to understand the talk, and we don't know how
to read. They know it well, they're familiar with it, they have
done much studying. But we only understand that it is like this,
and we only obey orders. . . . Because our eyes are closed and
our ears are covered, we don't know how things are, what it is
that God truly wants. But those who know Spanish well, they
understand what work we should do. That's how it is. In our own
minds we only understand if there's corruption and suffering
because of the government, where the problems have started,
where it created oppression. Well, *that* we understand, all of us.
But really, how to change this, how to solve it, we don't know,
and we don't know how to ask for it. That's what I understand
of these things.[28]

The authority that Catholic Pedranos grant the allied mestizos is further reinforced by broadly held notions among Pedranos, which differentiate between ordinary villagers and those with demonstrated expertise in religious, moral, and political matters, related to the earlier calpul
form of organization. This implies a strong sense of respect for knowledge, the capacity to reason, and the ability to promote social accord—
abilities commonly associated with elderly men who have gained high
positions in the community. In a similar vein, Pedrano Catholics recognize the bishop as their ultimate authority in both religious and political
matters and regard the pastoral workers as representing his authority.

Catholic Pedranos are aware of the unequal relationship with their
mestizo allies, and they reflect upon and comment on their complex dependency. One of the most experienced leaders of Las Abejas expressed
his feelings of inadequacy when he addressed a municipal meeting of
the association in fall 1995. Representing Las Abejas together with another delegate, he had participated in a preparatory conference in San
Cristóbal for the peace negotiations on indigenous rights between EZLN
and the Mexican government. The participants had been representatives of indigenous organizations as well as "specialists," mostly mestizo
middle-class intellectuals. Reporting about the conference and the document with the conclusions they had reached, he said it had been difficult

to fully grasp many of the new issues, while they had presented few problems for the mestizos:

> Those invited by the EZ have many responsibilities. They are doctors, anthropologists, "licenciados,"[29] and from other professions. That's why they know and understand everything that is written here [points at the document], and that's why they understand the situation of the indigenous poor. That's why sometimes we don't understand what they say to us. We don't know if it's good or if it's not good. . . . We will go over it [with you] in a minute, we'll read it, because the words are really complicated, much of it we don't understand.[30]

The sense of shortcomings in relation to mestizo allies applies to the sharp contrast in living conditions as well. For the delegates of Las Abejas at the conference, the material differences between Pedranos and mestizo advisors had been more palpable than usual during those days of close interaction. The meeting, the men reported, had been prolonged by several days, which put indigenous representatives like themselves in a precarious situation, since they had too little money to cover any extra expenses. They were provided with food and lodging in the former premises of the National Indigenous Institute, where they slept on the floor in halls with other men, but it was in stark contrast with the mestizo delegates, who were able to pay for quite different accommodations: "Our problem was that we don't have that much money. We didn't have any place to eat, only when they gave it to us for free. The others, in contrast, they slept in hotels. When you sleep in a hotel, the mattress makes you bounce like a ball! [General laughter.] There is color television, you can watch it lying on the bed. You are like a king! I say this because I went in there a little while, where the others sleep."

The man reflected on how settings like these made him lose his usual confidence, and that he shared this experience with many others: "When we are at home we feel really bold, we can quarrel, we can argue. I may even get into a fight with someone and hurt him. But these things we can only do here. When we get into dealing with very important issues there, we don't know anything. Well, that's what happening to us now. This national dialogue [the preparatory conference] seems very difficult to us."

But in spite of the unequal relationship to their mestizo allies, Pedrano Catholics are never passive recipients of the instructions and guidance they are offered. They always evaluate the teachings, and while they often follow them eventually, they question many issues and directly resist others, openly or by evasion. While the coordinating catechists usually back up diocesan authority, others, both catechists and regular chapel members, sometimes react with hesitation or outright rejection. Disagreements among Pedrano Catholics on whether to follow the direction promoted by the clergy has sometimes led to conflicts and secession by those diverging from the diocese's line, as will be discussed in chapter 7. With their growing political experience and confidence, Catholic Pedranos and their leaders have increasingly contested and at times dismissed the advice and goals of the pastoral clergy.

Still, Pedrano Catholics are maintaining their adherence to the diocese and the Catholic Church. Through their alliance with the diocese and the Fray Bartolomé de Las Casas Center for Human Rights, they assure themselves of continued assistance and protection. This was especially tangible during the violent aggressions against Catholic followers in Chenalhó in 1997 and the years of continued paramilitary threats that followed, when several thousand Catholic Pedranos lived in refugee camps in the municipality. Even when their own employees suffered harassment and persecution, the diocese and pastoral workers demonstrated loyalty and support that the Pedrano Catholics could count on in times of severe need and danger. The converts, on their part, continue to confirm their allegiance to their allies and to their position as authorities. Although the alliance is unequal, it is based on mutual commitment and trust.

BECOMING CATHOLIC

Many men and women who join the Catholics stay on the periphery of the group and eventually stop attending meetings; instead, for different reasons, some may opt to join other religious groups. It is a known phenomenon that Maya villagers in Chiapas often, and seemingly effortlessly, switch religious adherences. Many church members in Chenalhó, however, have come to take the new teachings to heart. A great number of the Catholics I met had been members for years, some since birth, and many will probably remain in the faith for life. And many of those who leave the Catholic group because of different political or personal conflicts still retain their Catholic faith as integral to their identity and daily life.

The converts, of course, vary in their understanding of the new teachings. There are differences between those converting late in life and those born into the church, between active churchgoers and those seldom attending, and between ordinary followers and experienced catechists. The adherents also differ in what attracts them to the new religion. It is often young, literate men who most easily grasp biblical discourse and who gain confidence when they notice how quickly they learn. However, those who have incorporated the new religion most deeply in their lives are frequently women who have become mothers, whether married, widowed, or divorced. They are likely to have little or no schooling to facilitate their Bible study, and often, women complain that they are ignorant and slow to comprehend the texts. Yet, bearing the primary responsibility for the health and care of their children, many women consider God as their steady companion and source of encouragement. Equally among women and men, however, I found a hope for social change, with the help of God. In the following chapter, I describe concepts and practices I believe most Pedrano Catholics share, but also important differences in perspectives.

PART II

Restructuring Maya Community

CHAPTER 3

Seeking God's Protection

Pedrano Catholics, who call themselves followers of the Word of God, have over time organized their diocese-affiliated congregation into a cohesive and highly coordinated community. The basic units of this community are the chapel groups; with distinctive social, political, and religious structures, each can be described as a village within a village. The chapel is the spatial center where Catholic villagers come together to worship. Here chapel members meet every Sunday to pray, listen to and analyze selected parts of the Bible, and discuss matters of mutual concern, including the political situation in the municipality and beyond. The Sunday meeting is also the arena for collective decision making; meetings of the respective chapel groups are regarded as the principal authority of the Catholic Pedrano community. Chapel groups are coordinated through a body of municipal-level catechist leaders.[1]

Their political association, Las Abejas, parallels this structure. Village-level Las Abejas groups include both Catholics and followers of costumbre religion. They hold meetings in the local school or, often, the Catholic chapel. Las Abejas groups are coordinated through a joint overarching leadership constituted by representatives from the village groups.

To some extent, the Pedrano Catholic community organization is structured along lines conferred by the Catholic Diocese of San Cristóbal. The connection with the diocese is intrinsic to its organization and expresses Catholic Pedranos' dependence on the religious and political authority of the diocese. These structures resonate with the modes of governance that emerged in Maya communities during the latter half of the twentieth century, such as assembly-based decision making, and leadership based on skills such as literacy, but they also integrate new elements, particularly the inclusion of women both as assembly participants and leaders.

I suggest, however, that in important ways, Pedrano Catholics have shaped the Catholic community along lines that reflect the continuing importance they give to long-standing Pedrano notions of community, worship, and leadership. Like the earlier calpul subdivision system and the present villages, Catholic village chapel groups are formed as localized, largely endogamous corporate groups that strive for social and political cohesion, in which both kinship and locality play a role in defining membership. The municipal-level coordination of the chapel groups also draws on the earlier calpul organization, incorporating the representatives of the chapel groups into a joint political leadership that ensures political equity.

Furthermore, Pedrano Catholics share the concern both of the earlier calpuls and later parajes and ejidos with constituting the local community and the whole of the municipality as collective entities upholding an intimate relationship with special patron deities. Villagers have traditionally given reverence and offerings to divinities in exchange for protection and well-being. Likewise, Pedrano Catholics aim through their devout worship to uphold a communal relationship with God that ensures his guardian protection, both on the village level through the chapel groups, and on the municipal level in joint ceremonies where the local chapel groups are represented.

Like practitioners of "traditional" Maya religion, called "costumbre," Catholic Pedranos emphasize the difficulty for ordinary men and women—the "creyentes" (believers)—to approach the divine, and thus the need for expert knowledge and guidance. It is the catechists who hold this role. In contrast to costumbre practitioners, however, Pedrano Catholics grant the ultimate religious authority to outsiders—the non-Pedrano clergy of the Catholic diocese; a subordination they explain as the result of their own lack of knowledge in a religion that so obviously has arrived from the outside.

In spite of this hierarchical leadership, Pedrano Catholics are creating a form of veneration that is highly participatory in character and that contrasts with the practice of costumbre. Using the communal assembly—

the Sunday service—of the chapel group as a base for worship and theological reflection, communication with God is in a sense "democratized"; in principle, accessible for all. Through their multiple participation, Catholic followers express religious veneration and create bonds of mutual obligation with the divine.

Thus, I suggest, the Catholicism practiced by Pedrano Catholics is a dynamic reorientation of their relationship with the divine, which draws on Roman Catholic and Pedrano costumbre thought as well as the secular, participatory assembly. The efforts of the converts to constitute this new community of veneration is the focus of the present chapter. In the subsequent three chapters, I address how Pedrano Catholics have organized their religious community and its form of governance, and how their religious interpretation forms the basis for a new collective identity.

THE CATHOLIC ALLIANCE WITH GOD

The followers of the Word of God are creating a new form of alliance with the divine. Like costumbre practitioners, I suggest, they strive to uphold a relationship to God that ensures his guardian protection. They also hold the religious community as the central entity for establishing such a relationship. Similar to what Richard Wilson (1995:204) found among Q'eqchi' Catholics in Guatemala, religion for Pedrano Catholics is still "the sacred ground on which the community is imagined." The character of the divine has changed, however. Rejecting, at least on the surface, the existence of the costumbre guardian deities the *anjels* and the Holy Earth, most Catholic Pedranos have ceased to perform ceremonies for them. Although they continue to have patron saints, Catholic Pedranos generally emphasize that saints are not gods, and most do not direct prayers to them. Instead, they are turning to a universal God, a God seen as shared with all humans.

The converts depict God as having an explicit purpose for human existence, including the desire for humans to live without suffering. In this sense, the Catholic God is regarded as less ambiguous than the costumbre deities. God is seen as attentive, benevolent, and offering comfort and consolation. His concern for the well-being of humans is considered to extend to every woman, man, and child individually. God sees everything and is troubled both by suffering and bad deeds. Catholics must strive to know and understand how to live according to God's will, to avoid sin, and not to be lured to deviate from God's path by the temptations of the devil. Humans are expected to give praise to God and to endeavor to understand and implement God's intentions. Many converts integrate God into their everyday life, and their moments of prayer, at home or in the chapel, take the form of a daily or weekly report, an account of their concerns since their last prayer.

The primary vehicle for worship for Pedrano Catholics is the collective gathering at the weekly Sunday service in the group's chapel. In many villages, shorter prayer meetings are also held on Tuesday and Thursday late afternoons. By attending these gatherings, the members strive to pay respect to the Word of God and to take another step in learning how to interpret its significations. Catholic followers lacking a chapel in their own village attend services in the chapel of a neighboring village or hold smaller gatherings in someone's home.

Each chapel group has a patron saint as a special protector for whom it holds a yearly festival led by the catechists, sometimes inviting neighboring chapel groups to join in. The chapel groups hold further ceremonies in accordance with the Catholic liturgical calendar, such as Christmas and Easter, sometimes with ritual enactments lasting for several days. Chapel group members also show their devotion to God through various household-oriented ceremonies, such as prayer ceremonies for the sick, when chapel members led by a few catechists visit the home of the ill person. Life-cycle ceremonies such as the prayer ceremony following the birth of a child are commonly performed in the family's home, with a few catechists leading the prayers, while the death of a chapel member is a concern of the whole chapel group, with catechists and chapel members participating in the wake and funeral at the lineage burial ground.[2] An increasing number of Pedrano Catholics celebrate Catholic sacraments for other life-cycle events such as first communion and marriage.

The Catholic community also performs ceremonies on a joint municipal level. The most important are the yearly festivals for saints, mass prayer ceremonies, and pilgrimages to seek God's protection during special troubles, and since 1998, monthly and annual commemorative

Festival for San Martín, patron saint of the Yibeljoj chapel group, 1995. Catechists perform a ritual change of the saint's clothing in a cloud of incense smoke. Photo by author.

masses for the victims of the Acteal massacre. During my stay, the municipal capital of Chenalhó was the center of Catholic celebrations to the saints represented in the old municipal church. Meanwhile, the Catholic center in the village of Yabteclum was the venue for large Catholic prayer ceremonies combined with a mass held in the village church. The purpose of these prayer ceremonies was to ward off the acute danger of war and, it was said, to soften the heart of the government toward the Zapatistas and other members of the opposition, like themselves. With the Acteal massacre in 1997, the village of Acteal became the new ceremonial center of the Pedrano Catholic community, where most municipal-level ceremonies take place, including the annual festival of San Pedro led by the neotraditional cargo-holders (see chapter 4).

In the same way as calpuls were formerly represented in municipal-level religious ceremonies, all village chapel groups are represented in the current Catholic municipal-level ceremonies. This is formally expressed through the participation of a zone chief from each of the five zones that divide the Catholic congregation, as well as—ideally—catechists from each chapel group. Most celebrations are led by the zone chiefs and leading catechist coordinators, whose role is similar to that of cargo holders in costumbre religion. But in contrast with costumbre ceremonies, individual members of the respective village chapel groups are not represented through a cash contribution to ceremonial expenses. Instead, the active participation of as many chapel members as possible is urged, especially in the large prayer ceremonies. Those who are able will often leave their homes before dawn to take part in the ceremonies, carrying a day's ration of food and water.

The spiritual node of the Catholic community, however, is the local Sunday service. During my fieldwork in 1995–96, I particularly followed the Sunday services of the Catholic group in the village of Yibeljoj in the northeastern section of Chenalhó, where I was staying with the family of one of the catechists. The Catholics here formed a relatively large and stable group within a highly factionalized village. It was also one of the larger groups of Catholics in Chenalhó, with about 120 adult members, in a village of 540 adults.[3] Due to the paramilitary persecutions in the late 1990s, most of these families today live in a separate section of the village, called Nuevo Yibeljoj, where they have built a new chapel, their own school, and a clinic, which has only reinforced the characterization of the Catholic group as a village within a village.[4] I will describe in detail one of the Sunday meetings and discuss the enterprise in which the Yibeljoj chapel members, like other Catholic Pedranos, are engaged—trying to be true followers of the Word.

A VILLAGE CHAPEL MEETING

On the Sunday morning of June 9, 1996, around sixty adults and an even greater number of children had gathered by nine o'clock in the yard outside the Catholic chapel in the central barrio of the village of Yibeljoj. The vast majority of the adults were, as always, women. Most chapel members had come on foot from the different barrios of Yibeljoj, but a few lived in neighboring communities. While they waited for the catechists to come out of their preparatory meeting in the old chapel building, it was a welcome time for relaxed socializing, and there was much small talk and laughing, the women sitting together on the grass while most men sat on low log benches. Most families had been members for years and were well acquainted with one another.

The chapel grounds contained several buildings surrounding a large grass courtyard. The chapel, built in the early 1990s, was a large building of raw concrete bricks with a corrugated metal roof. Across the chapel yard were three simple wooden buildings: the former chapel, now used by the catechists for preparatory meetings and for the parallel Sunday service for children; the kitchen where meals were prepared for festivals and other large gatherings; and the small clinic of the Catholic health promoter, with rudimentary equipment. The whole chapel area (of perhaps nine hundred square meters) was enclosed by a fence. No one in the village who was not specially invited or wished to become a member of the Catholic community passed through the gate.

Earlier in the morning, my host had left for the chapel while the rest of us were still eating, because, as the leading catechist, he had to prepare the agenda of the Sunday meeting with the other catechists. While I did the dishes together with little Jesús, his mother, Antonia, and the other women of the lineage compound were getting ready. They stood around the tap in the shared backyard, washing and braiding shiny ribbons into their hair. Like their mothers, the girls had put on clean huipil blouses, while some of the boys managed to escape the procedures, leaving early with their well-groomed fathers. When we were ready, the women locked the doors to their respective homes, and we went up to the chapel and joined the others.

When the catechists came out from their meeting and unlocked the large blue-painted chapel door, people stood up, gathered their children, and began entering the chapel. The large chapel hall was dusky after the bright sunshine outside, in spite of the electric bulbs, and the dirt floor made it seem even darker. The chapel hall, like all the other Catholic chapels I visited in Chenalhó, was filled with rows of simple wooden pews divided into two separate sections for men and women with an open aisle between them. Small children and young girls sat down with their mothers on the right side, while several of the older boys chose to join their fathers on the more sparsely populated left side. Some teenage boys sat together in the back, ready to sneak out for some air when the session got too long. The front rows were designated for the catechists, in Yibeljoj all male, and the most elderly men and women, in recognition of their status. At the head of the hall was the altar, a simple table holding a wooden case with a small statue of the chapel group's patron saint, San Martín de Porres, and decorated with a tablecloth and fresh flowers.

The chapel meeting was led by the catechists, who now stood up at the head of the hall. As usual, it was one of the senior catechists who opened the meeting by addressing the assembled chapel members. I found him to be the most fatherly and perhaps most forgiving of the catechists, admonishing but also full of humor and sensitivity. He began:

> Men and women, we have come to listen to the Word of God and we have lived for another week. Now we will begin to pray to God, we will all pray to God, men and women, and we know how it should be. We mustn't stop praying to God since we are living in great suffering; pray that God be with us and protect us, that God have mercy on us, that there be no more suffering. In the meantime, we must enjoy our lives, men and women.

After mention of chapel members who were sick and had asked to be included in the prayers, the prayers began. One of the other catechists placed a row of candles on the floor in front of the small altar. This was an expression of the revival of costumbre rites in which Pedrano Catholics are engaged. When all the candles were lit, the catechists knelt in a line facing the altar, their backs to the congregation. The assembled men and women also knelt in front of each bench, the women pulling their shawls over their heads. The oldest catechist, a man who was still strong and rather stern, now led the sequence of classic Catholic prayers that initiated each prayer meeting, most of them recited in Spanish. The congregation followed in a collective murmur. After this sequence, the "free" prayer in Tzotzil followed, led by the same catechist. This was the moment where each chapel member could address God with what troubled her or his heart and ask for God's help. It was always the most emotional moment of the whole Sunday service and perhaps the most important for those who had come. The oldest catechist initiated the prayer with standardized phrasing and then began an improvised address to God, speaking on behalf of all the chapel members. Then the congregated men and women joined with their own simultaneous prayers, praying aloud in semi-chanting voices, some animated, and many women crying. The prayer lasted for several minutes, the collected voices intermingling and filling the chapel almost like a choir. In contrast to costumbre prayers led by the *kabildo vinik*, there was usually no music during Catholic prayer. However, the collective, singsong murmur of all the gathered worshippers created a comparable monotonous and almost trance-inducing sound, using the repetitive falling scales typical for costumbre prayers, a "holy noise" that, like the costumbre use of flute and drum, seemed to mark the extraordinary transmission of human address to the divine realm. Then, one by one, the voices grew silent, and finally only the leading catechist could be heard until he closed with, once more, formal Catholic phrasing in Spanish. Everybody sat up on the benches again, and the catechists let people collect themselves before the service continued.

The prayers I could hear around me often used the parallel metaphoric couplet phrasing typical of costumbre prayers, and sometimes also a costumbre-influenced imagery, the person describing herself as being at the hands and feet of a deity, whose gaze and care she asks to be reached by (cf. Gossen 1974:161; Eber 2000:185). Church members also employed the petitioning and humble self-presentation often used in costumbre prayers. In interviews, I asked some chapel members what was said during this collective, free prayer. One woman explained that they ask God to send them the Holy Spirit so that their hearts might be open and able to keep his holy words. Another said she asks God for help in finding food, that he bless her house and cure diseases. She asks him for strength and life, she said. Several said they ask forgiveness for sins; for example, for losing their temper or quarreling with family members. One woman told me that she also asks for help understanding God's words in the Bible text that will be read during the service, and for the ability to respond well to the questions.

After the prayers, the three core members of the chapel's conjunto, or music band, came up to the front of the hall and sang two songs with the congregation, who stood up in their bench rows. Today, the second song was the "Hymn to the Synod" in Spanish, which was a diocese composition and very popular among Maya Catholics throughout the diocese. In the refrain, which most knew well, I believe people referred as much to their highly esteemed bishop Samuel Ruiz, still in service at the time, as to Christ:

> You are our Lord, our shepherd
> Defender of the poor and humble
> You are our Lord, our shepherd
> Walk with us and there is nothing to fear.[5]

Before turning to the reading of the scripture, it was time to offer some guidance to the "creyentes," the chapel members. First, the president of the chapel group asked the creyentes to stay in the chapel during the services and not go outside to buy sweets or to chit-chat: "We have to listen to the commandments [*mantaletik*]; that's why we have come." Then, several of the catechists in turn alluded to what the president had said and transitioned into general moral advice to keep faith in God. The catechists were aware that chapel members could be offended by their admonishments and tried often to soften their remarks and make people laugh. Because on this day, the lecture on how the converts ought to behave was particularly extensive, one of the catechists felt the need to add: "Don't take it badly. [Don't think,] 'how can he tell me that? Next week I won't come!' You mustn't react like that, men and women. Don't get angry. This is to learn the commandments, to learn how to be good, men and women."

Then it was time to listen to the Word of God, today Romans 16:1–6.[6] The catechist leaders at their meeting in Yabteclum intended the text by Saint Paul to stimulate discussion about the role women should have in the work of the diocese and the Catholic community in Chenalhó. In the passage, Paul praises women who have worked at his side to spread the Word of Jesus Christ, and he admonishes the Romans to receive them well and respect their work. All the chapel groups use a Tzotzil translation of the Bible. In Yibeljoj, the text was read without any explanation of the context. Most catechists were only functionally literate, so they usually read the text in a monotonous, slow voice, halting and repeating passages that were hard to pronounce. These conditions sometimes made it onerous for the audience to pay attention and follow the text. This Sunday, many chapel members were already half-drowsing, tired

by the long preceding sermon. Some of the infants were crying, add-
ing to the difficulty of hearing the reading, until their mothers nursed
them. The difficulty in understanding the text, however, seemed only to
further emphasize its sacredness. I often found the presentation taking
on the form of a reverent reading of a holy and obscure code brought to
the group from God through the diocese, and I knew that many of the
creyentes would only blame themselves if they did not understand.

After the catechist finished reading the passage, he read three questions about the text for chapel members to discuss, which had been prepared at the monthly catechist meeting in Yabteclum. On this day, the
questions addressed how women could contribute to the work of the
chapel groups. On most Sundays, however, the first one or two questions
would address the Bible text more directly, asking, for example, in relation to the account of the Pharisee: "How did Jesus regard the behavior
of the rich man?" The final question would ask the chapel members to
draw parallels with their own lives and times, such as: "How can we help
today so that God will be pleased with us?"

After the questions had been read to the group, the creyentes were
ushered out to the chapel yard to discuss possible answers among themselves. The men and women sat in separate groups in the yard, and another catechist read the verses from the Bible an additional time. Then
each group chose a secretary. Teenagers were frequently chosen, as they
were more likely to be literate. On this day, however, it was a sturdy and
confident woman in her late twenties, the wife of the most junior catechist, who volunteered to be secretary for the women. At first, the discussion among the women was hesitant, and many said they had not
understood and did not know what to think. Little by little, however, several spoke out and some gave lengthy arguments about how the church
needed women to attend the meetings, pray, and reflect, and that they
should support one another. The secretary listened calmly to the different contributions of the women sitting around her on the grass, taking
the role of chairperson, and summarized the answers in the notebook
she had been given. When she had finished writing, she signaled to the
catechists who were waiting—the group of men had already finished—
and we all returned to the chapel, where the two secretaries read out the
respective answers. On other Sundays, the discussions were sometimes

Women in the Yibeljoj chapel group discuss the Sunday service questions about the Bible, 1996. Photo by author.

held inside the chapel, and after some initial talk with their neighbors, the creyentes would be encouraged to stand up and share their thoughts. During some meetings, they were told to come up to the front and speak into the conjunto microphone so everyone could hear. Usually, more women than men would volunteer to speak, although speaking in public was associated with much embarrassment for many women.

After the creyentes had suggested answers to the questions, it was the turn of the catechists. In a lengthy speech, one of the catechists elaborated on the significance of the biblical text and questions, attempting to relate it to his listeners' daily lives. The catechists consider this phase of the service, called "the supplement," highly important, since it is here that they can influence and guide the chapel members' understanding of scripture and Catholic doctrine.[7] It is therefore also considered the most difficult catechist task, since it requires skill not only in theological reasoning but also in making a cultural translation to the time and lives of the chapel members. Today, however, the task had been given to one of the newer catechists, who after a self-effacing introduction explained

what Saint Paul had said in the text and why the apostle had meant that
women were important in spreading the Word of God. Thanks to the
contribution of women such as Mary, the mother of God, the catechist
said, the Word of God could multiply. "If she hadn't worked, it [the
Word] would not be known. But since she believed in God, our Mother
Mary, it became manifested in the whole world, and that's why we still
are listening to it." The important role of women did not end in those
times, he continued:

> No, we're continuing the labor here also, since both men and
> women are contributing. . . . Every time women are called to meet-
> ings in Yabteclum, or to go on commissions to San Cristóbal, well,
> that is their work. That's how it is today, men and women. You
> women, see how the women of the past were in your situation, and
> how women today are still respected. They are teaching you what
> it is that God wants, how the women of the past worked. So you
> should listen to the convocations [to meetings] that come, what
> God wants, because it's the work of God.

The catechist was aware, of course, that women's role in Chenalhó is
quite different from the role he was encouraging them to take. He also
knew that Catholic men had difficulty accepting these changes. Thus,
he directed his next words to the men, admonishing them to respect
women and their words, and to take their opinions and the information
they brought from meetings into account. After he had finished, one of
the senior catechists added some further explanations. By now, many
creyentes had problems paying attention, and in combination with the
heat and the constant noise from the small children, some were over-
come by sleep, others by restlessness that made them stir and murmur
to bench neighbors.

The meeting was coming to a close, as there was no political information this Sunday from the Pedrano Catholic center in Yabteclum. On
other Sundays, however, catechists or other chapel members who had
gone to a meeting or event would now give reports with political news
and proposals. If there were political or practical issues to be discussed,
debates could sometimes be lengthy, with men and women getting to
their feet to voice their opinions and the catechists commenting and
explaining until a joint decision could be reached.

In closing, the catechists reminded the creyentes of upcoming events: the women's course in Yabteclum the coming Tuesday and Wednesday, and the next special prayer meeting in the chapel on Thursday. It would be the last of three special prayer meetings on consecutive Thursdays to ask God to calm the increasing political tensions in Chiapas and make the government comply with the demands that the EZLN had made as a condition of returning to peace negotiations. After the last information, the meeting ended and people began to leave the hall. It was one o'clock in the afternoon, rather early in comparison to many other Sundays. The families who had some distance to walk home first sat on the ground in the shaded parts of the courtyard to have a light meal, brought by the wives. Most drank the corn drink *mats'*, "pozol," carried in small plastic containers. Those living close by, including my host family and myself, left to drink *mats'* in their own homes. Little by little, the chapel yard was emptied, the chapel again closed and locked.

COMMUNAL CATHOLIC APPEALS TO GOD

Pedrano Catholics' notion of communal veneration differs from that held by practitioners of costumbre religion. In the practice of costumbre, the family and community petition for divine protection of *kuxlejal* (life) by performing specific ceremonies. The strength of these ceremonies depends on the full representation of all petitioners, through monetary contributions, as well as on the skill of the performance, with great focus on the liturgical language of prayer. In costumbre theology, deities are portrayed and addressed as awesome beings of "flowery countenance." Humans, on the other hand, are described as small, feeble plants at "the hands and feet" of the deities, imperfect and sometimes annoying for the deities. Therefore, human communication with the divine is a precarious affair (Eber 2000:154). Any adult villager who follows costumbre is expected to know how to perform certain prayer ceremonies on behalf of the household—at home, out in the field, or sometimes before the saint in a church. However, these prayers are made with a certain apprehension, as Guiteras Holmes describes (1961:295), since people commonly feel inadequate when addressing deities. Today, few ordinary costumbre villagers are left who still practice these prayer ceremonies. In Chenalhó, as in most Maya societies, the direct appeal to costumbre gods is performed primarily by ritual experts: the *kabildo vinik* and the cargo holders (cf. Gossen 1974). They carry out communal ceremonies at the village and municipal level on behalf of all villagers; each family of the collectivity is represented by the money it contributes. These prayers, as well as those of the healer (*j-ilol*), demand specialized knowledge and competence, the memorization of long, set sequences, and the ability to elaborate and improvise. Only certain persons are seen as possessing the necessary liturgical skills as well as the state of spiritual and social maturation and sophistication that are demanded; cargo holders acquire this competence gradually during their successive offices.

Pedrano Catholics, in contrast, emphasize the importance of communal, active participation. Certainly, catechists are the religious leaders of the Catholic community. They define the spiritual, moral, and theological training that creyentes should work toward and they are thus crucial to the appropriate performance of veneration.[8] Catechists are central to Catholic ceremonies, opening and leading all prayers and other rituals. However, they do not usually perform ceremonies on behalf of the chapel members. For Pedrano Catholics, one's level of ceremonial expertise and fluency with liturgical language are only moderately significant in prayers; any man or woman is regarded as equally capable of communicating directly with God. Instead, Pedrano Catholics describe *kuxlejal* as something they petition for through the repeated attendance and prayers of the chapel members in weekly chapel meetings as well as through their continuous struggle to understand and implement the Word of God. It is through these dedicated efforts that they show their veneration, and for their sacrifice, their lives will be protected by God. Encouraging the followers to continue these efforts, a catechist said at a Sunday service: "It's life [*kuxlejal*] we are seeking, by being here in the church." A creyente woman spoke up to agree: "Our work is to be in the church to listen to the commandments, to listen to what the catechists say. We have to pay attention although we don't hear well, although it doesn't enter into our minds, into our hearts, although we are very stupid. At least we are here."[9]

Pedrano Catholic prayer ceremonies, whether they take place at home, in the village chapel, or at various municipal-level sites, are truly collective events where catechists and creyentes kneel down and pray together, the largest ceremonies gathering thousands of participants. The strength of Pedrano Catholic prayer, I believe, is perceived to be achieved not by liturgical complexity but through the multitude of participants, even when those participants are ordinary creyentes, praying without special skills. Therefore, although Pedrano Catholics can address God wherever they are, most seem to save their prayers for the chapel meetings, since individual prayers are not seen to be as powerful as those performed in a group. One of the devout creyente women in Yibeljoj, a mother of six, explained why so many women came to the chapel meetings: "Really, it's better that between all of us we pray. Perhaps in this way our Lord may attend us, when we bring our prayers together, when we put our hearts into it. That's what the women say."[10] While the costumbre practitioner is dependent on ritual experts to pray on her behalf in many spheres of life, the individual Catholic can be described as dependent on her local community of Catholics to ensure that God will hear her appeal. In this way, I suggest, Pedrano Catholics have retained the central costumbre notion of the importance of shared, collective veneration but have transformed this notion to an ideal of multiple participation, making human appeal to the divine "democratic" and participatory (cf. Wilson 1995).

Pedrano Catholics seem to regard prayer ceremonies as performative events, not just humble petitions to God, which stands in contrast to the view of the pastoral clergy and diocese dogma. Pedranos generally perceive prayer ceremonies for the sick, for example, as a summoning of God and his divine power to cure. The prayer itself, if performed with the right heart and strength, has the capacity to heal. Pedranos may further reinforce prayers by combining them with fasting, sometimes over three consecutive days.[11] Catholic villagers share this notion of the performative force of prayer not only with costumbre practitioners, but also, it appears, with followers of the Protestant churches in Chenalhó.[12] However, like costumbre practitioners, Pedrano Catholics also feel significant trepidation in approaching God. This is particularly associated with the task, requested of each chapel member, of learning how to interpret his Word.

UNDERSTANDING THE WORD OF GOD

To become Catholic, as understood by Catholic Pedranos, is a gradual process in which one learns to interpret and reflect upon the Word of God; that is, the Bible.[13] The Tzotzil term *sk'op jtotik* (Word of our Father/God) is used to refer both to the Catholic prayer meetings and the Bible. Through patient efforts, studying and reflecting upon his words, the villagers hope to know and understand God's intentions and wisdom more and more. By this means, they believe, they will gradually learn to live in accordance with God's will (cf. Scotchmer 1986:214). Without understanding God's Word, the catechists often told the creyentes, there is no real belief, for until then, one has not seen the face of God. Creyentes, too, seem to regard their own and others' success in interpreting the Word as a measure of the commitment of their heart.

In this labor, catechists have a central function as specialist interpreters. In contrast with Protestant villagers, few Catholic creyentes read the Bible in their homes, and although many own a Tzotzil Bible, they are not expected to advance their knowledge by themselves, but through the catechists' guidance. As the primary interpreters of the Word of God, catechists are expected to absorb the theological knowledge defined and provided by the diocese clergy. This knowledge is intimately associated with literacy, the Spanish language, and educated urban mestizos, especially, of course, the bishop and clergy of the diocese, and ultimately, the pope. The Bible appears as a divine message, as it were, that has arrived by way of this literate world, in which most Pedranos still feel badly inexpert.

Thus, the base of catechist authority is quite different from that of the costumbre religious leaders. It implies a rejection of the earlier association in Chenalhó between spiritual maturity and advanced age, which was especially noted if the person had held prestigious cargos. In the Pedrano Catholic community, while elders are still respected, they are often regarded as less apt in understanding God's commands than the young who have schooling.

On the other hand, the distinction between catechist and creyente is fundamental for Pedrano Catholics and made continually. The Tzotzil term used in Chenalhó for catechist is *chol-k'opetik*, for which the conventional meaning is preacher or prophet.[14] The term for creyentes is *jch'unolajetik*, which my host translated as "listeners" or "obedients," since "they believe in all the commandments from God."[15] I do not know if the Tzotzil terms were chosen by the diocese or by Tzotzil catechists. However, they seem to capture the gist of how Pedrano Catholics perceive the difference between the two categories of Catholic Church members and the normative relation between them, with the creyentes listening to and following the catechists' directions. Creyentes appear to find in their new religion not only comfort but also an obligation to live up to the expectations of the catechists and clergy. I often heard creyentes speak of themselves as persons with little knowledge who need to be informed and advised by catechists, while catechists describe creyentes as a group that should be given enlightenment and guidance, and that can be manipulated and misled by catechists of bad faith. These separate roles are reinforced at every chapel meeting, where catechists guide and admonish the creyentes to live according to what is expected of true believers. While catechists can be demanding and sometimes even harsh when addressing creyentes in their sermons, they often speak softly, respectfully, and with much humor. I usually found a strong sense of solidarity between catechists and creyentes, based on a common understanding of shared life-worlds and difficulties.

THE QUESTIONS

The central vehicle for transmitting knowledge of the Word of God to the creyentes has for many years been a series of questions about the weekly Bible text that catechists pose to the chapel members during the Sunday service. "The Questions" were introduced in the Pedrano chapel groups around 1984 as part of the so-called *tijwanej* method described in chapter 2, used by the diocese with the aim of making the teaching of scripture more dynamic.[16] Although the diocese describes the questions as a participatory and democratic tool, I found that Catholic Pedranos felt anxiety about the use of the questions, which to some degree reinscribed the hierarchical relationship between the Pedrano Catholic community and the diocese.

Pedranos generally applauded the use of the questions. Senior catechists told me that previously, catechists would lecture on the weekly text while the others sat and listened passively, often without grasping much of the message. With the questions, however, the creyentes are asked to reiterate the fundamentals of the text that just has been read to them, thus making them listen more intently. Further, they are asked to reflect upon parallels between the events or relations described in the biblical text and their own lives today, and what this should imply for their own behavior. With the questions, the chapel members also began to evaluate their position in Mexican society. Drawing parallels with conditions Jesus condemned during his time on earth, Catholic villagers began to define their lives as characterized by marginalization and exploitation, where they suffered abuse by the rich and those in power. Pedrano Catholics told me repeatedly that it was with the advent of the questions that their political reflection began. One of the newer catechists in Yibeljoj said: "They [the questions] are there so we can begin to wake up the creyentes. So that they begin to think and begin to understand, for example, the situation for the first believers. But it's not enough just to listen. . . . The questions are needed for them to dwell or reflect upon in their heads and in their hearts how corruption has come, and injustice."[17]

But first and foremost, catechists described the questions as an instrument to advance the creyentes' understanding of the scripture. The questions require the creyentes to listen attentively as the biblical text is read, and to analyze its possible significance. This perspective was shared by creyentes, and many said the questions were a help to them. One woman argued: "It's very important. . . . It's not a bother. They're good to develop our ability and give us some experience, it's no problem. It's what our Heavenly Father wants, that I will have more knowledge in my head and my heart. Then I can answer the questions."[18] Another creyente told me: "Well, I think they are good because this way we learn the Word of our Lord well, and how our lives are. We answer the questions so that in this way we can find heaven."[19] Quite a few of the creyentes in Yibeljoj had ventured to answer at least some of the questions during Sunday services, and many told me they had gained confidence from their increasing ability to interpret the Bible and to speak in public. One woman said: "I didn't understand before because there were no questions, but now I understand all that the Word of God is. We understand

well why we are suffering, thanks to the help of the catechists who explain it to us very well. Now we understand perfectly that not only those
of the past suffered, but also we today."

Villagers nevertheless view learning to understand the Word as a slow
and difficult process that gives rise to anxiety and self-abasement. Since
the questions demand individual participation, they are understood as
a yardstick and demonstration of one's capacities, and they are commonly described as the most difficult part of the chapel meetings. To
know how to interpret the biblical text and answer the questions is seen
as requiring intelligence and skill that many feel they do not possess.
When I asked creyentes about the questions, they usually complained
about their own inadequacy and lack of intelligence for learning. Both
men and women tended to say they were not good at understanding or
thinking and often had to fight the drowsiness they felt during chapel
meetings. One creyente said the parish nun sometimes came to her in
dreams at night to comfort and encourage her; if she kept on going to
the church service, she would learn to grasp the import of the biblical
texts and the questions:

[The nun said:] "Don't be sad, don't worry. You'll get there if you
give it your best," she told me. "Keep on going, don't quit," she
told me.
"But I can't keep it in my heart," I told her.
"It will stay there little by little. Give it your best. It won't stay in
your heart without your effort."
That's what I dream. But I believe that one day—I can see it
before me—one day it will happen that I can answer, but only if I
do my best, and if there are no [other] obstacles, that's what I tell
myself.[20]

The apprehension associated with the questions and the interpretation of scripture is widespread in the municipality. One of the senior catechists told me that in all chapel groups many people had difficulty responding and instead sat silent. Therefore, he said, many people did not
want the questions, but wished for the earlier form of catechist-oriented
lectures. The questions were difficult for the catechists as well, especially
for the new ones. Only by going to the monthly catechist meetings at the

municipal level, where the questions are drafted and discussed, could they learn to master them.[21] One catechist with only a couple years of service described how for him the questions were a test of his biblical understanding, which he often failed: "Well, for my part I feel I can't contribute with anything. Because I know I don't know much. I see that sometimes the creyentes know how to speak very well. Then I feel in my heart: 'Why is it me who's a catechist, why aren't they?' That's what I think. Do you know why? Because among them there are those who know how to speak very well, who are very good at extracting the meanings. Sometimes it's not until then that I myself get it, thanks to them! That's the situation."[22]

The strain caused by the questions appears to be reinforced by the setting of chapel meetings, which draws on the school model, with catechists as teachers and creyentes as pupils. The seating in the chapel hall, the use of the question-and-answer form, and the employment of texts and writing all reinforce this impression. I asked one creyente whether the questions reminded her of school, which she had not liked very much. She answered: "That's how I feel. It's as if we're going to pass an exam. [With the questions,] it became more difficult. We feel like we're doing an exam in school. Now we don't know what to say sometimes."[23] In Yibeljoj, it was obvious that the creyentes who appeared to feel the least secure in answering the questions usually were those of older age who had the least school experience.

To understand the anxiety related to the questions, one must understand its associations with the mestizo leadership of the diocese and the literate, urban world. Catholic villagers told me the bishop wanted them to respond to the questions to show that they understood God's words. The catechists collected the written responses to the questions after each Sunday service and brought them to the catechist meeting in Yabteclum, where they were handed over to the nun. Both catechists and creyentes told me that the answers were then brought to the bishop.[24] Since Catholic Pedranos find that they still lack an adequate understanding of the Bible, most describe their answers as incomplete. Their weekly responses to the questions are thus loaded with both duty and embarrassment, seen as a manifestation of their own mediocrity and inadequacy, and the remoteness of the advanced wisdom of the clergy and bishop. Through the instruction and guidance of the diocese clergy, the converts nevertheless hope to progress in their knowledge.

The perceptions Pedrano Catholics have of the questions highlight the hierarchical relationship between the diocese and its converts. Although the explicit intention of the diocese is for the questions to encourage critical reflection and social analysis, the creyentes are very alert also to the meta-language of the weekly setting, which implicitly communicates their inadequate knowledge and dependence on the diocese clergy. Learning the Word of God thus implies for many converts a desired movement from a state of ignorance to enlightenment.

The converts' trepidation with the questions and their high regard for the Bible and the diocese clergy seem to be furthered also by conventional Pedrano notions of the importance of expert interpretation of hidden meanings. For costumbre practitioners, it is ritual experts such as the *j-ilol* or the *kabildo vinik* who are able to provide insightful interpretations of the divine and hidden realm—the "otherworld"—in order to uncover the true meaning (*sjam-smelol*), which is not easily accessible to ordinary villagers (Arias 1975:38–39; Eber 2000:61). This relates to a long Maya tradition of regarding truth as opaque, accessible only through specialist interpreters (Edmonson 1993:72–73; Gossen 1999:253–59). Pedrano Catholics, too, regard the divine will as obscure, making human interpretation dependent on specialists. However, following the Pedrano Catholic community ideal of collective participation, creyentes are expected to gradually learn to interpret for themselves. Despite being ordinary villagers without formal education, they are asked to explain what God has intended and said. Thus, the anguish of Catholic creyentes before such a task reflects a feeling of insufficiency any ordinary costumbre villager would share. One catechist, seeing the insecurity in the creyentes' answers about the weekly text, tried to comfort and hearten them:

> First I would like to say, all of you, when we listen to the Word of God and its meaning, men and women, young ones, don't be afraid of the Word of our Father, men and women all. . . . We don't ask of you all your strength, only that you make some reflection, for example, on the questions. Therefore we ask you now, men and women. Sometimes you see that one of you speaks; you, older sis-

ter, say another thing, and so do you, young boy, and you, younger
brother. You open your eyes. But [the rest of you] don't speak in
the plenary sessions. But that's the way we do it. "The Word of
God," we call it, so don't be afraid of the words.[25]

LIVING THE WORD OF GOD: FOSTERING
A NEW MORALITY

Pedrano Catholics demand of themselves that they learn to implement
the Word of God in their daily lives. Like the Protestant Mayas that David Scotchmer (1986:214) describes, their goal is "the establishment of
a new order of equality, service, and love." The ability to approach this
new order depends on the work of each individual and the joint efforts
of the group. To live in accordance with the Word of God is generally
seen as demonstrating that God's teachings are fully understood and
taken to heart. Thus, Pedrano Catholics are attempting to construct a
new morality, and in the process, reconstituting themselves as moral
subjects. While the catechists are the most determined protagonists in
this undertaking, creyentes appear largely to embrace the project. Empathy and respect for one another, help for those in need, nonviolence,
and lifelong monogamy are commonly held out as key norms to follow.
Church members are also expected to restrict their use of alcohol. Since
excessive alcohol use is a common problem in Chenalhó, as in other
Maya communities, the Catholic drinking restrictions are appealing to
many villagers as a way, for example, to keep their husbands from heavy
drinking (see also Eber 2001b; Kovic 2005). The use of the term "her-
mano" for fellow members of the Catholic Church is associated with this
sharing of common ideals, ideals that many converts regard as morally
superior to those of other villagers.

For practitioners of costumbre religion, personal conduct should be
true to "the way of the ancestors." Tradition defines morally acceptable
behavior. Guidance on how to live in accordance with tradition is found
from elders, especially pasados, the former cargo holders, who are considered to have the most knowledge of ancestral ways. The ancestors may
also reveal themselves in dreams to individual men or women to give direction and safeguard traditions (Arias 1975:38; Eber 2000:143, 210–11).

For Pedrano Catholics, in contrast, guidance is found in the Bible and is mediated through the catechists with the guidance of the pastoral workers. Thus the catechists claim only partial competence to formulate the norms valid for the Catholic Pedrano community. Instead, catechists must rely on Catholic experts outside Chenalhó to help them learn and understand the norms they wish to follow.[26] I often heard catechists describe pastoral workers as role models for how to live as good Christians and compare them to the dedicated, humble, and self-sacrificing first apostles.

Catechists hold that chapel members should constantly evaluate their behavior in relation to God's commands. Failure to follow the teachings is described as sin caused by weakness of character and sometimes by the temptations of the devil. Catechists describe how some people lose this battle, converts who succumb to temptation and choose to leave the Catholic community (cf. Warren 1978:116).

Catechists often emphasized the right, even obligation, of converts to evaluate the behavior of other chapel members. If a man commits a fault; for example, by getting drunk, they should not gossip behind his back but address the person face-to-face to guide him to the rightful path. This implies a form of "communalization" of the concern for individual spiritual maturation, which appears to be very different from conventional Pedrano thinking. While costumbre practitioners also expect conformity to norms and may comment on and even criticize the behavior of others, ordinary villagers do not usually interfere as long as a person's behavior is not directly harmful to others. To openly address and criticize another person's behavior, I was told, is regarded as inappropriate and offensive (see also Eber 2000:137–38). The avoidance of direct criticism is further strengthened by the fear of causing anger or jealousy, which may motivate the offended person to strike back with witchcraft. Catholic Pedranos, in contrast, especially the catechists, emphasize that all chapel members are dependent on one another to ensure that they live up to the standards expected of them, and therefore they should offer and gratefully accept mutual, tactful guidance. An important function of the Sunday meetings is to provide the creyentes with such guidance from the catechists.

Pedrano Catholics should also spread the Word of God to those not yet sharing it. While they do not actively missionize among non-Catholic villagers, catechists encourage the creyentes to share "the Good News" ("la Buena Nueva") that God has brought them, and by their lives to inspire others to become a follower of the Word. Villagers who express interest in learning more about Catholicism are encouraged to join the chapel group and start attending the Sunday services, thereby gradually expanding the Catholic community.

The work of making the Word known, however, is associated with hardships, Pedrano Catholics say. It is especially hard for the catechists, who spend long hours on church-related work without monetary compensation and have to neglect their own work of supporting their families. Worse, the Catholic faithful risk persecution. Conflicts with costumbre followers and the massive, politically motivated persecution and violence they have been exposed to, especially during the latter part of the 1990s, are frequently compared to the harassment the first apostles experienced. Pedrano Catholics often describe the hardships they suffer as a sacrifice made for their faith. Many, particularly the catechists, talk of their readiness to suffer for their belief in God and for spreading his Word. They express faith in divine justice; if they put their lives in the hands of God, goodness and justice will prevail.[27]

CHANGING RELIGIOUS AUTHORITIES

The choice to join the Catholic community and thereby reject the guardianship of costumbre deities might appear to be a daring decision that risks the safety of oneself and one's family. Practitioners of costumbre religion emphasize that religious veneration should be performed by the community as a whole, all households represented by the ritual specialists. A failure to represent the entire group may signal disrespect to the deities and call forth their retribution (Pérez Pérez 1992:90–93). However, women and men I talked with frequently explained that they had joined the Catholic group precisely to find divine protection either urgently for a sick child, or for the future assurance of good health.[28] All the Catholic and Protestant chapel groups offer prayer rituals for the ill, and in moments of urgent need, a family may turn to a chapel group instead of to the customary village healer, the *j-ilol*, and then remain as a member of the new group.

Nevertheless, to become a member of a Catholic or Protestant group implies a dissociation from the religious community of costumbre followers. It is a challenge to conventional Pedrano norms and faith as well as to the basis for religious authority. Both Catholic and Protestant Pedranos hold that there is only one God, and while most acknowledge that costumbre practitioners also believe in God, they claim that the costumbre worship of other divine forms is idolatrous. Protestants, and some Catholics as well, have refused to contribute money for the *mixa* prayer ceremony for the *anjels* and the Holy Earth. In contrast with Protestants, Catholics perform ceremonies for the saints. Many Catholic couples even take on traditional cargos in the municipal center. But as a collectivity, the Catholics define the festivals to the saints organized by cargo holders as costumbre religion and instead hold their own separate celebrations.

The converts' rejection of costumbre deities and their abstention from crucial ceremonies and money contributions present a danger to the life and well-being of all of Chenalhó, from the viewpoint of traditional Pedranos. Traditionalists have argued that by this failure to manifest a unified reverence for the divine, the deities may be angered and strike the whole community (Pérez Pérez 1992:115). Thus, ever since the first Pedranos converted to the "new religions," the converts have been met with suspicion and criticism by other villagers and regarded as showing disrespect for the ancestral customs of their people and the Chenalhó collectivity (Eber 2000:210). I heard both Catholics and Presbyterians saying they suspected traditional ceremonial leaders (*kabildo viniketik*) of attempting to use their powers to bring sickness and death upon the converts as punishment for this disrespect (see also Pérez Pérez 1992).

A further charge made against both Catholic and Protestant chapel groups is that they have introduced new criteria for defining the basis of religious knowledge and leadership. Local specialist competence is presented as no longer sufficient. Instead, the authority is granted to religious clergy from the outside and to their principal text, the Bible. Other villagers have described the converts as followers of new and alien religions. A Presbyterian pastor from Yibeljoj told me that the converts were ridiculed for relying on external doctrines: "Some say that the evangelicals only study the words of foreigners. The Bible, they say, comes from the foreigners, from other countries. From people like you, who live in other countries, the gringos, the Germans, they say.[29] They don't believe it's the Word of God. That's why they make fun of us and get angry at us."[30]

At times, Catholics as well as Protestants have chosen to challenge costumbre authorities and their prerogatives face on as definers of the divine and channels for human veneration. They have claimed their right to profess the religion of their choice, referring both to the Mexican constitution and to authorities of their own church.[31] In contrast to several other Maya municipalities, most notably neighboring Chamula, Pedrano municipal authorities have yielded to the influence of the new doctrines. The main battles with converts took place in the 1950s and 1960s. Since then, religiously tinged conflicts have arisen only sporadically, primarily concerning the *mixa* contribution. The different religious groups in Chenalhó have been able to find compromise solutions that have permitted a mutually tolerant coexistence. Instead, conflicts have revolved around more openly political issues and the control of the municipal government (see chapter 7).[32]

From the 1990s on, the Catholic community in Chenalhó has adopted a more conciliatory attitude toward costumbre faith and traditions. Both parish clergy and their followers have softened their earlier critical attitude. Their new tolerance was propelled by the diocese project "Teología India" (Indian Theology), a project consistent with the ideas of liberation theology on enculturation (CENAMI 2000). For Pedranos, the conciliatory approach was further strengthened by the cultural revivalist discourse of the indigenous movement in Chiapas that gained force starting in the early 1990s. The work of the Indian Theology project in Chenalhó has been led by a small group of catechists supported by the parish clergy and the CENAMI institute in Mexico City.[33] The group has printed several bilingual pamphlets describing important costumbre ceremonies and prayers. The Catholic catechists of the group, applying a liberation theology perspective, make an effort to define the core principles of what they consider to be the autochthonous, traditional Pedrano religion that display respectful veneration of God. Their goal is to promote the incorporation of such beliefs and ceremonies into their own Catholic community. For many Catholic followers, the teachings of Indian Theology present a way to reconcile the doctrines of the Catholic community with beliefs they still hold, associated with costumbre religion and their historic past. Others, who have distanced themselves more fully from costumbre beliefs and practices, have openly criticized the revivalist project. Nevertheless, Pedrano Catholics have incorporated various costumbre rituals into their own ceremonies. A *kabildo vinik* and traditional musicians are today likely to be invited to initiate important masses and prayer ceremonies. The leaders of Las Abejas have also included various traditional cargos in their system of governance. Still, the interpretive framework by which this revitalization is performed is based on Pedrano Catholics' special orientation to the divine.

CHAPTER 4

Organization of the Catholic Community and Las Abejas

The organization of the Catholic community and Las Abejas at the village and municipal levels combines new and old forms of community-making and leadership. In this chapter, I describe this special blend, whereby Pedrano Catholics have created a highly participatory yet rather authoritarian form of governance. Politically, the way both the Pedrano Catholic community and Las Abejas are organized manifests a conscious attempt by the members to create structures free of government dependency and interference, in an approach similar to that taken by many other groups in Chiapas in opposition to the government. Pedrano Catholics regard the official municipal administration of Chenalhó as being co-opted by state interests and often feel excluded and discriminated against by its authorities. To a significant degree, they have instead created their own municipal structures, similar to that of the Zapatista autonomous municipality. These structures also mediate and facilitate Pedrano Catholics' interactions with Mexican institutions and officials. The primary ceremonial and political center for Catholics in Chenalhó today is the village of Acteal—the seat of Las Abejas—while the village of Yabteclum serves as the center for catechist municipal coordination.

The dynamic between the two Catholic community bodies—Las Abejas and the catechist coordination of the chapel groups—is complicated. The catechist leadership once functioned as the sole coordinating and ruling body of the Pedrano Catholic community at the municipal level, through which the catechists, on behalf of their congregation, decided whether and how to act as a unified group in both religious and political matters. During my stay in 1995–96, the direction of Las Abejas was still subsumed

115

under catechist coordination. Now political leadership has been increasingly taken over by Las Abejas. The catechists today are no longer considered the primary leaders of the Catholic community but find their
authority paralleled, sometimes contested, by the leaders of Las Abejas.
The situation has been further complicated by the split of Las Abejas in
2008 into two separate organizations due to political differences between
its members. What I describe in this chapter refers to the time before this
division and is still largely valid for the organization that has retained
the official name—Sociedad Civil Las Abejas—and the seat in Acteal.[1]

THE VILLAGE CHAPEL GROUP

Catholic chapel groups in Chenalhó vary in size from only a handful of
worshippers in some villages to several dozen in others; they provide cor-
respondingly varied bases for community formation. The larger groups
almost constitute full-fledged communities that function as separate
entities within the highly factionalized villages. Catholic chapel groups
are but one of several village factions that all, to some extent, operate
as exclusive social and political units. During my fieldwork in 1995–96,
the tension between the different factions in Chenalhó was increasing,
although the degree of interaction between the groups varied between
villages. In various villages, like Yibeljoj, the different factions had their
own small stores and health promoters, as well as connections with mestizo doctors who would occasionally make pro-bono visits to the municipality. Although villagers would also seek services at establishments of
other factions than their own, this categorization was part of village life.
During a village's general community assemblies, the men participating
would side with their faction on any controversial issues. Most of the
political decisions were made in separate meetings of each faction. For
Catholic villagers, such decision-making arenas were the Sunday chapel service and the local meetings of Las Abejas, which also had some
costumbre villagers as members. After the period of escalating conflicts
and paramilitary violence in 1997 and the ensuing years of high tension
and suspicion between groups, factional life has again assumed a more
stable, albeit tense, character.

Membership in the different groups fluctuates considerably over time.

During my stay, fifty-two households in Yibeljoj were members of the Catholic chapel group. One catechist told me he knew of an additional thirty-one households that had been members previously but had left the group. Many villagers apparently have individual reasons for leaving, including lack of faith or enthusiasm, or conflicts with group norms. I heard of at least a couple of men who had left the group after they had taken a second wife, which only is accepted by costumbre norms. Some people chose to join other religious or political groups, while others remained unaffiliated. Quite a few villagers left collectively in connection with conflicts concerning the political direction of the Catholic group.

Paradoxically, the internal fissioning of Catholic chapel groups may partly stem from an apparent effort to achieve social and political cohesion within the group. Disagreements between chapel members are supposed to be worked out through collective discussions so that the group may act in concord. Permanent differences of opinion are regarded as highly problematic and disruptive. The emphasis on social conformity may be related to a continuous striving among Mayas to maintain the social cohesion of their communities, because social harmony is regarded as protecting the health and well-being of each individual (Guiteras Holmes 1961:308; Gossen 1994). The striving for consensus may also reflect an attempt by catechists to control chapel group politics. If differences in opinion cannot be worked out, catechists appear to prefer to drive out dissidents rather than accommodate them in the group. Catechists of opposing standpoints in a chapel group also appear to prefer to leave, along with their followers, if they have no prospect of success in directing the group.

Kinship and Locality

To some extent, Catholic group formation, like that of other new political and religious groups in Chenalhó, transcends both kinship and locality, instead drawing members from different lineages and barrios of the village. This is apparent in villages like Yibeljoj, to which families from various communities and lineages have moved over the past few generations in search of land, causing members of the same lineages to be dispersed over several barrios.[2] Nevertheless, in looking closely at the pattern of factional adherence in Yibeljoj, I found that villagers' choice of religious and political affiliation seemed to be influenced by both kinship and residence.[3] In fact, the political and religious factions appeared to a significant extent to be organized as localized groups of allied patrilines, similar to the former calpuls.

Most religious and political factions in Yibeljoj were dominated by only a few lineages. In the Presbyterian group, one lineage dominated both in numbers and by its control of the leadership. In the Catholic chapel group, almost 70 percent of the households, thirty-five out of fifty-two, belonged to only five lineages.[4] Each of these lineages had six or more houses in the group. These five lineages also held all but two of the various leadership posts. During my fieldwork, one lineage was especially influential: the Nichim family, the family of my host.[5] Brothers in this family held positions as leading catechist and three out of the four conjunto members, and their late father had been chapel president. His widow, my host's mother, was still in charge of food and drink preparation at large chapel celebrations, and the chapel kitchen was her domain. The majority of the women who assisted her in the kitchen were wives of those of her sons who held posts in the chapel group, or her divorced or unwed daughters. When I was in the chapel kitchen amid the hectic work or the cheerful sharing of food after the labor was completed, I felt as much at home as I did in the lineage compound of my host, surrounded by almost the same women.

Residence appeared to be another important factor when people chose affiliation. Almost all factions in Yibeljoj drew their members from mainly one or two barrios each. Of the Presbyterian households, all but two were located in the same two barrios, the majority in the barrio where the Presbyterian chapel had been built. Of the Zapatista households, about half were located in a single barrio, where they constituted a large majority. Catholic villagers referred to that part of the village as "the Zapatista barrio." Although that barrio also had the greatest mixture of lineages in Yibeljoj, it showed considerable political cohesiveness over time. During some years before the Zapatista rebellion in 1994, almost all in the barrio—thirty-one of its total of thirty-eight households—were members of the Cardenista party. And preceding that period, in turn, most had been members of the Partido Socialista Trabajador (PST), I was told. The costumbre members of the PRI also lived predominantly in one barrio, as did the small number of Pentecostals and those who were still members of the Cardenista party. In fact, the Catholics were the group with the most dispersed members, living in three barrios. (A fourth barrio had only one Catholic household.)[6] During my stay in Chenalhó, I heard even entire villages referred to as a "Zapatista" or "PRI" village.

Without diachronic data, one can only speculate about whether the factional concentration in a few barrios reflects the extent to which people are influenced by their neighbors when choosing political or religious affiliation, or whether families of the same faction have moved to the same barrios to live close to one another. However, my data from Yibeljoj indicates that men tend to be highly influenced by members of their closest patriline in their choice of group. Women, in contrast, are expected to follow the affiliation of the patriline that they marry into, regardless of any earlier adherence. The influence of kin on men's choices was especially notable when members of the same patriline lived close together. Men tended to be part of the same faction as their neighboring father, older brothers, paternal uncles, and cousins. This was especially prominent in lineages whose individual houses covered a large interconnected area—the whole compound tended to be affiliated with the same political or religious group. In contrast, married sons who lived in different barrios from their parents often belonged to other factions. The importance of residence was also apparent in kinship groups where the older generation of brothers was distributed over several barrios, each man with his adult sons living nearby. The people in each of these lineage segments often belonged to different factions. Thus, it appears that when parents lack land to give their sons to build their homes on, patrilineal influence lessens and the sons exercise the freedom to join political or religious groups of their choice. With land increasingly scarce in most Pedrano villages today, one can expect that patrilineal influence on men's choice of factional adherence will continue to decrease.

In many factions, villagers further strengthen kin-based cohesion by practicing endogamous marriage. In Yibeljoj, the Presbyterians applied a strict endogamy, their leaders prohibiting Presbyterians from marrying persons who were not members of the church, unless they were willing to convert. Catholics, too, tend to marry other Catholics, frequently from their own chapel group, a practice enforced both by catechists and parents. In my interviews, I found that parents were particularly insistent on choosing devout Catholic boys for their daughters to marry. Marrying a non-Catholic would most certainly imply that the girl would have to abandon the church, since few men accept their wives' being members of a group other than their own. Picking a Catholic boy also ensures that the future husband will share the norms of the girl and her parents—most importantly, the Catholic restrictions on alcohol use and the ban on polygamy. If the husband breaks these norms anyway, the wife can find help from the catechists to try to make him change his behavior. The parents of devout Catholic boys also seem to prefer Catholic brides for their sons, although this requirement is not as important as the reverse. While leaders of politically oriented factions may not be equally active in enforcing group endogamy, it is probable that parents hope to find sons-in-law who are members of their own faction so that their daughters, and future grandchildren, can remain in the group.

Chapel Group Leaders

Catholic chapel groups are led by catechists. Like traditional Pedrano authorities, Catholics may receive their calling to become catechists through a dream where they are approached by a messenger of God (see also Eber 2000:52–58). Aspiring catechists need the chapel group meeting's approval to begin serving and to receive the requisite training. Each chapel group also has a board that is responsible for collecting and administering pooled resources and for chapel maintenance, though their authority is subjugated to the catechists. Chapel members who hold positions on various temporary committees, or as health promoters or members of the conjuntos, the music bands, also have a certain authority and status due to their network of contact with and knowledge about the broader Catholic and mestizo society.

The chapel leaders, usually through the board, can request the contribution of money and labor from chapel members, which is announced at the end of Sunday meetings, when monetary contributions are collected. Money, labor, or in-kind contributions such as firewood and tortillas are requested for large festivities of the chapel group, to construct and maintain chapel buildings, and for the annual week-long catechist course at the Catholic municipal center in the village of Yabteclum. At times, pooled resources are also used to help chapel members in difficulties. In addition, Catholics are often asked to contribute money at the separate meetings of Las Abejas.

During my stay, chapel members often found the repeated collection of money and resources burdensome. That did not mean they questioned the right of the chapel leaders to demand these contributions from the members. The extraction of money and organization of corvée labor have been a long-standing characteristic of villages and earlier calpul units in Chenalhó and other highland Maya communities, as well as of customary subdivisions all through Mesoamerica (Hunt and Nash 1967:265; Thomas 1979; Mulhare 1996a:97). In Chenalhó, as noted in chapter 1, it has been the principales of each village who call together the local men to perform communal labor duties and who collect and administer a form of "tax" from each household known as "cooperación" by Pedranos, in Tzotzil called *ak' tak'in* (literally "give money"), used to cover public works and ceremonial expenses.[7] In the Catholic community, this corporate economy is now justified with biblical references. I often heard the individual contribution described as a service to God and an act that pleased God since it expressed the ideal of sharing. Catechists often admonished the creyentes to respect this ideal.

Catechist Leadership

The position of catechist is of the utmost importance to the Catholic community and encompasses many, or even most, of the roles of "traditional" Pedrano leaders, going far beyond the typical catechist functions prescribed by the Catholic Church. The position can roughly be divided into three fields, although they are intimately linked and can be said, rather, to be different aspects of the same form of authority: religious, moral, and political.

The central and most explicit task of catechists is of course religious leadership. It consists of leading the appeal to God in prayer and ceremonies, and to function as expert interpreters of the Bible, the Word of God. It is their knowledge of the Bible and their competence as interpreters that define and legitimize their religious authority. With this competence, they must guide the creyentes' worship, ensuring that their veneration is performed in such a way that it pleases God, willing him, as it were, to extend his protection.

Furthermore, catechists are expected to offer moral guidance to the creyentes on how to live in accordance with the Word, similar to the guidance offered by the traditional pasados. Catechist counsel is offered during chapel service but also in private contexts. If a family experiences a crisis, a pending divorce, or some form of conflict, catechists may be called on to mediate and offer guidance. Sometimes moral counseling is combined with prayer ceremonies in which God is asked to give the sinful person the strength to change. Catechists may also be asked to present marriage petitions to prospective parents-in-law, similarly to the way costumbre villagers turn to lineage elders or pasados. If the catechists assist with the marriage, I was told, the spouse and parents will be assured of moral support from the catechists in case the other spouse later violates chapel group norms. On the other hand, the authority of catechists in moral matters is sometimes contested. Especially when it comes to family matters, the guidance of a catechist is not always well received. One woman told me that husbands who are advised to change their behavior may get angry and reply: "No one is going to come here and tell me what to do! It's not as if I'm asking him for money or that he is going to offer me food; I'm providing for myself!"[8] Thus, catechist authority must be negotiated and is, of course, most easily granted by those who identify themselves as dedicated creyentes.[9]

Catechists are also the political leaders of the chapel groups, and to a significant extent, they steer the political direction of the Catholic community. During Sunday service in the chapel, creyentes are encouraged to discuss issues that come up, and they often vent their varying opinions. In the end, I found that the word of a catechist weighs the most heavily in discussions, often resulting in consensus decisions in line with the catechist's standpoint. Catechists are commonly regarded as having better political judgment than creyentes because of their understanding of the Word of God and their access to political information outside the sphere of most followers. It is important to note that catechists cannot force the creyentes to accept decisions that most disagree with; instead, they must convince the chapel members that their suggestions are reasonable. Their authority and continued legitimacy as leaders rely on their ability to be in tune with the sentiments of the chapel members and present suggestions that will not collide with theirs too drastically. Further, catechists need to demonstrate that they live according to ideals considered truly Christian and unselfishly serve the creyentes. Those who are able to incorporate political and religious skills with socially responsible conduct achieve legitimacy and thus influence as leaders.

The integration of religious, moral, and political authority is a long-standing characteristic of leadership in Chenalhó, as in many other Maya societies. In several aspects, the catechists have a role similar to that of cargo holders, where couples hold offices—cargos—in the civil-religious hierarchy of the municipal center. In contrast with the lifelong positions of village ceremonial leader (*kabildo vinik*) or traditional healer (*j-ilol*), cargos are taken by "ordinary villagers" who increase their competence, prestige, and power through repeated service (see, e.g., Guiteras Holmes 1961:72).

In the past few decades, however, Pedrano positions of leadership have increasingly separated the religious, moral, and political domains of authority. The various new posts at the local level, such as municipal agent or those of the ejido committees, are secular offices implying no religious authority. Even the civil-religious cargo holders in the municipal government are no longer seen as religious authorities by those who do not practice costumbre religion. In fact, many question their political and moral authority, accusing them of political corruption and co-optation, and of immoral, illegitimate rule. Thus, in contrast, the leaders of the Catholic community, as well as those of the various Protestant groups, can be said to bring these three dimensions of leadership together again.

A significant departure from both traditional and new leadership offices in Chenalhó is that women, too, have access to the catechist position. Still, the great majority of Pedrano catechists are male. Because the catechist role and competence are largely modeled on positions of leadership formerly held only by men, women catechists are seen as challenging this utterly male territory and often find themselves subordinated to their male colleagues (see chapter 5). The wives of male catechists hold a less conflictive role. Although the catechist position is individual and not held by couples as traditional cargos are, catechist wives partly parallel the role of cargo-holding women, such as preparing food for large festivals of the chapel groups. Some catechist wives participate in the tasks carried out by their husbands, visiting and praying in homes of followers. The wives of the deacons and pre-deacons (deacons-in-training) have an even more explicit role as companions in the duties borne by their husbands, and the couples perform many of the ceremonies together.

MUNICIPAL-LEVEL CATECHIST GOVERNANCE

The local chapel groups of the Pedrano Catholic community are aligned in a municipal-level structure with coordinated leadership and actions. This structure exists parallel to the "official" politico-religious municipal government, which is concerned only with costumbre religion. With its centralized yet umbrella-like structure, the Pedrano Catholic community shares significant features with the former organization of Chenalhó back when the municipal ruling body was constituted by representatives from each of the calpul subdivisions. The Catholic center in the village of Yabteclum functions in a similar fashion, as a governing body representing the local chapel groups in the municipality. The highest leaders consist of zone chiefs representing the five "zones" or regions into which the chapel groups are organized; coordinators of the different work areas of the municipal-level organization; and a few pre-deacons and deacons. While the municipal government designates special messengers to bring orders and information to the local communities—formerly principales, and today, municipal agents—the catechists serve both as members of the confederate ruling body and as messengers to the individual chapel groups. Like the municipal government of Chenalhó, the municipal-level leaders of the Catholic community function as intermediaries to authorities outside Chenalhó; which are, for the Catholics, primarily the Diocese of San Cristóbal and the Fray Bartolomé de Las Casas Center for Human Rights, but also official federal and state institutions.

During my stay, the parish priest did not participate in the regular meetings and courses of the Catholic community, except at especially crucial encounters. His principal authority lay in his performance of the sacraments. Today, the priest has a more active role and meets regularly with catechists. Being a liaison to the parish priest is the special responsibility of the "consejo parroquial," a person chosen for two-year terms by the catechist representatives.[10]

The center for the catechist coordination is in the village of Yabteclum, located in the geographic center of the municipality, which carries a significant symbolic role as the former capital of the Chenalhó municipality. The Catholic center consists of a set of buildings located right next to the old church of Yabteclum. During catechist meetings and other Catholic gatherings at the municipal level, participants meet, eat, and sleep on center premises.

THE YABTECLUM MEETINGS

The decision-making body of the Catholic community is the monthly catechist meeting in Yabteclum, usually lasting two days, where zone chiefs, coordinators, deacons and pre-deacons, and regular catechists come together. Each chapel group is expected to send at least one catechist to these meetings.[11] Extra catechist meetings are called when issues arise that need to be addressed rapidly. The meetings are prepared and led by the zone chiefs, pre-deacons, and the coordinators of the different work areas, all of whom thereby hold considerable sway over the presentation of the issues at hand and the discussions that will lead to joint decisions. During my stay, the pastoral worker participated in, and partly guided, the preparation of the agenda for the meetings, but she stayed in the background during the actual meetings. She only intervened when she deemed it necessary to direct the discussion or explain certain positions. The language of the meetings was always Tzotzil, including the agenda, written on a flip chart, and written work materials. Although the nun had a basic command of Tzotzil, she usually asked one of the coordinators to interpret when she wanted to talk to the group at length. The nun was assisted by two indigenous Tzotzil-speaking lay nuns who were part of the all-women "indigenous missionaries" group under the tutelage of the Hermanas del Divino Pastor. These two women had grown up in conditions similar to those in Chenalhó and were often called on to be cultural and linguistic interpreters between the nuns and the catechists.

At a catechist meeting, zone chiefs report on events or special problems in their zone. They are responsible for ensuring that the chapel groups in their zone function well; they advise local catechists on how to prevent and resolve conflicts, increase attendance of followers, and so on; and they spend much time making the rounds of various chapel groups during the Sunday services. Zone chiefs are experienced and well-respected catechists, all of them men during my stay, who have been appointed by the other catechists and may serve for many years before the position is rotated to another person. During the catechist meeting, ordinary catechists of the individual chapel groups may also give reports or raise issues to complement what is addressed by their respective zone chief.

Coordinators of the different thematic work-area groups attend catechist meetings when they want to report from their respective group on issues of interest to the whole Catholic community. The work areas include Indian Theology, the diocese-wide network called Pueblo Creyente, CODIMUJ (the Diocesan Coordination of Women), the more general area "women," the catechists for children, and the conjuntos. Several of the work areas link the Pedrano Catholic community with other parishes of the diocese, with whom the representatives meet regularly to exchange news and discuss shared concerns.[12] The coordinators that take part in the preparatory sessions of the catechist meetings are able to wield more influence than the others. Several of the top area coordinators during my stay were women, and they had gained significant status and influence. Meetings will also receive other members of the Catholic community who have important information to share; for example, on recent political events of concern to the community. The group will debate important issues, and if needed, the catechists in attendance will propose what the Catholic community's response should be.

In principle, decisions made at the catechist meetings have to be affirmed by the individual chapel groups. At the following local Sunday service in each village, the catechists will present the issues to be decided on, as well as other information and news, and explain the motivation for the proposals from the Yabteclum meeting. In practice, chapel members

Catechist zone chiefs and coordinators at recess during a catechist meeting in Yabteclum, 1996. Photo by author.

often take these proposals as mandates. Even after sometimes lengthy discussions, I found, the followers ultimately accepted the Yabteclum proposals.

The catechist meetings evidently also define and develop the ongoing religious work of the Catholic community, for the primary purpose of the meetings is to prepare for Sunday services the following month. At the meeting, catechists read and discuss the Bible texts that will be addressed, so they will have a foundation for the reflections they will lead in their respective chapel groups. During my stay, the catechists also wrote the two or three questions about the texts for the creyentes in each village chapel group to discuss and answer. The written responses to these questions were brought back to Yabteclum the following month.

Those attending the catechist meeting in Yabteclum have the right (as does the official municipal government of Chenalhó) to request the contribution of labor and resources from local chapel members for municipal-level activities. The Catholic center in Yabteclum was built by the contributions of individual chapel groups. The chapel groups also take care of its maintenance and provide cooks, food, and firewood for the yearly catechist courses.[13]

The center hosts the annual week-long catechist courses, which are prepared and taught by the pastoral workers and the highest echelons of catechist leadership. All chapel group catechists are expected and encouraged to attend the courses every year as part of their continued religious training. Through the guidance catechists receive from the pastoral workers, their biblical interpretation evolves in line with the diocese's perspective. They also develop methods to culturally translate Catholic dogma for the creyentes of their respective chapel groups. The courses treat biblical themes, church history, and Pedrano costumbre religion, the latter as part of the Indian Theology effort to integrate Catholic and traditional religious thought. Sometimes, more secular issues are addressed as well, such as Western doctrines on health and hygiene. After the annual course, the catechists will offer shorter, adapted versions of the courses for creyentes in the central village of each of the five zones. The catechists also integrate crucial themes from the course into the sermons they deliver throughout the year.

SOCIEDAD CIVIL LAS ABEJAS

Any political action Pedrano Catholics take vis-à-vis other groups in the municipality or outside Chenalhó is likely to occur through the political association Sociedad Civil Las Abejas. Pedrano Catholics founded Las Abejas in 1992 to protest an attempt by the PRI municipal government to attack oppositional catechists. After the Zapatista uprising in 1994, Las Abejas merged with Sociedad Civil, which was a peacekeeping network in the municipality connected with the broader diocese, and the association positioned itself in support of the EZLN demands and in opposition to the federal government.[14] Las Abejas also has a large number of non-Catholic members, most of whom practice costumbre religion, and has gained followers in several of the neighboring Maya municipalities: Pantelhó, Chalchihuitán, Simojovel, Zinacantán, and Tenejapa. However, Catholic Pedranos continue to dominate the association both numerically and politically, and the discourse of the group is highly influenced by the liberation theology perspective of Pedrano Catholics.

After the paramilitary persecution in 1997, culminating with the massacre of unarmed Catholics in Acteal, and the enormous international attention that followed, Las Abejas would increase considerably in strength and status. It also grew geographically, having begun with a membership solely of people from Chenalhó. The leaders of Las Abejas coordinate the contacts with Mexican and international NGOs, churches, and intergovernmental organizations like the European Union that offer political and monetary support, and they also administered some of the aid to the thousands of members who were forcibly displaced from their homes during four years. Las Abejas leaders organize the reception of the stream of visitors and human rights observers who arrive in villages with Las Abejas members, and they issue monthly public political statements. Today, Acteal, the seat of Las Abejas, is considered the definite center of the Catholic community, both by Pedranos and outsiders, and the primary arena where Pedrano Catholics come together to constitute and manifest the municipal-wide Catholic community. Acteal has since the massacre also become the ceremonial center of the Catholic community, as noted earlier, with highly politicized religious ceremonies performed regularly at the new chapel and the memorial tomb for the victims of the massacre.

It was the growth of Las Abejas after the massacre that shifted the power balance between Las Abejas and the municipal-level catechist coordination in Yabteclum, sometimes resulting in tensions between the two groups; for example, concerning their unequal access to resources. To improve coordination and communication, catechist leaders and Las Abejas leaders have started a body for joint governance, a group amounting to about fifty persons who meet regularly in Acteal.

Las Abejas has an umbrella structure similar to that of the municipal-level organization of the chapel groups. The base of Las Abejas is made up of village-level groups comprising Catholic and costumbre villagers who hold regular meetings to discuss and decide the activities and positions Las Abejas should assume. Similarly to the Catholic chapel services, and contrasting with the regular village assemblies, the meetings of Las Abejas are open to women, who usually make up the majority of participants. During my fieldwork in 1995–96, about thirty-five village-level Las Abejas groups were active in Chenalhó; all held regular meetings, often hosted in the local Catholic chapel. In 2008, Las Abejas had in total forty-three village-level groups, some of them in the above-mentioned neighboring municipalities (Schlittler Álvarez 2008:52). Each village-level group has one or more leaders, depending on its size, elected at a village meeting. The leaders—called representatives—plan the agenda for and preside over the meetings of the village-level group.

Like chapel groups, the local Las Abejas groups are coordinated and governed on a municipal level through regular meetings of the village-level representatives. During my stay, the venue for these meetings was rotated between different villages. Today they take place in Acteal. The meetings are presided over by the top leaders of Las Abejas—the members of the board. During my stay, the board was composed of mainly middle-aged men, several of whom were catechists. At least one was a founder of Las Abejas. I found that the authority of the board members was significant, and although lively discussions were held on different issues at the municipal-level meetings, if the board members presented clear suggestions for action, there was seldom any opposition. The majority of the village representatives were non-catechist young men, in contrast to the board members, and several were of costumbre religion. In the municipal-level meetings I attended, usually only two or three of the representatives were women. Even though they were experienced catechists, in contrast to most of the men, they were quite marginalized politically. Even today, few women are chosen as representatives and never, it seems, as board members.

As with the catechist leaders of the chapel groups, the representatives of Las Abejas bring the municipal-level agreements before the local groups to be affirmed—or rejected—by the members. They also update local members on political developments. A local member described the news that had reached her village group through the representatives during the tense period of negotiations between the Zapatistas and the federal government in 1996: "They talk about how the conflict is going and about the suffering. They bring information and explain. They inform us about politics and how the peace negotiations continue, or if there are more conflicts. The leaders will quickly tell their people if there will be war."[15]

Local members would usually accept the proposals that came out of the municipal Las Abejas meetings. Local Las Abejas meetings were nonetheless important arenas for engaging the members in the decision-making process. By taking part in both the frequent village meetings of Las Abejas and Sunday services of the chapel groups, Catholic villagers managed to keep up-to-date on all political developments of concern for their Catholic community, locally and regionally, and actively participate in determining their own collective involvement. Like catechists, Las Abejas leaders also have the right to request the contribution of labor and resources from the local members for activities on the central level, usually to cover travel expenses of the representatives.

At present, the Las Abejas board consists of a president, secretary, treasurer, three substitutes, and a personal secretary of the president who takes care of many of the day-to-day matters. Added to the core leadership are positions such as the members of the legal committee that processes the claims to indemnify the survivors of the Acteal massacre. They also handled the claims, now settled, for the stolen property of the displaced. An ejido commissioner handles land issues and disputes, and a lay judge deals with, for example, interpersonal disputes, including divorce settlements.[16]

In addition, Las Abejas has installed a hierarchy of traditional authorities, similar to the cargo positions of the municipal government of Chenalhó, such as regidor, alférez, capitán, and alcalde. This includes an alférez for the figure of San Pedro, the patron saint of Chenalhó, which Las Abejas, like the Zapatista autonomous municipality, has "recuperated" as their patron saint (the "official" celebrations of San Pedro are controlled by the PRI-ist municipal government). The neotraditional authorities hold no formal political authority over Las Abejas or its members but offer counsel and guidance and today play an important ceremonial role in the celebrations and demonstrations taking place in Acteal.[17]

All of these officials are elected to one-year terms by the general assembly of Las Abejas and installed at the start of the new year, like the cargo holders of the official municipal government (Schlittler Álvarez 2008:54). Board members and other officers reside semi-permanently in Acteal during their terms, which is also similar to the practice of the officials of the municipal government in the Chenalhó capital.

Some of the former leaders of Las Abejas, including founding members with long experience and numerous contacts, exert considerable de facto influence over the board, especially when actual board members are insecure about handling the demanding interactions with external actors, from official institutions to NGOs (see Tavanti 2003:17–18). Their role parallels the influential role of traditional pasados in Chenalhó and demonstrates the continued sway of seniority in spite of the increased authority of younger men.

The various leaders of Las Abejas serve without pay, similarly to the catechists. Pedranos regard this as an important demonstration of one's willingness to dedicate a considerable amount of time and effort to the service of the Catholic community. This willingness to serve without remuneration also resembles the costumbre ideal of cargos—paying service to one's community. However, this demand makes it hard for persons with very scarce resources to enter time-consuming offices, since they cannot afford not to work full-time for their family.

Las Abejas embraces a great number of work areas, each with its own membership base and coordinators or boards. Some are registered legally as non-profit organizations ("asociaciones civiles") or cooperatives. Many have received funding directly from foreign NGOs, such as Peace and Diversity Australia, which finances an array of small projects.[18] Those working in the area of autonomous education ran independent schools in several of the camps for displaced people. The health promoters, who used to pertain to one of the work areas of the catechist-led organization, formed their own association in 2006, OSECAPIACH, which receives financial support from the French NGOs Espoir Chiapas and Médecins du Monde.[19] In the area of communication, Radio Chanul Pom (Radio Las Abejas) began broadcasting in 2003 with sixteen hours of daily radio transmissions in the Chenalhó area, a mixture of music and short informational bulletins.[20] The radio is since 2009 part of the new Las Abejas organization based in Nuevo Yibeljoj. The organization with headquarters in Acteal has a new radio station called Radio Almantal Yu'un Lekilal. Since 2005, a group of videographers has made several productions, and in 2009 they incorporated as Colectivo de

Las Abejas youngsters learning to make videos through Colectivo de Comunicación Koman Ilel, 2011. Photo by José A. Jiménez Pérez.

Comunicación Koman Ilel. The Acteal Choir, which formed in 1998, has made two records and various tours of Mexico and abroad. In 2006, several Pedrano women formed Grupo de Mujeres Mayas de Las Abejas (Tsoble Bats'i Antsetik Yu'un Chanul Pom, the Group of Maya Women of Las Abejas). Their goal is to strengthen the still-marginalized position of women in Las Abejas and to increase their active participation.[21]

Las Abejas has also created two cooperatives aiming to offer an improved economy for associated members. In 1999, the cooperative union Maya Vinic was formed, which consists of about five hundred members producing principally coffee but also honey. The members come from thirty-six villages in Chenalhó, Pantelhó, and Chalchihuitán. The cooperative owns a central storage and roasting facility in San Cristóbal and exports coffee to North America, Europe, and Asia, much of it certified as organic and fair trade. Maya Vinic markets its products through international partners such as Higher Grounds Trading Company and Cooperative Coffees in the United States, Arabejas in Switzerland, and Ataka Trading Company in Japan.[22] And finally, women formed a small artisan cooperative, Maya Antsetik, in 2001 to make and sell woven and embroidered textiles.[23] Through the projects developed by Las Abejas, Catholic Pedranos have strengthened their own community's independence from the broader municipality of Chenalhó. They have also developed structures increasingly similar to those of the "official" municipal governance, further emphasizing their rejection of the present municipal institutions, controlled by PRI.

MANTAL: LISTENING TO THE LEADERS' COMMANDS

As stated earlier, the responsibility for decision making in both the Catholic community and Las Abejas falls to the village-level assemblies of the respective group. At these meetings, the members—women as well as men—may attend, voice their opinions, engage in discussion, and finally, come to a joint decision. The assemblies provide a highly participatory ground for political decision making, the local members determining the direction their whole organization should take. However, I found that the authority of catechists and the leaders of Las Abejas is significant, with local members usually accepting proposals of the municipal-level

meetings of leaders. This reflects, I believe, the long-standing importance in the eyes of Pedranos of a hierarchical differentiation between
authorities and regular villagers.

The notion of *mantal* epitomizes catechist authority, I suggest, conflat-
ing both the religious and political domains. Pedrano Catholics use the
Tzotzil term *mantal* (*mantaletik* in plural) to refer to the teachings and
"orientations" the catechists give the creyentes, stemming from scripture and thus from God. The term signifies "order" or "law," but also
"instruction" or "convocation."[24] The expression *ta jch'un mantal* means
simultaneously "obey," "respect," and "believe," I was told. The association of *mantal* with catechists can be seen as an indication of the high
authority Pedranos cede to their leaders and the weight they give to their
directives.

By obeying the *mantal*, creyentes express their commitment and subordination to the authority of catechists, and ultimately, to God. Thus,
one catechist said in a Sunday service: "We have to believe [obey] the
commands [*mantaletik*] that our Lord tells us, those he has written." At
the same Sunday meeting, a creyente woman drew a parallel between
obedience to the commands and the respect creyentes should show God:
"If we [women] did not come [to the chapel], if we were not searching,
we would not be working for the Lord. There are also the commands
[*mantaletik*] brought by the catechists. If they come to inform us, we have
to obey. Therefore, those who understand have to work together. Together we will do the work."[25] Creyentes also use the term *mantal* to refer
to the messages and proposals catechists bring from Yabteclum. Thus,
what the catechists referred to as a tentative suggestion I often heard
creyentes describe as a final decision and a command. I also heard them
use the expression "the representatives from Yabteclum" to refer to catechists bringing information about a certain question, indicating that
they see the catechists as representatives of the governing center.

In Las Abejas as well, suggestions brought from the municipal-level
meetings by the local representatives appear to be generally perceived
as *mantal*—a command rather than a suggestion. Local members of Las
Abejas often described their acceptance of the central commands as an
expression of respect and trust that their leaders, who were regarded
as competent and better versed than themselves, would make the right

decisions. A Catholic member in Yibeljoj spoke of this trust almost joy-fully: "In Sociedad Civil [Las Abejas], people obey the orders [*mantal*]. They listen to what the representatives say from wherever they have brought the messages. We agree to listen to them, we truly agree. We take what they say into consideration. We don't disobey the leaders."[26] She said this was the case for all organizations in Chenalhó. The leaders of the respective groups were respected and obeyed, and they in turn re-spected the members. When I commented that this resembled the obe-dience villagers used to show their leaders in the past, she agreed.

The authority of catechists and Las Abejas leaders relies to a high de-gree on their capacity to be intermediaries to spheres outside Chenalhó; especially, of course, the Catholic Diocese (cf. Wilson 1995:185, 203). By virtue of being trained and continually informed by the diocese, cat-echists are acknowledged as the bishop's messengers. The *mantal* that is sent out from the Yabteclum center to the village chapel groups is often referred to as originating with the bishop. By obeying the *mantal*, crey-entes express their commitment and obedience to the diocese and its representatives, including pastoral workers and catechists.

Las Abejas, on its part, functioned relatively independently during my stay and was influenced only indirectly by the pastoral workers and their directives. Las Abejas meetings were held with no pastoral workers or other mestizos present, and the members determined the structure and agenda of the organization. But the members also clearly recognized the bishop as the supreme authority of Las Abejas; although not all members were Catholic, they identified with the bishop's objectives: establishing peace with social justice. Furthermore, as described earlier, the leaders of Las Abejas frequently consulted with diocese advisors and allied NGOs, especially the Fray Bartolomé de Las Casas Center for Human Rights, before making important political decisions. After the paramilitary per-secution, Las Abejas leaders have found themselves in greatly increased demand as intermediaries before national as well as international actors. To guide the leaders in this capacity, the Jesuits took on the role of men-tors of Las Abejas and assisted the organization in establishing several of the new projects and work areas.

The role of mediator, for both catechists and Las Abejas leaders, re-quires specific skills. Important competencies are, as noted earlier, bilingualism, literacy, knowledge of mestizo society and institutions, and understanding of how internationally funded projects are organized and administered. Though not all catechists can read and write, the great majority are functionally literate, and they are improving their proficiency through the constant use of notebooks and written texts; a Bible or notebook in the hand is virtually the sign of a catechist. These skills are considered even more important for Las Abejas leaders (cf. Tavanti 2003:17–18). Accordingly, like the other new positions of authority that have emerged in Maya communities during the last century, and in contrast with conventional costumbre cargo-holders and pasados, old age is not accorded special merit. Most catechists are young or middle-aged. During my stay, the representatives of Las Abejas were even younger, except for the board members. Many seemed attracted not only by the political agenda of Las Abejas but also by the bridge that the association provided to Mexican society and modern urban life. With the intense interaction with foreigners and international NGOs after the Acteal massacre, many young Las Abejas members have found the means to further their skills in various areas, some even going to San Cristóbal to study at the high school level, which few Pedranos did in the past (Schlittler Álvarez 2008:61). Jaime Schlittler Álvarez even talks of an "Acteal generation" of young Pedranos who are increasingly influencing the political discourse of Las Abejas (2008:61). As noted, however, young people are usually considered as lacking the proficiency and experience required to carry the full weight of leadership. Catholic Pedranos thus continue to value more conventional Pedrano qualities of leadership such as accumulated expertise and prestige.

For catechists—and to some extent Las Abejas leaders—their dependence on the diocese makes their role fairly complex. On the one hand, they need to function as autochthonous authorities of the Pedrano Catholic community, responsible and responsive to their followers. On the other hand, they need to represent and answer to the pastoral workers and bishop and even the Fray Bartolomé de Las Casas Center for Human Rights. This delicate, dual nature of Catholic leadership is especially visible in the role of the zone chiefs, deacons, and key catechist coordinators, who function both as the main leaders of the Pedrano chapel groups and as the people in charge of disseminating diocesan teachings.

They depend on the respect and approval of both sides to maintain their position. During my stay, some of these leaders were finely attuned to the ideas and goals of the pastoral worker and shared her concern with transmitting them to the broader Catholic community. When regular catechists sometimes hesitated or rejected her teachings outright, these leaders struggled to find convincing arguments.[27] At the same time, these men were those most respected by the other catechists and most influential in the decision-making process because of their qualities of leadership and theological expertise. The authority of the main catechist leaders is thus highly dependent on skill in balancing these different demands for loyalty and representation to both Catholic Pedranos and external allies.

EXTERNAL AUTHORITIES

During my stay, I frequently saw individual villagers, catechists, and Las Abejas representatives make journeys to San Cristóbal to deal with cases for which they previously would have turned to the municipal government. The diocese, and to a lesser degree, the Fray Bartolomé de Las Casas Center for Human Rights, function as additional authorities of the Pedrano Catholic community and Las Abejas, which strengthens their independence from the official municipal leadership of Chenalhó. Now, they turn to the diocese or the staff at the Center for Human Rights for advice on how to proceed. Thus, for example, a catechist I knew went to the Center for Human Rights for advice on his sister's divorce from an abusive husband, which eventually led to a settlement between both parties. People seeking advice from the diocese sought out one of the more highly placed advisors, usually by visiting the diocese office next door to the cathedral in San Cristóbal. They also visited the convent of La Nueva Primavera on the outskirts of town to find one of the nuns of the Hermanas del Divino Pastor or the indigenous lay nuns working in Chenalhó at the time. Only then would the persons sometimes choose to address themselves to the municipal authorities in Chenalhó, guided by the advice they had received.

The support from the diocese and allied NGOs not only supplements that of the official municipal authorities of Chenalhó but has also provided Catholic villagers with leverage in internal municipal disputes. By taking complaints of abuses by the municipal government before the Center for Human Rights, and if the situation is deemed serious, receiving help in bringing the case before higher bodies, Catholic Pedranos are able to challenge the previous hegemony of the municipal government. This outside support has clearly affected Catholic influence on municipal politics, as will be described in chapter 7.

And finally, when Pedrano Catholics must interact with "official" mestizo society, institutions, and authorities, they frequently, as described in chapter 2, seek counsel and assistance from their "allies" in mestizo society—the Catholic Diocese and a few select NGOs. Pedrano Catholics often appeal to institutions and authorities as a collective unit, having already discussed and agreed on the matter in previous meetings of chapel groups or Las Abejas, and tasking the leaders to act as intermediaries. When individuals or smaller groups have particular concerns to be handled with official institutions, they again rely on their adherence to the Catholic community, turning to their leaders or mestizo allies to function as advisors, backup, or representatives. Acting through these channels, Pedrano Catholics are attaining the means and confidence to claim rights and equal treatment, somewhat reducing the discrimination they otherwise encounter.

CHAPTER 5

Re-gendering Political Agency

As argued in the previous chapters, Pedrano Catholics are both reproducing and changing earlier ways of constructing community in Chenalhó. Perhaps the most striking change concerns the relation between gender and participation in the public, political sphere. While this sphere has conventionally been restricted to men, women today are increasingly present and active in this arena. These changes have not only affected the construction of male and female gender but also transformed the political life of the community. Whereas politics was formerly a male, lineage-oriented matter, it has become more pluralistic and possibly more communitarian in character—at least within the different politico-religious factions.

Pedranos generally express a communitarian ideal that highlights their mutual concern for ensuring a livelihood and survival. Ideally, this concern unites husband and wife, the different kin-groups of a village, and the local communities of the municipality. This ideal is also expressed in the cargos—the offices of the municipal civil-religious ruling body—which are held by married couples and where both men and women have important ceremonial roles (Rosenbaum 1993; Eber 2000). The public, political sphere, in contrast, has been constructed as an exclusively male field of decision making and alliance building, where men fill all positions of political leadership. With the changes in political structure imposed by state reforms in the twentieth century, it appears that women were even further excluded from communal politics. The male dominance of the public and the political is also expressed through the fealty to patrilin-

eal interests that is still reflected in village politics. To some extent, Pedrano society can be described as a grouping of patrilines that compete
for influence in community affairs. Although decision making based on
consensus is preferred in the communal assemblies, men's primary loyalty appears to have been to their patriline. To a significant degree, this
loyalty is today superseded by loyalty toward one's faction. But because
religious and political adherence appears partly to follow lineage lines,
as was argued in the preceding chapter, factional affiliation and loyalty to
one's closest lineage members may amount to the same thing.

Women are represented in the communal assemblies only through
the adult men of the household headed by their father or husband, and
they are expected to identify with and be loyal to its interests. A woman
can have a certain influence on her husband's position in different matters, but her political agency has necessarily been only indirect and has
depended on her husband's willingness to discuss issues and make joint
decisions with her. Furthermore, in contrast to men, women have had
limited possibilities to come together with other women outside their
kin group to share experiences and reflections. Because of the highly
segregated life-worlds of women and men, women have been largely confined to their lineage household compound; first that of their fathers,
and after marrying, that of their husbands. Thus, women have had little
possibility of transforming their concerns and interests into political action if these did not coincide with the concerns expressed by men in the
political arena.

In the Pedrano Catholic community, however, as in the other new
politico-religious groups, the public, political sphere is no longer exclusively male. Most, if not all, groups allow and even encourage women to
participate in meetings, study the information, and voice their opinions.
Women have embraced the new possibilities for public agency, participating actively and in large numbers in Catholic and other new groups,
often even constituting the majority at meetings and religious services.
During my stay, women did not commonly phrase their new demands
in terms of human rights or citizenship, but their arguments often contained a strong claim for justice. In this chapter, I aim to depict both the
scope and complexity of these changes.

GENDER SEGREGATION

Men and women have traditionally had quite different access to political agency, related to the social segregation of men and women in Chenalhó that is upheld by norms of women's propriety, patrilocality or virilocality, and gendered divisions of work and the public sphere. Overall, men and women tend to live in separate social spheres with distinct obligations and expectations.

Men usually have ample opportunities to form both social and political relations with other men outside their lineage. As described earlier, all positions of political leadership in Chenalhó have been held by men, both those in the municipal center and at the village level. The central arena where men form a political collectivity is perhaps the communal assembly—the arena for village-level decision making introduced by agrarian reform—of which all men are full members. Men may also work collectively in corvée labor tasks decided by the communal assembly—on the village school or on the communal plot of land. Furthermore, men often have time to socialize with friends. In the afternoon, after eating and resting after working in nearby fields, they frequently leave home again to pass the time with male friends in the village, playing basketball or chatting. Taken together, the male sphere of life, work, and politics in Chenalhó sets the scene for strong male collectivities with dynamics that are able to "move things."

The male public sphere extends beyond the borders of Chenalhó. For at least a century, many Pedrano men have temporarily left the municipality to find work, and this necessity has increased dramatically in the last few years. Men also go to urban areas, principally San Cristóbal, alone or in the company of other men, on family errands or on behalf of the village or their organization or church (cf. Leyva-Solano 1995). As a result, most men have considerably more experience of mestizo society than women do, as well as access to knowledge and skills that are important means to political influence in Chenalhó.

Women with similar skills and experiences, in contrast, are often the object of criticism by their families and neighbors and may feel ostracized by their community (Eber 2000:192; see also the experiences of "Antonia," Eber 2011). Most women rarely have a reason or the means to leave the municipality, and many have little practice and competence in dealing with mestizo society and city life, not to mention limited knowledge of Spanish. Therefore, women often feel at a loss in mestizo-dominated environments (cf. Rostas 2003:183).

Within their own community, women's opportunity to create bonds with women outside their own kin-groups has been limited. Everyday interaction with unrelated women has often been sporadic: encounters at the village store, by the spring or river where women wash clothes and fetch water, or on the way to collect firewood or work in the field. Both the productive and social spheres of a woman are to a large extent circumscribed by the boundaries of the household and the lineage compound.

According to the prevalent norm of patrilocality, a man and his wife will usually live in or close to the house of his parents after marriage. If a father has enough land, he will give portions to his married sons to build their own houses for their families, preferably close by. Sometimes the houses of the same patriline cover a considerable area, where adult brothers, their parents, and their paternal uncles with their sons and families all live in proximity. Their children feel at home running between the households to play and listen to the small talk of adults. In the village of Yibeljoj, one the largest lineage compounds consisted of twenty-one houses, amounting to almost half of their section, or barrio, of the village, both in size and number of houses.

For a woman, the norm of patrilocality means that she will leave her own family upon marriage, often in her lower or mid-teens, and join the household—and the political or religious adherence—of her husband and parents-in-law, sometimes entailing a move to a different village. Although her relationship to her family of origin often continues to be important and close, contact may be quite infrequent. In her new home, the woman will be subject to the authority of her husband, and especially in her daily tasks, her mother-in-law. Since the house is where a woman spends most of her time and carries out her work, her quality of life is very much dependent on the family she marries into.

For women growing up in very poor or abusive families, marriage has long been their principal means to try change their situation. Several women in Yibeljoj told me that by marrying, they grasped at the chance to live in a home with enough food and proper clothes. Parents, on their part, may choose to marry off their daughters at a young age to have fewer mouths to feed, which implies the risk that the girls end up in uncaring families (Freyermuth 2003a:239). Women who become widows or decide to leave abusive husbands are usually accommodated, along with their children, in the home of their parents or other relatives. With the increasing number of young couples marrying without the consent of the girl's parents, however, the woman lacks this safety net if the marriage fails to gain acceptance by her parents (Kovic and Eber 2003:4).

After some years, most young couples are able to construct their own home, whether on lineage grounds or not. In families where the lineage houses are close together, women can head their own households and yet help each other with more strenuous tasks, watch and comfort each other's children, and have time to sit down and talk while working on their handicrafts. Throughout the day, much of a woman's work revolves around the kitchen and yard, preparing food and feeding her family, taking care of the children, and attending to her poultry. Women who are married to brothers in a lineage compound become part of a female collectivity together with the mother-in-law and the unmarried, divorced, or widowed women of the patriline. This is the circle of women with whom they usually have the closest relationships after marriage, besides their own mothers and sisters. This was the case with my own hostess, Antonia Ruiz, who had her own household with her husband but shared the yard and water tap with her mother-in-law, her husband's divorced sister, two sisters-in-law, and an unmarried female relative of her husband. These women were an important help and company to each other, and shared worries, laughter, and social and political news. Because the patriline had been devoted to Catholicism for some decades, the women also attended chapel meetings together and shared the faith and preoccupations of the church group.

In spite of the ideal of reciprocal dependency and respect between the spouses, a woman is usually expected to serve and obey her husband and is exposed to the whims of his temperament. Many women suffer physical abuse from their husbands, especially when the husbands are drunk. Most women are taught to be submissive and obedient as children, and many learn to accept physical punishment as a means to correct their behavior (Freyermuth 2003a:381). That does not mean a husband is considered morally justified in beating his wife, and a woman can take a physically abusive husband before the authorities of the municipal government for reprimand, temporary arrest, or divorce. Nevertheless, as shown by Anna María Garza Caligaris (2002), authorities tend not to accept a divorce, but pressure the couple to try to reconcile. Women, on the whole, have also lacked alternatives because there are few means for divorced women to support themselves and their children, as women traditionally do not own land on their own. Today, however, with better access to schooling and skills in Spanish and literacy, a growing number of young women prefer to delay marriage in order to attend secondary school, or to seek employment, often as domestic workers, in urban areas outside Chenalhó. Some women decide not to marry at all, saying they do not want the abuse and subservience they have seen their mothers or sisters endure, or to be limited to household work (Freyermuth 2003b; Kovic and Eber 2003:4).

Of course, some women traditionally have had access to wider networks and prestige through the various occupations open to them. In the role of *j-ilol* (healer) or traditional midwife, they have moved freely between households and gained both a degree of authority and the opportunity to interact with other women and men (Eber 2000). Women have also been cargo holders in the municipal center jointly with their husbands, and with equal prestige. Depending on the cargo, a woman performs specific ceremonies and together with other cargo-holding women is responsible for the preparation and serving of the huge feasts served to other cargo holders and guests at ceremonies. After completing her cargo, she, like her husband, will be treated with deference and respect (Eber 2000:81, cf. Rosenbaum 1993:152). As a cargo holder, a woman can create important contacts with women from other communities on which she can draw later in life (Rostas 2003:173).

However, women do not hold cargos that involve political leadership or where they must be accessible to the public to receive complaints and settle disputes. One woman told me: "It seems that they [women] don't solve problems, only the men do that, like the suplente, the alcalde, or the regidores. Not women."[1] Nor do women hold any of the newer posts of village leadership that the federal government introduced, such as

municipal agent or school committee member, which men occupy without any accompanying role for their wives (cf. Rostas 2003:183). And the
introduction of communal assemblies, which opened up village governance for more participatory decision making, did not strengthen wom-
en's political agency because they are barred from attending. As these assemblies also elect people to hold the new local leadership posts, women
are excluded from such voting. The reason community assemblies are
closed to women, I was told by both men and women, is that women
do not work in the fields (see Arias 1975:27).This exclusion from the
assemblies may possibly stem from formal federal regulations of the assemblies for ejidos and agrarian communities, which restrict attendance
to the formal holders of land titles—in most cases men. However, in the
general communal assemblies, this principle has been extended, since
teenage boys living at home participate in the assemblies once they fin-
ish school and start to work full-time with their fathers in the field.

I was also told that women are not considered men's equal in their
capacity to reason and take part in deliberations for the common good.
A woman explained: "Women have not been respected. Men say that
women cannot reason, that only men have the right to have opinions. . . .
Women don't come to the assemblies, only men. When there are some
problems to solve, only men will come. The women are not involved,
they are not called."[2]

Nevertheless, in recent decades, a growing number of women are finding the means to broaden their physical and social sphere. The formation of religious and political organizations, improved access to schooling and infrastructure, and an increased need to find extra sources of
income have in different ways changed relations within the family and
the position of women in the public sphere. The Catholic community is
one of these organizations.

ACQUIRING POLITICAL AGENCY

The new religious groups that emerged in Chenalhó, as in other Maya
municipalities, offered one of the first public arenas where women could
actively take part. In the Catholic prayer meetings in Chenalhó, women
are part of a collectivity that turns to God with their worries about the

health and welfare of their children. In the company of other church members, they can complain of fatigue, family problems, or their own shortcomings, and receive comfort. In the mutual reflections of the groups wherein they compare biblical texts with their own lives, they can articulate their personal hardships and share them with others. As full participants at these meetings, they take part in the decision making of the chapel groups, which includes approving would-be catechists and electing people to other positions in the chapel leadership. As suggested by Susanna Rostas (2003) regarding Protestants in Tenejapa, the new churches provide women with a space where they can gain agency independent of their husbands, and a means to attain spiritual as well as social strength—all eagerly welcomed by many women.

During the same period that the new Catholic and Protestant churches were gaining followers in Chenalhó, women also began to engage in other arenas. One of the first fields for women's collective organization in Chenalhó was created through cooperatives making and selling handicrafts to the tourist market. Since the late 1960s, several artisan cooperatives have emerged from state-run development programs directed at

Women filling the Yibeljoj chapel at Sunday service, 1996. Photo by author.

the rural indigenous population. By the late 1980s, Chenalhó had four cooperatives, three of which were related to PRI or official institutions, while one was independent (Eber and Rosenbaum 1993). Since then, several more independent cooperatives have emerged, such as Tsobol Antsetik, whose members are adherents of the Zapatistas or Las Abejas, and the now-defunct Maya Antsetik, part of Las Abejas. The cooperatives have not only given women a new source of income—creating more independence from and sometimes friction with their husbands—but also the experience of all-women arenas of work, organization, and leadership, and of interacting with mestizos in San Cristóbal (Eber 2001a). Another important field of organization among women is that of healthcare, likewise initially sparked by state programs. Traditional midwives, *j-ilol* healers, and other types of healers in Chenalhó have become part of the statewide Organización de Médicos Indígenas del Estado de Chiapas (Organization of Indigenous Doctors of the State of Chiapas, OMIECH), which also includes men as members (Garza Caligaris 2002:130–31). Some of these cooperatives and associations are part of the broader politicization of Maya women and are seeking ways to change their position both within the family and in broader society. Their members at times join encounters with other women's organizations in San Cristóbal (Hernández Castillo 2006b).

Women in increasing numbers have also joined various groups of political opposition emerging in the municipality, whether political parties or civil organizations, such as the former Cardenista party, the Zapatista autonomous municipality, and Las Abejas. All of these organizations allow women to participate in their respective assemblies where the members discuss their concerns and make joint decisions. In most of these groups, women hold positions of leadership, albeit lower-level positions. In the Zapatista support bases, for example, women participate on a par with men, attend assemblies and other meetings, and hold positions as low-level leaders (Eber 2000; Garza Caligaris 2002). And at the local Las Abejas meetings in Chenalhó, the vast majority of participants are women. At some of the Las Abejas meetings in Yibeljoj during my stay, women and their children even filled the entire meeting hall, leaving only two rows of benches in front for the male elders, obliging the other men to line up against the walls. In the municipal-level meetings of Las

Abejas representatives, women are still a small minority, as noted earlier. But Las Abejas has formed several internal groups consisting primarily or solely of women: besides the now-closed cooperative Maya Antsetik, for example, the Acteal Choir and the Group of Maya Women of Las Abejas.

The male leaders of the various politico-religious organizations usually applaud the presence and active participation of women. In the Catholic community, for example, catechists publicly promote and support women's attendance at chapel group meetings. They often encourage women to take an active role in the meetings, answer the questions, and express their opinions. In some village chapel groups, the male catechists even make an earnest effort to motivate women to become catechists. During my stay, the nun and the catechist coordinators also tried tactfully to initiate a discussion of the general subordination of women in Chenalhó. They questioned the authority of family patriarchs in the Catholic community and asked the other male catechists if there were "pharaohs" in their own homes. They emphasized the role of women in the Bible as evangelists of the Word of God and women's importance to the work of their own chapel groups (cf. Gil Tébar 2003:151).

The push to include women appears to be generated by allied organizations and churches outside Chenalhó, reflecting changing ideals in mestizo Mexican society. A young woman of the Cardenista party explained how the change came about among Pedrano members of the party: "The leader came to say that here, not only men have rights, but women have rights, too. Women, too, can defend their people. That's what the leader said. And that's what we understood. And so we nominated women, the women who are smart, so to speak. And that way he brought us together and had us form base committees."[3] Women's participation in the Catholic church groups also drew support from the higher-ups, a woman told me: "Women have the right to participate, that's what the command said."[4] Inside the diocese, the work of CODIMUJ is explicitly intended to strengthen women's role in the chapel groups and beyond, and during my stay, it was also the aim of the nuns from Hermanas del Divino Pastor working in Chenalhó, albeit through low-key and non-confrontational methods. In addition, after the Acteal massacre in 1997, several of the international NGOs that decided to support the work of Las Abejas have endeavored to further strengthen women's role through various projects they have funded (e.g., Schlittler Álvarez 2008:51).

These changes have nevertheless encountered considerable resistance. The presence and active participation of women in various group meetings implies a challenge to male authority. Furthermore, the role of women as leaders contests conventional boundaries of both male and female genders. Although many men favor the presence and participation of women in theory, at times they have problems accepting the consequences in reality.

Assembly Participation: Challenging Male Authority

One area of dispute concerns the claim I sometimes heard that the use of reason to solve problems is a capacity primarily held by men. But when women voice their opinions in the meetings, they demonstrate that they, too, have this capacity. Rosa Sántiz Pérez, an assertive Catholic woman in Yibeljoj who sometimes spoke at chapel meetings, explained the change the new organizations have brought: "Before, women were not respected. . . . Only men had the right to speak their opinion, that's what men said. Now, instead, they say both men and women have the right. So they say. Now, we [women] can say what we want, whatever we like. Sometimes the women are better at reasoning, and at times we don't agree with what the men say. So, it seems like we women can also reason."[5]

Women's claim to intellectual competence is often taken as a challenge of men's capacities. At one of the Sunday services in the Yibeljoj chapel group, the male catechist addressed the men specifically on this matter: "Listen, men, everybody has to be respected; you cannot say 'I'm the man, it's I who decide, the woman knows nothing!' You can't say that, men. You can't say that. We have the same thinking, the same reasoning, we have the same duties if we pay attention, men and women; we have the same blood. That's why they [women] have to be respected, too."[6]

To defend their prerogatives, Catholic men sometimes belittle women's words and opinions, often indirectly, through patronizing attitudes and phrases. They may portray women's knowledge as too limited or inadequate to permit an analysis of the question at hand, whether a religious matter or an assessment of political events. In the Yibeljoj chapel group, male catechists or conjunto members sometimes told me, as I read the papers with the chapel members' responses to the weekly Bible questions, that I really should not bother to read the women's answers, since they were less correct than the men's.

The public participation of women also breaches the principle of male representation of the household practiced in the regular communal assemblies. For many men, leaders included, it is a humiliating dismissal of their own role and a public loss of face if their wife, daughter, or sister speaks at the meetings of Las Abejas or the chapel group. A man may therefore obstruct her active participation by letting her know he does not accept it. Thus, although women are present at the meetings and encouraged to speak by the leaders, they often remain silent. Margarita Arias Ruiz, one of the leading women catechists in Chenalhó during my stay, known for her boldness and quick wit, described this enforced silence of women:

> If the women and girls don't want to speak, it is because they are afraid of their husbands. If they go to the meeting, they will be scolded. "Why are you speaking if I am not? I don't care if you know how," the husband says. . . . "Why are you speaking if I'm not speaking?" they say to their daughters. There are some who are pleased that their daughters participate, even old men, because they learn to speak there. Those are the ones who have a good heart. But those who don't have a good heart feel jealous. They say, "You are shaming me," if we speak.[7]

The ideal of women's participation in meetings is challenging for women as well. Many women find it highly uncomfortable to speak at gatherings where men are present (see also Garza Caligaris 2002:144). For both men and women, the experience of hearing female voices in such public contexts is new. Many remain mute, while others shield their bowed faces with their shawls before and after speaking. One woman in Yibeljoj said: "We women are very shy and easily embarrassed. Only those who can really express themselves participate [actively]. . . . We don't all participate as we should because it makes us women very embarrassed, yes, very embarrassed." In contrast, she added, some young men "talk just to hear themselves talk."[8] An old woman explained how difficult it was for her to voice her reflections on the questions during the Sunday chapel service: "Sometimes I think something, but I can't spell it out. It's because I can't get beyond my embarrassment. That's why I don't speak even if I understand what they say, for example the question about the Holy Spirit. . . . It seems as if I just keep it stored in a basket."[9]

Apolonia Sántiz Jiménez, my host's mother, described the tongue-tied anguish that speaking involves for many women, even when male catechists encourage them to voice their opinions: "We don't know what to say. The men tell us to participate, to speak; that women can't remain suppressed but should be taken into account. That women have value, also. [They say:] 'We cannot be the only ones talking, you women must also participate. Talk,' they tell us. But we don't know how to speak, we don't know what to say. Like this, we're closed."[10]

Gradually, however, women are gaining a public voice in the collective gatherings of Catholics. Many women in the Catholic chapel group in Yibeljoj told me they had managed to gain the confidence to speak at the meetings of the chapel and of Las Abejas, and that other women had learned the same way, one step at a time. At the chapel meetings in Yibeljoj, where most participants were women, more women than men usually spoke up, even though most women sat silent. While women were more passive at the meetings of Las Abejas than in the chapel gathering, there too, some took the floor. Apolonia Sántiz said she appreciated those women: "There are women who really know how to speak in the meetings. They participate and say what they feel in their hearts, they say how they are suffering because of corruption."

It is notable that at gatherings with only women, such as the special Catholic meetings and workshops held for women in Yabteclum (see below), women showed no discomfort whatsoever at speaking in public. At the gatherings I attended, I was amazed to see otherwise silent and shy women, some of them old, stand up even in large groups of women and speak out with clear and unhesitating voices, showing that Pedrano women also carry the Tzotzil tradition of being eloquent speakers.[11] Catechist Margarita Arias Ruiz commented on this difference: "If there is a meeting of just women, they will speak, although still only a few, because they are still afraid. But little by little, they are learning. They say: "Although we think a lot about what we want to say, it doesn't leave our mouths," that's what they say. If men are present, they [women] are embarrassed because sometimes we don't know how to speak well. But here [at the meeting] we don't care if we don't know how to speak, as long as we speak, since we are all women here."[12]

Women's public participation in the new politico-religious groups contests the conventional female gender role in other ways as well: women's expected confinement to the domestic domain and their responsibility for the household (see Eber 2000). Since women tend to be more active chapel members than their husbands, they may wish to attend chapel meetings regularly while their husbands may not. But Catholic women in Yibeljoj sometimes complained to me that attending services alone with their children was frowned on. The husbands might get upset if women leave their homes unattended or are not present to serve meals. Many men also get jealous, suspecting that the woman will meet other men. Rumors may also arise among the neighbors, which would humiliate the man (see Kovic 2003b:135 on similar accusations against participants in the diocese-wide women's network, CODIMUJ). Close contact or small talk between men and women outside of the immediate family is generally considered improper and may give rise to gossip and criticism, directed especially at the woman. Thus, a woman must always protect her reputation; when she runs errands outside the home or community it should be in the company of a chaperone, at the very least a child.[13] Male catechists, too, may forbid their wives to attend special gatherings for Catholic women, although their official role is to encourage women to attend. One woman I knew, who was married for ten years to a man who drank and beat her, described how wives of drunkards have to tread a careful balance between their own wish to attend the meetings and their husbands' demands: "There are many women who come alone to listen to the Word of God while their husbands go out drinking. When our meetings end very late, the women will worry, 'Now my husband will get mad because he is drunk.' That's why the poor women become sad."[14]

Gatherings that take place outside the home village are the most problematic, since the participants will be away for one or two days. I heard of several Catholic women who were beaten on their return from the special all-women workshops held in Yabteclum. The violent reactions of men were in no way unique to the Catholic community in Chenalhó. I learned of various women in other Maya communities who were beaten and sometimes even killed by their husbands because they went to meetings for their artisan cooperative or other gatherings (see also Nash 1993:127–29; 2001:182).

As a result, many women have to negotiate carefully with husbands or parents in order to attend the various gatherings. They may, however, find some confidence in the conviction that their participation is the will of God. One catechist woman said: "There are also catechists who are jealous. Therefore they don't let their wives or even their daughters leave. It's because they do not yet know what our God asks of us."[15] Women find additional moral support from fellow members and chapel group norms, which stress that women ought to attend meetings. Thus, many husbands yield and allow their wives to go. Women often try to facilitate their impending absence at faraway meetings by preparing meals for their families and arranging with a sister- or mother-in-law to look after children who remain at home, as well as their poultry. Even so, the majority of those who attend such gatherings are childless women or women whose children are grown. Others have only one small baby, or children old enough to be patient throughout the meeting if they cannot be cared for at home. For Catholic women with several young children, it is usually impossible to attend the women's meetings in Yabteclum.

Women Catechists

The changing public role of women is especially tangible for women catechists, who have entered radically new territories for women.[16] While catechist women express contentment and pride in their work, they sometimes encounter serious conflicts for breaking established gender norms, as do women leaders of other organizations.

Although women traditionally have been *j-ilol* healers or held cargos jointly with their husbands, those customary positions differ in character from the new positions of leadership. Catechist women take on the role of specialized interpreters with strong personal faith who must guide both men and women in their chapel groups in the process of learning and understanding the Word of God. They have direct access to news about current political events and must direct the agenda of the Catholic community. The women who make up part of the group of coordinators

Women catechists gathered for discussion at a meeting in Yabteclum, 1996.
Photo by author.

that prepares each catechist meeting in Yabteclum constitute the highest Pedrano Catholic leaders together with their male counterparts. Although during my stay, most of the women catechists were silent in groups with catechist men, their confidence and proficiency as leaders were visible in meetings with female creyentes. In the typically gentle, humorous, and supportive way of Pedrano catechists, they encouraged the women to reflect on the issues at hand.

Their male counterparts often contest the power implied in the new leadership role of catechist women. In the village chapel groups, women catechists are often subordinated to the male catechists and sometimes find themselves obstructed in their tasks as leaders. Margarita Arias Ruiz explained how the work situation of women catechists depends on their male colleagues:

> There are villages with catechists who respect the women [catechists] and who prepare the tasks for each Sunday equitably. But there are others who think that women shouldn't work in their village, that only the men should work with the Word of God. Some respect the women and others do not, because they don't want to feel inferior to the women. And as for the women, although they want to speak, there are men who just tell us to wait. But there are others who respect us. "What do you want to say? You can do it," they say, and, "You will give the information [to the chapel members] first and then I will continue if there is anything left to add," that's what they say. There are some catechists who are good.[17]

Catholic men have, at times, even questioned the authority of women pastoral workers, who are otherwise considered to have high prestige. One catechist told me that the nuns' directives had been rejected during the period when many Catholics refused to contribute to the money collections for the costumbre *mixa* ceremony. At one meeting, a nun had tried to convince those gathered to contribute, but was told that they did not have to listen to her, since she was a woman. The nun replied that she was sent by the bishop, who was a man, but the argument was not accepted; she, the messenger, was still a woman.[18]

The authority of women catechists is further weakened by their unmarried status. At the time of my fieldwork, all women catechists in Chenalhó were single and childless except one who was a widowed mother.[19]

In Chenalhó, as noted, a person is usually not recognized as socially mature until she or he marries and has children. While male catechists have attained this status, female catechists have not. This is also reflected in the terms of address. As unmarried women, the women catechists are still called "girl" (*ts'eb*) instead of "woman" (*ants*) by male catechists and others, even when they are older than the speaker. Because of their socially juvenile status, the words of female catechists are often not given the same weight as the words of men or even married creyente women. Male catechists sometimes told me that "they don't know what they're talking about since they have no husbands and children."

The demands on Pedrano wives and mothers make it impossible in practice for a woman catechist to be married.[20] Besides weekly Sunday services, catechists have to attend many meetings at the Yabteclum Catholic center and in Acteal, enroll in the annual weeklong courses for catechists, and take care of an array of other tasks outside the home. Not only are the workloads difficult to combine with those of a wife and mother; it is also very hard, if not impossible, to find a husband who agrees to such a combination of tasks. Therefore, women who want to be catechists, and have parents who support their choice, opt not to marry as long as they remain catechists. Instead, they continue to live at home, where they struggle to combine the responsibilities of catechists with the tasks required of them at home to help support the family.[21]

Thus, in contrast to male catechists, catechist women remain subject to the authority of their parents. They must obtain permission to leave for meetings, which is especially hard to obtain for meetings outside Chenalhó, since parents are concerned about their daughters' reputation and safety. Furthermore, the women have little or no money of their own if they do not, for example, weave and make embroidery to sell. Since most parents cannot afford to defray costs such as public transportation, women catechists usually have to walk for hours to meetings in Chenalhó—in contrast to many men who arrive by truck or microbus—and can rarely afford to attend distant meetings.

Catechist women also have to defend their reputations against gossip that may arise about their chastity. Their journeys to meetings and other gatherings, and their work and socializing together with men, frequently give rise to malicious rumors in their home villages (cf. Rosenbaum

1993:47–48; Forbis 2006:196). They must find chaperones to accompany them to all meetings, usually another female catechist. A former catechist in Yibeljoj told me she had resigned her position when she lost her traveling companion: "When I finished primary school I started going there [to the meetings of catechists], but I don't anymore because I'm a girl and I can't go alone with the catechists. . . . I had a girl colleague [catechist] but she married. I tried to find another, but I didn't find anyone. Therefore I stopped going to the meetings."[22] Even with chaperones, however, rumors may arise, causing problems for the women as well as their parents. Ernestina Arias Guzmán, one of the catechist coordinators in Chenalhó in the mid-1990s, then in her thirties, who combined self-confidence with a delicate and humorous manner, explained to me what kind of rumors women catechists have to cope with, while the other catechist women present nodded their agreement.

> Men of costumbre or other men say we're no good. They say we are only committing sins with our sweethearts, that's what they say. And some say that we are no longer decent women. They say we are no longer decent because we walk alone to other places, looking for a husband. That's how they spread rumors about us so that no one [no suitor] will come to ask us to marry him. . . . Young men and older men and women talk like that. But even so, we don't care. The important thing is that it's not true what they say. And we know we are not doing anything bad. Instead of going around watching us, they should look out for their own reputation![23]

The other catechist women who were assembled on this occasion laughed at Ernestina's words. Margarita Arias Ruiz, Ernestina's colleague and friend, added that the rumors are not only hard on them, but also difficult for their parents to bear.

> They [the neighbors] go around saying that we're no good anymore; that we are walking alone and looking for a husband. They say many things. That we speak with men or laugh with men to seduce them, that's the kind of things they invent. . . . They invent our crimes and then they speak with our parents, who take it in and begin to scold us and even hit us sometimes with a belt. . . . Sometimes, and I think it is the same for my friends here, when I come home, a rumor has arrived before me. I notice that my father isn't speaking to me, that my mother doesn't answer me, because of all

the rumors they have been told. That's what my parents have to live with, but it's all lies.

While catechist women are problematic role models for some creyente women, for others, they are a source of great inspiration. They have not only gained more freedom, but influence and personal intellectual development. One afternoon in the yard outside my host family's house where we sat shelling beans, one of my host's sisters told me how much she admired the catechist women. She could see the intelligence and determination in their eyes, she said. She wished that she could have had the opportunity to become a catechist when she was young, she continued, instead of marrying and becoming bound to a family.

Forming Shared Demands

In spite of various obstacles, women appear to have gained increasing self-confidence and assertiveness from these experiences and from recognizing and articulating shared concerns with other women. Women's newfound participation and leadership in the Catholic community, as well as in the other new religious and political groups and cooperatives, are a significant change in the life of many women in Chenalhó. Through this change, Pedrano women have begun to publicly exercise political agency, both individually and collectively (Eber 1999; Eber and Tanski 2001).

In the meetings of the Catholic chapel groups and Las Abejas and its various affiliated associations, women are informed directly of news on a broad variety of issues not filtered through their husbands or other relatives. As one shy but committed Catholic woman stated: "It's good that we participate. In this way, we learn about what is going on."[24] By attending the meetings, women have access to information that allows them to form their own opinions, even ones that may differ from those of their husbands. Being affiliated with these political and religious groups has provided women with possibilities to create new and extensive social bonds with other women outside their father's and husband's lineages (Eber and Tanski 2001; cf. Gil Tébar 2003:151). To some extent, these are parallel to the collective networks of men, although women are more restricted in how and when they can socialize.

The Catholic community also offers women the possibility of expanding their mobility beyond the municipality at events such as the diocese pilgrimages and the demonstrations arranged by allied organizations in San Cristóbal or elsewhere inside or outside Chiapas. Many Catholic women eagerly welcome these occasions to publicly manifest their faith and political demands together with large masses of people, and to leave Chenalhó. For catechist women, there may be opportunities to participate in regional meetings for the diocese work areas; for example, Indian Theology or CODIMUJ, where they meet with women from other municipalities and states (see Kovic 2003b). Within Las Abejas, the Acteal Choir and the Group of Maya Women of Las Abejas have made it possible for women participants to travel to encounters far away, and for the latter group, to join large-scale political gatherings. Representing Las Abejas, women delegates have traveled as far as the Vatican in Rome and the United Nations in Geneva.

As a consequence, women are able to compare their experiences with other women to a greater degree than before. At the time of my fieldwork, there was no formalized women's group in the Catholic community or Las Abejas, but under the "women" work area of the Catholic community, the female catechist coordinators and the parish nun organized gatherings of women in Yabteclum. In these gatherings, participants discussed topics seen as especially relevant to women, ranging from women's health and the role of women in the Bible, to the daily life of Pedrano women, their work, and their relation to men. Women who participated in these meetings gave reports to the other church members back home at village chapel group services, thereby bringing women's experiences and interpretations out into the shared public sphere of Catholic Pedranos. They sometimes raised issues or presented political information to their chapel groups that originated at those meetings.

Some of these all-women gatherings promoted reflection and discussion about the situation of women in their families. In one workshop, planned and prepared by a mestizo woman from Mexico City, the women discussed the lives of Pedrano women and compared their workload to that of men. They found that although the men toiled very hard in the fields, they often had free time when they came home in the afternoon, and most of them spent leisure time with friends after eating their meal.

Women, on the other hand—the participants said—were busy until late in the evening, last to bed and first to rise in the morning.[25]

At the same workshop, participants were asked to comment on a series of drawings the mestizo facilitator had brought of a bird in a cage, where the cage door was gradually opened and the bird eventually flew out. Asked to choose which picture could serve as a metaphor for her own life, woman after woman stood up to speak. One woman, an unmarried catechist, said she identified with the fifth and last picture, where the now free-flying bird was looking in on a bird in a closed cage. "That is me," she said with smiling confidence. "I am the bird that is free and wants to help other women come to the meetings so they, too, learn new things." Another woman said she was like the bird in the cage with the door half-open. She was sometimes able to go chapel meetings and learn things she did not know before, she said, which she liked, but at times her husband got angry that she wanted to leave. He would beat her and make her stay home. Many other women pointed at the pictures where the bird was in the cage as a representation of what they sensed were highly restricted lives.

For many Pedrano women, life is the fulfillment of an endless array of chores, carried out first in their parents' house, then in the house shared with their husband. Hard work and poverty take their toll. In church meetings, I saw many women sit with worn bodies and dazed eyes, children pulling at their skirts and perhaps an infant at their breast. Their lack of sleep—and often, nutrition—made it difficult for several to follow and participate in the reflections and discussions, and many would sit mute, some, they told me, feeling ignorant and slow. I heard from a Tzotzil lay nun working in the neighborhood municipality of San Pablo Chalchihuitán, how a Catholic woman there had complained, worn out, about how the conditions of her life, particularly the long hours working for her family around the cooking fire, dragged her down. "I cannot think," the woman had said, "because my head is all filled with smoke."[26]

Through their shared encounters and reflections, Pedrano Catholic women sometimes try to change certain aspects of their lives. After participating in the Catholic workshop in Yabteclum described above, one of my host's sisters decided to try to make her sons and husband ease the burden of her own duties. She told them they could wash their own clothes and serve themselves the already-prepared food when they were hungry instead of demanding that she serve them. The husband and oldest son, perhaps ten years old, flatly refused. It's too late, she complained to me, with a regretful smile. Women may also seek help from their church group to change their husbands' behavior in conformity with the group's moral code. This may include pressure to stop drinking—especially in Protestant groups where alcohol is usually banned—to avoid using violence, and not to take a second wife, otherwise accepted in many Maya communities. If the man breaks these norms, the wife may get support from church leaders, who visit the couple to offer counseling. Other women find support for deciding on their own whom to marry, or not marrying at all (see Robledo Hernández 2003 on Maya Protestants in Teopisca).

Through the new groups, women are questioning conventional expectations of them, and sometimes openly criticizing male privileges

Women at a protest in Acteal on August 12, 2011, marking two years since the Mexican Supreme Court decided to free Pedrano men sentenced for committing the Acteal massacre. Photo by José A. Jiménez Pérez.

and traditions that they believe unjustly limit and subordinate women. This forms part of a broader contestation of conventional gender roles among indigenous women, where, for many, the Zapatista Revolutionary Women's Law has been an important instrument, its ten articles defining the rights of women. In state-level meetings of CODIMUJ and nationwide meetings of the National Council of Indigenous Women, for example, women from different communities and ethnic groups are reformulating what it implies to be a woman, indigenous, and poor, both in their own communities and in relation to national society (Kovic and Eber 2003; Hernández Castillo 2006b; Speed, Hernández Castillo, and Stephen 2006).

In the Pedrano Catholic community, as in many other groups, women are increasingly affecting the social and political agenda of their groups, introducing new concerns into the political sphere, and sometimes contesting those of men. Perhaps the first dramatic impact of women's voices in the Catholic community was achieved in the latter half of the 1980s, when Catholic women started campaigning against men's excessive use of alcohol and against the sale of alcohol in their villages (Eber 2000:230–31; 2001b). By 1988, linking up with a broader critique in the municipality against unrestricted sales of alcohol, the campaign managed to gain the support of the municipal government, which imposed a sales tax on alcohol and restricted selling to weekends only. Several villages imposed even further prohibitions on the sale and use of alcohol (Morquecho 1992:53; Eber 2001b). Many of the generally shared concerns of Pedrano women found resonance in the discourse of the Pedrano Catholic community and became part of the broader preoccupations of the whole group. Thus, for example, women's worries over how to cure sick children were incorporated into a critique of the lack of clinics and doctors, seen as part of the general oppression of indigenous peoples.

Catholic women collectively have also aimed pointed criticism at national politics and state repression. They complained about the military presence in Chenalhó, for example, which was increasingly intrusive after the Zapatista uprising. In the summer of 1996, Catholic women who had gathered for a course in Yabteclum discussed rumors that soldiers in the neighboring municipalities were leaving poisoned food in people's homes, and decided to present a written petition to the PRI municipal president, asking him to withhold an invitation he was allegedly considering for the military to establish a base in the municipality.[27] The women read the presence and behavior of soldiers as being part of a government strategy to intimidate those who opposed the PRI in the indigenous communities. The massacre in Acteal, in which most of the victims of the paramilitary attack were women, became a blatant demonstration of the truth of this allegation, because the paramilitaries were seen as supported by the Mexican government. Thus, before and after the massacre, Catholic women have continued to resist any military presence. When the government installed an array of military base camps in the municipality in early 1998 with the explicit intent of controlling the paramilitary groups, the women regarded this not as protection but as increased intimidation and danger. A large group of women formed a live front, pushing out the soldiers who were aiming to create a military base near the refugee camp in X'oyep; the photograph of the encounter became one of the most famous symbols of the conflict in Chiapas (see the mural based on this photo, page 224).[28]

Women appear to have been instrumental in the decisions made by Las Abejas refugees during 2000 and 2001 to return to their homes after living for several years as displaced persons in the internal refugee camps that hosted thousands of families of Las Abejas after the paramilitary persecutions.[29] The decisions to return were made against the advice of pastoral workers and allied NGOs, and were not a position shared by everyone in Las Abejas. However, women were suffering the most from the irregular life in the camps. A return to their home communities presented a chance to resume self-sufficiency in their own households and restore their life to something approaching normal.

By articulating their experiences and needs, women in the Catholic community are challenging the former male dominance of the political agenda. They are also challenging the conventional code of patrilineal loyalty. As with the alcohol issue, women may express viewpoints and launch issues that do not necessarily represent the views of men in their particular household. Women who voice their criticism against the conventional gender order destabilize men's authority and control of the political agenda, which leads to schisms and sometimes conflicts.

Nevertheless, women demand that these concerns be taken into account and even supported. Thus, one could say, they extend the ideal of reciprocal complementarity and respect, which should ideally guide the relation between spouses, into the public sphere of the Catholic group. In this sense, the participation of women might add a "communitarian" and multivocal dimension to the political life of the Catholic community. While women continue to struggle for their opinions to be taken seriously, they appear to be gradually transforming the makeup of the public, political sphere, no longer "an exclusively male system of formal governance" (Stephen 2006, referring to similar changes among Zapatista base communities in the Tojolabal region).

Pedrano women often express their political participation as a "right": a right to go to meetings, a right to speak. However, during my stay, I did not hear women use the broader rights discourse for these claims: a notion of universal human rights or rights established in the national constitution. This was partly due to the low-key guidance of the diocese nun, who did not talk about rights conventions, and a lack of exchange with the more outspoken feminist mestizo women in San Cristóbal who served as advisors to several of the artisan cooperatives of Maya women in the highlands. Today, I continue to find little use of rights language concerning women's demands in official communiqués from Las Abejas, including those few written by women. Instead, women marshal moral arguments for their demands, primarily by referring to their important role in the sacrificial struggle for change, embodied by the many women who died in Acteal.[30]

CHAPTER 6

Suffering as Identity

Catholic Pedranos are engaged in a reconstruction of their collective identity, in which their experience of suffering from poverty and persecution has taken on a new and central role. The village and ethnic group still provide the principal loci of identity, but ethnic identity has been extended and augmented with other allegiances and belongings. Catholic Pedranos often define themselves as part of a translocal community of Catholics and as members of a global humanity. In this vast community, they want to be recognized as equals, but also as a people holding a unique position. In this chapter, I explore the formation of this identity and of what I call a Catholic Pedrano moral theology of suffering. As I will further detail in chapter 8, this moral theology has provided the foundation for their demands for universal rights and the perspective through which Catholic Pedranos can interpret the massacre in Acteal.

The cosmological universe depicted by Pedrano practitioners of costumbre, or traditional religion, is highly localized. The deities are considered the creators and owners of the landscape and the natural forces, and they put conditions on human use of this landscape. In this universe, costumbre Pedranos, like other highland Mayas, define themselves as representing humanity, literally calling themselves *bats'i vinik-antsetik* (true men and women). Cosmologically, they are the only relevant people. The theological focus is on their relationship with the divine powers in this sacred landscape.

The theologically relevant universe is different for Catholic Pedranos. Their cosmological situatedness, it could be said, is in a "social" landscape that transcends the immediate region and society to include, ultimately, the entire world. In Pedrano Catholic theology, Catholic Pedranos do not represent *the* human beings, as the true men and women, but see themselves as part of a global humanity and a global Catholic congregation.[1] Pedrano Catholics share their relationship to God with other humans, since God is seen as the universal creator. All humans are equal before him, and all are subject to his love and concern. Thus, the converts often express a fundamental notion of brotherhood or sisterhood with humanity as a whole, which translates into a moral discourse on justice and, by extension, on human rights. In this sense, Pedrano Catholics, similarly to the diocese, regard human rights as natural law; the rights preceded their formulation in human laws (see Speed 2008:39–42).

But within this global humanity, Pedrano Catholics define themselves as belonging to the category of poor, indigenous peasants, for whom they believe God holds a special love and a particular interest. Their distinctive relationship with God is motivated by the trait that sets them apart from the broader humanity: their suffering. It is as a "suffering people" that Catholic Pedranos enter the scene of a universal humanity and are defined as a people especially dear to God. The emphasis on their suffering, of course, finds a strong resonance in the liberation theology perspective of the diocese. For liberation theologians, God reveals himself in the suffering of the poor. Jesus's crucifixion is not an offering on behalf of mankind, but a historicization of "the suffering experienced by God in all the crosses of the oppressed" (Webster 1984). The poor and suffering are regarded as those closest to God, and through their suffering and pain, more motivated to know God. Thus, they become models for others in their striving for salvation (Webster 1984).

NARRATING PEDRANO LIVES

During the year I spent in Chenalhó, I constantly heard Catholic villagers talk about the origin of Pedrano suffering, the reasons for their present state of poverty and oppression, and the hope of escaping it with the help of God and his messengers—their Exodus. Told in meetings of the church groups or Las Abejas, in catechist courses, or face-to-face in informal small talk or interviews, these stories came from women and men, creyentes and catechists. Although differently elaborated and detailed, the stories were highly consistent in their central themes and formed what I would like to call a local Catholic narrative about past, present, and future Pedrano life. The Pedrano Catholic story line integrates various other narratives and perspectives—Catholic liberation theology, the Gospels, and the politicized discourse of indigenous organizations and the Zapatistas— into a joint text.

Through this story line, Pedrano Catholics inscribe themselves in a biblical narrative, where they identify with the poor and suffering for whom Jesus spoke. Furthermore, the converts, particularly catechists, identify with Jesus's apostles as messengers of the Word of God. Described as their exemplary predecessors, the biblical apostles are thus made part of the ancestral body of the Pedrano Catholics. One of the principal means for developing this interrelation is the weekly set of questions at Sunday services in the village chapels, where creyentes are encouraged to compare society at the time of Jesus with their own. At these encounters, as well as at Las Abejas meetings, participants draw frequent parallels between the biblical past and modern Pedrano life.

The story line also includes a new appreciation for Pedrano costumbre religion and mythology, promoted by the catechists of the Indian Theology project. While this reevaluation was still emergent during my stay, it has since gained considerable force, notably in the efforts by Las Abejas to incorporate various traditional leadership positions and ceremonies. The parish priest, Pedro Arriaga, explicitly supported this process during his term. The reinterpretation of costumbre religion is influenced not only by the theology of enculturation promoted by the diocese— incorporating autochthonous Maya forms of spirituality—but also by the new regard for indigenous history and culture furthered by the indigenous movement in Mexico and elsewhere. In the politicized formation of a Maya identity, Pedrano Catholics, like members of indigenous organizations throughout Chiapas, are attempting to define what constitutes Maya traditions and values, and contrast them with those conceived of as Western. In this context, local traditions in Maya communities are seen as part of a unique pan-Maya cultural heritage, passed on from Maya ancestors since before the Spanish colonization. This heritage should not be disregarded, the protagonists hold, but recognized and recovered.

The narrative Pedrano Catholics tell is a linear sequence of events. In this respect, it may seem to present a clean break with the cyclical-time narrative of costumbre theology and general Maya religious thought (e.g., Gossen 1974; Edmonson 1993). Through its linearity, the Pedrano Catholic narrative manages to offer both an explanation of the causes of past and present suffering and a promise of its eventual abolition. This undoubtedly explains some of its strong appeal to Catholic villagers.

Nevertheless, there are strong cyclical themes in the Pedrano Catholic narrative as well. One such theme concerns the hope for the future achievement of a condition free of suffering, a state of harmony which Pedrano Catholics sometimes describe as characteristic of the original indigenous society. The other theme concerns the reestablishment of what is perceived as an authentic Maya relationship to God. Converts often say this relationship became corrupted and distorted by the colonizers and the mestizo government. Influenced by the work of the Indian Theology group, many Pedrano Catholics hold that their work as messengers of God includes the restoration of Maya values and respect for the divine in cooperation with costumbre elders, thereby recreating a true and autochthonous worship of God. With the cessation of suffering and abuse, the original state of reverence and harmony will be restored.

Gary Gossen has proposed that there is an incompatible difference between the cyclical time of Mesoamerican temporal order and the linear progressive time of the "competing" ideologies in the Maya region, such as "Protestantism, Marxism, Reform Catholicism, and development programs." He argues that the new ideologies "must either acknowledge and accommodate to this ancient ideology or demand its eradication. Comfortable coexistence is unlikely" (Gossen 1983:5). This is not necessarily the case. In Chenalhó, I found that Catholics were telling and retelling central themes of the Pedrano Catholic narrative to explain historical processes and to express anger, worry, and hope. The integration of both linear and cyclical themes in the narrative, I suggest, makes it compelling and highly meaningful for those telling it, offering both a vision of change and a sense of possible reestablishment of order.

Religious narratives may offer especially forceful ways to reflect upon and change social realities, a process through which people reconstitute their individual and collective identities and social memories. Quoting John Peel's (1995) work on Christian missionizing in Nigeria, Ruth

Marshall-Fratani argues that religious narrative can be a highly political discourse since it offers the possibility of agency: "'Narrative empowers because it enables its possessor to integrate his memories, experiences, and aspirations in a schema of long-term action.'" She continues: "The narratives of contemporary conversion to Pentecostalism involve the same process of reinventing history in order to bring order to a chaotic present and a new shape to the future" (Marshall-Fratani 1998:289). The liberation theology narrative is thus not unique in its political potentiality, although it is perhaps particularly explicit in its projection of social and political change.

The Pedrano Catholic historical narrative is under continuous formation, propelled by various sections of the Catholic community. Reflecting the centralized structure of the Catholic community, principal themes are promoted and partly authored by the catechist coordinators and the pastoral workers, and then presented, discussed, and modified at the village chapel services. One important arena for developing the narrative components is provided by the catechist courses held for a week every year. In the following, I will attempt to describe the principal stages in the narrative, referring extensively to the catechist course held in February 1996, which was led by the zone chief catechists and the Indian Theology group.[2]

The Golden Time: The First Mayas

Many among the leading Pedrano catechists and Las Abejas leaders, as in the broader indigenous movement, possess a strong notion of an autochthonous Maya society characterized by a harmonious social order and a respectful veneration of the divine. It is commonly depicted as an original state free of suffering and poverty. This was also the message conveyed in the catechist course in 1996. The catechists referred to pre-colonial Maya societies in Yucatan and Guatemala as "our Maya ancestors."[3] They described the ancient Maya societies as guided by principles of equality and complementary dualism; for example, between men and women; a social order in accordance with the will of God.

The notion of a harmonious, pristine state appears to relate to common Pedrano conceptions held also outside of the politicized discourse of the indigenous movement. Elders told me that in the past there had been almost no illnesses in existence; those had come later. A pamphlet produced by the Catholic Indian Theology group describing costumbre curing by the *j-ilol* healers reads: "Before, there were not many deaths due to diseases. There were only curing prayers for the small spirit, for envy and for death; they did not get sick at that time."[4] On several occasions, I also heard villagers refer to a lost state of social harmony, when the elders knew how to solve problems with words and reason, without getting emotionally heated. For costumbre practitioners, this perception of the past is associated with the original state of human veneration of the gods.

In costumbre mythology in Chenalhó, as in other Maya societies, creation is described as a series of successive attempts to create humans who are conscious of the importance of venerating the deities. The first creations were failures, since these more primitive forms of humans neglected to give thanks to the deities and were therefore destroyed. The present time is seen as the creation where humans have finally fulfilled these demands and can therefore be considered real humans.[5] A costumbre elder, the *kabildo vinik* of Yibeljoj, who was invited with three other elders to the catechist course in 1996 to share their knowledge of Pedrano creation stories, described the first unsuccessful attempts of the deities to create humans: "The land and the sky were created as well as the animals. And the humans received their mouth and eyes, their nose, face, and hands. They were well made, but they didn't answer. They couldn't talk. They couldn't give thanks to the deities. The gods said, "Let's see if they become smart." But the humans didn't know the meaning [of worship]. This didn't look good, since they didn't know how to give respect."

Another of the invited costumbre elders described the last, successful, creation. Now humans were made who learned to speak and give respect to the deities through the teachings of the saints that today are patron saints of the Tzotzil municipalities around Chenalhó. This was how Chenalhó evolved, with its ceremonies and ways of respecting the gods. The man concluded:

This is how we multiplied here on earth. That's what I've heard. Now they knew how to think, and to see that they should pray at the mountains. And to pray at the crosses which are standing at each of the springs. And they decided they should offer candles when they prayed to God. They began kneeling and asking forgiveness for their sins. In this way, they thought we could multiply. So I've heard that they said [the now deceased elders], that from all this we could multiply. And [I've heard them speak] about how life entered the springs, how the *anjels* came to be there, in the mountains and the springs, because that's how our Mother left things, back in that time.[6]

When the catechists interpreted the costumbre creation stories during the course, they focused on the importance of venerating God in order to be full, moral humans. The catechist coordinators encouraged course participants to recognize the Pedrano costumbre ceremonies as their ancestral Maya heritage, one that truly acknowledged and revered

Costumbre elders invited to the catechist course in Yabteclum describe the creation of the world and the origin of Pedrano religious ceremonies, 1996. Man in black is the *kabildo vinik* (ceremonial leader) of Yibeljoj. Photo by author.

God, and to identify this reverence with their own Catholic faith. Because such teachings partly contradict earlier diocese criticism of costumbre ceremonies and beliefs, they were met with several heated discussions on the part of other catechists during my stay. Still, many Pedrano Catholics, perhaps especially the regular creyentes in the chapel groups, accepted the idea of respect for the costumbre form of veneration, at least on a theoretical level. Most villagers have grown up with parents or grandparents who were costumbre practitioners, and although many converts have turned their backs on the beliefs of their elders, many still feel great respect and awe. When the topic was addressed in the Yibeljoj Sunday ceremony a couple of months after the catechist course, the chapel members seemed to easily embrace the recognition of costumbre ceremonies. One of several men rose to claim: "We have not left, we have not deserted the ways of our ancestors. We have it in our hearts, here in the midst of the Word of God." Another man said: "The customs of the Maya of the past, of our Maya ancestors, are very good, the way they respect our Father. They use incense, they use candles, they cense the cross, they cense the saints. That is our custom. We know that we respect all of it: the cargo holders, the gods, the crosses, what the *kabildo* [*vinik*, ceremonial leader] does, well, we have it all in our hearts."[7]

This revivalism has later, especially since 2006, focused increasingly on the broad Maya heritage, with repeated reference in the communiqués of Las Abejas to the Maya pre-colonial text *Popol Vuh* from the Quiché in Guatemala, and the battles there described between good and evil forces (Schlittler Álvarez 2008:61–62).

A Time of Repression and Suffering

The period of a pristine, disease-free state of harmony is described as having ended abruptly both in the Catholic Pedrano narrative and by costumbre practitioners. For the latter, the "fall" seems to have been caused either by the carelessness of people or deceit by the deities.[8] Catholic Pedranos, however, describe the fall as caused by the arrival of the Spanish colonizers. One of the groups at the catechist course in 1996 handed in the following written historical description in a session to explain their present situation: "When the Spaniards entered into our territory they brought suffering, as they did wherever they came. They didn't think that the traditions of our father-mothers here in our land were important, and everything we had ended up in their hands."

These phrases eloquently sum up what I found to be one of the central and broadly shared themes of the historical narrative of Pedrano Catholics. From a great number of Catholic villagers I received the same explanation for their suffering: it was the result of the colonization of their land and society by outsiders. The colonization was described as having brought death and pain but also continued domination by these outsiders—today the mestizos. While not all villagers were familiar with the nationality of those first invading their land, they were defined as non-indigenous and were associated with the present-day mestizos. A junior catechist in Yibeljoj described how the disastrous arrival of the Spanish created the inequalities that still continue:

> I don't know what year, but when the rich came, they brought corruption, and poverty began. Now it's more than five hundred years ago, it seems.[9] Since then, there are the rich and the poor, who are also oppressed. Before, the poor were like slaves. They had to carry all kinds of things and obey orders. When the owner of the ranch wanted to go to San Cristóbal, they had to carry huge things. Now it's less, you hardly feel the abuse. But you know, when we buy things, they are badly made. They only want us to waste our money. All they ever do is trick us.[10]

People describe the present day as a continuation of the colonial situation, characterized by unjust exploitation, poverty, and suffering. Mestizos, the government, and the rich are all seen as descendents of the colonizers and as the protagonists in the repression that Pedranos and other indigenous peoples suffer. Many Pedranos have the finca times in vivid memory, especially those who have parents or grandparents who lived and served on the former fincas in the municipality. Both of the parents of Apolonia Sántiz Jiménez, my host's mother, had served on the finca in Los Chorros in Chenalhó, and she had heard many disturbing stories about those times. The present government of Mexico, she contends, displays a similar wish to enslave indigenous people.

> At that time, my father and mother suffered a lot. It was not very good. There were many slaves in my parents' time. There were

many poor, suffering people. At that time, my parents worked as "baldíos" [sharecroppers]. Both my father and mother were poor. My mother told me: "We were poor at that time, we were under the landowner, we were baldíos. When we went to the river, he followed us with his whip. We carried 'panela' [unrefined sugar]. We didn't have clothes, we were very poor."

But now, the government wants to do the same to us. It wants to make us into servants. The government wants be our father [i.e., the one others obey], it wants to make us servants and bother us. Now it doesn't think about giving anything. The same thing is happening now as at that time when the Pharisees were bothering others. Now it is the government that wants to bother us, it keeps molesting us. The government is sucking our blood today.[11]

Like Apolonia Sántiz, Pedrano Catholics often make comparisons to biblical times. They do not hold that the state of oppression and poverty is unique to themselves. Identifying with the poor people of biblical times, the converts often call them "indigenous." I asked a young creyente woman in Yibeljoj if there were similarities between life today and at the time of the Bible. She answered unhesitatingly: "Yes, there are similarities! The way it was before, so it is now today. Before, they suffered a lot and also today there is suffering. . . . They suffered, they killed each other, there was disease and everything, they suffered a lot. There was the flood as well. . . . Today we have suffering because of the government. It wants to take the land away from the indigenous people."[12]

The fear of losing their land is widespread among Catholic Pedranos, who all depend on their small land plots to support their families, at least as supplemental income. The fear was reinforced by an experience from a couple of years before my fieldwork, when a foreign natural-gas company had come to investigate discoveries close to the Yibel mountain near the village of Majomut. Catholic villagers told me that the company had been forced to leave since it could not find any more gas. I was often told that this was brought about thanks to the prayers and fasting performed by the Catholic community. This, Pedrano Catholics said, demonstrated God's intervention to protect their lands, and the power of prayer.

With the creation of the North American Free Trade Agreement (NAFTA) and the constitutional changes opening up ejido land for privatization, many felt a new threat hanging over their lives.[13] For many Pedranos and other Mayas, the notion of free trade, although often only vaguely conceptualized, has become a symbol of the government's betrayal in selling Mexican land and resources to foreigners. A young catechist referred to this agreement when I asked him what injustices he found today: "It's like we said, that free trade will come. It's because it's no good for us since we are a poor and small people. The rich feel they are in control, they come to invade our lands so we'll leave. This way, we live in oppression here. We also have no land, the rich ones have occupied the lowlands. That's the situation we're in. We're among nothing but rocks. We're no better off than animals."[14]

In a meeting of Las Abejas in fall 1995, one of the leaders, Antonio Gutiérrez, described the threat of the new governmental reforms, but also the resistance people would put up before giving up their lands: "[The government] is saying to us that's we're good for nothing, that we might as well die, that we're a disturbance upon the earth. But nevertheless, here we are, still surviving. We can still defend ourselves with machetes and sticks." Several of the men who had gathered there replied: "We sure can." Gutiérrez continued: "Their plan is that when they've finished killing us, then they will be able to easily occupy our lands to get the oil, the raw material, put free trade into practice—Article 27 [of the constitution] and other modifications of the laws—and then appropriate the territory. That's why life will get very difficult. But as we said, we're still alive, although we're full of fleas!" People laughed at this and murmured among themselves in their seats, while Gutiérrez concluded: "But we have really important work to do."[15]

Many converts, especially the catechists, hold that their domination by the mestizos, who are described as governed by a thinking that favors inequality and exploitation of those below them, has also contaminated the Pedranos themselves. In the same meeting of Las Abejas, a man commented on how the sons of the respected Pedrano leader Manuel Arias had not followed the admirable path of their father to serve their people, despite their education. He concluded: "What I see is that it seems like we are learning the culture of the mestizos, the fat ones. That's why we don't make any progress."[16] In the catechist course in 1996, Antonio Vázquez, leader of the Indian Theology group, offered a characterization of the mestizo mode of thought as one guided by principles such as hierarchical divisions and individualism: "In the thinking of the mestizos, they favor one above the others; that there is a boss and that the others respect him; that there is someone who is below, squashed. That's the idea of the mestizos, governments, the rich. . . . That is why we have suffering. . . . But the idea God has is not like this. We should be equal, working together."

At the course, the coordinators contended that typical mestizo behavior was shown by Pedrano men who tried to boss other men around or dominate their wives. They also said that some people get hot-headed and provoke conflicts with others. This, one of the coordinators said, is contrary to both their authentic Maya culture and the will of God: "God doesn't want this. He wants us to be united."

The government is often blamed for orchestrating the desecration and corruption of Pedrano and other Maya values. In the catechist course, one of the men said what I had heard many converts state: that the government had caused the divisions and violence among Pedranos and made son stand against father, father against son, husband against wife. Consequently, the man said, this situation weakens the power of the indigenous peoples, which is also the intention of the government. This man, like many other Catholic Pedranos, maintained that the ultimate goal of the government was the obliteration of indigenous traditions and the very existence of indigenous peoples.

The experience of the paramilitary persecution in 1997, culminating with the massacre in Acteal, has only driven this point home for Pedrano Catholics. Seen as set up and supported by the government, the paramilitary bands of Pedrano men are regarded as a genocidal attack against the whole people of Chenalhó. These experiences further prove to Catholic Pedranos that they are enduring persistent suffering caused by the Mexican government.

Waking Up and Spreading the Word

Throughout my stay, I heard Catholic Pedranos stress the importance of becoming aware of the oppression they live under and the reasons why they suffer, thereby turning it into a liberating force for change. People often described this process as an awakening: opening one's eyes and seeing reality. They also emphasized that this is done with the guidance of God. This, then, is the present stage of the Pedrano Catholic narrative; of seeing the truth and taking action. In a Sunday service of the Catholic group in Yibeljoj, a middle-aged woman, Marcela Pérez, rose to speak: "We are seeing our suffering. Here in the midst of the Word of God we see our suffering. Therefore he will solve it. He is watching his people, our Lord. Therefore one can see that we, with the Word of God, want to find a solution."[17]

Catholic Pedranos tend to describe the suffering they endure as a source of the power required to know God and to change the bad situation. In another Sunday service, a creyente woman, in response to a question on the role of women in the church, said that their shared experience of suffering should be transformed into political action:

> Well, the [prayer] meetings began because of our suffering. We're not doing it for fun, and not out of happiness. It's out of sadness. That's because we can't sit and be sad in our homes. It's better to go out to listen, to know, how the others are handling their suffering, there where they are suffering; every people, in every village, in every municipality. That's why we go out. There we will learn if the [federal] government respects us or not, and the governments of each municipality. Because sometimes soldiers enter the municipalities, they come to trouble us. And we can write this on a banner to bring to a demonstration if they continue to trouble us. If the soldiers come to trouble us, well, we'll write it on a banner, we get together to shame the government through a demonstration, that's what they say. . . . If we are content, we don't think [about things]. In contrast, if we feel anguish, well, then it's better that we come together and share our thoughts.[18]

For Catholic Pedranos, change will take place through the work of realizing God's will. In this work, the messengers of the Word of God hold an important role, taking it as their task to spread his word. The converts, especially the catechists, describe themselves as such messengers. As such, they claim, they are part of a long tradition of which the founders were the apostles, the disciples of Jesus.

Biblical Role Models At Sunday services in Yibeljoj, I often heard both catechists and creyentes describe the work of the apostles as the ideal of how they themselves should behave and spread the Word. Like the first apostles, they should show humility, people often said, and not ambitions of their own. They should feel empathy, especially for those who are worse off, and not identify with those of power and wealth. They should strive for cooperation and social equality, and not create conflict but work toward social harmony and unity. They should show respect and obedience to God's commands. The model presented by the apostles was also addressed in the catechist course in 1996. One of the course participants said of the first apostles, reporting on his group's discussion on the topic: "They helped one another. They sold their lands and they sold their possessions, and they helped the humble and the poor who had nothing." These values, Pedrano Catholics believe, were set by Jesus and should guide the work of Pedrano catechists and creyentes. They should be reflected in their conduct both with other members of the Catholic community and with non-Catholic villagers, as well as outsiders.

The clergy of the Catholic Church should of course also follow these ideals. In their interpretation of the history of the Christians and the Catholic Church, Pedrano Catholics see many bishops and popes as having forgotten the meaning of Jesus's teachings, having been corrupted by greed and personal ambition and becoming indistinguishable from the rich and powerful who abuse the poor. In short plays, "señas," through which the participants in the catechist course presented their group discussions, the corrupt bishops were portrayed with the emblems attributed in irony to the powerful: sunglasses, bodyguards, and a desk to sit behind, unless they were standing on a chair to elevate themselves above their people. While each group's skit elicited much laughter among the other participants watching, they provided harsh commentary on a Catholic Church that was found to have lost its original message, in part. Considered one of the principal representatives and defenders of apostolic values is Pope John XXIII, who convened the Second Vatican Council, completed in 1965, and who is identified with liberation theology ideas. Most admired by Pedrano Catholics was Bishop Samuel Ruiz of their own diocese, as well as the clergy working in his tradition, all seen as true heirs of the first apostles.[19]

Defining themselves as heirs of the first apostles as well, the converts link the Pedrano Catholic community with the apostles of biblical Israel and the many messengers that thereafter have spread God's Word across the world.[20] By sometimes referring to the first apostles as *totik-me'tik* (our father-mothers), the spectrum of ancestors of the Catholic Pedranos is expanded. It now includes not only the ethnic Pedrano ancestors, who were costumbre practitioners and thus at least partly defined as of a different faith, but the Christian apostles.

The incorporation of the biblical apostles in a Catholic Pedrano history contrasts with the portrayal of non-indigenous characters in Chamula costumbre theology, as analyzed by Gossen (1983). Finding that all important actors in Chamula mythology are either white or black, and that none are indigenous, Gossen wonders if this expresses a subordinated Chamula identity. He concludes, however, that the case is the opposite; Chamulas "historicize" others ("Europeans, Mexicans, Guatemalans, Afro-Americans, Jews and gringos"), whereby these are placed in the past, defined as part of earlier and more primitive creations. Their role is to negate Chamula social order, "in order to foreground and frame and favor an always-emergent Indian community in the present." Gossen continues: "The bad guys become, as it were, members of their own ancestral lineage" (1983:467; see also Gossen 1999).

Pedrano Catholics do the opposite. The apostolic forefathers are presented as heroic and highly respected models, not only for them but also for non-indigenous Catholics. By linking themselves to the apostles, Catholic villagers associate themselves with greatness and devotion to God. Constituting themselves as inheritors of the ideals of the first apostles, and thus in some sense, as descendents, they create a continuity that transcends not only the lapse of two thousand years but also continents and ethnicities. Pedrano Catholics incorporate themselves into a universal Catholic community as part of a long history of Christian messengers originating with the first apostles of Jesus, where they themselves become role models for all Catholics.

Simultaneously, the Spanish colonizers, mestizo authorities, and the rich, as well as the popes and clergy corrupted by their own greed, are portrayed as the negation of the social order and morality upheld by the converts and the first apostles. These categories of people are structurally similar to the first, failed creations of primitive humans, since they do not truly worship God. They are in this respect not fully human. Thus, like costumbre Chamulas, Catholic Pedranos maintain themselves in a cosmological and moral center by defining contemptible humans as their polar opposite. In contrast to costumbre practitioners in Chamula as well as Chenalhó, however, Catholic Pedranos also claim their morality to be universally legitimate by positing the founders of worldwide Christianity as their own ancestors and models. The persecution that Pedrano catechists and creyentes experience enforces the connection they make with the first messengers. The comparison gives comfort and encourages them to continue in spite of the difficulties.

Costumbre Role Models   The first Christian apostles are not the only models for the converts' role as messengers. During the catechist course in 1996, catechists of the Indian Theology group encouraged the participants to seek good examples also in Pedrano costumbre mythology. Although the approach appeared to be novel for most of those present, the rather bold and innovative parallels drawn were met with interest and approval.

Among the costumbre figures, it was especially the deity Ojoroxtotil who was held out as an example of good and unselfish behavior on behalf of his people. Ojoroxtotil is one of the principal Chenalhó deities, or possibly a manifestation of God.[21] There are several myths about how he once walked on the earth and did grand deeds to make human survival possible, defeating such dangers as the jaguars and the Bone Eating Woman, who were devouring humans.[22] At the catechist course, a group of the catechist coordinators acted out various sequences of the myths in an elaborate play in the yard outside the church, with an enthusiastic audience that tried to recognize the various themes from the myths, familiar to most. In the assembly afterward, the participants were presented with an interpretation from a Pedrano liberation theology perspective. María Vázquez Gómez, catechist and member of the Indian Theology group, offered her perspective on the work of the deity when humans were exposed to dangers from malevolent forces:

MV: Back in that time, there was a lot of suffering. People did not reproduce; they were becoming extinct because of the jaguars. They were becoming extinct because of the Eater of Bones, the woman who eats bones. They had a very painful situation in that time. But when our Father Ojoroxtotil came, he saw the situation of his children and saved them when they were suffering. He saved them. Our Father Ojoroxtotil had no house, no chair to sit down on. He walked a lot and saw the truth. . . . It was our Father Ojoroxtotil who made salvation. He was a liberator, one can say. But now, also, we have a liberator. There is someone who resembles Ojoroxtotil, who has dedicated himself to freeing us from our situation and the way we are manipulated. [She is here alluding to Bishop Ruiz.] Today, who is like the jaguar, the devouring jaguar?

Various: It's the rich.

MV: Yes, indeed, friends, it's them. We, here, too, are becoming extinct. We are suffering because of oppression. We're living with a lot of suffering.

Together with the catechist coordinators, the participants drew essential parallels between the myths and their own lives, looking at the malevolent forces threatening human life. Figures such as the Bone Eating Woman were compared to the government, pretending to be good hearted while in reality scheming how to deceive people. One myth describes how Ojoroxtotil defends himself from the Bone Eating Woman by turning into stone, which causes her to lose all her teeth when she tries to eat him. Coordinator Antonio Vázquez made this into another parable: "The stone symbolizes the people, it signifies that the people make themselves very strong and mobilize their power, that the people get strong so that the teeth cannot penetrate." Ojoroxtotil was described as a model of personal sacrifice, humble poverty, and dedication to his people, all traits highly valued for messengers of the Word of God. Like the apostles and the Christian messengers of today, Vázquez said, Ojoroxtotil was persecuted by people who said he was the devil.

The Pedrano liberation theology readings of classical Chenalhó myths, although new to most of the participants of the course in 1996, highlight values that Pedrano Catholics commonly present as central for Catholic messengers and leaders: showing selfless dedication to the well-being of the people; bravely resisting ominous powers. These interpretations also

Catechists act out a Pedrano myth at the 1996 catechist course. The deity Ojoroxtotil lies sleeping while the jaguars sit and prepare their attack, unaware that he has magically glued them to their seats. Photo by author.

emphasize that costumbre creation stories define respect and veneration for the divine as the mark of true humans. Thus the catechists attempted to integrate what are defined as core costumbre values with Catholic values, describing the mythic costumbre ancestors as bearers of true apostolic values, while also affirming themselves—as Catholic Pedranos—as true humans, since they know how to respect God.

The Future: Liberation as Exodus

When I talked to Pedrano Catholics, I was struck by how their vision of the future alternated between two positions: on one hand, trust in God and their own work for change; and on the other hand, fear that their poverty and suffering might continue and even increase. Most villagers described the sense of an ever-present threat of further-deteriorating living conditions.

Besides more government cutbacks on credits and subsidies, villagers fear that their land will be taken by foreigners and the rich, and that the government will force them back into the state of near slavery of former generations. Ever since the beginning of the armed conflict between EZLN and the government, there is also trepidation that the war will be renewed. After the emergence of paramilitaries in Chenalhó in 1997 and the mass flight of villagers who belonged to Las Abejas and the Zapatista support bases, the most pressing fear has been the threat of renewed paramilitary attacks. In spite of their trust in God, Catholic villagers express no certainty that things will go well.

In spite of their fears, Catholic Pedranos cherish the hope of a future liberation from suffering. This hope for the restoration of justice, faith, and moral values, both in Chenalhó and in the broader world, is placed on the realization of God's will. One day, Catholic villagers say, the Kingdom of God will be created, free from poverty, illness, and suffering; they will be free and find the good life, as told in the Bible.[23] When this will happen is uncertain. Only God knows, villagers would tell me. However, here and now, Catholic Pedranos already see themselves as involved in the work leading to what they call their liberation, their "Exodus." The story of the Exodus of the Israelites offers an evident and hopeful parable, describing both the misery of an enslaved and oppressed people and how God intervenes so that they are able, after a long struggle, to liberate themselves.

Exodus is a central theme for liberation theologists, and it has greatly influenced the work of Samuel Ruiz and the San Cristóbal diocese (e.g., Fazio 1994:117). The narrative of Exodus is regarded as pointing to "the liberating intervention of God," which is understood to have taken place in actual history, embracing not only religious but also social and political liberation (Gutiérrez 1996:220–21). The Exodus and the life of Christ, who struggled against the oppressors of his time, for liberation theologists form the two key events in the biblical drama about God's taking the initiative in seeking the liberation of mankind; the resurrection of Christ is God's promise that justice will triumph and everyone will be liberated (Ferm 1991:47–48).

The work of Pedrano Catholics to change their living conditions is nourished by this hope for the coming realization of God's will. In a meeting of Las Abejas in fall 1995, one of the leaders drew the parallel to the biblical Exodus to encourage those gathered to have faith that their prayers would affect the outcome of the ongoing peace negotiations with the government and thus eventually lead to the end of oppression.

> We mustn't be disheartened about praying to God. Keep your spirits up, just like the catechists here. I'm also a catechist. What did the Israelites do when they liberated themselves from slavery? They prayed a lot and God heard their requests and supplications. In this way, they liberated themselves from oppression and slavery. And in the same way, we will liberate ourselves also. But we have suffered oppression longer. Now it's been 503 years. The Israelites, in contrast, had only suffered for 400 years when they were liberated by Moses. Therefore we have already suffered too long. But do you know why? It's because we get tired of praying to God. Therefore we have to make a greater effort, my friends. We have to keep praying to God. When we see a problem we just have to pray to God because by ourselves we don't know how to solve it.[24]

The liberation they seek should include the recognition and reestablishment of true Maya values, and the reconstruction of Chenalhó as a unified and harmonious community. Here, the work of the Catholics is seen as central, since they consider themselves to be those who truly attempt to seek cooperation and mutual understanding with other groups. In the catechist course in 1996, coordinator Antonio Vázquez drew a parallel with the resurrection of Jesus:

> What does "resurrection" mean? That the people revive their traditions, that they revive their cultures, their way of life, and that they begin to show respect again. Therefore we are looking, together with our friends [of costumbre] and with people's way of life, for ways to revive the traditions and the [traditional] way to solve problems. . . . That's why we want to study [Indian] Theology. Yes, because we want to get ready so that the new earth and the new heaven may come. We are searching for the new life, but it requires that we all be engaged in this.

While the converts have a clear idea of what their everyday, local tasks consist of in the work for liberation, there is less agreement about how to accomplish broader political and social changes. Much hope has been put on the Zapatista demands, which Pedrano Catholics have supported, and over the years, they have formed alliances with associations and networks close to the Zapatistas to demand social justice. However, the

Zapatista struggle is problematic for many Catholic villagers since it is highly confrontational, and many prefer less conflictive methods.

For Pedrano Catholics, the ultimate agent affecting their future is God. Thus, for many converts, the fundamental way to affect the course of things is through prayer and other ceremonies that call on God. An elderly creyente described how she put her faith in God, and how he had helped them to escape earlier dangers: "God has helped us miraculously. He gives us his power and his blessing. It's not because we have a lot of strength and courage, but because we pray to God. That's what I've heard and that's what I've seen."[25]

A MORAL THEOLOGY OF SUFFERING

Catholic Pedranos are far from the only ones in Chenalhó who decry the hardships of their present lives. As noted, most Pedranos describe suffering and the poverty causing it as characteristic of life in Chenalhó. Suffering is described as the trait that differentiates Pedranos and other poor, indigenous peasants from mestizo and foreign people, and it has come to form an integral part of the collective identity of Pedranos as well as of other Maya peasants in Chiapas. The concept of indigenous suffering also has a widespread moral connotation. Although not all Mayas hold wealthy mestizos responsible for their poverty, most seem to agree that the relation between mestizos and indigenous peasants is exploitative and disrespectful and therefore contributes to undue suffering among the Mayas.

The notion of suffering is present also in Pedrano costumbre cosmology. Although here, too, suffering appears to have certain moral aspects attributed to it, the focus is principally on how to behave to limit the extent of pain. Perhaps one could say that suffering here is dealt with on an existential and generalized level. From the wording of costumbre prayers and the dictates for performing ceremonies such as the Prayer for Life and the *mixa* ceremonies, hunger, illness, and hardships appear as ever-present conditions of human existence. While costumbre villagers try to minimize this suffering, they cannot expect to be totally free from it. Suffering is depicted as caused by human dependency on hard physical labor and exposure to circumstances beyond human control, but also by the malicious deeds of others. Thus, humans turn to the deities for help and safety. They petition them to protect human life and health as well as their crops. By showing due veneration to the deities, humans can induce them to minimize suffering (Guiteras Holmes 1961:285; Arias 1975:32, 39). The deities are often represented as caring and comforting, the "Embracers and Carriers" who, like parents, look after their children. On the other hand, costumbre deities may also allow attacks from demons or bring suffering upon humans as punishment for sins they have committed. By capturing or in other ways harming the soul of a person transgressing the prescribed norms, deities may bring him or her disease and even death (Guiteras Holmes 1961).

There is also an "ethnic" dimension to the vulnerability of humans in costumbre cosmology, where the malevolent powers take on the appearance of mestizos. Thus, the Earth Lord is commonly described as a mestizo plantation owner who demands that Pedranos work for him (Eber 2000:251). This association between destructive, even evil forces and mestizo attributes, including physical traits, is common throughout the Maya region (see Vogt 1969; Gossen 1983, 1994; Watanabe 1990; Wilson 1995). Mestizo symbols may also be used to express authority, such as the office desk that God is described as sitting behind in some prayers. The saints, even the patron saint San Pedro, are usually described as mestizos, and in prayers, both saints and *anjels* may be addressed as *kaxlan*, "mestizo" (Arias 1975:56n4; Eber 2000:251).

While costumbre cosmology may emphasize Pedrano vulnerability and sometimes associate mestizo traits with forces both powerful and malevolent, the suffering of Pedranos does not appear to be attributed, theologically speaking, to the power of mestizos. Instead, in prayers and ceremonies, costumbre practitioners underscore the personal and collective possibility and responsibility to limit suffering by honoring the deities and behaving in ways that do not attract evil powers.

When Catholic Pedranos refer to the suffering of Pedranos in prayers, sermons, and theological discussions, their descriptions bear important similarities to both costumbre notions and popular Maya perceptions of suffering as an ethnic marker. However, as seen in their historical narrative, they are reinterpreting the character and causes of suffering, and they give the denunciation of indigenous suffering a central place in their cosmology. Both catechist and creyente Pedranos explain their suffering as the outcome of the unequal relationship between indigenous people and mestizos. Inequality is described not as an inevitable condition of human life but as caused by exploitative and discriminatory forces orchestrated by other humans.[26] Accordingly, those exposed to suffering are regarded as victims of intentional callous treatment. Pedrano Catholics consider the Mexican government to be the agent ultimately responsible for indigenous poverty and suffering. The government and its allies are described as the adversaries of Pedranos and other poor indigenous peasants, intent on profiting from their labor and land, and if necessary, harming them if they object and resist.

In costumbre theology, such actions are, as noted earlier, commonly depicted as typically mestizo and attributed to deities such as the Earth Lord, described as a dangerous mestizo who can capture Pedranos for slavery (Eber 2000). For Pedrano Catholics, however, the divine is benevolent. The evil forces that they do depict within the sacred realm—the devil and demons—do not appear to have any distinct mestizo traits. Instead, the Catholics seem to make the harmful mestizo-associated traits external to the divine and locate them in the highest secular authority, the federal government.

Catholic Pedranos define the suffering among indigenous peoples as contrary to the will of God and therefore as unjust in absolute terms. One day, converts maintain, God will put an end to this injustice. God has become for the converts "the moral center of an immoral universe" (Lancaster 1988:203), providing a sense of justice in the midst of injustice. Thus, the Tzotzil term *jvokolil*, commonly used by villagers in Chenalhó to refer to their hardships (see chapter 1), is imbued by Pedrano Catholics with highly moral connotations. In the politicized discourse of the converts, *jvokolil* denotes not only suffering, but suffering that is unnecessary and unjust.

Against the backdrop of the broader narrative of exploitation as causing the suffering of the indigenous poor, personal experiences of suffering are explained and condemned. Hardships and humiliations—of waiting a day, unattended, at the clinic; of the substandard price received in San Cristóbal for one's handicraft; of the worries about a son going off alone to work for mestizos in a distant state—are shared and acknowledged. Catholic villagers are thus translating their experience of poverty and abuse at the hands of mestizos and the government into a discourse on ethnic relations whose inequality is seen as violating God's will and the rights every human is granted by God. By defining their suffering and poverty as contrary to God's will, the converts morally denounce their predicament in a theological discourse that claims validity outside of Chenalhó as well. As we will see in later chapters, Catholic Pedranos are backing these claims by referring also to international human rights regulations.

SUFFERING AS A VIRTUE

Catholic Pedranos do not describe suffering as a purely negative experience, however. Influenced by the perspective of liberation theology, they think of suffering as something that brings humans closer to God. While God loves all humans, converts say, he holds special love and care for those who suffer. Through the suffering of Catholic Pedranos as well as other impoverished Mayas, they are seen by God and given the balm of his compassion and love. My host's mother, Apolonia Sántiz, explained to me how God and his messengers loved the poor and not the wealthy, both in the time of Jesus and today:

> We believe that our Lord came at that time for us, to love us. He came to die for our sake, for his children, at that time; he came for his children, our God. That's how he came, to love. He didn't come for the rich, our Lord. He didn't come for those who are rich. He came for the poor, our Lord. That's how it was at that time. And that's how it is still today, where the apostles' work has continued [by others]. It continues to the present day. There are still those who pay attention to our humiliation and our suffering. Now it is our Father, the bishop, who is looking after the poor, the humble. Just like he once came to do in this world, our Lord, when he came at that time. It continues to the present day, the work of the Lord, taken up by our Father, the bishop. That's how we see it.[27]

Suffering is also seen as causing people to love and respect God, since it creates a longing for comfort and consolation that can be found with him. Therefore, Catholic Pedranos often explained to me, their suffering makes them turn to God when the body aches from hard work, when the children are sick without adequate medicine, when there is not enough food. For those who are not suffering, they said, it is easier to forget God. A young catechist said: "The rich put their faith in their wealth; they no longer know that there is a God. They put their faith in all their money."[28] Thus, the degree of suffering not only differentiates people, but also defines people's relation to God. The poor respect and venerate God, and God loves the poor more than he loves anyone else.

Suffering, Catholic Pedranos argue, is an experience that molds people's character, making them more humble and sincere. Poor people, who are used to having almost nothing, villagers explained, are also less greedy and selfish than the rich. They are concerned instead with the needs of others and willing to share the little they possess. Thus, the poor and suffering are more apt to fully understand the teachings of Jesus and more capable of implementing them in their own lives.[29]

As a result, converts say, poor, indigenous peasants are an example to other people who are not suffering. Like the first apostles, the poor help to implement the Word of God by living in accordance with God's will. Thereby, they are able to reciprocate some of God's love. However, the poor also risk falling into corrupt behavior. The implementation of the Word of God must constantly be reflected upon, then, and strengthened by the encouragement of the catechists, in turn guided by the diocesan clergy.

Catholic Pedranos turn poverty and suffering, previously a burden and a stigma, into a virtue that places them in a unique position to understand God and gives them privileged access to God's love. Instead of being the last and most despised, the poor and suffering become the first before God, and those who can teach others. Thereby, I suggest, Catholic Pedranos manage to particularize their relationship with God within a broader humanity that they now see themselves as part of. Whereas in costumbre theology Pedranos are the true humans, in Pedrano Catholic theology they are the chosen humans within a global humanity. Furthermore, whereas costumbre practitioners create bonds of interdependence with the particular deities of the surrounding landscape, Catholic Pedranos create bonds of particularized interdependence with a God who is seen as universal, embracing the whole of mankind. Through this alliance, Pedrano Catholics hope to receive special protection and care.

PART III

Opposing the State

CHAPTER 7

Political Opposition and the Acteal Massacre

Pedrano Catholics have gradually constituted themselves as a community in opposition to the Mexican government. They have increasingly regarded the state, once their ally, as an antagonist responsible for the poverty and marginalization they experience as indigenous peasants. Through the tools and structures for political reflection and organization lent by the Diocese of San Cristóbal de Las Casas, along with their own emphasis on grassroots participation, political consensus, and the authority of leaders, Pedrano Catholics have made their municipal Catholic organization into a powerful and effective base for reaching joint decisions and organizing unified action. In this chapter, I explore how Pedrano Catholics from the early years of conversion until the late 1990s and especially after the Zapatista uprising in 1994, through Las Abejas, came to take an increasingly adversarial position toward the Mexican government, and the consequences this had.

Crucial for Pedrano Catholics has been to undertake political actions that they regard as true to their faith. Their ongoing discussions and evaluations are guided by the moral discourse and collective identity by which they position themselves in relation to the broader society. They have also made an effort to find a line of action they believe to be shared by the diocese. After the Zapatista uprising and for several years thereafter, most Pedrano Catholics felt that their role in the larger struggle for justice was to demand change but also to be mediators between the conflicting parties, promoting justice and peace through prayer and avoiding violent and disruptive conflicts. This was also the role identified with Bishop Samuel Ruiz. This political posture is to some extent explained

195

by common Maya notions about the importance of upholding social equilibrium and concord; agitation and disruption are regarded as "hot" and potentially dangerous.[1] In general, the Pedrano Catholic community and Las Abejas appear to have attracted villagers who are relatively careful politically and apt to stress the need for concord, in contrast to those joining the Zapatista support bases. However, Pedrano Catholics still differ on how outspoken their opposition to the government should be, which has sometimes led to diverging positions and fissions among the members.

In the escalating conflict in Chiapas, national interests have also been at stake. The Catholic community, along with Las Abejas, became part of an increasingly unruly mobilization of indigenous poor that challenged state control and PRI dominance at both the municipal and national levels and demanded far-reaching changes in Mexican society. Eventually, despite their efforts to eschew aggressive methods, this made Las Abejas the target for the worst violent persecution in Chiapas during the whole period following the Zapatista uprising, culminating in the massacre in Acteal on December 22, 1997.

FORMING A POLITICAL OPPOSITION

Pedrano Catholics began to act politically as a group as early as the 1970s. In 1974, they were central in nominating the alternative campesino PRI candidate to the municipal presidency in Chenalhó, in opposition to a faction supporting a teacher candidate (Arias 1994:390–91; Eber 2001a). Probably due to the involvement of the Catholic community, this political campaign was the first in the municipality to engage the massive participation of women (Garza Caligaris 2002:97). In the late 1970s, many Pedrano Catholics joined the first opposition party in Chenalhó, the Partido Socialista de los Trabajadores (Socialist Workers Party, PST). However, not all Catholic villagers agreed with their position. The differences in party choice were possibly related in part to the diverging positions of different lineages and villages. Support for the PST was primarily found in the northeastern *olon* section of Chenalhó. An additional and important factor, similarly to later years, was the position of the diocese and the local clergy. There was no support from the diocese in favor of the PST, and for this reason, it seems, many Pedrano Catholics rejected the party and criticized its political militancy.[2] In Yibeljoj, where a large number of Catholics had joined the PST, chapel members complained to me that the PST supporters had transformed the chapel meetings into political rallies, forgetting the Word of God. Party alliance was seen as conflicting with membership in the church. One of the senior catechists explained: "They did and wanted whatever their leaders said; they accepted it. But since our 'hermanos' [also] give orders, or rather the bishop, they didn't want to accept these [diocese orders]." He concluded by explaining why he and others like him had resisted the party: "There is a section in one of the Gospels that says, 'no one can serve two masters.'"[3]

Other Catholics, who had favored the political activism of the PST, told me it was the militancy of the party, such as advocating land invasions of nearby fincas, that caused the clash with several of the catechists. One woman in Yibeljoj who had joined the PST said: "They [catechists loyal to the diocese] didn't want to pit themselves against the government. They say we can't make problems. The catechists even say that it's not in the scriptures, and that we just have to cope with the fact, if we don't have anything."[4] Tellingly, it was the position not supported by the diocese that was forced to acknowledge defeat in the ensuing struggles over the Pedrano Catholics' political direction; the PST-affiliated catechists and creyentes left the chapel groups.

THE FORMATION OF LAS ABEJAS

Pedrano Catholics increasingly took positions in opposition to the government, however, in tandem with the gradual politicization of the diocese. In 1992, when Catholics formed the first human rights committees in Chenalhó, linked to the Fray Bartolomé de Las Casas Center for Human Rights, they began to discuss issues of human rights, access to land, the changes to Article 27 in the constitution concerning the privatization of ejido land, and how to form a municipal-wide resistance to such threats.[5]

Then, in late 1992, a series of events led to the formation of the Las Abejas political association. Various versions of this history exist, both

among Pedranos and outsiders, some gaining almost mythical propor-
tions as an example of indigenous resistance and mobilization, or of the
collective struggle for women's rights. Here I present my own partial
understanding of the history, drawn from several different and partly
contradictory accounts, but mainly from the description one of the main
persons involved gave me in 1996: Mariano Pérez Vázquez, a leading catechist in the Tzajalch'en village. His version, less heroic than most, describes what I've found to be an ongoing concern of Pedrano Catholics:
to balance political demands with negotiation and avoidance of open
conflict.

The origin of the events, it appears, was a land conflict between members of a family in the villages of Tzajalch'en and Tzanembolom in the
northern part of the *olon* section of Chenalhó. Two elderly sisters, with
their husbands and adult sons, claimed the inheritance of a large piece
of land, which their brother refused to give them, referring to customary law in Chenalhó according to which only sons may inherit.[6] This
conflict evolved into factional strife where each side pulled in other villagers for support. The brother's supporters belonged to the PRI, the
majority from Tzanembolom, and the supporters of the sisters and their
sons belonged to Solidaridad Campesina-Magisterial (Peasant-Teacher
Solidarity, SOCAMA), the majority from Tzajalch'en.[7] The leading catechist in Tzajalch'en, Mariano Pérez Vázquez, described for me how he
and other Catholics in the village initially assisted the sisters' families
in their attempts to petition for the land to offices outside Chenalhó.[8]
Pérez was also a human rights committee member and a former municipal agent of Tzajalch'en and had knowledge of legal procedures. Eventually, however, Pérez told me, the Catholics decided to withdraw their support, since tensions were escalating and both sides in the dispute were
threatening to use arms to get control of the land. They tried to calm
the conflict and suggest reconciliatory solutions between the two parties.
This greatly upset one of the sisters' sons, who was the municipal agent
in Tzajalch'en. When he said he wanted to summon the state police to
the village as protection against possible attacks from the other side, the
community assembly, including the Catholics, resented such police involvement, Pérez said, and confiscated the keys to the municipal agency
office where a radio communication system was located.

Some ten days later, a large meeting was held in Tzajalch'en, which, according to Pérez, was with the National Indigenist Institute (INI) to apply for credits for coffee production. According to other sources, Las Abejas was formed at this meeting on December 9, 1992, in support of the two sisters and as a defense against possible attacks by their brother's group. Las Abejas had representation from twenty-two communities and was under the auspices of the Society for Coffee Producers of Tzajalch'en (Hidalgo 1997; Tavanti 2003). After the meeting, Pérez said, while taking part in birthday celebrations at the house of a Catholic family, he and the others gathered there heard shouting and learned that the son who was the municipal agent had been ambushed and shot, together with two of his brothers, by a group of heavily armed men. Pérez and some other men brought the injured to the truck they had summoned from the municipal capital through the radio at the municipal agency, now deciding to also call for the support of the state police. But on arrival with the injured at the Chenalhó capital, they were arrested and taken to the jail in San Cristóbal, accused of having carried out the assaults. Since one of the injured, the municipal agent, died during the journey in the truck, the charges included murder.[9] Shortly afterward, the wives of the three ambushed sons were assaulted and robbed in their homes, and one of them was raped. Pérez said that the relatives of the sons who were shot initially accused them of the ambush because of the earlier decision of the Catholics to withdraw their support and lock the municipal agency, thus blocking access to police protection.

The imprisonment of Pérez and four others, most of them Catholics, caused an uproar among Pedrano Catholics and was interpreted as an attempt by the municipal president to attack Catholics—both individuals and the entire group—because they had begun to threaten the hegemony and arbitrary rule of the municipal authorities and PRI.[10] Catholics from throughout Chenalhó mobilized to pray and defend the jailed men (Kovic 2003a), and they received legal and strategic assistance from the pastoral workers and the Center for Human Rights of the diocese. To protest the unjust arrests and demand the release of the men, they also organized pilgrimages to San Cristóbal, and from there, marches on five consecutive days to the prison outside town where the men were being held (Hidalgo 1997). Calling themselves "Las Abejas" (The Bees), the politically mobilizing Pedrano Catholics now gained public attention. On December 24, the pilgrimage consisted of five thousand persons (Kovic 2003a). Through the diocese-wide Pueblo Creyente network, Las Abejas garnered support from Maya Catholics from various other highland municipalities; on January 4, 1993, eight hundred villagers from seven municipalities participated in the protests (Kovic 2003a). One of the Catholic Pedranos organizing the protests from Chenalhó, Antonio Gutiérrez, told me in 1996 that the sight of the long row of men and women marching together looked like a swarm of bees, which gave them the name Las Abejas, one of the many explanations that exist today for the choice of name.

On January 7, 1993, all five arrested men were released since no evidence could be presented to prove their guilt. The two men who had survived the ambush and the three assaulted women named villagers from neighboring Tzanembolom as their aggressors. Only two of the accused men were caught, and the sisters did never inherit the land, Pérez said.

The arbitrary arrest of the men from Tzajalch'en was condemned by the National Commission of Human Rights, and the case, as well as Las Abejas, gained a reputation in the region. For the first time, the Pedrano Catholics had manifested their political force outside the municipality. However, I was told, not all chapel members agreed with or took part in this openly oppositional stance toward the PRI and the municipal government. Many of those who disagreed lived in the southwestern *k'ajal* section of the municipality.[11] As a result, many of them left the Catholic community, some returning a few years later.

THE ZAPATISTA UPRISING: TAKING A POSITION

When the news reached Pedranos about the Zapatista occupation of several municipal buildings in highland Chiapas on January 1, 1994, and the ensuing days of attacks by the Mexican military, many were afraid of becoming the target of military aggression from either side. The Zapatista Army of National Liberation (EZLN) constituted, for most Mayas, an unforeseen revolt against the national government. When I later talked with Pedrano villagers about this period, they said they had feared most of all that the government would be provoked to strike back ferociously.

Even villagers who were loyal to the government and the PRI told me they had been afraid of its potentially destructive powers and that they would be the next target: "Because if the government turns against us, it's bad. Because then we will all die."[12] Due to EZLN's open and armed confrontation with the PRI government, many were therefore alienated from the uprising.

In spite of these fears, however, it appears that the rebellion and the Zapatista demands for improved living conditions for indigenous peoples gave rise to widespread excitement among Pedranos, as among other Mayas, regardless of political affiliation (G. Collier and Rus 2002). Many found strength in the Zapatistas, who with their ski masks, weapons, and bold confidence became something of Maya supermen, heroes who finally stood up against the government and the wealthy. Thus, an increasing number of Mayas began to support the EZLN demands for political and social change. For Catholic Pedranos, the crucial issue was whether they should join Zapatista support bases emerging in Chenalhó or promote a less confrontational form of support of the Zapatista demands.

During fall 1994, the Catholic Diocese provided a way for many Catholic Pedranos to express support for the Zapatista struggle while at the same attempting to stop the use of violence, and it was therefore embraced by a vast number of Catholics. Chapel groups throughout the diocese were encouraged to name representatives for what was called the Peace Process, instigated by Bishop Samuel Ruiz. Each community was to choose a representative from those villagers who wanted to be part of the pacifist movement. Non-Catholic villagers were invited to participate as well.[13] This effort was part of a broader attempt since the beginning of the uprising, led by the diocese and various civil associations in the state, to form a unified civil society that promoted a peaceful solution to the conflict. This broad coalition explicitly referred to itself as "la sociedad civil" (the civil society) (see Nash 2001:135, 160).

In Chenalhó, this initiative soon achieved a formal political structure, drawing on the political experience and organization of Las Abejas and the representatives of the human rights committees in the Pedrano Catholic community. Reflecting the broader civil mobilization in the state, Pedranos came to refer to the formalized association in Chenalhó in its first years as the "Sociedad Civil." In practice, the association merged with and became identical to Las Abejas.[14] During this period, it appears, the village-level groups of the association were formed, as well as a municipal-level governance constituted by representatives from the village groups. Sociedad Civil Las Abejas became an integral part of the Catholic community in Chenalhó.

Pedranos initially joined Sociedad Civil to find protection. Ever since the first weeks of open warfare in January 1994, there was a threat of further attacks from the Mexican army in its search for Zapatistas. In Chenalhó there was also a rumor, I was told, that the Zapatistas would protect and evacuate only the villagers who were part of their own support bases if the war arrived, leaving the others to their fate. The formation of what was described as "a civil society united in a process of peace" gave the affiliated villagers a certain feeling of safety. Therefore, the association also attracted Pedranos who were not Catholic, the majority of them costumbre practitioners, but also Protestants and even villagers supportive of the PRI government. However, the vast majority of the members of Sociedad Civil were Catholic, and they eventually steered the political direction of the association. Increasingly, Sociedad Civil Las Abejas became identified, both by its own members and other villagers, as being against the government and for the demands of the Zapatistas. The difference between it and EZLN, it was argued, was its promotion of pacifist methods to reach those demands.

Catholics as well as other Pedranos identified the political position of Sociedad Civil Las Abejas with that of the diocese and Bishop Samuel Ruiz. Members often told me that the bishop had created Sociedad Civil in Chiapas to serve as a buffer between the Mexican army and the Zapatistas, promoting a solution to the conflict through reason and dialogue. This was seen as similar to the role of the National Mediation Commission (CONAI) in the negotiations between the EZLN and the government, over which Bishop Ruiz presided.[15] Within Chenalhó, I was told, Sociedad Civil Las Abejas ought to assume a CONAI-like role as mediators and peace promoters, trying to ease and solve conflicts between the different municipal factions and promote unity instead. One of the catechist coordinators in Chenalhó said: "We're small mediators, in every community, so there won't be confrontations, so war won't come."[16] Of great importance for Catholic Pedranos was that the bishop's stance in the conflict, and hence, that of Sociedad Civil, was seen as reflecting the will of God, proclaiming justice for the poor but without violence.

At this point, Pedrano Catholics also stopped voting for the PRI in elections. Despite earlier criticism of the government, I was told, the chapel members had continued to give their votes to PRI candidates. One chapel member, Rosa Sántiz Pérez, described how the new position evolved:

> Samuel [the bishop] is the one who is helping us, he makes us see reality, he awakens us, he makes us see that we are suffering. This is how we turned against the government. In the past, we were delighted with whatever it sent us. Now, the government [mistakenly] thinks that we will all surely continue to accept whatever it sends us. [But] people have begun to organize because they became aware. It's Samuel who woke us up, who guides us so we won't fall asleep again. He makes us see that the government is fooling us. It's because we became aware, that the first of January [of 1994, the date of the EZLN uprising] happened. The gringos almost penetrated our territory. Our lands were already sold. [She refers to the NAFTA free trade agreement and the privatization of ejido lands.] We started to notice this when our Father Samuel showed us the truth, together with the army that is in the jungle [EZLN]. Thanks to them, the foreigners didn't enter. . . . They [the EZLN] didn't agree that we should suffer, therefore they came to defend us. The first of January, they learned that we were sold out by the government. That's truly how it was; from that time we learned that, we were sold. Who received the money? It [the government] sends us a little PROCAMPO [federal program for peasants], but it's all from the sales price for our lands; it's the money from our lands. Before, there were many who weren't aware, now we are beginning to notice things. That's how it is, that's how we woke up.[17]

Through the Sociedad Civil Las Abejas, Catholic villagers became active participants in a political panorama that extended beyond their own municipality. Again and again, in meetings of the chapel groups and Sociedad Civil Las Abejas, I heard people describe political events taking place that were considered significant for Pedranos, repeating a phrase that linked the local village to wider spheres: "here in Mexico, here in Chiapas, here in our municipality, and here in our village where we live." This interrelation not only sprang from a keen interest in how political events on different levels of society affected local developments. It also expressed the notion that they, through Sociedad Civil Las Abejas, were engaged in a struggle for social change that extended far beyond Chenalhó. One of the chapel members in Yibeljoj explained: "The Sociedad Civil exists in other nations, not only in the state of Chiapas. . . . It is the poor who have come together like this everywhere."[18]

THE BREAK WITH ZAPATISTA CATHOLICS

Not all Catholic Pedranos were content with the passive support for the Zapatistas that Sociedad Civil Las Abejas offered. Instead, they wanted to take a more active role in the struggle as an integrated part of the EZLN structure. Since this collided not only with the position of other Pedrano Catholics, but also with the position of the diocese clergy in the parish, it caused a fracturing of the Catholic community in Chenalhó.

In contrast to many other municipalities in Chiapas, there appear to have been no Zapatistas in Chenalhó prior to the January 1 uprising.[19] During 1994, however, villagers who had shown interest in the movement received visits from representatives of EZLN and began to discuss whether to join the ranks. Zapatista support bases with connections to the wider EZLN structure gradually formed in the municipality, attracting villagers of different religions.[20] Like Sociedad Civil Las Abejas, each Zapatista village support base in Chenalhó held weekly meetings and was linked by representatives to the municipal level and the regional zone (see also Eber 2001a:54). Many of those who joined the Zapatista support bases were Catholics, both catechists and creyentes. A Catholic Zapatista explained how they had reached the decision after several informational meetings: "Now we were aware of the struggle. We said yes, because we liked what we heard. Because among the Word of God [the Catholics], there was no way forward, no road to follow. So we found it was good, the Zapatista Army of National Liberation. Therefore we joined to support them."[21]

The choice to join the Zapatista support bases was met with criticism from other Pedrano Catholics as well as the diocese clergy working in the municipality, I was told, who advocated for a pacifist struggle. The Zapatista demands could be supported, the nuns maintained, but one should not be part of the actual organization since it was willing to use armed violence. Many of the Pedrano catechist coordinators also took this position. Backed by the weight of the diocese, they were able to make this the "official" position of the Catholic group in Chenalhó. Thus, the catechists and creyentes who had become members of EZLN parted ways with the Catholic parish and were no longer recognized by the diocese. But they did not abandon their Catholic identity and faith. Instead, they developed a structure of chapel groups and catechist leadership similar to that of the "official" group of Catholics (Eber 2001a). Although this group is independent from and unrecognized by the diocese, diocese clergy have at times offered them religious services and other support. However, as part of the local Zapatista support bases, they answer politically only to the Zapatista leadership. The "official" Catholic group, in contrast, together with the association Sociedad Civil Las Abejas, continues to receive recognition and support from the diocese.

These diverging loyalties—to the diocese and to the EZLN—have come to characterize the work of the respective groups. The Zapatista Catholics have often argued that Sociedad Civil Las Abejas is overly careful and passive politically since the members are too closely bound to the diocese and the political line of the clergy. Many Catholics of Sociedad Civil Las Abejas complained in turn, during my stay, about the politics of the Pedrano Zapatistas, which they found to be far too provocative and self-interested, leading to the failure of the many attempts at cooperation between the two groups. Many within Las Abejas claimed that the Pedrano Zapatistas were not "real" Zapatistas; the real ones were in the Lacandon jungle (see also Tavanti 2003:143–44).

SUPPORTING ZAPATISTA DEMANDS

During 1995 and 1996, Pedranos of the diocese-linked Catholic community were thoroughly engaged in what they had defined as their role in the conflict: to support the Zapatista demands for political and economic change, and to try to calm the conflict through mediation and prayers to God to forestall any more violence. Many members of Sociedad Civil Las Abejas regarded the Zapatistas as the leaders of the actual struggle, the results of which would benefit the others. A young Catholic man of

Sociedad Civil told me: "Sociedad Civil is like the EZ[LN], only that it wants peace. EZ, it's the leader. It leads the way to see how it can achieve the well-being of the peasants. . . . It's the Zapatistas who will solve it. The Civils [members of Sociedad Civil Las Abejas] are peasants, they will only have well-being if the Zapatistas succeed."[22]

Pedrano Catholics frequently described Chiapas as a state in turmoil, where indigenous villagers in all communities were hoping and struggling for an end to their poverty and suffering. The presence of large numbers of Mexican army troops in the state, some regularly passing through Chenalhó en route to the military installation in neighboring Pantelhó, was seen as representing a repressive and hostile government. Especially after the expulsion in summer 1995 of three foreign priests working in the diocese, the government was also perceived as a threat to the bishop and the diocese clergy, for whom church group members showed their support by gathering in large prayer ceremonies. Ever since the escalation of the campaign against Bishop Ruiz in spring 1995, Pedrano Catholics, like many others, feared that he might be removed, because both the Vatican and the Mexican government disliked his political stance. All of this compelled Pedrano Catholics into action to try to control and change the situation.

At the village group meetings of Sociedad Civil Las Abejas, usually held every other week, Pedrano Catholics continually discussed the political situation and what their role should be. The chapel groups also took part in the political mobilization through the weekly village Sunday services as well as the monthly catechist meetings in Yabteclum. Since all the members of the "official" Catholic community were members also of Sociedad Civil Las Abejas, the actions decided on in the chapel groups were parallel to, and not always easily distinguishable from, those of this organization.

One of the principal forms of participation was prayer. Throughout my stay in Chenalhó in 1995–96, the Catholic chapel groups held different types of prayer ceremonies, at chapel-group level or at the municipal level in Yabteclum, to support the peace process and forestall a renewed outbreak of war, appealing to God for his intervention and protection. God was petitioned to "cool off" the overheated situation to avoid increased conflict and violence. Such ceremonies were particularly crucial when the Zapatistas declared "alerta roja" (red alert) to warn against imminent attacks by the federal army. Every prayer meeting was usually performed while fasting and lasted the entire day, divided into three sets of prayers with breaks in between. Pedrano Catholics prayed for God's help to make the government and EZLN leadership use, as they said, words and reason instead of violence. Chapel members usually described the prayers as the most important contribution to preventing war. A young Catholic woman explained: "Prayer is needed so it [the conflict] comes to a good resolution, so there will be understanding between [Zapatista subcommander] Marcos and the government. It takes prayer for them to understand the words of Marcos." Otherwise, she added, there would be war.[23]

In addition, the chapel groups pooled the supply of corn on several occasions to feed people in Zapatista support bases in the Lacandon jungle, who, the catechists explained, were unable to work in their fields due to the military presence in the area. The corn was collected at the end of Sunday services and brought to the catechist center in Yabteclum, from which it was sent to the diocese center in San Cristóbal. These collections were organized at the diocese-wide level.

Pedrano Catholics also undertook to support the peace negotiations between EZLN and the Mexican government that took place in the neighboring Tzotzil municipality of San Andrés Larráinzar during fall 1995 and early spring 1996. For most Pedranos, as for other Mayas, the negotiations, commonly referred to as "the dialogue," were considered an extraordinary event, for indigenous delegates from the region were sitting face-to-face with the government's representatives to discuss the future of the indigenous peoples, witnessed by the entire nation. EZLN and the government had agreed that the dialogue should be divided into a total of six thematic sections, the first addressing Indigenous Rights and Culture, including issues of local self-determination and the right to territory and resources. The next sections were to cover issues such as "Democracy and Justice," and "Welfare and Development."

Through Las Abejas, Pedrano Catholics supported the negotiations in two ways. In October 1995, and again in June 1996, Las Abejas, together with other indigenous organizations and independent mestizo advisors, was invited by EZLN to participate in the large preparatory meetings in

San Cristóbal to discuss what the principal demands at the negotiations should be. In addition, Las Abejas Sociedad Civil regularly sent members to the seat of negotiations in San Andrés Larráinzar to participate in the so-called peace belt, "cinturón de paz," which formed a cordon of people surrounding the building where the dialogue was taking place, aiming to protect the delegates. The peace belt, seen as representing civil society in Chiapas, was composed of members from various civil associations, the majority of them Maya villagers of the Catholic Diocese, who received accreditation by CONAI. There was also a human cordon of the Red Cross and another of members of Zapatista support bases in Maya villages throughout the highlands. Surrounding them all was a fourth cordon, consisting of uniformed members of the Mexican military police. Pedranos of Sociedad Civil Las Abejas described their participation in the peace belt as an important sacrifice to support the dialogue as well as a way to stay informed about developments in the talks. At the village-level meetings of Sociedad Civil back in Chenalhó, the delegates

Soldiers from the Mexican military police in San Andrés Larráinzar during the peace negotiations between EZLN and the Mexican government, 1996. Photo by author.

who had last been to San Andrés would report on the negotiations, and the assembly would decide who should be the next to go.[24]

The decision made by the Catholic chapel groups and Sociedad Civil Las Abejas to stop receiving government aid, manifesting their rejection of the former patron-client bonds with the state, was regarded as an important form of resistance. The most common support in this period, from the PROCAMPO program, consisted of cash payouts to support small-scale cultivation of basic grains (see Harvey 1998:214). The members contended that the money was a way for the government to lure villagers back to the PRI without offering any lasting changes. In fact, federal institutions sometimes formally requested a display of political loyalty for people to receive aid programs; for example, by presenting a PRI registration card and having no known affiliation with parties or groups of opposition (G. Collier and Quaratiello 1999:142). Conversely, beginning in spring 1996, there was a growing resistance among Catholics, and many others in opposition in Chiapas, to pay the electric bills, which were seen as outrageously high and a way for the federal government to milk poor peasants of the little money they possessed.

But the rejection of state support proved an economic strain too difficult for many families to bear. While some accepted the aid under the critical eyes of fellow members, others chose to leave their groups. The economic pressure was intensified by the frequent contributions of money and resources the members were asked to make to Sociedad Civil Las Abejas, and for the Catholics, to the chapel groups as well. The catechists and Las Abejas leaders urged the members to endure the economic sacrifices. Their ability to resist the government's offerings was described as a sign of their commitment to integrating God's will into actual personal behavior. The political struggle, one of the Las Abejas leaders told me, must be fought hungry and suffering (cf. Eber 2001a:57).

To demonstrate diocese unity and support for the peace process and the bishop, Pedrano Catholics participated in mass pilgrimages in San Cristóbal during 1995 and 1996 that each drew between ten and thirty thousand participants from the whole diocese region, almost all Maya Catholics. In Chenalhó, Pedrano Catholics always maintained that the bishop had called for the pilgrimages, although they were formally summoned by Pueblo Creyente. The pilgrims congregated on the outskirts of San Cristóbal and walked in procession through town to the cathedral, concluding with a mass, often held by the bishop, more often than not in the company of bishops and pastoral workers from other states. The pilgrimages were organized to demonstrate criticism of government actions or attitude, such as its passivity in the peace negotiations, but they were free from political slogans or banners. Instead, the pilgrims carried religious banners, flowers, and censers, asking God's help to change the attitude of the government (see Kovic 2005:171–75). During this politically tense period, the pilgrimages were forceful political manifestations expressing a vast unity among Maya Catholics of the state in their political demands. They were equaled in size only by the demonstrations of the Zapatistas, together manifesting the broad indigenous backing for the Zapatista struggle, whether civil or armed. Thereby, they also indicated the potential for mass mobilization and social unrest, should either Bishop Ruiz or the EZLN leadership be removed.

Furthermore, through Las Abejas, Pedrano Catholics cooperated with other organizations in the region in supporting Zapatista demands. They chose mainly to ally with mestizo-dominated associations that focused specifically on seconding the EZLN attempts to pressure the Mexican government. Las Abejas did not close ranks with other civil indigenous organizations in the state, such as the State Council of Indigenous and Peasant Organizations (CEOIC), the umbrella organization formed in January 1994 in support of the Zapatista demands; or the Democratic State Assembly of the People of Chiapas (AEDPCH), which CEOIC became subsumed under, together with various mestizo organizations.[25] Instead, Las Abejas preferred to send representatives to the broader gatherings of the Mexican left, called the National Democratic Conventions, convened by EZLN to muster Mexican opposition to the PRI and support for Zapatista demands for political and constitutional changes.[26] It also supported the mestizo journalist Amado Avendaño, who under the banner of the socialist Party of the Democratic Revolution (PRD) was the candidate with broad support on the left in Chiapas in the state gubernatorial elections in August 1994, losing to PRI in an election many regarded as fraudulent. Avendaño and most mestizo-led organizations broke out of AEDPCH in 1995 and formed the Civil Zapatista Movement (MCZ), which Las Abejas joined. Las Abejas often turned to Avendaño

Pedrano Catholics march in a demonstration in San Cristóbal de Las Casas for the Civil Zapatista Movement (MCZ), with a total of three thousand participants, August 1995. Photo by author.

for political counsel. In spring 1996, Las Abejas decided to become a formal part of FZLN, the Zapatista Front for National Liberation, a nationwide network of mainly mestizo civil associations that supported the demands of EZLN.

As in other matters, the forms of collaboration Pedrano Catholics chose were very much guided by advisors in the diocese. One of the Las Abejas leaders told me that the decision not to join AEDPCH was based on the recommendation they had received from an advisor in the diocese who claimed that AEDPCH was too closely affiliated with the government. The diocese clergy, as well as most mestizos working in the NGOs based in San Cristóbal, tended at this time to be rather skeptical of the indigenous organizations, which sometimes diverged from the political strategies of EZLN, and advocated that the political struggle should focus on the Zapatista peace negotiations with the Mexican government. Furthermore, some of the Las Abejas leaders held that the indigenous AEDPCH organizations had sold out by accepting grants from the government, which clashed with Las Abejas's position of non-collaboration with the state. Thereby, it was said, these organizations displayed their lack of interest in truly participating in the struggle of EZLN and making sacrifices for the struggle.[27]

THE FIGHT FOR MUNICIPAL POWER

The existence in Chenalhó of both Sociedad Civil Las Abejas and Zapatista support bases meant that a majority of Pedranos now publicly opposed the PRI government and had severed many of their ties with state institutions. While Chenalhó, like most highland Maya municipalities, had previously been a PRI stronghold, the ruling party now found its base there marginalized, its control of the municipality uncertain. Thus the municipality entered into the broader political combat in Chiapas, with all major antagonists involved: the federal and state PRI governments, EZLN, and various churches and organizations. This contributed to the escalating tensions, simultaneously strengthening the political agency of each of the factions in Chenalhó and undercutting their power to dominate the political and social life of their own municipality.

During spring 1995, Las Abejas and the Zapatista support bases decided to nominate a joint candidate in the municipal elections to be held in October of that year. The candidate was a Zapatista, Javier Ruiz Hernández, but he would run under the banner of PRD, the largest left-oriented oppositional party in Mexico (CDHFBC 1998a; Hernández Castillo 1998). The alliance between Las Abejas and the Zapatista support bases under a PRD banner had already been successfully tried in Chenalhó in 1994 for the federal and state elections on August 21 of that year. In Chenalhó, PRD had gained 63 percent of the votes, which was a historic defeat of PRI in the municipality (CDHFBC 1998a).

But the coalition was short lived. Seeing how little support the PRI candidate would be able to garner for the municipal elections in October 1995, the Zapatistas decided to install the PRD candidate ahead of time in June 1995, before the elections, forcing the sitting PRI authorities out of the municipal presidency.[28] Less than a month later, on July 15, the PRI faction managed to summon hundreds of armed mestizo state and federal police to the municipal center of Chenalhó, along with fifteen hundred agitated PRI-leaning villagers, to reinstall the PRI municipal authorities (cf. Eber 2001a:54). These dramatic events not only polarized PRI supporters and opponents in Chenalhó, they also broke the alliance between Zapatistas and Las Abejas, since the latter had not agreed on the installation of the PRD candidate and found it far too provocative, as members voiced in several subsequent meetings of Sociedad Civil Las Abejas that I attended. During the coming year, I was repeatedly told that many of the politically most cautious members of Sociedad Civil Las Abejas had left the association after this incident, since they felt they had been lured into militant actions they did not agree with.

There was no longer a unified opposition against PRI for the municipal elections of 1995, so it was likely that the municipality would remain in PRI control. Therefore, Zapatista support bases began to consider a withdrawal from the formal municipal organization to form their own independent power structure (Eber 2001a). Las Abejas members, in contrast, were still anxious to fight for the municipal presidency and discussed the possibility of putting up their own candidate. But in a municipal-level meeting of Las Abejas in early August 1995, the representatives decided to abandon the idea. The deciding factor was the report from a Las Abejas commission who had been sent to San Cristóbal to consult with highly positioned advisors in the diocese. The delegates reported that they had been told to forget about the elections and instead focus on the nationwide consultation, or referendum, the EZLN had convened for August 27.[29] If a large number of people in Chiapas participated in the consultation and showed their support for EZLN, the delegates had been told, PRI would have to leave state government. This would, in turn, open up the municipal governments to parties of opposition.[30] Those attending the Las Abejas meeting decided to follow this recommendation. However, though participation in the consultation was high in Chiapas—more than 150 thousand—it was fewer than Las Abejas had hoped for and did not force the PRI governor from power.[31]

Thus, when municipal elections were held on October 15, the only party in opposition to the PRI was the Frente Cardenista. The members of Sociedad Civil Las Abejas decided to participate but leave their ballots blank to show their protest against PRI's dominance, while the Zapatistas in Chenalhó, like many Zapatista support bases throughout the state, decided to boycott the elections. Thus the elections became a walkover victory for the PRI, which won with the support of only 21 percent of the registered voters in the municipality.[32] A new period of PRI rule was a given. In a last attempt to prevent a PRI municipal government, Zapatista villagers occupied the municipal building at the end of December 1995, when the new authorities were about to take office. Within a few days, the police had again dislodged the occupiers and the new PRI municipal president was reinstalled. In April 1996, the Zapatista support bases declared the establishment of an autonomous municipality, thus publicly withdrawing from the formal municipal structure.[33]

Now Chenalhó had become divided into three separate political structures, each with its members dispersed in villages all through the municipality. One was the Zapatista autonomous municipality, which chose as its capital the village of Polhó, located in the northeastern *olon* section where the leadership was seated. The governing structure partly reproduced that of the official Pedrano municipality, with similar officials at the village and municipal level, including municipal agents and a municipal government (Eber 2001a:55). From Polhó, the municipal president, Javier Ruiz Hernández, led the Zapatista support bases residing in thirty-three villages and seventeen barrios of the municipality (CDHFBC 1998a:9). The village was renamed San Pedro Polhó, taking San Pedro as its patron saint in a symbolically significant repossession of the saint from PRI dominance.

The second structure consisted of the political association Sociedad Civil Las Abejas and the Catholic community with its chapel groups. As described above, these were the Pedrano Catholics that continued to be an integrated part of the diocese, in contrast to the Zapatista Catholics, who had broken away. The municipal governance of the Catholic community was centered at its facilities in the village of Yabteclum, while Las Abejas had no geographical center at that time, instead rotating the municipal-level meetings of the leaders between different villages.

The third, and smallest, structure was the official PRI-controlled municipal government, with its center in the capital town, San Pedro Chenalhó. Its followers included both die-hard party supporters and others who remained with the party out of what villagers described as tradition; many were alienated and worried about the oppositional factions. During this period, almost all Presbyterian Pedranos were affiliated with PRI.

An additional, and now marginal, political group consisted of the members of the party Frente Cardenista, the majority living in the northeastern *olon* section of the municipality. The Cardenistas with whom I spoke identified politically with both the Zapatistas and Sociedad Civil Las Abejas. The members were often militant and used land occupations as a political tool in their demands for improved living conditions. After the Zapatista uprising in 1994, the Cardenistas in Chenalhó had lost most of their members to the Zapatista support bases, which were perceived as being even more militant and having the potential for a substantial political impact. Now the party was no longer a significant political actor, though it was the only opposition party to front a candidate in municipal elections. In the 1995 municipal elections, the Cardenistas had gained two posts in the municipal government and therefore had some political influence.

Not all Pedranos had chosen a faction. A number of villagers tried to steer clear of any claims of committed support. During my stay, these were often defined as "costumbre," implying adherence to the traditional religion, and usually, at least passive support of the PRI. Some villagers were regarded as being in between groups, having deserted their previous allegiance. Others, who were unaffiliated but more often than not opposed to the PRI, were referred to by their more formal status as "independents" (Eber 2001a:55).

Most villages in Chenalhó contained members of various or all of these factions. The division of families, villages, and the entire municipality, and the fact that the actual municipal power, allied with the federal government, lay in the hands of a group representing only a small minority of the Pedrano population, gradually increased the tension in the municipality.

PARAMILITARIES, MASS FLIGHT, AND THE ACTEAL MASSACRE

By early fall 1996, the relationship between the various factions in Chenalhó had become highly polarized. Villagers were forced to declare a position in the escalating conflict and to demonstrate loyalty toward their own group. This polarization reflected the growing political tension in the state. In spite of the successful signing of the first set of Peace Accords on Indigenous Rights and Culture in February 1996, the negotiations between EZLN and the federal government broke down in the summer of the same year.[34] The Zapatistas declared that they would not resume the dialogue until a series of demands had been fulfilled, including the withdrawal of army troops from the conflict area. Instead, the militarization of the state increased, making Chiapas the most militarized state in Mexico, with severe effects on indigenous communities (Nash 2001).

In addition, a number of paramilitary groups had begun to appear, primarily in the northern region of the state, terrorizing Zapatista villagers and others who were critical of the government, and there was increased harassment of the staff of different NGOs (e.g., Harvey 1998:232–36). Although the Mexican government has denied involvement in these paramilitary groups, incriminating documents exist, as I argued in the introduction, that testify that the paramilitaries have been part of a broader counterinsurgency strategy of the government. In 1996, there were rumors that paramilitary groups were about to appear in other regions besides northern Chiapas. Chenalhó was a not unlikely target. It was the only highland municipality besides San Andrés Larráinzar that had an autonomous Zapatista municipality, and in addition, the presence of a large group of pro-Zapatistas: the diocese-linked Las Abejas.

The increasing schisms in Chenalhó initially led to struggles among the different factions over their respective spheres of control.[35] For the Catholic community, the struggle concerned the use of the village of Yabteclum as their municipal-level center. During spring 1996, PRI members in Yabteclum, displeased with the Catholic presence, had cut off the water supply to the buildings of the Catholic center on several occasions. By the time I left Chiapas in July 1996, the PRI activists had forbidden the Catholics to use the Yabteclum church and the center for their meetings, hanging a padlock on the gate to the compound. Subsequent negotiations between the Catholics and the municipal agent of Yabteclum and with the municipal president produced no results. The catechists decided not to force their way in, choosing instead to hold meetings in the chapels of alternating village chapel groups.[36]

While the Catholic community found its municipal "territory" diminished, the Zapatistas tried to assert—or even expand—theirs. In a written document from August 16, 1996, the president of the Zapatista autonomous municipality claimed that the "sandbank" in the village of Majomut was part of the autonomous municipality, and that anyone else trying to exploit the gravel would be arrested. This area had been occupied since 1994 by Cardenistas who eventually had formed an association and bought the right to the territory.[37] However, since part of the land was inside the boundaries of a barrio of Polhó, the capital of the Zapatista autonomous municipality, the ownership rights could be debated. With the construction of the paved road to Pantelhó that was then going on, the sandbank, located just off the road, was a highly lucrative property.

In response to this Zapatista takeover, the Cardenistas in Majomut sought support from the ejido of Los Chorros, where some of the Majomut Cardenistas were from. Since the 1970s, the ejido had been trying to gain the rights to the territory of the Majomut village because there was not enough land for the new generations of villagers in the ejido. Now an unusual alliance was formed between the PRI and Cardenistas against the Zapatistas and their autonomous municipality, which was considered to be far too presumptuous and intrusive (e.g., Sistema de Información Campesino 2007). The collaboration was facilitated by the joint governance of the municipality after the outcome of the fall elections. Soon, this pact was directed also against members of Las Abejas, since they were regarded as pro-Zapatista. The polarization of alliances followed in villages all through the *olon* section of the municipality of Chenalhó.

The friction between the two groups of factions in Chenalhó grew during spring 1997, with both violent confrontations and attempts at negotiations. In May, the Zapatistas in the ejido of Puebla in eastern Chenalhó refused to contribute money to the construction of a road connecting Puebla with a community in the municipality of Tenejapa.[38] In response, PRI villagers detained three Zapatistas and later ambushed the Zapatista commission on its way to liberate the men, killing one. Fearing that they would also be attacked by the PRI villagers, several hundred Las

Abejas villagers from the village of Yaxgemel, the place of the ambush, fled to two neighboring villages (CDHFBC 1998a).

In June, Pedrano Zapatistas were accused of shooting two police officers in Chenalhó. The same month, the PRI municipal authorities and those of the Zapatista autonomous municipality met to discuss the sandbank, but the meeting was interrupted due to new mutual attacks. The PRI-affiliated municipal authorities of Chenalhó asked CONAI and COCOPA, the national mediating commissions, to intervene to set up a dialogue between the factions. They also asked for more police forces to be sent to the municipality to ensure order, which was granted. The federal elections on July 6, 1997, created more turmoil in Chenalhó. The Zapatista autonomous municipality called the elections a mockery and burned forty election booths throughout Chenalhó, demanding compliance with the Peace Accords signed by the federal government and EZLN before they would trust the government (Balboa and Henríquez 1997).[39] The same month, the municipal president ordered all the municipal agents to make lists of who in each village were adherents of PRI, and who were not (Bellinghausen 1997).

By early fall 1997, paramilitary groups were being formed in several Pedrano villages, all located in the northeastern *olon* section. The paramilitaries, dressed in black uniforms, were principally recruited from the many young, landless Pedrano men in the ejidos, who found access to weapons and were trained in the use of firearms by persons from outside the municipality (Aubry and Inda 1997b; CDHFBC 1998a). From mid-September, beginning in the ejidos Los Chorros and Puebla, these groups started demanding "taxes" from all inhabitants to pay for their expenses, such as ammunition. Those who refused to pay were beaten and arrested. They also forced villagers to participate in the harassment of Zapatista neighbors.

Now began what eventually was to become a mass flight of villagers who belonged to either the Zapatista group or Las Abejas; they were driven from their homes at gunpoint. Others left in fear of attack, or to avoid supporting the paramilitaries. On September 17, families belonging to both the Zapatista support bases and Las Abejas fled from Los Chorros, fearing for their safety. A large number of their houses were burned. On October 15, almost five hundred villagers were driven from

Tzanembolom, and two weeks later, twelve hundred villagers were driven from C'anolal (CDHFBC 1998a). Both of the latter attacks were directed against villagers of Las Abejas and the Zapatista support bases. There were also smaller clashes between PRI followers and Zapatistas in several villages, and Zapatistas were accused of killing four in Yaxgemel, which the autonomous council denied.

With alarm spreading in the municipality, both Las Abejas and the Zapatistas mobilized large demonstrations in the early fall to protest the persecutions. Both groups claimed that the paramilitaries were backed by the PRI government and armed and financed by the public security police of Chiapas by directive of the state governor, Julio César Ruiz Ferro (Balboa 1997; Bellinghausen 1997). They also accused the PRI municipal authorities, led by the municipal president, Jacinto Arias Cruz, of supporting and protecting the paramilitary groups.[40] To denounce the acts of aggression against their members, both groups made frequent reports to the Fray Bartolomé de Las Casas Center for Human Rights. The center repeatedly condemned the acts of violence in Chenalhó and demanded criminal investigation of the incidents. State authorities investigating some of the acts of violence in Chenalhó during the fall claimed that they found no violence to report.

Las Abejas and the Zapatistas diverged in their strategies for dealing with the aggressions. On more than one occasion, the Zapatistas employed armed violence during the conflict, killing a debated number of Cardenista and PRI-favoring villagers.[41] In contrast, Las Abejas members in some villages initially acquiesced, under threat of violence, to participating in the harassment of Zapatista neighbors, before deciding to flee rather than be accomplices. There are no reports that Las Abejas members have used violence against the PRI and Cardenistas. Following their ideal as promoters of peace, Las Abejas members instead frequently took the role of mediators, trying to calm the conflict or, in later stages, to facilitate negotiations between the Zapatistas and the PRI municipal authorities (Bellinghausen 1997; CDHFBC 1998a).

PRI members and Cardenistas in the municipality accused their antagonists of being the tools of outside interests: the Catholic Diocese and the Fray Bartolomé de Las Casas Center for Human Rights. In early October 1997, the municipal president of Chenalhó accused the Center for Human Rights of destabilizing the municipality. A month later, he accused the parish priest, Miguel Chanteau, of being behind "everything that was happening in the municipality" and threatened to kill him.[42] These charges were supported by pro-government forces outside Chenalhó, further spurred by a media campaign against the Center for Human Rights and against CONAI, the mediation commission that Bishop Ruiz presided over. The Pedrano Cardenistas were backed up by their party higher-ups; a spokesperson from the Cardenista party state committee stated that the Zapatistas in the region were responsible for the violent acts in Chenalhó (CDHFBC 1998a; see also Sistema de Información Campesino 2007).

In early November 1997, the violence reached Yibeljoj, the village where I had lived during my fieldwork. By October, there had already been rumors of a paramilitary attack from neighboring Los Chorros, and most villagers had escaped for several days to hide in the mountains or neighboring villages. After their return, the Yibeljoj villagers made a non-aggression pact after negotiations led by the municipal agents of the village (there were two that year) and the school committee. The leaders of the different factions in the village agreed to keep peace and not let themselves be drawn into the conflicts.[43] However, on November 10, PRI members from Los Chorros entered Yibeljoj and demanded that each family pay 335 pesos as a "war tax," or they would be evicted. The next day, there was an initial attack against villagers in one of the barrios, the families again fleeing up into the mountains. In a larger attack on November 16, all Las Abejas and the Zapatista support base villagers were driven from their homes and their houses looted (CDHFBC 1998a). The PRI municipal agent of Yibeljoj, who was part of the unity pact, was caught by the PRI members from Los Chorros, who, as punishment for the pact, beat and tied him up, and then pulled him behind a truck along the road. This I was told by my former host in Yibeljoj, who a few days later called me in Sweden from San Cristóbal. His family had left Yibeljoj before the attacks since his wife was about to give birth. Because of the conditions in Chenalhó, they wanted the safety of a hospital. He had learned about the attack from a villager coming to San Cristóbal who told him that their house was ransacked and all their things destroyed, his catechist papers scattered along the road outside their house. The sign on their house, saying "Civil Society/Peace/Neutral Zone," had been plastered with mud. The majority of the houses in the village, he had been told, were now deserted. A few weeks later I learned by phone from one of my Pedrano interpreters that most Catholics from Yibeljoj were living in the refugee camp in the village of X'oyep, including my host and his extended family.

By now, the number of displaced villagers could be counted in the thousands. Some had found shelter in San Cristóbal and others at the homes of relatives in safer villages in Chenalhó. The majority, however, were hosted in villages in the *olon* section in Chenalhó, where Las Abejas and the Zapatistas set up makeshift camps for displaced members of their respective group. Through the municipal structure of each organization, corn was collected from their village groups and brought to the camps, providing a ration, I was told later, of not more than a couple of tortillas per day.[44] The host families in the villages with the camps made extra sacrifices to assist the bereaved refugees. For shelter against the cold and the rains that had begun, the displaced had only torn plastic sheets and banana leaves, and the ground was quickly transformed into mud. The majority had left their houses with no time to bring a change of clothes or blankets, and so they were constantly wet and dirty. The situation was rapidly becoming precarious and there was still practically no outside help for the displaced. On November 21, eighty displaced families of Las Abejas in the camp in X'oyep sent an appeal for help to the Center for Human Rights in San Cristóbal, stating that they lacked the most basic necessities. The board of Las Abejas also sent out appeals.[45]

Now the situation of the refugees was beginning to receive national attention through newspaper and television coverage and the report of an international observation mission.[46] The photographs of the misery in the refugee camps shook many Mexicans, and NGOs and individuals began to mobilize aid to the refugees, much of it channeled through the Catholic relief agency Caritas.[47] The state government, while previously denying that there were more than six hundred displaced persons in Chenalhó, now declared that there would be humanitarian aid for the displaced. The municipal president of Chenalhó, Jacinto Arias Cruz, said there were an additional two thousand displaced PRI members.[48]

The presence of paramilitaries in Chenalhó was the subject of additional attention and concern and was denounced by NGOs, journalists, and intellectuals. The paramilitary violence was described as only the latest example of a statewide strategy of low-intensity warfare—instigated and directly promoted by the state and federal governments, along with military and police bodies—against indigenous villagers who were opposed to the PRI government (see, e.g., Ramírez Cuevas 1997). The police forces in Chenalhó, stationed at this time in about ten villages, were accused of harassing anti-PRI villagers, while protecting pro-PRI villagers who were harvesting coffee in fields that belonged to the displaced (Petrich 1997). In late November 1997, Zapatista commandant David stated that the developments in Chenalhó were part of the government's attempt to destroy the Zapatista support bases.

In early December, the leaders of both the PRI and the Zapatista autonomous municipality agreed to meet for negotiations. Representatives of Las Abejas were observers, together with several human rights organizations, while CONAI served as mediator. Although certain agreements were reached in the first meetings, the negotiations broke down after mutual accusations that the other group had violated the non-aggression pact. On December 18, CONAI and the Fray Bartolomé de Las Casas Center for Human Rights issued a press communiqué warning that the breaking-off of negotiations would increase the violence in the municipality. They also asserted that the involvement of interests outside the municipality was making negotiations more difficult (CDHFBC 1998a). Villagers in Acteal informed the Center for Human Rights that PRI supporters were firing shots to create fear and were spreading rumors of imminent attacks on displaced villagers, reportedly to make the families flee once more (CDHFBC 1998a:52; Procuraduría General de la República 1998:73).

On December 22, about sixty to eighty men in uniforms entered the village of Acteal with the intention of killing Zapatista and Las Abejas villagers, many of whom were displaced and living in either of two refugee camps in the village (Procuraduría General de la República 1998:79).[49] The Zapatistas, however, had already left the community after hearing the increasingly clear rumors. The group of Las Abejas members, in contrast, including both local villagers and displaced people who were in the camp called Los Naranjos, had decided not to let themselves be driven away. By most accounts, they were gathered in the chapel, praying, when the attackers arrived around eleven o'clock in the morning. When they heard the shots, panic broke out and men, women, and children ran out and tried to escape, many stumbling down the steep hill toward the river. The attackers were not interrupted by the public security police stationed a few hundred meters down the road.[50] Thus the shooting was able to continue all day, the men walking around to find those who had hidden in ditches or caves. When the last of the assailants left the village in the late afternoon, those who had hidden successfully walked warily back to the center of the village. They found bodies littered everywhere. In all, forty-five persons were killed. Twenty-one were women, nine were men, and fifteen were children. Four of the dead women were pregnant. Sixteen persons were injured, most of them children.

AFTER ACTEAL

The Acteal massacre transformed Chenalhó into a society under military siege. On December 27, 1997, the government installed twenty military camps in Chenalhó with two thousand soldiers, establishing several checkpoints along the main road to control all incoming and outgoing traffic. During 1998, the Zedillo government increased its military control of the whole conflict zone in Chiapas, strengthening the coordination of the Mexican army, the public security police, and federal and state police (SIPAZ 2001). There was also a series of operations directed at Zapatista autonomous municipalities. With the military presence and public attention that followed the massacre, further paramilitary aggressions appear to have been discouraged. However, members of Las Abejas and the Zapatista support bases have continued to report that armed paramilitary groups with access to high-caliber guns still exist in various villages, and some still fear renewed attacks.[51] The men and women of Las Abejas also perceive the presence of the Mexican army as a threat, representing a hostile and powerful government that even orchestrated the massacre. In 2009, there were still two military bases in the municipality.

Chenalhó became a society of refugees, as well. After the massacre, an additional four thousand villagers fled their homes. Now one-third of the Pedrano population, or around ten thousand people, lived in camps, the majority in the municipality of Chenalhó. Most of the Las Abejas displaced members lived in camps in the villages of X'oyep, Tzajalch'en, and Acteal, while Zapatista villagers stayed primarily in Polhó, but also in a separate Zapatista camp in Acteal. A few hundred people from both groups were in small camps in San Cristóbal. About two thousand of the displaced were pro-PRI villagers. The displaced increasingly received aid from the International Red Cross and the Red Cross of Mexico, Spain, and Germany. The European Union decided to initiate major support for the displaced in Chenalhó as well as the displaced in other regions of Chiapas, which they channeled through the International Red Cross.[52] With the aid, the camps could be improved, with better shelter and modes of providing for the transport and distribution of food and water. To discourage renewed paramilitary aggressions, the Fray Bartolomé de Las

A mural in Chenalhó depicts displaced Catholic women in X'oyep protesting against the Mexican army's attempt to position a base adjacent to their refugee camp (after a photograph by Pedro Valtierra). Note the bees in the air, symbolizing the women's political allegiance to Las Abejas. Photo by Marco Tavanti.

Casas Center for Human Rights coordinated the continuous presence of national and international peace observers. As protection against paramilitary attacks, the center also organized contingents to accompany Las Abejas members to harvest coffee in lowland fields at harvest time.[53]

In May 1998, I returned to Mexico, anxious to visit my host family and other friends and acquaintances in Chenalhó, most of whom were now staying in the camp in X'oyep. Foreigners were not allowed to visit Chenalhó, but at the military checkpoints stopping the minibus I was traveling in, I claimed to be on my way to Pantelhó, at the end of the road. My former host waited for me by the path leading from the road to X'oyep, together with his oldest children and a couple of men whom he had asked for help in carrying me and my wheelchair all the way to the camp. On their backs along the hilly path—trying to feel less like a colonial-style mestizo and more like any disabled relative they would carry—I was full of anticipation about meeting the familiar faces again. As we arrived, I saw the camp, spread out on a wide field and up and down the surrounding hillsides. In the center was an outdoor chapel. The camp still consisted of quite a few plastic tents of simple construction, but many families had been able to buy planks and construct houses. I was led to the home of my host and was able to greet all of his extended family again. Formerly sharing the same compound, they were now scattered throughout the camp and came down from the hillsides to see me.

It was a sunny day, children playing and people busying themselves with things. Many of the men in the camp were better dressed than they would otherwise have been able, in clothes brought by the aid organizations. There was now regular delivery of water and food, although in scarce quantities. But there was a dislodged feeling to it all. Most, like my former host family, had to share a house with several other families, often unrelated by kinship. My hostess served a meal she had cooked in a large kitchen hut that she shared with unrelated women. As I sat by my family's house, trying to take it all in, several of the other Catholic women I knew from Yibeljoj came up to me and told me, in tears, about the horror they had lived through and the misery of their present lives, and their fear that the aid on which they had become dependent would disappear.

Camp life for the displaced lasted almost four years, until agreements were made with municipal and state authorities for villagers to return home en masse in 2000 and 2001 (see chapter 9). In 2011, the municipal government of Chenalhó still remained firmly under the control of the PRI.

CHAPTER 8

Martyrdom and the Claim for Rights

Pedrano Catholics describe the victims of the Acteal massacre as martyrs, killed in their struggle to end their poverty and marginalization, despite being pacifists who had made an effort to avoid direct confrontations with other community members and the state. They blame both fellow Pedranos and state officials at various levels for the violence Pedrano Catholics have endured. This martyrdom is the basis for the moral pressure Las Abejas exerts on the Mexican government today and to a great extent informs their political claims.

Since the 1997 persecution and massacre, Pedrano Catholics have strengthened their identity as a suffering people subject to oppression and as an example for others who struggle for peace with justice. They no longer confine their political role to that of intermediaries supporting the Zapatista struggle. The Acteal martyrs are said to have died in a struggle that extends beyond Chenalhó to include people of all continents, indigenous and non-indigenous. This understanding of the massacre has been affirmed and fortified by the enormous international attention that Las Abejas has received since the massacre. Representatives of governments, the United Nations, human rights organizations, and churches, as well as celebrities, journalists, and activists, have come to Acteal and the camps of the displaced to take part in testimonies from the members, serve as peace observers, or provide support for the work of Las Abejas. Through their interaction with these various actors, Pedrano Catholics have advanced their use of globalized notions of human rights, justice, and suffering. Through a Pedrano Catholic moral discourse that refers to Christian norms as well as international regulations on human rights, they today demand both legal justice concerning the massacre and broad social change.

THE WORLD AS WITNESS

After the events of 1997, Chenalhó was no longer just one part of the broader political conflict in Chiapas and Mexico; it had come to emblemize this conflict, and outsiders ascribed the violence to various explanations depending on their political perspective on the broader conflict. The massacre drew enormous attention and became headline news in Mexico and abroad. It ignited national and international discussions concerning the political state of the country and the forces spurring the violence in Chiapas. Questions were raised about whether the paramilitary aggressions were protected and even orchestrated by the top echelons of authority in Chiapas and the nation, or whether it was an expression of purely internal family and community conflicts inside Chenalhó, aggravated by the local Zapatistas.[1]

The crisis brought on by the Acteal massacre would shake the reputation of the Mexican government as viewed by other heads of state around the globe. For many, as John Ross notes (2007), "Acteal became synonymous with human rights abuses in Mexico." While foreign governments and media offered a variety of interpretations about who was responsible for the massacre, there was a general pressure on the Mexican government to clarify the possible involvement of state authorities, the military, and the police in arming and training the Pedrano perpetrators. The massacre and the persecution that preceded it gave reason to doubt the ability or interest of the Zedillo government in controlling the violence in Chiapas and in finding a solution to the political unrest. The United Nations as well as international human rights associations now looked at conditions in Chenalhó when evaluating the human rights situation in Mexico. The massacre caused the European Union to question whether to proceed with its planned free trade agreement with Mexico and to criticize the lack of human rights protections in the country. In February 1998, the European Union sent a delegation of over two hundred representatives to Mexico on an International Civil Commission for Human Rights Observation. Their report, based on interviews with civil associations and government officials in Chiapas, was presented to the European Parliament.[2]

The violence in Chenalhó thus led to a severe crisis for the Zedillo government, making it keen to demonstrate both its political stability and its respect for human rights. President Zedillo denied any government involvement and ordered an immediate investigation by the federal Office of the Attorney General (PGR).[3] Under pressure from opposition parties, Interior Minister Emilio Chuayffet was let go on January 3, 1998, replaced by Francisco Labastida Ochoa. Four days later, the governor of Chiapas, Julio César Ruiz Ferro, was replaced by Roberto Albores Guillén. The new governor, in turn, fired nine state government officials in the police agency and other agencies that had been widely criticized for negligence and possible involvement in the crimes.

The official government explanation of the violence, however, has been tightly confined within the borders of the indigenous municipality. In the report released by the Office of the Attorney General at the end of 1998, the paramilitary groups were called "security and vigilance committees" formed by PRI and Cardenista supporters to "safeguard order and protect themselves because of the presence of EZLN supporters in the municipality," who were said to have fostered an atmosphere of illegality and violence (Procuraduría General de la República 1998:76). The massacre was described as the result of inter-community conflicts in Chenalhó stemming from feuds over power and resources between groups and families that had been going on for several decades.

By the end of 2007, a total of about 80 Pedrano men had been sentenced and convicted for involvement in the massacre, plus the Pedrano municipal president of Chenalhó, with sentences ranging from two to thirty-five years. Besides the municipal president, another 14 low-level public officials—members of the military or the police—were sentenced. In contrast to him, these were convicted for indirect responsibility: for not interfering during the massacre, or for carrying weapons without permission (CDHFBC 2007a). The lawyers representing the victims as well as those defending the accused have criticized the legal process for being slow and full of irregularities. Between August and November 2009, alleging fabricated testimony and illegally obtained evidence, the Mexican Supreme Court released 29 Pedrano men who had been sentenced to prison for their involvement in the massacre, while 16 men were granted new trials and were all released in 2010 and 2011. Of the 81 Pedranos who were sentenced for involvement in the massacre, a total of 54 persons had been released by 2011 (CDHFBC 2011).[4] During 2012, there were further releases of Pedrano men who had been formerly sentenced for the massacre. To date, no higher-level officials have been sentenced.

In contrast, for many Mexicans as well as foreigners, Las Abejas and those killed in the Acteal massacre have become the emblematic victims of political violence and injustice directed at the Maya population in Chiapas, for which the Mexican government is held to be directly or indirectly responsible. The paramilitary aggressions caused outrage among international supporters of the EZLN and were seen as part of a broader attempt to halt the Zapatista uprising. Chiapas support committees in Latin America, the United States, Canada, and Europe mobilized a range of protest actions. The largest demonstration abroad was held in Rome on January 26, 1998, with almost sixty thousand participants. Within the first few weeks of the massacre, a total of more than two hundred thousand people had participated in demonstrations in front of Mexican embassies and consulates in twenty-seven countries; the demonstrators held the Zedillo government responsible for the massacre (e.g., Paulson 1998). In Mexico, both in Chiapas and nationwide, indigenous and peasant organizations, human rights associations, and popular and student movements mobilized massive protest actions—demonstrations, communiqués, and fasting vigils—holding state authorities responsible for the violence against Pedranos opposed to the government.

The protesters have for the most part criticized the government for not fully investigating the events, for not sentencing higher-level officials, and for continuing to deny the existence of paramilitary groups in Chenalhó. Many also extend the blame to a globalized neoliberalism said to abuse and marginalize the world's most destitute populations. Las Abejas is frequently depicted as engaged in a global struggle against such political and economic oppression. Observers usually emphasize Las Abejas members' refusal to use firearms. The paramilitary aggression they suffered in spite of their pacifism is seen as further underlining their status as victims, as well as the grotesqueness of the violence.

This symbolic role that Las Abejas has acquired is evident from the high number of visitors the organization receives every year. Especially in the first decade after the massacre, Acteal was one of the central destinations on any visit outsiders made to the conflict zone in Chiapas with the intention of meeting indigenous representatives. Often, these tours also include the Zapatista centers of Polhó or Oventic in neighboring San Andrés Larráinzar.[5] The stream of visitors is still considerable, consisting of representatives of foreign parliaments, commissioners from the United Nations, human rights associations, support committees, and independent individuals. A long procession of domestic and foreign journalists from the press, radio, and television has come to Chenalhó. Internationally celebrated personalities have also felt compelled to come, including the writers Susan Sontag and José Saramago, Nobel Peace Prize laureate Rigoberta Menchú, and the former first lady of France, Danielle Mitterrand. The musician Manu Chao and his band Radio Bemba, who became something of icons for the global anti-neoliberal movement, gave a concert in the neighboring Pedrano Zapatista village of Polhó in December 2000.

A large number of visitors has consisted of peace observers from Mexico and abroad, often referred to as "campamentistas" in Spanish. The observers stay a minimum of two weeks in a village with a high number of Las Abejas members, where they are expected to document military troop movements, signals of paramilitary activities, and any violation of the villagers' human rights. By their mere presence, it is hoped they will discourage such violations from taking place.[6] The presence of observers was considered especially important while there were still camps of displaced villagers, but observers have continued to accompany Las Abejas villagers after they returned to their original communities, because of the continued threat of paramilitary violence. Many of the observers work in support committees for Chiapas in their home countries and will disseminate information about the political situation in Chiapas after their return. For many years, they also exerted pressure on the Mexican government to halt the violence and accept the Zapatista demands.

Because most Las Abejas members are of the Catholic faith, many politically engaged Catholic as well as Protestant groups inside and outside of Mexico have also embraced the association and pay frequent visits, many as peace observers, to Acteal and other villages with a concentration of Las Abejas members. These groups include the Christian Peacemaker Teams and the ecumenical Strategic Pastoral Action, both based in the United States.[7] For many who are sympathetic to Zapatista demands but troubled by the use of violence, the pacifist Las Abejas has been held out as an admirable example of civil Maya resistance (cf. Eber 2001a). Such groups, especially the Christian Peacemaker Teams, have also worked to strengthen the identity and activism of Las Abejas members as people engaged in religious-based nonviolent resistance, promoting different forms of public protests, such as praying before military checkpoints in Chenalhó, where they participate together with Las Abejas members (Tavanti 2003:179–86).

The international attention has also brought crucial economic support to the displaced. The European Union and the International Red Cross provided, as noted, shelter and a food supply for the camps. When the displaced families finally returned to their original villages, the construction of new houses was partly financed by the European Union, the Spanish and Mexican Red Cross, and funds from the state of Chiapas.

Las Abejas has, as noted earlier, begun to work in cooperation with a broad range of associations from various countries that wish to support different kinds of development projects among Las Abejas members. These groups provide financial and organizational support for defined projects, ranging from installing ONIL stoves and corn grinders, to supporting health promoters, to projects such as "Organizational Strengthening and Project Management" and "Women's Empowerment."[8] To a certain extent, these groups have also influenced the internal organization and agenda of Las Abejas.

Acteal and Las Abejas have even attracted activism tourists, such as those participating in the so-called Reality Tours organized by Global Exchange that aim to give, according to its website, "a better understanding of popular movements and modern day social struggles in Mexico."[9] For several years, the program included visits to communities of Las Abejas members affected by the paramilitary violence. In 2001, this meant an overnight visit to Nuevo Yibeljoj, the new village where formerly displaced Catholic villagers from Yibeljoj live, where the tourists were welcomed with a ceremony and an account of the massacre by one of the Las Abejas representatives, who told "how he heard shots during the massacre, ran to Acteal and found pools of blood everywhere."[10] While Global Exchange no longer includes Las Abejas in its tours, they have been replaced by "fair trade travel" organized by Higher Grounds Trading Company, which supports the coffee exports of the cooperative Maya Vinic of Las Abejas.[11]

Las Abejas has reciprocated the international exchange; its members have been invited to places in and outside Mexico. Their chief ambassadors have been the Acteal Choir, formed after the massacre, which has traveled with conjunto musicians all over the country. Las Abejas representatives have also gone abroad to the United States, Guatemala, El Salvador, Colombia, Italy, Spain, Portugal, Switzerland, Germany, France, Denmark, and Sweden to speak about the persecution in Chenalhó and the work of their organization. In 1999, three of the children injured in the massacre traveled to Washington, D.C., to receive medical examinations to determine further treatment, accompanied by Chenalhó pastoral workers and a representative of Las Abejas.[12]

One of the official international recognitions of Las Abejas with the most political significance was when the French Republic granted the association its Prize for Human Rights on December 11, 2001.[13] Las Abejas was represented by Agustín Vázquez from Yibeljoj, who received the prize from the hands of French prime minister Lionel Jospin; Vázquez was accompanied by Bishop Emeritus Samuel Ruiz and the former parish priest in Chenalhó, Miguel Chanteau. The rationale for the award stated that Las Abejas received the prize "for their struggle against racial discrimination and the defense of the rights of indigenous populations in the state of Chiapas." But undoubtedly the most palpable expression of the symbolic importance of the Acteal victims for outsiders is the huge sculpture called "Pillar of Shame" that stands at the entrance to Acteal. Made of black bronze, it portrays a group of more than fifty painfully twisted human bodies. The monument was erected in 1999 on the initiative of the National Indigenous Congress and the cultural association CLETA and created and donated by Danish artist Jens Galschiot. The inscription on the statue reads: "This sculpture has been erected to denounce the encroachments of the Mexican state on the indigenous population. May the victims be remembered and honored forever; and may

Las Abejas logo. Photo by José A. Jiménez Pérez.

the perpetrators be brought to justice and tried for their crimes against humanity."[14] The pillar has become part of the Las Abejas logo used today on all their communiqués.

THE POWER OF MARTYRDOM

Members of Las Abejas are very much aware of the role they have been given, and they actively take part in influencing public perception of this role. They know that the national and international attention has been crucial for protection against renewed paramilitary attacks and for ensuring the constant supply of food and aid during the years of displacement as well as funding for various kinds of projects. The intense interaction with concerned and supportive Mexicans and foreigners—both in the villages and at the municipal center in Acteal—has strengthened the sense among Las Abejas members that an international community of people believes that their lives as impoverished, marginalized, and persecuted indigenous peasants are unjust (see also Tavanti 2003:174–75; Schlittler Álvarez 2008:60–61). As one Catholic man in Yibeljoj reportedly said to U.S. visitors on the Reality Tour in 2001: "We don't feel alone. Because you are with us."[15] The broad international network developed by Las Abejas has provided political support for their demands and serves as a constant reminder to the Mexican government that Chenalhó is under international scrutiny. The close relationship with an international community has also influenced the perception Las Abejas men and women have of the political violence they have experienced, further influencing them to see the massacre as a sign of how exceptional both their suffering and struggle are.

The massacre in Acteal and its victims have become something members and leaders of Las Abejas constantly refer to. In ceremonies, political statements, and even the daily broadcasts of the local radio station of Las Abejas, Radio Chanul Pom, there are constant allusions to the victims and their spiritual and political importance (e.g., Schlittler Álvarez 2008:52). These various expressions form part of an intense cultivation of martyrdom that has developed.

As described in chapter 6, before the Acteal massacre, Pedrano Catholics already had articulated an identity as a suffering people especially loved by God. This identity has become greatly strengthened since the massacre. The victims are seen as the embodiment of the suffering of Pedrano Catholics and other members of Las Abejas in their struggle for liberation. A common phrase of Las Abejas members is that the victims were killed "when they were engaged in prayer and fasting to ask God for peace and justice for the entire people."[16] Thus, the victims are described as martyrs of this struggle who were willing to die for their cause. In the words of Las Abejas board members, "We believe that God has made a covenant with us through the blood of the martyrs of Acteal. We can have peace in Chiapas, but before a new child will be born, a

Women holding crosses with the names of the Acteal martyrs, during a protest against criminal impunity and crimes of the state, August 12, 2011. Photo by José A. Jiménez Pérez.

covenant with the people of Chenalhó was to be made. God has chosen this people. All this attention of the world to Acteal is because of this covenant" (Tavanti 2003:95, from a group interview made in 1999). Furthermore, the victims are martyrs in the long tradition of those bringing the Word of God, as the killing is seen also as an attack against their Catholic faith (cf. Schlittler Álvarez 2008:49).

By defining the victims as martyrs, Catholic Pedranos and members of Las Abejas attempt to transform the terror and fear created by the massacre and the broader paramilitary persecution into something purposeful that may even bring hope for change. The dead martyrs hold the promise of resurrection. The victims are described as bringing strength and hope into the struggle of Las Abejas, their blood "serving as fertilizer for the flowering of the struggle" (Schlittler Álvarez 2008:46; quote from interview with catechist coordinator Antonio Vázquez). Instead of being a senseless and devastating deed, the massacre becomes a verification of Pedrano Catholics' incessant fight for truth and justice. The forty-five martyrs provide faith and hope to the survivors and to all others engaged in the struggle to spread the Word of God. Thus, their death was not in vain; the government tried to "kill the seed, but the seed has multiplied" and brought trepidation to those in power.[17] In this way, the deaths are portrayed as a sacrifice that gives life to others (Schlittler Álvarez 2008:46). Therefore, Las Abejas leaders can even exclaim "¡Viva el masacre!" (Long live the massacre!) and have participants at the mass respond "¡Viva!"[18]

The diocese clergy have actively contributed to the construction of these deaths as martyrdom, for martyrs play an important role not only in the Catholic Church as a whole but also in liberation theology in particular (e.g., Sobrino 2001; Lundberg 2004). In the words of Bishop Arizmendi, the victims died "for their faith, being the apostles of the Gospels, for defending the human rights of those who are marginalized, for their search for peace, justice, and reconciliation."[19] In the monthly mass in Acteal held on November 22, 2007, parish priest Pedro Arriaga stated: "God has chosen this people to suffer the martyrdom of his son, so that the blood of these people will be spilled like the spilled blood of Christ. These people suffer the martyrdom of our Lord and their blood will serve to make the Catholic Church grow" (Schlittler Álvarez 2008:48, my translation from Spanish). Because some regard the massacre as an attack on the Catholic Diocese and its political influence in the state, the diocese's depiction of martyrdom can be seen as a way of clearly incorporating the victims and thus Las Abejas into the broader Catholic Church. In a sense, it also depoliticizes the factional, local- and state-level combat in which Las Abejas took part, instead describing the massacre as a more general attack against the faith of the victims and their broad search for social justice and peace (Schlittler Álvarez 2008:49).

The diocese's focus on the victims as martyrs in a struggle not only for peace and justice but also for reconciliation expresses the need to forgive rather than to foster feelings of revenge—while still demanding legal punishment of the perpetrators—and to find ways to reconcile with Pedrano villagers of opposing groups. Pedrano catechists and leaders of Las Abejas have also pushed for this nonviolent posture, in line with the position of Las Abejas since its foundation: to work for conciliatory and nonviolent means in the struggle for social justice.

Acteal became the new ceremonial core of the Catholic community in Chenalhó after the 1997 massacre and is now often referred to as "the sacred land of the martyrs of Acteal." A large open-air chapel with a sloping roof has been built on the site. The victims of the massacre are buried, not in their respective lineage cemeteries, as is the custom, but collectively in a memorial tomb next to the chapel, with photos of the dead on a wall and enough space for groups to pray (cf. Schlittler Álvarez 2008:57). In another newly constructed chapel resides the statue of San Pedro together with a statue now called the Virgin of the Massacre, a figure of the Virgin of Guadalupe that was hit during the shootings. The little statue, dressed in the clothes of Pedrano women, is wrapped in a white bandage where the bullet entered. The bandage is changed in a yearly ceremony as a manifestation that her wound has not healed. At Easter, the Virgin is taken on a pilgrimage to other villages in the municipality to visit Catholic chapel groups. The procession also arrives in the Zapatista center of Polhó, where the Virgin is received by the patron saint of the autonomous municipality, San Pedro.[20]

Every twenty-second of the month, a commemorative mass and ceremony are held in the chapel, with a larger commemoration on the December 22 anniversary. These masses, Pedranos have told me, will be observed until justice is obtained and all the perpetrators sentenced. The masses are organized by the Las Abejas board together with the parish priest. While the parish priest and Pedrano catechists and pre-deacons lead the religious ceremonies of the mass, the Las Abejas board runs the political component that is always part of the mass, including the reading of the monthly communiqué with a political message to the broader public. The board members and other Las Abejas authorities, all dressed in traditional ceremonial clothes, also initiate the ceremony with a procession starting at the Pillar of Shame monument, circling it three times before descending the stairs to the outdoor chapel.

In certain months, particularly on the December anniversary, the mass draws Las Abejas members from the entire municipality and numerous Mexican and foreign visitors. In 1998, the first anniversary of the massacre was commemorated with an imposing ceremony with between five and ten thousand participants, including sixteen priests from Mexico,

Memorial mass in the Acteal outdoor chapel on the tenth anniversary of the massacre, 2007. Photo by José A. Jiménez Pérez.

France, and the United States. In 2007, the tenth anniversary of the massacre was remembered with a large memorial service, also celebrating the fifteen years since the creation of Las Abejas. It was preceded by two days of workshops, named the National Encounter Against Impunity, where various examples of state violence and impunity—the failure to bring perpetrators to account—were discussed with participants from fifty different national and international organizations.[21]

In other months, the mass is more sparsely attended, with the majority of the participants consisting of foreign visitors, many of whom are peace observers. This was the case with the mass I attended in June 2006. I was struck by how the commemorative mass on such occasions, with few Pedranos present, has become first and foremost a means to integrate and emotionally engage visitors in the struggle of Las Abejas and the plight of its members. At a certain moment of the mass, they are even asked to come to the front of the chapel to introduce themselves and give the reason for their visit, demonstrating, as it were, the global expansion and weight of the cause of Las Abejas (see also Schlittler Álvarez 2008:60).[22]

One of the most elaborate mobilizations dramatizing Acteal martyrdom was the national pilgrimage to Mexico City and the Basilica of Guadalupe that Las Abejas members undertook in fall 2000, together with members from the Maya organization Xi'Nich, based in eastern Chiapas. On their two-month journey covering more than 1,300 kilometers on foot, the approximately 250 pilgrims gained nationwide attention and some international coverage as well. The pilgrims called on the nation to recognize their plight and cause, and their emphasis on the Acteal martyrs contributed to both the pilgrimage's moral and political force (Moksnes 2000).

The discourse on martyrdom has given further weight to Las Abejas's political demands. In the board's monthly written communiqués, wherein they present demands or aim accusations at the Mexican government, they usually mention the deaths of the victims and often state the number of years and months since the massacre.[23] In these demands for change, Las Abejas often maintain that they are backed by an international community that regards the victims as martyrs also of their own struggles. All of the Las Abejas communiqués, which besides being read at mass are also e-mailed, are directed to a global imagined community of support and concern; they are addressed to "the national and international press," "national and international human rights organizations," "social and political organizations," and "public opinion." The global role ascribed to the martyrs is depicted in a particularly powerful communiqué sent out in the year 2000 by the Las Abejas board on August 9, which the United Nations has declared the International Day of Indigenous Peoples. The board members of Las Abejas in the statement not only denounce the massacre and their poverty, but situate Acteal and Chenalhó in an international arena of struggle for justice supported by peoples on all continents:

> Many people, thousands and perhaps millions, in the different continents of America, of Europe, of Africa, of Asia, and of Australia, people of different faiths, of different social and political organizations, learned about what distorted rhetoric has always tried to

conceal. Many of them have come to visit us, to express solidarity with us, to offer a shoulder to console us, to help ease our immense pain. So many have cried with us and afterwards wiped the tears of us the survivors, the men, women, boys, girls, elderly men and women, there where the blood was spilled of those who, in praying and fasting, were seeking peace for all peoples, indigenous and non-indigenous. Many have come to learn for themselves, many have discovered the lies that the tongue of the government has spread. But they all embraced us and lifted us up. Therefore, today, we have the strength to shout, because our forty-five brothers and sisters died in order to live.

In a similar vein, in a communiqué on April 20, 2009, the Las Abejas board wrote: "We convoke the peoples of the world to mobilize together with us and demand punishment of those responsible [for the massacre] and also that we as one people pass the word from generation to generation about what happened in Acteal."

DEMANDING UNIVERSAL RIGHTS

The focus on martyrdom has come to govern the type of demands that Las Abejas pose to the Mexican government. Since the massacre, much of the political work of the group has focused on the 1997 events and on achieving what is defined as justice for the crimes committed against the members. Their central demands are for conviction of those guilty of orchestrating and executing the massacre and persecution, and indemnity for the lost homes, harvests, and belongings. The work has involved lengthy legal proceedings filed by Las Abejas representatives, usually with the assistance of the Fray Bartolomé de Las Casas Center for Human Rights. Las Abejas describes the massacre as a crime of the state.[24] Both Las Abejas and the Center for Human Rights have further defined it as a "crime against humanity."[25] Thus, perhaps the main objective of Las Abejas's struggle has become the recognition and bringing to trial of the Mexican government's involvement at the time. In this, they coincide with the Center for Human Rights, which maintains that without official recognition of the massacre as part of a counterinsurgent strategy, there can be no conditions for long-term solutions to the conflict in Chiapas (CDHFBC 2009b:25). Representatives of both groups went to Mexico City in June 2009 to protest the impending release, described above, of various Pedranos sentenced for the massacre, and the lack of a legal trial of high-level officials, including former president Ernesto Zedillo. Representatives of Las Abejas held "a day of fasting and prayer" in front of the Supreme Court and presented letters and documents to the High Court and Mexican president Felipe Calderón (Las Abejas communiqués, June 8–9, 2009).[26] Besides these demands, Las Abejas continues to present demands for broader social change to end their poverty and marginalization in Mexican society. They often describe the eradication of poverty as a prerequisite for making possible a lasting peace with justice and dignity, "paz con justicia y dignidad" (e.g., Schlittler Álvarez 2008:51).

Pedrano Catholics have backed these political claims by referring increasingly to international human rights regulations. The paramilitary

Leaders of Las Abejas with the former bishop of the Diocese of San Cristóbal de Las Casas, the late Samuel Ruiz, in Mexico City, June 9, 2009, protesting the impending release of men sentenced for the Acteal massacre. Photo by José A. Jiménez Pérez.

violence, perceived as being at the behest of the federal government, and the affirmation by an international support community of their identity as martyrs in a global struggle, have further motivated the converts to expand their political activity to involve an international arena of actors, including the United Nations. The appeal Las Abejas members make to universal rights reflects their increasing appropriation of the globalized human rights discourse in addressing both the Mexican government and these international actors. While the Las Abejas leadership more clearly employs and elaborates the language of human rights, ordinary members, too, appear to hold a fundamental and strongly felt notion of having certain universal and absolute rights.[27]

For the Catholic members of Las Abejas, I believe, the regulations issued by the United Nations and other international bodies are taken as the secular application of the universal justice that they regard as proclaimed by God. In what I have called a moral theology of suffering, Catholic Pedranos describe their suffering as contrary to the will of God. They proclaim the existence of universal values and their absolute right to live without the suffering brought by poverty and marginalization (see also Kovic 2005).

Certainly, it should be noted that highland Mayas in the past also referred to laws and official regulations to defend their needs and interests. Since early colonialism, leaders of Maya societies in Chiapas have turned to legal and political institutions; for example, to protest land invasions, denounce unjust treatment by hacienda owners, or protect their political autonomy (for a series of such appeals, see Vos 1994). Today, however, appeals to official regulations are made in language referring to rights, both rights as Mexican citizens and universal rights backed by international laws and conventions.

The founding of Sociedad Civil in Chenalhó in the early stage of the Zapatista uprising was undertaken, even then, with reference to international regulations that would ensure people's right to physical protection. Sociedad Civil, which soon merged with Las Abejas in Chenalhó, was considered by its Pedrano members to be organized in accordance with international agreements that would guarantee the safety of its members. Many members said it was the United Nations that had made and enforced these regulations, although most had only a vague notion of the institution as such.[28] These rules, Pedrano Catholics repeatedly told me during my fieldwork in 1995–96, delineated the protection of civil populations during wartime and bound the conduct of the Mexican government as well as their Zapatista adversaries. To signal their belonging to Sociedad Civil—the unarmed, neutral civil society that was created throughout the diocese on the initiative of the bishop—affiliated Maya villagers all over Chiapas put up poles with white flags on their houses and painted signs on the house walls that said, "Civil Society/Peace/ Neutral Zone."[29] These signs, I was told again and again in Chenalhó, served as protection against military attacks. Sebastián Gómez, a Catholic, explained: "If the government bombs where it is marked 'Neutral Zone,' the government will lose. If the Zapatistas shoot in the neutral zone or construct a base there, this also can be denounced. It should immediately be communicated to the [Center for] Human Rights and the Mexican Red Cross so they can evacuate [the civilians]. Making warfare is not allowed in the neutral zones, that's what it says in the law."[30]

Sociedad Civil was said to have intimate ties to various independent institutions outside Mexico, a fact regarded as bolstering their cause and guaranteeing the application of law and justice. A leader of Sociedad Civil Las Abejas said: "We're connected with the National Commission of Human Rights, with the foreign organization of Latin America, and with the organization of the United Nations—that's the very root.[31] There's no reason to fear. Wherever we go, we're not afraid."[32]

During my stay in 1995–96, when Catholic Pedranos used the term "human rights" (the Spanish term "derechos humanos" is also used when speaking Tzotzil), they usually meant the Fray Bartolomé de Las Casas Center for Human Rights. Thus, people would say, "They're from Human Rights," or "We went to speak to Human Rights," when referring to the center.[33] The members had scant familiarity at the time with the broader concept of universal human rights. Las Abejas representatives, as well as the human rights committees of the Pedrano Catholic community, attended various weekend workshops offered by the Center for Human Rights to learn about the human rights concept. There they became more acquainted with how the notion of rights can be used to express demands for basic needs and what obligations the state held to fulfill such needs.[34]

After the experience of paramilitary terror, held to be orchestrated by a state employing impunity to protect its actions, the authority that international regulations represent has grown even more crucial to Catholic Pedranos. The United Nations is almost seen as a new ally. Las Abejas leaders now repeatedly appeal to UN officials for support and protection while they denounce persecution in Chenalhó and petition for support in the claims they direct toward the Mexican government.

The first interaction between Las Abejas and the United Nations took place in April 1998, when Las Abejas sent catechist María Vázquez Gómez as a representative to the meeting of the UN Human Rights Committee in Geneva, Switzerland. Vázquez, a member of the Indian Theology group and native to Acteal, had lost nine family members in the massacre, among them her brother Alonzo Vázquez Gómez, catechist and zone chief.[35] In her address before the committee and an auditorium filled primarily with governmental delegates, she held the Mexican government responsible for the massacre. During the week she attended the UN meeting, Vázquez also met with various journalists and representatives of governments; she was accompanied by representatives of Mexican human rights associations who were then in Geneva. Together, they presented the Acteal massacre as the most blatant case in a long stream of human rights violations in Mexico.[36]

The same year, 1998, Las Abejas sent a letter to UN Secretary-General Kofi Annan in which they criticized the state governor for obstructing the investigation of the massacre and asked for UN intervention to establish justice and peace in the state.[37] Within a week, Las Abejas received a reply from Annan, who said he would be following the conflict in Chiapas and the investigation of the massacre closely. The letter from Annan was read out at the memorial ceremony held in August for the victims of the massacre.

Las Abejas has also contacted several UN special rapporteurs and commissioners. In 1999, they wrote to the Representative of the Secretary-General on Internally Displaced Persons, Francis M. Deng, asking him to pressure the Mexican government to accept the San Andrés Peace Accords to make possible a safe return of the displaced in Chiapas. In 2002, Deng was invited on a mission to Mexico, and during his journey, he visited Chenalhó and interviewed Las Abejas.[38] In 1999, Las Abejas

representatives met in Acteal with the UN Special Rapporteur on Ex-
trajudicial, Summary, or Arbitrary Executions, Asma Jahangir.[39] In her
report to the UN Commission on Human Rights, she included a special
section on the Acteal massacre that confirmed much of what Las Abejas members had consistently argued. Jahangir concluded that "armed
paramilitary groups continue to operate freely and threaten the lives of
the indigenous people," and that there was a "culture of impunity" in
the country.[40] In November 1999, Las Abejas representatives addressed
Mary Robinson, the UN High Commissioner on Human Rights, at a
meeting between Robinson and Chiapas-based NGOs in San Cristóbal.
In response, Robinson described the Acteal massacre as an example of
the lack of enforcement of justice in Mexico and said she would ask the
authorities to respond to the demands for a just investigation.[41] In March
2002, it was the turn of the UN Special Rapporteur for the Right to Adequate Housing, Miloon Kothari, to meet with Las Abejas representatives
in Acteal. Kothari affirmed that the question of human rights should be
given priority in Chiapas, and that he found the problem of housing to be
intimately related to the right to the land, urgently needing a solution.[42]
As in their other encounters with UN officials, Las Abejas members took
his statement as an affirmation by the United Nations of their precarious
living conditions and the acute need for improvements. Furthermore, in
2005, Las Abejas and the Fray Bartolomé de Las Casas Center for Human
Rights appealed to the Inter-American Commission on Human Rights
(IACHR) to try the involvement of the Mexican state in the massacre,
and in 2009, delegates from Las Abejas and the center presented evidence on the case before the IACHR in Washington, D.C.[43]

   In these various addresses to international bodies, demands expressed
in communiqués, and legal cases pressed in Mexican courts, many of the
rights claimed by Las Abejas are within the sphere of civil and political
rights. In a communiqué in 2006, Las Abejas forcefully demanded the
application of these rights:

> Justice is far from being the desire of the federal government and
> the Office of the Attorney General (PGR) of this country, which
> demonstrates ungovernability, partiality of justice, exclusion, dis-
> crimination against indigenous peoples, where we see the persis-
> tent violation of our human rights. We deserve equal and respect-

ful treatment. It cannot be that the Mexican state continues to violate our human rights as victims and that Mexico continues to live in a state of impunity. This is the reason we have turned to the Inter-American Commission on Human Rights by sending a letter demanding justice in the case of Acteal.[44]

Other demands by Las Abejas, such as those for housing, schools, health clinics, and better pay, concern the so-called second generation of rights: economic, social, and cultural rights (cf. Collier and Collier 2005:456). In contrast to their demands for civil and political rights, however, Las Abejas members do not express these demands in explicit rights terms or with reference to the UN covenant that establishes these rights. This difference may reflect the predominant focus of the Fray Bartolomé de Las Casas Center for Human Rights on violations of civil and political rights, as well as the right to self-determination for indigenous groups. Although the center, as described earlier, takes a holistic stance on rights, I have seen little or no indication that it has implemented any articulated processes for demanding the implementation of second-generation rights nor instigated such procedural discussions among Maya groups.[45] Rather, Las Abejas men and women, like others in the indigenous movement in Chiapas, mostly refer to these latter rights in broad terms as a right to social justice—in short, to freedom from poverty. Although by convention these rights are defined as individual, the members, as well as the center, usually categorize them as collective (CDHFBC 2005:19, cf. Harvey 1998:27).

Las Abejas members demand, furthermore, the collective rights of indigenous peoples. Here they align themselves with the Mexican indigenous movement in challenging the notion that democracy can be achieved without the full recognition of Mexico as a multiethnic country (e.g., Burguete Cal y Mayor 2002). It is as a distinct, self-governing people that Catholic Pedranos conceive of their participation in the nation-state. In a 2000 communiqué, Las Abejas leaders wrote: "The government of Ernesto Zedillo refuses to recognize that besides the mestizos, we indigenous people exist, too, and that we have the right to be different and to have rights as indigenous peoples."[46] A central document that Las Abejas explicitly refers to is ILO Convention 169 concerning Indigenous and Tribal Peoples in Independent Countries, which the Mexican

government has ratified. The group also refers to the San Andrés Peace
Accords on Indigenous Rights and Culture, signed by EZLN and the
Mexican government in 1996, which it demands that the government
adhere to. The San Andrés Peace Accords have become, for Las Abejas
and most other indigenous organizations in Mexico, a significant land-
mark for their aspirations to indigenous self-determination and equal
participation in the Mexican nation-state and their constitutional right
to ethnic difference.[47]

During my stay in 1995–96, the demand for autonomy, which EZLN
presented in the peace negotiations, was still rather unfamiliar to Catholic Pedranos. Because the relative autonomy of their municipality had
not protected them from political corruption and abuse by the broader
society, the benefits of autonomy were not self-evident. Some of the catechists, however, were already familiar with the ILO Convention 169 on
indigenous rights and tried to describe the convention to the members.
On one occasion in summer 1995, I watched a video presentation about
the ILO convention in the Yibeljoj Catholic chapel, arranged by the catechists, who had borrowed the equipment and video from the nuns. But
because the film was in Spanish and the catechists had little background
to explain the content, the screening was mainly an evening of diversion
for the many families who had gathered. The interest among catechists
and Las Abejas leaders grew, however, especially after their participation
in the preparatory meetings of the negotiations in 1996. In his report
from one of the preparatory meetings of the peace negotiations, Las
Abejas leader Antonio Gutiérrez described the implications of the new
concept: "There, they said that the demand is for autonomy. The demand is for the law of the people. . . . 'Autonomy' means how the municipality should be governed, how it should behave toward the people.
Whether it should obey the people who elect the municipal president or
whether it should obey the state government."[48]

The Pedrano Catholics ultimately appropriated the demands for
autonomy as an integral part of their discourse on justice and rights.
They have begun to conceive of autonomy as a way to decrease state
authorities' control and protect Chenalhó from the type of involvement
by government, military, and police interests they see as responsible for
the paramilitary violence in 1997. Through the demand for autonomy,

Pedrano Catholics demand the right to govern themselves and to control state development programs directed at them. Autonomy, further, is seen as a protection for Pedrano territory and its resources against encroachment by national and foreign companies, which is feared especially after NAFTA. Thus, the fulfillment of the San Andrés Peace Accords has become one of the central demands of Las Abejas members. However, the legal reforms that the Mexican Congress finally approved in 2001 were significantly weaker than the original accords and have been severely criticized by the EZLN and most indigenous organizations in the country, including Las Abejas (e.g., Hernández Castillo 2006a). In a communiqué on May 22, 2001, the leadership of Las Abejas protested against the reform and demanded the constitutional acknowledgment of their right to autonomy, land, and political participation in Mexico:

> The reform that the legislators approved does not recognize the collective rights of indigenous peoples, nor their autonomy, nor their right to territory and natural resources, nor other rights crucial to our development. . . . We want to be included in making proposals that ensure real economic and cultural development benefiting our indigenous and non-indigenous brothers and sisters in Mexico. We want alternatives and just solutions to our demands, we who live in poverty.

Las Abejas has also used the autonomy argument to protest against the project called Plan Puebla Panamá, created in 2001 on the initiative of Mexican president Vicente Fox, a multigovernmental project of large-scale investment and development stretching from the nine southernmost states of Mexico to Panama. In 2008, the project was transformed into Proyecto de Integración y Desarrollo de Mesoamérica (Mesoamerican Integration and Development Project), with a total of ten countries participating, including Colombia. The project focuses on large infrastructure and energy projects to stimulate trade and commerce, and includes some investments for social development, such as, for example, health and environmental projects.[49] In Chiapas, the focus is on the large-scale cultivation of biofuels, the construction of hydroelectric dams, and the formation of so-called "ciudades rurales" (rural cities), seen as a measure to reduce poverty (Zunino 2010). By moving indigenous villagers from their dispersed communities to newly constructed houses in municipal centers, they are supposed to gain improved access to social services and salaried employment.[50] In 2011, only a few Maya municipalities had been transformed to rural cities, but various, including Chenalhó, were in the pipeline.

Las Abejas, like members of indigenous and social movements throughout the countries involved, have vehemently condemned the project—today known as Proyecto Mesoamérica—as a neoliberal attempt to privatize and extract natural resources for the benefit of multinational corporations by displacing indigenous peoples from their lands. In a communiqué of November 22, 2010, the board of Las Abejas wrote: "Our land, territory, and natural resources are threatened by the mining companies, dams, highways, ciudades rurales, etc. Those projects are a joke and the death of our communities and people. [We are] rejecting all mega-projects imposed on our territory by the transnationals." The communiqué ends, "Yes to the life and self-determination of the original peoples of Mexico!"

RELYING ON GOD AND THE LAW

Pedrano Catholics' increasing demand for the application of international rights regulations has practical ramifications. For centuries, Pedranos have had few other means to respond to abuse and violence besides highly risky direct confrontation. Maya leaders in the past have turned to higher authorities to protest unfair treatment, but the outcome was arbitrary and uncertain. When their lives were threatened, people usually either escaped into the woods and mountains or moved away. Catholic catechists and Las Abejas leaders, however, deem flight to be a strategy of the past. Instead, they say, chapel members should place their trust in God and the rule of law. The catechists in Yibeljoj made just such an admonishment during my stay in May 1996, when the villagers feared an attack by relatives of two men from a neighboring municipality who had been lynched in the village, accused of being murderers.[51] At one of the extra prayer meetings of the Catholic chapel group after the lynching, the three principal catechists took turns admonishing the creyentes not to listen to the rumors buzzing around in the village and run away to the mountains, as many had done on the two previous nights. Instead, they should let God be the judge of what should take place. One of the cate-chists said: "In truth, men and women, it's too bad that we don't have any courage. The truth is that we don't believe in what our Lord tells us. . . . Thanks to God I've never run away, ever. I've never slept in the moun-tains. It's because I put my trust in God. . . . What I really want to ask of you is to have more confidence in God. And this would be possible if we paid more attention to the Word of our Father, if we held the Word of our Father in our hearts."[52]

Ordinary chapel members urge this trust as well. One woman in Yibel-joj described the work of Sociedad Civil Las Abejas as a matter of staying in place and putting one's fate in the hands of God: "Those of Sociedad Civil talk about the suffering that comes. . . . [The leaders say:] 'Don't flee, don't be afraid. Only God knows if there will be more fights, if an-other one will begin or if here it will end.' That's what they say."[53]

The decision not to flee expresses not only a reliance on God, but also a demand to be recognized as subjects with rights that are defined and protected by law and convention. Sociedad Civil's declaration of "neutral zones" was an expression of such a demand for the application of the in-ternationally agreed upon protection of civilians during warfare. During my fieldwork, Catholic villagers repeatedly told me that if soldiers came to their house and harassed them, they would look for the pamphlet they had been given and show the soldiers that they were protected by international law.

During the paramilitary persecutions in fall 1997, Las Abejas villagers, acknowledging a superior danger, opted to flee in spite of their earlier resolve. With a renewed threat of attacks in December—paramilitaries shooting near several of the refugee camps to scare people—the dis-placed people discussed whether to flee once more. Those in X'oyep, I was told afterward by displaced friends there, had decided they were rel-atively well protected. Surrounded by villages with large groups of armed Zapatistas, the paramilitaries were not likely to risk an attack there. Ac-teal, in contrast, was more exposed. Even the Zapatistas in Acteal chose to leave the community. But the members of Las Abejas in Acteal, I was told, decided to not flee, believing that as unarmed civilians they should not suffer military aggression. Led by the catechist and zone chief Alonzo Vázquez Gómez, the Catholics shielded themselves only with prayers to

God and the demand that the Geneva Convention on the protection of civilians in warfare be followed. Their choice to stay was thus an attempt to transform their unarmed and passive vulnerability to a moral demand for the right to remain unharmed.[54] The failure of this shield to protect them has not caused the survivors to question its validity, but is seen as further proof of the monstrousness of the aggression.

In the narratives that Las Abejas members have formed about the Acteal massacre, one of the central accounts is about the now mythical last words of Acteal catechist Vázquez. These words capture the members' portrayal of the aggression as a violation both of the will of God and of international law. They also manifest the Christian martyrdom and innocence of the victims. In the midst of the shooting, Vázquez is said to have run toward his wife, who was falling to the ground with her baby. When he reached them, he saw that both were dead, and he spun around toward the men in black uniforms, crying out: "Don't shoot, we are the Civil Society!" Seeing them raising their weapons toward him, he lifted his face and hands to the sky, and just before being shot dead, he exclaimed the words that echo those of the crucified Jesus: "Father, forgive them, for they know not what they do."[55]

RIGHTS AND THE STATE

Pedrano Catholics have developed a moral discourse with claims of global validity, drawing on various translocal discourses—liberation theology, the notion of universal human rights, the indigenous movement, and the anti-neoliberal movement. By describing themselves as martyrs in a global struggle for social justice, and by condemning the Mexican government for violating their rights, and invoking the national constitution and international conventions ratified by Mexico, Pedrano Catholics implicitly state: "Do us justice by these terms that you have professed to share." This has been called the "politics of embarrassment" (Niezen 2000:128) or the "mobilization of shame," which can be effective as moral leverage when states are worried about their international reputation for protecting human rights (Keck and Sikkink 1998:97). With this tool, Las Abejas members, without any real power at all, are to some extent able to force the government at least to pretend to acknowledge and respond to some of their claims. This, I suggest, could be called a moral weapon of the weak (cf. Scott 1985).

To display its respect for human rights and the rule of law, the Mexican government has indemnified the survivors of the Acteal massacre and the displaced, and made sure that a number of Pedrano men were prosecuted and convicted as guilty of the massacre, although the majority were later released and there were no higher-level charges. The reform package of the San Andrés Peace Accords eventually accepted by the Congress was, to some extent, a recognition of indigenous rights in line with current state discourses on cultural pluralism, although considered highly insufficient by indigenous organizations.

But, overall, members of Las Abejas have seen few concrete changes in the actions of the Mexican state in response to their claims, especially concerning the reduction of poverty. To the contrary, it has become increasingly difficult for Pedranos and other Maya peasants to make a living. This has led to a dilemma for Las Abejas members about what their future position should be and raises questions about the extent to which there is any scope for them to exercise a rights-based citizenship. This will be discussed in the last chapter.

CHAPTER 9

Exodus? The Limits of Citizenship and Rights-Based Claims

The experiences that Pedrano Catholics have suffered are extreme. In the span of a few years, they have been subjected to far more persecution and violence than most groups in highland Chiapas. Also extraordinary is how rapidly Pedrano Catholics have integrated their struggle and plight into national and international movements for social justice, appropriating a globalized moral discourse of rights. Through this discourse, they have reinterpreted their collective identity and relationship to the broader society. They now define the Mexican state as an antagonist responsible for the enduring poverty of indigenous peasants and for brutally attacking those who dare to present claims for change. However, the extreme experiences and concerns of Pedrano Catholics elucidate processes of change shared with other Maya highlanders as well as other marginalized peoples who are striving to use global networks and rights discourses to alter their position in society. Furthermore, I argue, their experiences show the inherent limitations in the present possibilities of using citizenship and rights claims to improve one's living conditions.

As we have seen, Pedrano Catholics are today demanding a participatory and rights-based citizenship in the Mexican nation-state. They reject the poverty, subordination, and ethnic discrimination to which they have been subject. They demand to be treated instead as full citizens of the Mexican nation-state, with a voice, status, and rights that reflect the equality and justice they believe are proclaimed by God. In principle, the government is no longer perceived as a patron of whom to ask favors, but as an entity subject to a constitution and regulations that are accessible to the public for verification and control (cf. Harvey 1998:22).

Through denunciations, claims, and legal actions, Pedrano Catholics point out to the authorities the rights and codes established by Mexican law and international convention and demand they be followed. The rights they demand are general human rights—both civil and political rights, and economic, social, and cultural rights—though the focus since the Acteal massacre has largely been on their civil right to have those responsible for the violence prosecuted. In contrast to conventional rights discourses, however, Pedrano Catholics regularly emphasize that their demands for rights are collective and should be granted to all; they claim collective citizenship rights to social justice and to escape from poverty. And, like other indigenous peoples, Pedrano Catholics demand the collective right to indigenous culture, self-determination, and control of their land.

But the limitations and difficulties Pedrano Catholics face in exercising the citizenship to which they aspire are significant. With the current direction of national governance leaving minimal room for the kind of demands Pedrano Catholics present, and with the highly antagonistic stance Pedrano Catholics have taken against the Mexican state, they find themselves in what I would call a "trapped" claim for citizenship, constrained both in the scope of its political agency and in its prospects of having an impact.

First, Pedrano Catholics have little success in individually implementing their rights in a society where the indigenous poor still experience significant discrimination and marginalization. Instead, they exercise their citizenship and present their claims primarily as a collectivity, which somewhat strengthens their political agency. This collective form of action reflects a long-standing emphasis among Mayas on communal organization and cohesion. Mayas today are transforming their former tight-knit corporate communities into what could be called "translocal moral communities," held together by a religious or political ethos, through which they act in the broader national and international arenas.

Second, there are severe limitations to the extent to which Pedrano Catholics can exercise their citizenship even as a collectivity. Their principled demands for rights have brought few concrete outcomes. While several of the rights-based demands appear to resonate with official Mexican state discourse, few actual changes in government policy have occurred in response, but instead there has been a continued focus on economic governance that implies low pay for their agricultural products, low salaries, few employment opportunities, as well as continued scarce access to social services. Furthermore, there is the constant threat of continued violent repression against groups that stir up social unrest. Utterly distrusting the present state system, Pedrano Catholics and many other Mayas refuse to have any dealings with official authorities and political parties, or to accept any of the limited benefits they offer. Instead, they make an effort to create spaces of autonomous political agency free from state interference. But thereby, they drastically limit the political participation in national society that citizenship conventionally grants and expects, as well as closing off most routes to economic resources. For many men and women, the choice of political strategy involves a continuous evaluation between whether to hold these principled rights demands or to accept some pragmatic degree of state interaction. Las Abejas is one of the organizations that ultimately became divided over the issue.

Third, while Las Abejas, like other indigenous organizations, tries to break the bonds of dependence on the state, other dependencies have emerged in its place. As with many indigenous groups, Pedrano Catholics have developed alliances to non-state actors outside their own municipalities, effectively linking their local communal concerns and interests with those of broader groups of people which cross ethnic, class, and often nation-state boundaries. Through these alliances, Pedrano Catholics and Las Abejas members have lessened their political and economic dependence on the state. To some extent, however, these alliances recreate relations of patronage and dependence with new actors of greater resources and influence than themselves, who in turn influence the way Pedrano Catholics frame their political agency.

In this chapter, I address these acute dilemmas that Pedrano Catholics face and continually discuss and reflect upon. Ultimately, this chapter deals with the possibilities for rights-based struggles in the neoliberal setting and the scope of local oppositional agency—and, for Pedrano Catholics, the possibility of finding Exodus, their liberation from poverty and suffering.

EXERCISING COLLECTIVE CITIZENSHIP

As individuals, most indigenous men and women in Chiapas still have few opportunities for agency in the broader public sphere dominated by Spanish-speaking mestizos. Most Pedranos feel tightly constrained in their interactions with official and judicial institutions and are continually discriminated against by officials and other employees. However, in the many new groups that rural as well as urban Mayas have formed in the past several decades—Catholic and Protestant congregations, political and civil associations, and production cooperatives—their members have found ways to diminish some of these obstacles. As with the Catholic community in Chenalhó, these groups offer their members new perspectives and idioms by which to conceptualize and make demands on national society, as well as tools to address official authorities and institutions—whether in presenting joint demands or offering guidance and backup to individuals—often with the assistance of the respective leaders. Acting through the Catholic chapel groups and Las Abejas, and with assistance from the diocese and the Fray Bartolomé de Las Casas Center for Human Rights, Pedrano Catholics have significantly strengthened their possibilities for exercising their rights as citizens. Thus, it is in large part as members of particular collectivities, for example, Zapatistas or Pentecostal Mayas, that many, perhaps most, highland Mayas today take part in and act as citizens within the nation-state.

Many of these groups, including Pedrano Catholics, create a collective base for political analysis, decision making, and action. In local- and municipal-level meetings, members discuss and define their political demands and decide what to do as a unified collective. One example is that before an official municipal, state, or federal election, members of many of these groups collectively determine whether to vote or abstain, and if they vote, for which party or candidate. For the presidential elections in July 2006, members of Las Abejas told me the organization decided in meetings that they distrusted all presidential candidates and that the members would refrain from voting in order to express their political protest. Instead, they joined the Zapatista initiative La Otra Campaña (The Other Campaign) (see also Kenney 2007).

Pedrano Catholics also hold mass demonstrations to manifest their political demands, thus appropriating the public space normally controlled by mestizos (cf. Alvarez, Dagnino, and Escobar 1998:18). Through pilgrimages, participating in political rallies, or distributing communiqués, the villagers occupy physical and mass-media spheres to express their demands to a broad public and to state and federal governments.

The collective form of citizenship Pedrano Catholics have developed is related, as I have argued, to long-standing constructs of community among highland Mayas. Pedrano Catholics have constituted their community as a socially and politically cohesive collective with a special alliance with God, reminiscent of generations of Mayas before them. Drawing on earlier calpul forms of community, they endow leaders with significant authority. In this case, the catechists and Las Abejas leaders, as well as mestizo allies, especially the Catholic Diocese, often wield major influence over political and other decisions. At the same time, employing the communal assembly as the basic platform for decision making—a model that evolved in highland Maya communities during the last century—Pedrano Catholics make these decisions on a participatory basis. Today, both men and women take part in the decision-making discussions. The Pedrano Catholic community is thereby firmly established as an enterprise of both men and women. This trait distinguishes them from most civil indigenous organizations—where men dominate—but is shared by other religious groups, both Catholic and Protestant. With the heavy emphasis on cohesion, however, there is little room for divergent positions. While this strengthens collective agency, it makes the group vulnerable to strife and greatly limits the scope of individual choice.

The presence of these various religious or political groups in Chenalhó and other Maya municipalities signifies, of course, a considerable social change from earlier community forms. Each of the new politico-religious communities has defined its own way of addressing its members' concerns and trying to improve their living conditions. Their emergence has created polarized and sometimes antagonistic collective identities. The differentiation among villagers is reinforced by their diverging allegiances to actors outside Chenalhó. These external actors have become part of the internal dynamics of the respective Pedrano factions—offering ways to mobilize resources, gain increased influence, and create alliances against antagonists. In the past, conflicts in Che-nalhó were played out in a context where concern for the stability of social relations within the community was decisive in whatever action was taken. The new loyalty villagers feel toward their own specific faction today commonly overrides such concerns. Local conflicts often reflect, and are bolstered by, antagonisms on the regional and national level. Pedranos thus find themselves engaged in political and social processes that are partly beyond their control.

Perhaps contradictorily, however, the formation of the new groups is part of a reconstitution of local Maya society. The Catholic community in Chenalhó, while it contributes to the factionalizing process of the munic-ipality, provides a space where social cohesion, political legitimacy, and a shared identity can be reconstructed between the group members. Simi-lar spheres are formed by each of the new political and religious groups, transforming Chenalhó, like other Maya municipalities, into a mosaic of moral communities, each part of broader, translocal communities. Whether Pedranos will be able to recreate a sense of shared identity and trust that transcends these divisions remains to be seen. Many, perhaps most, Pedranos express sadness and regret over the division of villages and families. They occasionally make attempts, therefore, to bridge the differences between factions and find new modes of cooperation. Dur-ing my stay in Yibeljoj, the villagers formed several such temporary coali-tions. Perhaps these efforts point to the possibility of a new confederate model in Chenalhó that recognizes political and religious differences between the various groups but encompasses them within an overarch-ing structure.

The role of the collective and dependence on community leaders may decrease in the future. A growing number of Mayas are acquiring profi-ciency and confidence in interacting with the mestizo-controlled public sphere. It is becoming ever more difficult for mestizos to exclude Ma-yas from the public sphere of national society. Urban mestizos in many towns have also witnessed a rapid growth of the indigenous population, which is contesting public and economic arenas where mestizos have previously constituted the vast majority and exerted political, social, and economic control (Rus and Vigil 2007). Today, many mestizos appear to regard Mayas with new respect; others, with increased trepidation.

It is noteworthy, however, that also among bilingual, urban Mayas, "community" continues to be important. The many Mayas who emigrate to the urban shantytowns in search of subsistence, especially around San Cristóbal de Las Casas, create new communal organizations primarily through Catholic or Protestant congregations, but also through EZLN, indigenous organizations such as CRIACH, and all-indigenous trade unions (e.g., Rus 1997; 2009; 2010; Figueroa Fuentes 2000; Nash 2001; Kovic 2005; Moksnes 2011). These groups often seem to form coherent units with many resemblances to the Pedrano Catholic community. The role of leaders of these groups is often similar to that of the Pedrano catechists and leaders of Las Abejas; that is, as intermediaries to mestizo institutions and authorities. Thus, to a certain extent, even the urban Maya communities tend to structure and facilitate interaction with mestizo society for their members. The persistent importance of collective organization for highland Mayas seems therefore to demonstrate the capacity of these communal forms not only to offer continuous modes of organizing social life, but also to adjust to changing modes of political and religious agency.

DEALING WITH THE STATE: EXERCISING CITIZENSHIP, NEGOTIATING CLIENTELISM

Paradoxically, while an increasing number of Mayas demand rights that are established in the national constitution and international regulations that are acknowledged by the Mexican government, and employ a language of rights that appears to resonate with present neoliberal state discourse, the government shows less interest than ever in adjusting its national policies to these demands. Instead, it offers particularistic programs directed at poor families, such as Oportunidades, which most Mayas in opposition criticize for not addressing the roots of poverty. What they want to see are collective, large-scale, and long-term changes in Mexican society to address the marginalization of indigenous people and other poor people, changes for which they see few prospects with the current regime.

This poses a severe and very real dilemma for many Mayas: should they focus on the principled and long-term demands on rights, justice, and large-scale structural change, or concentrate on achieving concrete improvements in their present living conditions through the—insufficient and criticized—means offered by the government? Of course, this challenge reflects the classical conflicts between reformist and revolutionary strategies, and between idealism and pragmatism, and is present throughout the indigenous movement in Mexico (cf. Gledhill 1997; Hernández Castillo 2006a). In Chiapas, the different positions taken on this issue have led to severe divisions in the indigenous movement.

Some Mayas in the organized opposition hold that a certain amount of interchange with the state is the only viable route to resources; because state programs are financed by money the government has earned through its exploitation of cheap indigenous labor and produce, it is legitimate to reclaim the money. Many also argue that since access to these resources is their "right," the bureaucratic procedures required to achieve it are not morally tainted. However, not all agree.

Apart from the criticism of the general government policies, the experience of many years of a corporatist, authoritarian regime has bred deep distrust of the state. One suspicion is about the state's alleged endeavor to create patron-client bonds among the indigenous poor, exchanging state resources for political loyalty. The experience with these bonds of obligation makes it very difficult for Mayas to accept any benefits from the state without sensing an expectation of reciprocal loyalty, such as voting for the ruling party. To receive such a benefit may cause others to question one's claim of standing free and in opposition to the government. Another suspicion concerns the relationship that may evolve in any interaction between indigenous leaders and the state. This, likewise, is based on decades of state co-optation of indigenous municipal authorities, where these leaders were turned into caciques, local bosses who were no longer loyal toward their own villagers and sometimes amassed great political and economic power.

The profound distrust of state strategies has not changed with the transformation of state policies from corporatist to neoliberal in the past few decades, nor with the increasing democratization of the electoral system. The historic defeat of the PRI in the 2000 presidential elections certainly brought hopes for change, even though the winner was Vicente Fox and his right-wing Partido Acción Nacional (PAN), but these hopes have not been fulfilled. Many Mayas still perceive the state as constantly trying to entice the poor into paternalistic webs of dependency and compliance, to corrupt their leaders, and to divide the opposition by granting favors to some while exerting repression on others. In fact, as Claudio Holzner argues (2006:77), "clientelism has not gone away in Mexico and may even be strengthening in many areas" (cf. Fox 1997). Even federal programs that have been evaluated nationally and internationally as rather apolitical and "pro-poor" in character, such as the Oportunidades program of presidents Fox and Calderón (Rocha Menocal 2005), are still regarded with suspicion by many Mayas. This is especially so since Oportunidades only offers material or monetary support to individual families in exchange for reciprocal action, such as sending one's child to school or attending medical check-ups. Coupled with the dismantling of earlier pro-poor policies and reforms, initiated earlier with the PRI governments in the 1980s, many Mayas hold little hope that the government has any intention of changing the situation for the indigenous poor.

In this context, many Mayas find the principled demands for rights to require a position of strict "autonomy"; non-cooperation with the state, zero negotiation, and a refusal to accept any state programs or economic support. Las Abejas, the Zapatistas, and other indigenous organizations that hold this position regard any state interaction as a way to lure individual Mayas of the opposition back into bonds of clientelism and government loyalty.

Instead, these organizations wish to create spheres of political agency in which the government or other authorities cannot exercise the typical clientelist forms of control (cf. Foweraker 1990:16–17, in Hellman 1994:128). Various groups are also seeking economic alternatives outside of those controlled by global market forces and creating social and political institutions controlled by their own communities and responsive to their members' prioritized needs and interests (Stahler-Sholk 2007; Speed 2008). The Zapatista base communities, as Shannon Speed has shown (2008), do not even turn to the state to grant or affirm their rights, but describe their rights (to self-governance) as something they can effect independent of the state. Thus, they embrace rights discourse without subsuming themselves under state-controlled legislative structures (Speed 2008).

However, to find a long-term sustainable position outside of the structures of patronage presents an ongoing difficulty as long as the state does not change its overall politics. To say no to all state programs implies a considerable economic strain for families who have struggled for generations to secure their daily livelihood. This has led to serious tensions within various of these organizations, which I will describe here in some detail to show what issues are at stake.

The Splitting of Las Abejas

For the members of Las Abejas, diverging opinions on how to handle these conflicting postures led eventually to a rupture in the organization. In 2008, Las Abejas became formally and publicly divided into two separate associations, one retaining the headquarters in Acteal and the claim of official status (with a board formally elected by the remaining members), and taking the name Organización de la Sociedad Civil "Las Abejas." Sometimes it is referred to in Chenalhó as "Las Abejas de Acteal." The other has its office in the village of Nuevo Yibeljoj and has taken the name Asociación Civil Las Abejas, often referred to as "Las Abejas, A.C.", or "Las Abejas de Nuevo Yibeljoj." Both entities appear to have a reasonably strong membership base in communities all through Chenalhó, but the previously united members have had to choose which of the two factions to follow, and there is resentment and suspicion between the groups. In this climate of conflict, some Pedrano Catholics have chosen to withdraw from either organization.

Pedrano Catholics have a long history of trying to find equilibrium between a militant, or activist, position with strong and clear claims vis-à-vis the Mexican state, and a politically more cautious or conciliatory position. As described in chapter 7, conflicts over finding this balance have resulted in the secessions of those advocating more confrontational methods. Gradually, however, Las Abejas members have agreed on an antagonistic and non-collaborative stance toward the Mexican state and have refused to accept aid programs or pay for electricity. Many have also refused to send their children to public schools, instead developing a project of autonomous education with independent schools for which they received international funding for some years. The discussions on which strategies to choose have nevertheless continued, and certain issues have become sore areas of contestation between the members.

One issue concerns how to define an appropriate relationship with the municipal authorities of Chenalhó in a municipality with a continued paramilitary presence. This has centered particularly on the eventual return of the many thousands of displaced Las Abejas members after the paramilitary persecution in 1997. Many in Las Abejas aligned themselves with the posture of EZLN, believing that negotiations with the municipal authorities concerning such a return would only distort the real conflict at hand and allow the federal government to claim that there were no longer any paramilitaries in the municipality (CIEPAC 2002a). The Fray Bartolomé de Las Casas Center for Human Rights and the Jesuits working in the Chenalhó parish after the Acteal massacre have held this position—that Las Abejas should not return until all paramilitaries have been disarmed and there is no threat of further violence. Many Las Abejas members, however, have pressured the organization to bring camp living to an end. The first to go back were ninety-six displaced families from Yibeljoj that in fall 2000 decided to return to their home community. They established a new camp in the southwestern part of their former village, where they managed to obtain land. The camp gradually developed into a separate community in Yibeljoj, named "Nuevo Yibeljoj" (New Yibeljoj), with new homes, a school, and a Catholic chapel housing their new patron saint, the Virgin of Guadalupe. This return was against the explicit recommendation of their diocese advisors but with their acquiescence after the decision was made.[1] These different standpoints, some Pedranos told me, caused a rift with the diocese and Center for Human Rights, and some Catholic villagers even accused the mestizo advisors of being too comfortable, living in town, to understand the difficult conditions in the camps. But by emphasizing that the move was a "relocation" and not a "return," an agreement was reached that attempted to avoid any claim by municipal and higher governments that order and safety had been reestablished in the municipality, which was part of the official state discourse at the time.

While most Las Abejas members eventually agreed on the return of the displaced, they did not agree on the manner of accomplishing this return. To ensure the safety of those returning to their villages, Las Abejas leaders decided to engage in repeated negotiations with the municipal authorities in Chenalhó. In August 2001, a non-aggression pact, called a "treaty of mutual respect," was finally signed between Las Abejas and the PRI municipal presidency under the auspices of the Chiapas governor and officials from the federal government.[2] In fall 2001, the remaining displaced members of Las Abejas returned to their native villages. In contrast to the relocation of Yibeljoj villagers, the families now actually returned to their former homes if they had not been destroyed by the paramilitaries.[3] The treaty, which must be reaffirmed every year, initiated a process whereby some leaders of Las Abejas entered into an ongoing dialogue with the state government of Chiapas, which caused increasing distrust by others in Las Abejas (Schlittler Álvarez 2008:59).

Another, related, area of contestation has concerned the control of the municipal government. PRI is still ruling Chenalhó, but with the support of only a minority of the population since 1996. Some members of Las Abejas contend, as do the Zapatistas, that party politics, whether local or national, is a corrupt game not to be entered; they propose a boycott of all elections. On the initiative of others, nevertheless, Las Abejas put forth candidates for the municipal elections in 2001 and 2007 under the banner of PRD with a broad coalition of groups in Chenalhó, but lost both times to PRI, lacking the support of the Zapatistas. These election campaigns were criticized by other members of Las Abejas, who complained that they built on political coalitions with groups close to the paramilitaries.

The indemnity that the government paid out after the paramilitary persecution created still further tensions, since other members, considering themselves equally poor but without losses at the hands of the paramilitaries, received nothing.[4] Some members also held that the long dependence on external supplies during the years of displacement created an unhealthy orientation to outside sources of support (Schlittler Álvarez 2008:62–63).

Perhaps the most damaging disagreement, however, grew out of the negotiations with state governor Pablo Salazar during his term in office.

When Salazar became governor of Chiapas in 2000 under the banner of the PRD, he was supported by a broad coalition of parties and non-governmental associations including indigenous organizations, and there was considerable hope for change. Like many others, Las Abejas sent representatives to the negotiations initiated by the governor's administration to listen to the demands of civil associations (cf. Tavanti 2005:7–8). Las Abejas made a list of demands, ranked in order of priority, of which the first was legal justice concerning the Acteal massacre and the last were requests for public works such as roads, electricity, and water.[5] However, Salazar soon lost support from a large part of the indigenous and broader civil movement and was accused, especially by the Zapatistas, of not wanting to address the structural causes of the conflict in Chiapas and of instead creating divisions between organizations. Las Abejas members were torn over what position to take in relation to the governor. Some held that the Las Abejas representatives who handled the organization's negotiations with the Salazar administration became too enmeshed in the political game of the state and forgot to listen to their communities. The representatives were further accused of making deals with the state government, toning down the critique of the government in the monthly communiqués of Las Abejas in exchange for access to resources, and no longer giving priority to the demands for legal justice. One of my Las Abejas friends, critical of the negotiations with Salazar, said it should not be necessary to enter into this long process of negotiation and bartering to have one's request attended to; it should be enough to state one's rightful claims.

The position of those in Las Abejas who favored these negotiations, on their part, held that the government would not give anything voluntarily unless people insisted, even if those resources are their right. Furthermore, they held that those accusing them of corrupting the ideals of Las Abejas were satisfied with making public denunciations in the monthly communiqués of mainly symbolic importance. A friend from this side of Las Abejas described to me the successes negotiations with Salazar and other authorities such as the Health Ministry had achieved in bringing concrete gains to Pedrano villagers. People, he said, wanted to see real changes and were becoming discouraged by the lack of improvements.[6]

With the fracturing of Las Abejas in 2008, it was the faction proclaiming the principled position of rights demands and non-negotiation that took control of the official seat in Acteal as well as the official name, the group today regarded by most outsiders as the true Las Abejas and recognized by the Fray Bartolomé de Las Casas Center for Human Rights. The organization continues to send out highly political monthly communiqués and holds various forms of public demonstrations. One of their main demands continues to be the conviction of everyone guilty of or implicated in the Acteal massacre, and its designation as a crime of the state. The members align themselves with the broader national and international movement for social justice and against neoliberalism, denouncing, for example, the so-called Proyecto Mesoamérica—the multigovernmental project to stimulate trade and commerce, described in chapter 8—as well as various forms of human rights violations inside and outside of Mexico.

The other faction, now with the name Asociación Civil Las Abejas, moved its base to Nuevo Yibeljoj, where one of its main leaders lives. The members of this organization, like their counterparts, are also skeptical of state support and have discussed what support may or may not be accepted without risking co-optation and corruption. Most members have decided to refuse the family-oriented Oportunidades program. They do, however, accept basic state-provided services, since these are considered public necessities. Therefore, they continue to make applications to the state government of Chiapas for such services in villages where their members live, in Chenalhó and other municipalities, and have received funding, for example, for potable water, electricity, roads, schools, and housing.[7] This group has also lodged claims of hypocrisy toward the other for accepting funding and public works and thereby belying their public rhetoric. The leaders of Las Abejas in Acteal, in turn, have repeatedly accused this organization of doing the bidding of the Chiapas state governor and being part of the counter-insurgent strategy of the government.[8]

Both groups thus continue to demand large-scale social change and maintain that they have the right to government services. Both also regard the government as using co-optive strategies, offering goods to dominate and exploit the indigenous poor. They have made quite different choices, however, about how to handle this contradiction. Similar discussions of which position to take are now taking place throughout indigenous Chiapas.

The Splitting of Indigenous Chiapas

Since 1994, the year of the Zapatista uprising, many organizations have split in two, one retaining the official name, the other aggregating "independent" to the name, such as Asociación Rural de Interés Colectivo (ARIC) Independiente, to mark that the members regard it as standing free of government influence, in contrast to the other branch. Organizations and communities striving for far-reaching independence from the state often describe themselves as being "in resistance" (see, e.g., Swords 2007). For EZLN and various indigenous organizations such as Regiones Autónomas Pluriétnicas (RAP), this posture is related to the broader political project of indigenous self-determination, usually called "autonomía," implying various forms of self-governance and economic self-reliance. These autonomous projects are put into practice in spite of, and challenging, the highly limiting form of autonomy granted through the Ley de Derecho y Cultura Indígena, the legal application of the San Andrés Accords (see, e.g., Stephen 1997; Rus, Hérnandez Castillo, and Mattiace 2003; Speed 2008). The projects include autonomous political and judicial systems and the demand for the recognition of indigenous languages and cultures (e.g., Hernández Castillo 2006a). Many also try to find access to markets for their produce outside the control of transnational corporations, such as fair-trade or organic markets, sometimes through coffee or artisan cooperatives.

The most radical stance of autonomy and "resistance" is that taken by the Zapatista autonomous communities, which refuse any engagement with the state. In contrast with the years leading up to the 1994 rebellion, when Zapatistas accepted various forms of state programs directed to peasants in order to build up their forces, since 1996 the EZLN has demanded that its members reject all forms of government aid, including health programs and teachers' salaries (Barmeyer 2003; 2008:512). Instead, the Zapatistas have worked to develop far-reaching autonomous structures, including self-reliant production and trade, and certain collective forms of production and labor, partly drawing on old-

time calpul forms of community labor and taxes and forms of social security (Stahler-Sholk 2007; Barmeyer 2008). The Zapatista communities
have also tried to develop autonomous schools with volunteer teachers
recruited among villagers or international solidarity activists, and health
services offered through the visits of medical staff from, for example, the
Red Cross (Barmeyer 2003, 2008).

Economically, though, the Zapatista attempts at self-reliant structures
have mostly been insufficient to constitute reliable productive alternatives (Stahler-Sholk 2007). The schools wrestle with various problems,
dependent as they are on the rotation of local volunteers and the continuing support of Mexican and international activists offering teacher
training and materials (Barmeyer 2008:524). Thus the price of non-
acceptance of state support has been harsh for the Zapatista members,
resulting in large numbers leaving the EZLN from the late 1990s on,
deciding to accept various forms of state aid. Others have been banned
from the organization for receiving such aid (Barmeyer 2008).

Similar discussions on how to balance access to resources with political independence are found among indigenous people who have emigrated from their rural villages to San Cristóbal, the central town in the
Chiapas highlands.[9] The majority of these indigenous migrants live in
"colonias," shantytowns formed around the city center. Most or all of the
colonias that were formed after the Zapatista uprising in 1994 were created initially through land invasion (Rus and Vigil 2007). The municipal
government of San Cristóbal has generally accepted the regularization
of land holdings, paying economic compensation to the original owners and granting land titles to the new settlers, thereby also beginning
to develop access to urban infrastructure and public services. Many of
the inhabitants, however, do not want to enter into such a process of
regularization. By staying "independent," they say, not integrated legally
into the municipal bureaucracy, they will keep away from the clientelist
ties of the municipal authorities and the petitioning posture that many
regard as humiliating.[10] Furthermore, with legal titles, families begin to
sell their titles to others, which leads to new people moving in with varied
political and religious adherences, thus threatening the former unity of
the colonia. Some prefer, then, that their lots stay "unregularized" and
their colonia "independent," although this implies they will not receive

municipal public support for installations such as water supply, electricity, or school construction. Instead, the inhabitants construct their own streets or sewage system through pooled money and labor, sometimes by tapping into existing nearby electrical wiring or water pipes. Some refer to such water as "autonomous water" in Zapatista-style language, which, although ironic, contains a strong claim of having the right to such water, not accepting that the tapping be defined as a crime.

For others, however, this "independent" route is tiring after some years. First of all, they want the legal protection that a land title offers, making it possible to invest in improvements of their house and securing it for their children to inherit. Furthermore, to construct the colonia's infrastructure by themselves is costly, labor intensive, and slow. Independent, unregularized colonias are in notably worse shape than others: no paved roads, poor housing, no running water, and so on. In several neighborhoods, after ten or fifteen years as autonomous, some or most of the inhabitants have chosen to initiate the process of regularization, still, however, searching for strategies to maintain their political independence (Moksnes 2011).

Many politically organized Mayas in Chiapas contend that others are still looking for patrons to provide goods while disregarding the need for larger systemic change. A Catholic man told me in 1996: "People say that the government of Ernesto Zedillo is good, since it gives a lot of money, a lot of credits, that's what people say. 'This Samuel [Bishop Ruiz], he doesn't give anything,' they say."[11] Niels Barmeyer (2008:517) describes the complaint by a former Zapatista villager in 2001: "In her view, the EZLN had never really delivered anything of what was needed in the community and that the government was different in that respect. 'They might give only a little bit,' she explained, 'but at least they give something.'" Whether clientelist or not, the search for resources continues to guide the political choices of many families.

The autonomy-at-all-costs stance implies that EZLN and civil indigenous organizations also question participation in public elections. Maya people in Chiapas are generally skeptical toward political parties, which they often describe as uninterested in the living conditions of indigenous and poor people and as using clientelist practices, offering empty promises only to gain votes, and attempting to co-opt indigenous leaders with the (rare) offer of high-ranking offices (e.g., Hernández Castillo 2006a). Although a certain broad alliance between the PRD party and indigenous organizations has existed for some decades, this relation is shaky. While most indigenous organizations continue to make alliances with political parties before elections and encourage their members to vote, the Zapatistas usually boycott elections. Prior to the 2006 presidential elections, EZLN instigated the nationwide La Otra Campaña to mobilize the popular left in Mexico in an alternative political program instead of taking part in the elections, aiming for the writing of a new constitution.

The various positions of EZLN and indigenous organizations on how to relate to the state have deeply influenced the dynamics of the indigenous movement in Chiapas, leading to severe internal fissures. The EZLN was very critical of associations that collaborated with the Salazar state government after 2000, defining them as traitors, and has continued to hold this posture with the subsequent governors. It has condemned other organizations for cooperating with and accepting funding from federal and state institutions. Consequently, organizations that previously had a more-or-less functioning relationship with the EZLN, such as CIOAC and ARIC Independiente, are today defined as enemies. This has led to schisms and confrontations, sometimes violent, between members of these organizations and the Zapatista support bases (CIEPAC 2002b; Hernández Castillo 2006a), in addition to the ongoing antagonism that both the Zapatistas and the indigenous organizations have had with Maya villagers supporting the PRI and later, the PAN administrations. I will return to the dilemma about how to relate to the state in the last section of this chapter.

ALTERNATIVE ALLIANCES, NEW DEPENDENCIES

While many indigenous groups in Chiapas are shunning state patronage and resources, they are to some extent finding alternative support through other actors, ranging from churches, NGOs, and activist networks to multilateral institutions such as the European Union or the United Nations. These actors have in various degrees provided economic resources, access to the fair-trade markets, and other forms of support, as well as mediation with the Mexican state, its institutions and judicial system.

For Las Abejas, the alliances formed with outside NGOs after the persecutions in 1997 have been crucial but also have created new dependencies and forms of subordination. While Las Abejas received no outside funding before 1997, after the massacre it has relied heavily on such support, creating a new orientation toward "foreigners" as possible conduits to resources and other benefits (see Schlittler Álvarez 2008:60–63; cf. Speed and Leyva-Solano 2008:214). As argued by Jaime Schlittler Álvarez (2008:62–63, 68), this has led the organization to disregard its internal work with the village grassroots groups and created a distance between the leaders and regular members, which eventually gave way to the cleaving of the organization in two. To counter some of the influence of external organizations, EZLN decided on its part in 2003 that all NGO projects directed toward Zapatista communities had to be approved and coordinated by the Juntas de Buen Gobierno (Good Governance Boards) in the five Zapatista centers, called "caracoles," to ensure that the support accorded with EZLN priorities and was distributed evenly between the Zapatista communities (see, e.g., Stahler-Sholk 2007:57). For Las Abejas, similarly, all projects must secure board approval.

Furthermore, the degree of aid coming from NGOs, activist networks, and multilateral bodies is highly volatile and depends on the ebb and flow of political and ideological interest in the Maya region in the national and international arenas (cf. Bob 2005; Speed and Reyes 2005). Interest in Chiapas rose dramatically after the Zapatista rebellion in 1994 and decreased after 2000, forcing many NGOs working in the area to close various programs after some years, due to lack of funds (Benessaieh 2004; Tavanti 2005:7–8). Most of the outside funding for Las Abejas ceased in 2003, which forced them to close the autonomous schools and the women's textile cooperative, Maya Antsetik (Schlittler Álvarez 2008:63). The reasons for this decline in interest are various and could be attributed to the PRI's fall from power in 2000 and the expected democratization of the country, the switch of global attention by governments to the Muslim world after 2001, and the declining role that the often-silent Zapatistas and the increasingly complex indigenous political scene in Chiapas played in the anti-neoliberal movement (Benessaieh 2004; Tavanti 2005).

The dependence on international support groups is not only economic but implies an ideological adherence that sets the framework for how Pedrano Catholics can articulate their concerns and objectives. While the appropriation by Las Abejas members of global discourses on rights and indigenous ethnicity has offered them important tools for political agency, it also implies a kind of conformist integration, the members accepting that these discourses are granted relevance and legitimacy while others are silenced or disregarded. This becomes particularly clear in interactions with international organizations. In order for Las Abejas to receive funding for projects, or political support for their actions, it must be aware of and affirm, at least ostensibly, the ideals and priorities of the corresponding NGOs (cf. Gledhill 2003:215). Naturally, since the NGOs were attracted to Las Abejas in the first place because of its politico-religious stance, they already share certain values and frames of reference. Notwithstanding, these NGOs, together with the diocese clergy, have exerted considerable influence on the work and objectives of Las Abejas, such as enforcing its pro-Zapatista stance, its goal of gender equality, and its use of pacifist resistance—for example, holding sit-ins in front of military camps (see Tavanti 2003:145, 182). Such influence possibly even led to the radicalization of the organization and its posture critical of any state interaction, which eventually led to the splitting of Las Abejas. While these translocal discourses are well-received among some segments of Las Abejas members, perhaps especially, as Schlittler Álvarez notes (2008:61), the young and influential bilingual generation, they alienate other members, he argues. Barmeyer describes a similar dissociation in Zapatista communities, where the involvement and presence of foreigners and urban mestizos have made it difficult for villagers to identify with the projects and take an active part in their implementation (Barmeyer 2008:524; see also Baronnet 2008:120).

One important aspect on which Las Abejas members and the various supporting organizations agree is the shared construct of the martyrdom of those killed in the massacre, who are considered subjects of oppression, killed because of their fight for change. Among transnational activist and Christian organizations, this identification of Las Abejas with martyrdom has been a powerful tool for mobilization (cf. Keck and Sikkink 1998). The identity position of martyrdom, however, holds a difficult proximity to that of victimhood and its concomitant associations with pity and passive neediness. Although the members of Las Abejas talk of the martyrs as giving strength to their struggle, the continuous emphasis on the massacre also reinforces a petitioning stance of the members, asking for compassion and aid (cf. Schlittler Álvarez 2008:49–50). This stance has oriented the relationship of Las Abejas members to international visitors and organizations to a high degree—as those who can offer support.

The emphasis on "unique" martyrdom might also be hindering Las Abejas members' development of strong mutual cooperation with other indigenous organizations in Chiapas and Mexico. The group continues to relate primarily to mestizo-dominated groups in the neo-Zapatista network—the organizations that support the Zapatista demands. Possibly, of course, a horizontal collaboration with other indigenous organizations would provide less assurance of loyal support and protection, which the members still find they sorely need, especially in the absence of state funding.

EXODUS

So, then, what are the possibilities for Pedrano Catholics to find Exodus, becoming freed from poverty and suffering? Through the Catholic community and Las Abejas, many have found a sense of hope for change. In this hope, they have gained strength and determination, demanding a Mexico with room for themselves and their children. But since these efforts so far have provided little, if any, real material improvements, hope is wavering for many. This is exacerbated by the increased difficulty in securing a livelihood, with diminishing state programs and access to land. Some of my formerly energetic friends in Chenalhó are growing old with tired and disillusioned eyes.

Most members of Las Abejas and other indigenous organizations hold that their position as politically and economically marginalized citizens can only change with a different form of governmental regime, one that promotes social justice (see Kenney 2007). Since such a change is unlikely to take place anytime soon, some have opted for the position of autonomy, creating spheres where they can exert independent political agency. They are part of a growing number of social actors in Mexico and elsewhere who strive to stand independently from the state, articulating alternative political agendas (Hernández Castillo 2006a; Stahler-Sholk, Vanden, and Kuecker 2007; Speed 2008; Stahler-Sholk and Vanden 2011).

Some observers laud this position and find that it holds democratic potential with the promise of substantive global change. As such, these organizations can be described as part of the "place-based" resistance that Arturo Escobar (2004) argues constitutes a growing counter-hegemonic globalization based on subaltern practices of difference, enacting visions of an alternative global order that moves beyond the failed project of modernity.

Others ask what prospects this route has for accomplishing actual and long-term changes in people's living conditions. Will the posture in the long run only marginalize indigenous organizations further? David Chandler (2004) criticizes the autonomy posture as one of "political refusal rather than political participation," which, he argues, leads to only marginal global political impact. While keeping organizations from being "tamed" through interaction with the state, it is also, he argues, a choice to not challenge governing power. In the case of the Zapatistas, Chandler (2004:327) holds that the "rhetoric of global resistance coexists with a remarkable failure of the struggle to achieve any relief from abject poverty for the indigenous villagers of the area."

I cannot but wonder if the strict position of Las Abejas and the Zapatistas of non-acceptance of state support would look different if there had been more local discussions on how to press for economic rights and in what forms these rights can legitimately be granted. As described earlier, the various NGOs in Chiapas have not developed procedures for pressing such claims, but have been generally highly critical of organizations accepting government support. Instead, like various indigenous organizations, they have concentrated on the demands for civil and political rights and the rights of indigenous peoples to self-determination. But local self-determination on the whole provides few answers to the issues of poverty and economic marginalization; most Mayas in Chiapas live on land both meager and scarce, inadequate to provide sustainable self-sufficiency. Authors such as Nancy Fraser (2003:2) argue that without well-articulated and organized demands for economic change, "today's struggles for recognition" may be "serving to displace . . . struggles for egalitarian redistribution." She argues that the tension between struggles for recognition, expressed through identity politics, versus struggles for redistribution, "has dovetailed all too neatly with a hegemonic neoliberalism that wants nothing more than to repress the memory of socialist egalitarianism" (Fraser 2003:3).

The question, though, is what impact the organized demands for economic rights by Las Abejas and others might have when "democracy" has become a "small idea," no longer intended to have much effect on economic governance, as discussed in the introduction (Comaroff and Comaroff 1997:126). Neoliberal governance displaces not only the demands for economic justice, but also the economic sphere itself, to a sphere largely outside state governance. Thus, it "calls into question the strategy of gaining influence over the state in order to address economic hardships" (Shefner 2008:200). This, then, constitutes the trap that men and women of Las Abejas, and others, find themselves in.

In recent years, the notion of Exodus for a growing number of Pedrano Catholics has been transformed from a political project to one of migration. Seeing no actual improvements in their lives despite their long struggle, and with an urgent need to find actual means to support their families, more and more are emigrating today to distant cities or the United States in search of income. This is also the overall trend among Mayas in Chiapas, as well as among poor and middle-class mestizos. In 2008 alone, an estimated 136,000 persons migrated from Chiapas to the United States.[12] In spite of the severe difficulties of living as undocumented migrants, some 80 percent of the migrants never return (Pickard 2006). Jan Rus (2010:209) states that according to most observers, "since the Revolution of 1910 there has never been such a mass exodus from any Mexican state." The remittances migrants sent back to Chiapas were in 2009 about $712 million,[13] constituting a fundamental part of the economy for both the receiving families and the state of Chiapas. While most Pedrano Catholics still stay put in Chenalhó and Chiapas, they all now have relatives and friends who have taken the option that today appears to hold the most promise for escaping poverty: exit. For Pedranos like my host Mariano Pérez Sántiz, who so assertively told me during my early days in Chenalhó that their Exodus was a liberation from oppression that was to take place in their own lands, this is an immense tragedy. Today he, like many others, ponders whether he should advise his children to leave Chiapas and Mexico.

This mass migration is a testament to the failures of Mexican politics. It also expresses that many young Mayas, like poor people everywhere, are deciding they cannot accept the conditions their parents had to endure and instead are trying to take part in better opportunities offered elsewhere. In several U.S. cities today, they create loose-knit communities of migrant Mayas that help them deal with the challenges of living as migrants.[14] For people in the Chiapas highlands, the consequences of the failed government politics remain to be seen.

Notes

INTRODUCTION

1. Field notes, July 29, 1995.

2. The official name of the municipality today is Chenalhó, but it is still commonly referred to as San Pedro Chenalhó.

3. Costumbre theology is of course influenced by centuries of Catholicism. However, in accordance with emic terminology and for the sake of clarity, I use "Catholic" only to refer to those who have actively "converted" in the last decades and distinguish themselves from practitioners of costumbre religion.

4. Certainly, not all social movements employ rights discourses; see, for example, Ong 2006 on the preference for other expressions among Southeast Asian movements.

5. More-classic forms of political protest, such as labor and peasant movements, are also based on the articulation of collective identities but rarely demand the right "to be different."

6. With the start of the twenty-first century, parties allied with popular movements gained the presidency in several Latin American countries with programs contesting this neoliberal governance. The actual scope of alternative political routes is yet to be seen.

7. Hirschl's (2000) study was a quantitative-qualitative analysis of national high-court rulings involving the interpretation of human rights in New Zealand, Canada, and Israel, including all court cases since the constitutionalization of human rights in each country (1990, 1982, and 1992 respectively).

8. Interview with Margarito Ruiz Hernández, president of the indigenous organization Frente Independiente de Pueblos Indios (FIPI), October 1992.

9. Even the San Andrés Accords have been considered quite weak and insufficient in their development of indigenous political representation on regional and national levels (Diaz-Polanco 1998; Ruiz Hernández 2002).

10. Amnesty International (2010) reports a large increase in human rights

violations related to the Mexican government's combat against organized crime and the drug cartels, a development that has since only escalated.

11. E.g., March 12, 1975, letter to "Presidente del tribunal sup[remo] de Justicia, Palacio de Justicia, Tuxtla Gutiérrez, Chiapas," signed by nineteen members of Union Mexicana del Séptimo Día, protesting the arrest of their pastor, Domingo López Ángel (copy in possession of the author). Receiving little support from state authorities, the expelled villagers formed organizations, of which the largest and most militant was, and continues to be, Consejo de Representantes Indígenas de los Altos de Chiapas (CRIACH), constituted in 1984.

12. Cf. field notes, 1985–86.

13. Field notes, October 1992.

14. See, for example, the demands the Zapatistas submitted during the February 1994 dialogue: http://flag.blackened.net/revolt/mexico/ezln/ccri_di_demand_mar94.html (accessed February 26, 2012), or http://palabra.ezln.org.mx/ (accessed December 30, 2011).

15. The Independent Front of Indigenous Peoples (FIPI) and the Pluralistic National Indigenous Assembly for Autonomy (ANIPA) are both national umbrella groups of indigenous organizations. An estimated 15 to 20 percent of the Mexican population is indigenous, belonging to more than fifty-six language groups, and they reside all through the country, though the majority live in impoverished regions of the southern states. It is also there one can find the strongest indigenous organizations.

16. The SIPAZ (2001) document quotes a publication by Anaya Gallardo et al. (2000).

17. Bellinghausen refers to a study by Sierra Guzmán (2003).

18. In a May 4, 1999, telegram sent to U.S. Defense Intelligence Agency headquarters in Washington, D.C., the U.S. Defense Attaché Office in Mexico states that "army human intelligence teams were involved in training and supporting Chiapas indigenous armed groups." The telegram also holds, among other things, that "by mid-1994 the Mexican army had presidential approval to institute military teams in charge of promoting armed groups in the conflictive areas of Chiapas. The intent was to assist local indigenous personnel in resisting the Zapatista National Liberation Army (EZLN). Moreover, during the December 1997 Acteal massacre, army intelligence officers were involved in overseeing armed groups in the highlands of Los Altos, in Chiapas." The document was released in 2009 to the National Security Archives, a nonprofit organization at George Washington University, under the Freedom of Information Act. The telegram and a brief report from the National Security Archives are available at: www.gwu.edu/~nsarchiv/NSAEBB/NSAEBB283/index.htm (accessed December 30, 2011).

19. I have chosen not to offer much detail on the discourse and identity of

the nuns and other clergy of the diocese in order to avoid providing information that could be used against them, a precaution they asked of me.

20. The politico-religious map was drawn by a middle-aged man who wishes to be anonymous; he knew the lineage names for all villagers except women who had married into the village from other communities. With the lineage names, the map also became a map of kinship relations and showed which patrilines held large areas of adjacent houses and which had "segmented."

21. I was not allowed to pay for my lodging and meals, so I always brought back beans and other staples on my trips to San Cristóbal and tried to reciprocate in other ways the hospitality I was shown.

22. Like many other catechists who had received lessons on hygiene from the pastoral workers, my host had introduced his wife to the habit of boiling the drinking water for at least twenty minutes, which eased the strain on my Western stomach.

23. See chapter 7 for this division between Chenalhó Catholics. For closer descriptions of Zapatista Catholics, see Eber 1998, 2000, 2001a.

CHAPTER 1. POVERTY, MAYA COMMUNITY, AND THE STATE

1. Exceptions are the members of the semi-autonomous community of Santa Marta, who hold a separate ethnic identity. A number of Chamulas also live in Chenalhó, especially around the municipal center.

2. Interview in Spanish with Sebastián Jiménez, June 16, 1996.

3. Interview in Tzotzil with Lucía Gutiérrez Pérez, May 28, 1996.

4. Interview in Tzotzil with Rosa Pérez Sántiz and Rosa Sántiz Pérez, May 27, 1996.

5. Interview in Tzotzil with Manuel Pérez Sántiz, August 10, 1995.

6. Until the much-debated change to Article 27 of the constitution in 1992, it was not possible to sell ejido land to outsiders. Pedranos could until then buy ejido or communal land only if they became active members of the community in question and participated in the collective work and responsibilities.

7. Interviews in Tzotzil with María Sántiz, June 6, 1996, and Pedro Pérez Jiménez, June 16, 1996.

8. Programa de Desarrollo del Estado de Chiapas (PRODESCH) was founded in 1970 "to coordinate state, federal, and international development efforts in Chiapas" (G. Collier and Quaratiello 1999:62).

9. Before 1936, federal and state elections were taken care of by the mestizo municipal secretary, who filled out the ballots without involving Pedranos (Rus 1994:274). The municipal government of Chenalhó continued to be chosen by Pedrano elite authorities until the 1960s, when popular voting gradually became the norm (Arias 1985:121).

10. Interview in Spanish with Vicente Vázquez, April 22, 1996. The state party was initially called Partido Nacional Revolucionario (PNR) and was created in the 1920s by the elite who held power after the Mexican Revolution. In 1937 the party name was changed to Partido Revolucionario Mexicano (PRM), and in 1946, to Partido Revolucionario Institucional (PRI), which is also the label Vázquez used. The PRI remained in power until 2000.

11. Interview in Spanish with Antonio Vázquez, May 12, 1998.

12. See also Siverts (1965) and Gómez Ramírez (1991) on Oxchuc; Guiteras Holmes (1947, 1992) on Cancuc; Nash (1970) on Amatenango; and Gossen (1974), Pozas (1987), and Rus (2002) on Chamula.

13. The quotation refers to the conclusions made in the Viking Fund Seminar on Middle American Ethnology held by Sol Tax and Robert Redfield in 1949, which gathered the most influential anthropologists of the period working in that area.

14. For overviews of the discussions on the defining characteristics of the Mesoamerican subdivision system, see Hunt and Nash 1967; Mulhare 1996a, 1996b; Nutini 1996. There is limited data about social organization in Chiapas before Spanish colonization, but Calnek (1962:9, 27–31) describes how the small Maya highland states consisted of capital towns with surrounding subordinate towns and adherent villages, each social unit with ties to patron deities who offered special protection to the members, creating a "strong personalistic sense of relationship linking a community and its patron." Patron deities were often mountain deities and other nature-associated deities, manifested in caves, springs, or rivers, and caves were common sites for religious ceremonies, sometimes including sacrificial bloodletting (Calnek 1962:53–57; Megged 1996:5, 115). Ceremonies to deities at caves, springs, and hilltops are reported also in colonial documents (e.g., Wasserstrom 1983:78, 102–103; Vos 1994:203). For centuries, the subdivisions (calpuls) were used as units by the colonial administration for the extraction of taxes paid in labor, commodities, and other forms. An official from each calpul was responsible for collecting the tribute from the families of their section (Sherman 1979:299; Wasserstrom 1983).

15. The Spanish colonizers appear to have made Chenalhó (earlier called San Pedro Chinalhó) as well as Santa María Magdalena Tanjoveltik and Santa Marta Chupic (or Xolotepec) the political and religious capitals for the subdivisions that were affiliated with them. The latter two entities became semidependent parts of Chenalhó in the early twentieth century (Garza Caligaris 2002:59; cf. Calnek 1970). Magdalena became an independent municipality in 1999 with the name Aldama. Information on how the calpul units in Chenalhó were organized during the twentieth century is scant. I rely mainly on the invaluable monographs by Calixta Guiteras Holmes (1961) and Jacinto Arias (1985), a Pedrano anthropologist. I also interviewed two Pedranos, Sebastián Gómez (May 4–5, 1998) and Antonio Vázquez (May 12, 1998), who had considerable

historical knowledge acquired from their own interviews with elders. Few other Pedranos I spoke to were acquainted with the concept of calpul.

16. The figures vary, because sometimes only villages holding municipal agencies are counted, and other times sections, called barrios, of villages are also counted if they are large or semi-independent units.

17. In contrast to Guiteras, Vázquez said that when he was born in 1962, there were only five calpuls. These were Chojolhó, Taquiuc'um, Yabteclum, Polhó, and Tzanembolom.

18. There is little data on the extent to which calpul leadership was based on kinship. Gómez held that further back in time, calpuls were governed by leaders called *totil-me'il*, "father-mother," who held both political and spiritual powers (see also Guiteras Holmes 1961:163). Guiteras Holmes (1961:317) holds that the *totil-me'il* leadership had already disappeared after the so-called Caste War in highland Chiapas in 1868–70. *Totil-me'il* is also the term for ancestral deities (cf. Vogt 1969, 1976, on Zinacantán). For a similar leadership term and concept in Momostenango, Guatemala, see Tedlock (1992:74), and among the pre-colonial Quiché, see Carmack (1981:63).

19. "Principal" was the generic term ascribed by the early Spanish colonists to a person of the Maya nobility (Calnek 1962:89). Guiteras Holmes (1961:65) holds that the term "principal" was the name of "the special tax paid to the Royal Treasury."

20. The two calpuls formerly bore the names San Pedro Kukulhó and San Pedro Chenalhó, but it is unclear which was which (cf. Guiteras Holmes 1961:65; Arias 1985:119).

21. Arias (1985:119) says that the two calpuls practiced "reciprocal marriage exchange," which contradicts Guiteras Holmes as well as oral accounts by Vázquez and Gómez.

22. Since 1915, when Chenalhó became an independent municipality, the ruling body has consisted of the constitutionally required offices of municipal president, secretary, and judge, currently for three-year terms, which are the highest authorities both within Chenalhó and in relation to the outside (Guiteras Holmes 1961:19). It also has year-long civil offices such as "regidores," and religious cargos responsible for the celebrations of the saints, developed from the colonial "cofradías." Cargo positions are taken by married couples, the husband and wife having distinct functions. Pedranos often describe a cargo as a service to the whole community, but it is costly and often puts the couple in debt. However, pasados who once held prestigious cargos gain considerable status. In Spanish, the municipal government is called "ayuntamiento municipal." In Chenalhó, a cargo is called *ab'tel patan* (work contribution) or *nichim ab'tel* (flowery work) in Tzotzil, the latter referring to the cargos for the saints. The authorities of the municipal government are called *j-abtel jpatanetik*. For descriptions of the structure and tasks of the cargo system in Chenalhó, see Guiteras Holmes 1961,

Arias 1985, Köhler 1990, and Eber 2000. See Garza Caligaris 2002, and Rus and Wasserstrom 1980 for critical discussions on historical origin and changes.

23. Interviews with Sebastián Gómez (May 4–5, 1998) and Antonio Vázquez (May 12, 1998).

24. The term *mixa* stems from "misa," Spanish for "mass." The linkage to such divine protectors and the enactment of rituals maintaining these relationships varies between communities and over time. It appears that most local communities have established a relation to "local" deities such as *anjels* or the Earth Lord. For data from recent decades, see, e.g., Hunt and Nash (1967) and Laughlin (1969) for regional overviews; Pérez López and Ramírez Méndez (1985) and Köhler (1995:17–18 and n6) on Chalchihuitán; Vogt (1969, 1976) on Zinacantán, Pozas (1987:230) and Gossen (1999:16, 183–85) on Chamula; Gómez Ramírez (1991:163–70) on Oxchuc; Guiteras Holmes (1992:126–28) on Cancuc; Hunt and Nash (1967:257) on Tenejapa; and Nash (1970) on Amatenango.

25. Letter from Sebastián Gómez, September 1999. The deity Anjel is also called Ojov, "Owner," and owns and controls the mountains, caves, and springs, which are considered sacred gateways to the divine. See Köhler (1995:123–25) and Vogt (1969:302) for a discussion of the linguistic and theological origins of the term *anjel*. Mountain deities and similar divine guardians are also found among highland Mayas in Guatemala (e.g., Watanabe 1990; Köhler 1995:124; Wilson 1995). To facilitate comprehension, I am pluralizing *anjel* in English fashion: *anjels*.

26. There is also a notion of a less powerful masculine Earth Lord, as among neighboring Tzotzil peoples, who assumes a mestizo-like appearance and may force Pedranos to serve him (Eber 2000:251). For a discussion on Tzotzil gendered deities and the tension between male and female principles, see Rosenbaum (1993) on Chamula, and Wilson (1995:66).

27. Interview in Spanish with Sebastián Gómez, May 5, 1998.

28. The ceremony is also called *toy anjel* or *toy vits*, "praise the *anjel*" or "praise the mountain."

29. Some villages in Chenalhó have their own patron saints, celebrated with yearly festivals: the semi-independent community of Santa Marta, the former capital Yabteclum, and all the ejidos, which acquired their saints when they were founded.

30. Combined data from Arias (1985, 1994), Pérez Pérez (1992), Pineda (1995), CDHFBC (1998a), Melel Xojobal (1998–2001), and an interview with Cristóbal Sántiz Pérez, May 27, 1996.

31. Municipal-level meeting of Las Abejas Sociedad Civil, October 26, 1995.

32. Told to me by the uncle of the family in May 1998.

33. I have no data on when the office of municipal agent was introduced in Chenalhó. In neighboring Chalchihuitán, it was introduced in 1969–70 (Pérez López and Ramírez Méndez 1985:41). In 1998, sixty-two villages in Chenalhó had municipal agencies (Procuraduría General de la República 1998).

34. Interview in Spanish with Agustín Vázquez, June 16, 1996. See also Modiano 1990:182; Rockwell 1994; and Alfonseca 2005.

35. According to Vázquez, up to 1994, the teachers were those who in practice ran the communal assemblies.

36. On the exclusion of women from the public political sphere, see chapter 5.

37. Thus, the election of local officials is not open to women. Women participate in the today anonymous elections for municipal, state, and federal offices.

38. Interview in Tzotzil with Rosa Pérez Sántiz, together with Rosa Sántiz Pérez, May 27, 1996.

39. Interview in Tzotzil with Roberto Arias, June 7, 1996.

40. Instituto Nacional para el Federalismo y el Desarrollo Municipal 2003.

41. Although the conflict tends to be presented as one between teacher and campesino sympathizers, I do not know to what extent the opposition also was directed at the Arias family, who totally dominated the municipal presidency in the 1970s.

42. Arias (1994); Aubry and Inda (1997a); and interviews with María Sántiz, June 6, 1996 (in Tzotzil), Mariano Pérez Sántiz, May 8, 1996, and José Vázquez, May 15, 1998 (both in Spanish).

43. The official name was Partido del Frente Cardenista de Reconstrucción Nacional.

44. The figures were 13,522 in 1970 and 30,680 in 1990. See, e.g., INEGI 1992; Viqueira 1995:223–24.

45. In the 1995 municipal elections, only 21 percent of Pedranos voted for the PRI. In state and federal elections in 1994 and 2000, the PRI received only a minority of the votes in Chenalhó (35 percent of the votes in 2000.) Figures from Alianza Cívica.

46. Although various opposition groups have sprung up throughout the municipality, most have emerged in the northeastern, *olon*, section. This may be due to longstanding rivalry between the two sections; some Pedranos speak of people in the *k'ajal* section as more loyal to the municipal center, located in *k'ajal*. Furthermore, *olon* is the location of most ejidos, which are relatively politically independent from the municipal government.

47. The Acteal masacre and the factionalism that led up to it are described in detail in chapter 7.

48. Interview in Tzotzil with Rosa Pérez Sántiz, together with Rosa Sántiz Pérez, May 27, 1996.

CHAPTER 2. BUILDING ALLIANCES WITH THE CATHOLIC DIOCESE

1. Before 1957, the entire state of Chiapas was one diocese, seated in San Cristóbal de Las Casas. Only thirteen priests served the entire area (CENAMI

2000). In 1957 and 1964, separate dioceses were created for Tapachula and Tuxtla Gutiérrez, respectively, areas in which the majority of the population is mestizo. The Diocese of San Cristóbal de Las Casas, where Ruiz became bishop in 1960, covers the highlands and eastern lowlands, serving principally an impoverished Maya peasant population.

2. Unbaptized infants risk soul loss, regarded among Pedranos, especially those of "costumbre" religion, as a cause of illness, and if not restored, possibly death (see, e.g., Guiteras Holmes 1961; Arias 1975; Eber 2000). For a thorough discussion of Maya incorporation and interpretation of Catholic symbolism, see Early 2006 and 2012.

3. The previous bishop, Lucio Torreblanca, had also worked with some indigenous lay people, but their role and training were not formalized (Ruiz García 1993:29).

4. Besides the Hermanas del Divino Pastor, the diocese turned to the Hermanos Maristas (Marist Brothers) to establish the schools (Fazio 1994:78). In the years to follow, they founded six schools in the region, some intended specifically for the education of women catechists (CENAMI 2000).

5. Interview in Spanish with Pedro Girón, March 31, 1996.

6. Interview in Spanish with Esther Lorenzana, Hermanas del Divino Pastor, October 26, 1995.

7. Seven pastoral teams exist in the Diocese of San Cristóbal de Las Casas: Center, CHAB (Chilón, Arena, Bajachón), Chol, Tzeltal, Tzotzil, South, and Southeast. The Tzotzil team covers twelve parishes.

8. Interview with Padre Orlando, San Cristóbal, April 2, 1986 (see also Harvey 1998:73).

9. Besides deacons, there is also a high number of so-called "pre-deacons" ("prediáconos") in the diocese, that is, deacons-in-training, who carry out special tasks within the parish.

10. Interview with Felipe Arizmendi, "Arizmendi: Sueño con una diócesis con mayoría de sacerdotes indígenas," MOCEUP, April 19, 2008, available at: www.moceop.net/spip.php?article=469 (accessed January 2, 2012).

11. The two groups of lay nuns are Hermanas Autóctonas del Divino Pastor and Tsebetic Comunidad de Indígenas Misioneras. The former has an independent "convent" adjacent to the convent of the Hermanas del Divino Pastor in the neighborhood of La Nueva Primavera in San Cristóbal. The diocese recognizes and supports the groups to some extent, but their situation is rather precarious, since they have no order to grant them status or to support their livelihood, work expenses, and training. The members support themselves by horticulture and selling handicrafts.

12. The initiative for the First Indigenous Conference came from the state government to celebrate the five hundredth anniversary of the birth of Fray Bar-

tolomé de Las Casas, the first bishop in Chiapas, but Bishop Ruiz changed the focus of the meeting.

13. The literature on liberation theology in Latin America is vast. See, for example, Barreiro 1984, Berryman 1987, Boff and Boff 1993, Gutiérrez 1996. For case studies, see, for example, Lancaster 1988, Hewitt 1991, Levine 1992, Levine and Stoll 1997.

14. I never heard the term "*tijwanej*" in Chenalhó, where the method was referred to instead as the introduction of the "questions." See chapter 3 for a detailed discussion of how Catholic Pedranos perceive and employ the method.

15. Interview in Spanish with Pedrano catechist Antonio Vázquez, October 9, 1995.

16. Although Pueblo Creyente is ecumenical, including Protestants as well, the majority are Catholic and the association is a recognized part of the diocese structure (see Kovic 2005).

17. The human rights focus of the diocese was further propelled by its extensive engagement to assist the thousands of Guatemalan Maya refugees who fled to Chiapas from government and paramilitary persecution during the early 1980s (Kovic 2005:62–63; Speed 2008:41).

18. The Fray Bartolomé de Las Casas Center for Human Rights became an independent association in 1996. It is still, however, commonly associated with the diocese by indigenous villagers and others.

19. Quote is from the CDHFBC website: www.frayba.org.mx/sobre_nosotros .php?hl=en (accessed January 3, 2012).

20. Interview in Spanish with one of the first human rights committee members, Sebastián Gómez, October 1995.

21. Course in Human Rights, Yabteclum, April 19–20, 1996.

22. Miguel Chanteau was the eighth priest expelled from the diocese since the Zapatista uprising in 1994 (Paulson 1998). With the change of presidential administration, Chanteau was again permitted to enter the country in 2001 and took up residence in San Cristóbal.

23. Although moving away from Chiapas after his retirement, Samuel Ruiz continued to be regarded by Catholic Mayas as a close ally and protector. After he died on January 24, 2011, his body was brought to San Cristóbal de Las Casas, where mass was held in his honor in the cathedral, filled to its brim by Mayas and mestizos who wanted to show their respect. He was buried the following day in San Cristóbal.

24. The pilgrimage also protested the multigovernmental financial project called Plan Puebla Panamá, today known as Proyecto Mesoamérica. In the concluding mass, Bishop Arizmendi spoke against the PPP project (Henríquez 2002).

25. The newspaper *Expreso Chiapas*, May 7, 2009.

26. Interview in Spanish with Sebastián Gómez, October 1995.

27. Ibid.

28. Interview in Tzotzil with Juan Sántiz, June 6, 1996.

29. Licenciado—a person who has passed the academic exam of "licenciatura," comparable to a bachelor's degree—is commonly used by Maya peasants to refer to any person considered to be educated and having a prestigious profession.

30. Meeting of Las Abejas, Sociedad Civil, October 26, 1995.

CHAPTER 3. SEEKING GOD'S PROTECTION

1. During my fieldwork in 1995–96, about one hundred fifty catechists were working in the municipality in the Catholic group affiliated with the diocese (i.e., not including the Zapatista Catholics, who had separated from the diocese). The catechists were leading around three thousand followers in thirty-eight village chapel groups.

2. Like other Mayas, Pedrano Catholics also celebrate the Day of the Dead the first two days of November, although some have stopped making home altars with food gifts for deceased family members.

3. This number, based on information from a catechist, included family members who did not regularly attend chapel meetings. Between fifty and eighty persons attended each Sunday service during my stay.

4. In November 1997, most of the Catholics in Yibeljoj were forced by paramilitaries to leave the community; they lived as displaced people in a large camp in the X'oyep village until October 2000 (see chapter 7).

5. The Spanish lyrics are: "Tu eres señor, nuestro pastor/De los pobres y humillados defensor/Tu eres señor, nuestro pastor/Vas con nosotros, no hay nada de temer."

6. The diocese does not follow the universal Catholic liturgical calendar but has elected texts that it considers most accessible and fitting for the Maya communities, principally the Gospels but also other texts from the New Testament.

7. In both Tzotzil and Spanish, it was called "complementación."

8. See chapter 4 for a fuller description of the catechists' various leadership functions.

9. Sunday service in Yibeljoj, April 28, 1996.

10. Interview in Tzotzil with Rosa Sántiz Pérez, May 21, 1996.

11. On the similar importance of fasting in the broader Maya region, and also in pre-colonial times, see Early 1983:188.

12. The nun working in Chenalhó during my stay appeared slightly uncomfortable with people's strong belief in the potency of prayer but emphasized that praying for the sick is sacramental and very positive. She added that sometimes the sick would even be healed on account of their strong faith.

13. The Spanish expression "la Palabra de Dios" (the Word of God) is used commonly by the diocese.

14. *Diccionario tzotzil de San Andrés* (Hurley and Ruiz 1986).

15. Letter in Spanish from Mariano Pérez Sántiz, July 19, 1999.

16. Interview in Spanish with Sebastián Jiménez, June 16, 1996.

17. Interview in Tzotzil with Juan Sántiz, June 6, 1996.

18. Interview in Tzotzil with Marcela Vázquez Pérez, June 3, 1996.

19. Interview in Tzotzil with María Pérez Gómez, May 21, 1996.

20. Interview in Tzotzil with Rosa Sántiz Pérez, May 21, 1996.

21. Interview in Spanish with Sebastián Jiménez, June 16, 1996.

22. Interview in Tzotzil, May 1996. In case he might be embarrassed by this quote, I do not give his name.

23. Interview in Tzotzil with Lucía Gutiérrez Pérez, May 28, 1996.

24. During my fieldwork, the answers were kept on file at the nun's monastery, their use to be decided upon eventually.

25. Sunday service in Yibeljoj, April 28, 1996. The Tzotzil kinship terms the catechist uses are standard terms of address to co-Pedranos, denoting gender and relative age.

26. Pastoral workers have also attempted to influence the converts on issues such as nutrition, hygiene, Western healthcare and housing. Many creyentes have resisted many of these teachings, which are less clearly linked to the Bible.

27. See chapter 8 for how this emphasis on sacrificial suffering after the Acteal massacre in 1997 has evolved into the cultivation of martyrdom.

28. Although most Catholics appear to have entered the chapel group together with other families of their patriline, actual conversion was usually described as an independent decision of one's own family.

29. *Alemán* (German) is the old term used in Spanish and Tzotzil for white foreigners. It originally referred to the many Germans who owned plantations in the Sierra Madre region since the late nineteenth century, where many highland Maya men have worked. The term is becoming replaced today by "gringo."

30. Interview in Spanish with Agustín Sántiz Jiménez, October 1995.

31. E.g., interview in Tzotzil with Antonio Cuchillo Pérez, October 9, 1995. See also Pérez Pérez 1992:108.

32. In municipalities such as Chamula, municipal leaders have employed a religious discourse, accusing the converts of being against the "traditions" of their people, to maintain, also, political and economic control (e.g., Kovic 2005).

33. CENAMI is the National Center for Assistance to the Indigenous Missions, based in Mexico City.

CHAPTER 4. ORGANIZATION OF THE CATHOLIC COMMUNITY AND LAS ABEJAS

1. The full name, since the split is, "La Organización de la Sociedad Civil Las Abejas." The other faction has taken the name "Asociación Civil Las Abejas"

and has its seat in Nuevo Yibeljoj. The division of Las Abejas is described in more detail in chapter 9.

2. With a total population of about 500 adults in 1996, there were 39 different lineages in Yibeljoj in a total of 210 houses. The village had five barrios (village sections), three of which were dominated by a few large lineages, while the other two barrios were characterized by a conglomerated pattern with many lineages and not many large lineage compounds, possibly indicating that these barrios are more recently formed. In Chenalhó, as in many other highland Maya societies, descent is patrilineal, and the lineages are strictly exogamic.

3. The basis for my argument, besides general observations during fieldwork, is the politico-religious "map," described in the introduction, which I made together with a person from Yibeljoj. I have omitted any tables or other detailed information in this book since I use the actual name of the village.

4. A household, represented by a house, is the smallest localized unit of a patriline. All members of a household are usually members of the same religious or political faction. I will therefore refer to "houses" in the following descriptions of group affiliation.

5. The members of each patrilineage in Chenalhó carry a Tzotzil surname inherited from the father (for limited exceptions, see Guiteras Holmes 1961:69–70 and Pérez Pérez 1992:126), but these names are no longer used in official documents. A house is often referred to with the name of the patriline; the house of my hosts was called *sna' Nichim*, the house of Nichim.

6. A vast majority of the Catholic houses resided in two barrios, with eighteen and twenty-one houses respectively, and ten in the third barrio. In no barrio did the Catholic houses form a connected area of several lineages, in contrast to the Presbyterians and the Zapatistas in their respective barrios.

7. Interview in Spanish with Pedro Girón, March 31, 1996; cf. Guiteras Holmes 1961:65–66.

8. Interview in Tzotzil with Martha Pérez Sántiz, together with Marcela Pérez Sántiz and Antonia Ruiz Pérez, June 11, 1996.

9. See Kovic (2005:40) on the similar role of catechists as moral authorities and conflict mediators among Tzotzil Catholics in the outskirts of San Cristóbal.

10. Personal communication with Pedrano Catholics, October 2008.

11. Usually fifty to eighty regular catechists, of whom fifteen to twenty-five were women, attended the catechist meetings during my stay.

12. Most of the area groups use the Yabteclum center as a place to hold meetings and training, often under the guidance of a pastoral worker.

13. The cooks are Catholic village women who take turns coming to the center to make tortillas and other food. For the construction of the center, important support came from French volunteer work crews and donations, provided through the parish priest Miguel Chanteau and his contacts in France.

14. See chapter 7 for an account of the formation of Las Abejas in 1992 and the subsequent development of the organization.

15. Interview in Tzotzil with Marcela Vázquez Pérez, June 3, 1996.

16. Personal communication with Las Abejas members, October 2008. See also Schlittler Álvarez (2008:54).

17. Personal communication with Las Abejas members, October 2008.

18. See www.peaceanddiversity.org.au/ (accessed January 8, 2012).

19. OSECAPIACH stands for Organización de Salud, Educación y Capacitación de Apoyo por los Promotores Indígenas de los Altos de Chiapas. See http://espoirchiapas.blogspot.com (accessed February 26, 2012), and http://www.medecinsdumonde.org/gb/International/Mexico/Activities-2010 (accessed February 26, 2012).

20. Personal communication with José Vázquez Jiménez, October 1, 2008. In Chenalhó, there are also a Zapatista and an Evangelical radio station.

21. The website of Las Abejas is http://acteal.blogspot.com/. Koman Ilel's site is http://komanilel.blogspot.com/ (both accessed January 8, 2012).

22. See the Maya Vinic website: www.mayavinic.com (accessed January 8, 2012).

23. The women's cooperative ceased to function in 2003 due to lack of external funding (Schlittler Álvarez 2008:63).

24. *Diccionario tzotzil de San Andrés* (Hurley and Ruiz 1986). The Pedranos (all Catholic) who transcribed and translated my tape recordings usually translated *mantal* to Spanish as "orientación," "información," or "mandamiento." The term is also used in more daily activities; for example, for the orders parents give their children.

25. Sunday service in Yibeljoj, June 9, 1996.

26. Interview in Tzotzil with Rosa Pérez Sántiz, together with Rosa Sántiz Pérez, May 27, 1996.

27. During my stay, such schisms arose from attempts by the catechist coordinators of the Indian Theology group to convince the broader group of catechists to respect and even practice certain ceremonies of costumbre religion, to which many strongly objected.

CHAPTER 5. RE-GENDERING POLITICAL AGENCY

1. Interview in Tzotzil with Rosa Sántiz Pérez, May 21, 1996. The situation is similar in most Maya communities; see, e.g., Stephen 2006; Jolom Mayaetic, K'inal Antsetik, and Schweizerische Eidgenossenschaft 2007.

2. Interview in Tzotzil with Rosa Sántiz Pérez, May 21, 1996. One man told me the practice of excluding women dates from only a few decades ago, when the community assemblies were formalized with municipal agents, etc. When his father was a young man, both women and men participated in the assembly

(interview in Spanish with Antonio Vázquez, May 12, 1998). I have found no other data corroborating this.

3. Interview in Tzotzil with María Ruiz Sántiz and other Cardenistas in Majomut, June 15, 1996.

4. Interview in Tzotzil with Rosa Pérez Sántiz, together with Rosa Sántiz Pérez, May 27, 1996.

5. Ibid.

6. Yibeljoj chapel group, June 9, 1996. See chapter 3 for an account of this Sunday meeting.

7. Group interview in Tzotzil with about ten catechist women in Yabteclum, June 11, 1996 (with a female, non-Pedrano interpreter).

8. Interview in Tzotzil with Rosa Sántiz Pérez, together with Rosa Pérez Sántiz, May 27, 1996.

9. Interview in Tzotzil with Marcela Gómez Sántiz, May 22, 1996. Although shy in public meetings, Marcela Gómez was the only person in the Yibeljoj chapel group who approached me and asked me to interview her, and in the interview she spoke eloquently and without hesitation.

10. Interview in Tzotzil with Apolonia Sántiz, June 8, 1996.

11. No meeting I attended was totally without the presence of men. A few catechist men were normally present, lingering on the sidelines or occupied with practical arrangements, but their presence did not appear to bother the women.

12. Interview in Tzotzil with about ten catechist women in Yabteclum, June 11, 1996.

13. The avoidance of men is also regarded as a safety precaution. Women told me they were afraid of being sexually assaulted by men on paths, including by men from the same village (see Rosenbaum 1993:146–49 on similar fears among women in Chamula).

14. Interview in Tzotzil, June 1996. I have chosen to conceal the woman's name.

15. Interview in Tzotzil with about ten catechist women in Yabteclum, June 11, 1996.

16. Because during my stay there were practically no women leaders in Las Abejas, I here describe only the situation for catechists.

17. Group interview in Tzotzil with about ten catechist women in Yabteclum, June 11, 1996. While some spoke more than others, all contributed through their comments to give a quite homogeneous picture of the problems women catechists face.

18. Interview in Spanish with catechist Sebastián Jiménez, June 16, 1996. I don't know whether this argument took place in the monthly catechist meeting in Yabteclum or locally in the Yibeljoj chapel group.

19. The late husband of the woman had been a catechist. Upon his death, she took over the position.

20. Eber (1999) describes how the Zapatista base community in one village in Chenalhó for this reason has decided that only unmarried women can take positions of leadership.

21. Group interview in Tzotzil with about ten catechist women in Yabteclum, June 11, 1996. When I visited Chenalhó in 2006, some of the former catechist women had married, well into their forties, and had resigned their catechist position.

22. Interview in Tzotzil with Catarina Vázquez Pérez, May 20, 1996.

23. Interview in Tzotzil with about ten catechist women in Yabteclum, June 11, 1996.

24. Interview in Tzotzil with Rosa Pérez Sántiz, together with Rosa Sántiz Pérez, May 27, 1996.

25. Notes from the workshop "Mujer, Familia y Sociedad" in Yabteclum, July 25–26, 1995.

26. Told to me in Spanish by Pascuala Gómez in 1997, part of the Comunidad de Indígenas Misioneras.

27. See, e.g., Kovic and Eber 2003 and Speed 2003 on the special risks of the military presence to indigenous women, as compared to men.

28. The photograph was taken by Pedro Valtierra. For a critical reflection on the popularity of the imagery of unarmed indigenous women confronting soldiers, see Toledo Tello and Garza Caligaris 2003:111.

29. Conversation with Catholic Pedranos in October 2008.

30. See, e.g., "Comunicado de mujeres de Las Abejas," March 8, 2011, at http://acteal.blogspot.com/2011/03/comunicado-de-las-mujeres-de-la.html (accessed February 26, 2012).

CHAPTER 6. SUFFERING AS IDENTITY

1. See Wilson (1995) for a similar change among Q'eqchi' Catholics in Guatemala, who formed more inclusive identities based on class and pan-Maya ethnicity when they transcended the community as their basis for identity.

2. The course was held from February 26 to March 2, 1996, in the Catholic center in Yabteclum, and had about 120 catechist participants. The principal objective of the course was to prepare for the future nomination of Pedrano pre-deacons and to increase catechist knowledge of and respect for costumbre faith because the pre-deacons would also be carrying out sacraments such as baptism for costumbre villagers. I participated, passively, through the whole course.

3. In Tzotzil, *jtotik jme'tik maya'etik*, literally "our Maya father-mothers," or *poko' totil-me'il ku'untik*, "our father-mothers of the past." The societies referred to were Quiché, Tikal, Chichén Itzá, Uxmal, and Palenque.

4. In "Folleto sobre curandero: *Yich'el ta muc' j-ilol c'ac'al*," produced through the support of CENAMI, Mexico City. Eber (2000:156) describes how Pedranos

talk about a past when the ancestors, *totil-me'iletik*, guarded the souls of all Pedranos and ensured they would not get lost, hence, keeping all villagers in good health. Thus, no *j-ilol* healers were needed to cure illness (cf. Guiteras Holmes 1961:166).

5. Among Mayas in Chiapas and elsewhere, the present creation is defined as the fourth (e.g., Gossen 1974; Edmonson 1993:70). However, I heard Pedrano elders refer to the present creation as only the third. See also Guiteras Holmes 1961:313.

6. The man refers to "Our Mother," implying the powerful Holy Earth.

7. Sunday service in Yibeljoj, April 28, 1996.

8. In the booklet on costumbre notions of curing referred to above, diseases are, for example, said to have originated when people were careless with a talking saint-box, dropping it on the ground and thus calling diseases upon themselves. See Eber 2000:213 for more on the costumbre notion of boxes containing saints that can respond to peoples' petitions and questions.

9. The notion of 500 years refers to the year 1492 as the symbolic date for the beginning of the colonization of the Americas, which in 1992 indigenous organizations in Chiapas and elsewhere referred to as "500 years of colonization and resistance."

10. Interview in Tzotzil with Tomás Jiménez Sántiz, May 30, 1996.

11. Interview in Tzotzil with Apolonia Sántiz Jiménez, June 8, 1996.

12. Interview in Tzotzil with Belonia Vázquez Sántiz, June 4, 1996.

13. NAFTA, the free trade agreement between Mexico, the United States, and Canada, went into effect on January 1, 1994, and is commonly given as the main reason why the Zapatistas chose that day to initiate their uprising. The changes to Article 27 of the constitution, concerning the status of ejido land, were made in 1992.

14. Interview in Tzotzil with Tomás Jiménez Sántiz, May 30, 1996.

15. Meeting of Sociedad Civil Las Abejas, October 26, 1995.

16. Ibid.

17. Sunday service in Yibeljoj, April 28, 1996.

18. Sunday service in Yibeljoj, June 9, 1996. The woman spoke in the group of women who were discussing how to answer the questions given to the creyentes by the catechists (see chapter 3 for a description of this particular Sunday service).

19. Notable in these interpretations was the influence of the parish nun, who avoided portraying the then-current, conservative pope negatively, possibly to avoid alienating the converts from the global Catholic Church.

20. In the new Tzotzil Bible published in 1997, Chiapas and Israel are highlighted on the world map. There is also a chart comparing Hebrew and Tzotzil calendars (*Sch'ul C'op Jtotic Dios: Santa Biblia*, Sociedad Bíblica de México, 1997).

21. According to Guiteras Holmes (1961:313), he is the father of the sun and is invoked in prayers.

22. For a brief account of these myths, see Guiteras Holmes 1961:314.

23. E.g., interview in Tzotzil with Tomás Jiménez Sántiz, May 30, 1996.

24. Meeting of Sociedad Civil Las Abejas, October 26, 1995.

25. Interview in Tzotzil with Marcela Gómez Sántiz, May 22, 1996.

26. Certainly, I heard Catholic Pedranos state that all humans, including the wealthy, may experience suffering; for example, at the loss of a child, and also seek God for comfort. Such suffering, however, is characterized as individual and sporadic, not collective and continuous.

27. Interview in Tzotzil with Apolonia Sántiz, June 8, 1996.

28. Interview in Tzotzil with Tomás Jiménez Sántiz, May 30, 1996.

29. On notions within liberation theology of poverty as bringing privileged insight, see, e.g., Barreiro 1984; Berryman 1987, chaps. 2–3; Levine 1992:41–44. This prerogative of Pedrano Catholics is partly contradicted, or at least complicated, by their dependency on an urban elite from the Catholic Church to interpret biblical commands.

CHAPTER 7. POLITICAL OPPOSITION AND THE ACTEAL MASSACRE

1. This concept is related to a broader complex of hot–cold notions; e.g., Guiteras Holmes 1961; Vogt 1969. See also Early 2012 on Maya notions of social harmony.

2. The position of the diocese could be ascribed to a general scruple at the time to avoid encouraging combative activism such as land invasions or openly siding with a specific political party. It may also be related to the PST's being considered by many to have been created, or infiltrated, by the PRI to control oppositional movements.

3. Interview in Spanish with Sebastián Jiménez, June 16, 1996.

4. Interview in Tzotzil with María Sántiz, June 6, 1996.

5. Interview in Spanish with Mariano Pérez Vázquez, June 17, 1996.

6. The brother, Agustín Hernández López, was supposedly told by the communal assembly in his village to share the land, 120 hectares in all, equally between the siblings. He refused and decided instead to distribute half the land among men from neighboring villages who supported him (Hidalgo 1997; Kovic 2003a).

7. Conversations in Sweden with Diego Pérez Jiménez, a Pedrano, and Mexican journalist Luis Hernández Navarro, September 16, 2000.

8. Interview in Spanish with Mariano Pérez Vázquez, June 17, 1996.

9. Ibid., and "Comisión Nacional de Derechos Humanos, Recomendación

no. 34/93," report directed to the governor of Chiapas, Elmar Setzer Marseille, and signed March 12, 1993, by the commission president, Jorge Madrazo.

10. Pedrano Catholic friends told me in 2008 that two of the men arrested were Protestants. I have not seen this confirmed elsewhere, and I have no information on whether there was any mobilization among Pedrano Protestants in support of the jailed men.

11. Interview in Spanish with José Vázquez, May 1998.

12. Interview in Spanish with the Presbyterian pastor Agustín Sántiz Jiménez, a Pedrano, October 5, 1995.

13. Interview in Spanish with Sebastián Gómez, Chenalhó, October 1995.

14. Since 1998, the formal name of the association is Sociedad Civil Las Abejas; it is generally referred to as just Las Abejas. See chapter 9 on the organization's split in 2008.

15. The other mediating body was the Commission for Conciliation and Pacification (COCOPA), consisting of parliamentary representatives of the different political parties. In Chiapas, COCOPA was commonly associated with a pro-government position, while CONAI was identified as sympathetic to the EZLN demands.

16. Interview in Spanish with Antonio Vázquez, October 9, 1995.

17. Interview in Tzotzil with Rosa Sántiz Pérez, together with Rosa Pérez Sántiz, May 27, 1996.

18. Interview in Tzotzil with María Pérez Gómez, May 21, 1996.

19. One source indicates, however, that there may have been some combat training of young men under the cover of another organization.

20. Interview in Tzotzil and Spanish with members of a here-unnamed Zapatista support base in a village in Chenalhó, May 24, 1996. The EZLN consists of armed and trained soldiers, most based in the Lacandón jungle, and numerous unarmed support bases in regular villages whose members provide food for the soldiers and are part of the decision-making structure. The highest leaders are the Comité Clandestino Revolucionario Indígena-Comandancia General (Revolutionary Indigenous Clandestine Committee-General Command, CCRI-CG).

21. Interview in Tzotzil and Spanish with members of a Zapatista support base in Chenalhó, May 24, 1996.

22. Interview in Tzotzil with Cristóbal Sántiz Pérez, May 27, 1996.

23. Interview in Tzotzil with Belonia Vázquez Sántiz, June 4, 1996.

24. Those who went to San Andrés paid for their own transportation but were supported by extra money collected at the local meeting of Sociedad Civil Las Abejas. NGOs provided food and basic lodging in San Andrés, but the trip still implied a considerable cost and a loss of several days of work. Both men and women participated.

25. CEOIC split into a section loyal to the government and a section explicitly supportive of the EZLN. It was the latter part, calling itself CEOIC Indepen-

diente, that merged with AEDPCH. See Harvey 1998:211 for a nuanced description of this development.

26. The delegates were not admitted to the first convention in August 1994, since they arrived without credentials, but they presented a brief statement at the next convention in October. (Interview in Spanish with Sebastián Gómez, October 1995, one of the representatives to the October convention.)

27. E.g., interview with Antonio Gutiérrez, April 17, 1996. This position was shared by many of the government-oppositional mestizo organizations in San Cristóbal.

28. The new municipal president is not usually installed until January 1 of the year following the election. Zapatista villagers told me that it was one particular group of Pedrano Zapatistas that had decided to install the new president at once, which the others had accepted.

29. The National Consultation for Peace and Democracy, directed to all Mexican citizens, consisted of a written inquiry about what the future character of the Zapatista struggle should be.

30. Meeting of Sociedad Civil Las Abejas, August 8, 1995.

31. A total of 153,961 citizens participated in Chiapas through 1,362 assemblies in rural communities or filling out forms at "mesas" (tables set up in halls or outdoor squares) in urban areas. Figures from Alianza Cívica Chiapas, 1995. In Chenalhó, Alianza Cívica counted 7,592 participants, not including the Zapatista groups, who, I was told, sent the results directly to the EZLN leadership, CCRI-CG.

32. Of those actively voting, PRI received 91 percent of the votes, or 2,947 votes. Frente Cardenista received 270 votes. The number of registered voters was 13,737. The annulled, or blank, ballots were not counted. (Figures presented at a meeting of Sociedad Civil, October 26, later confirmed with Alianza Cívica.) The outcome was similar in Maya communities all over the state, with almost 70 percent abstention.

33. Autonomous municipalities, paralleling the formal, PRI-controlled municipal governments, were created by Zapatista support bases in several Maya municipalities from 1996 on. The leaders are elected by communal assemblies within the Zapatista support base of each village.

34. The government had neglected to process the signed Peace Accords and participated only passively in the new round of negotiations beginning in June, which was interpreted as a lack of real intent to solve the conflict peacefully. The EZLN refused to resume the dialogue until a set of demands was met.

35. For a detailed account of the events in Chenalhó in 1996–97 leading up to the Acteal massacre, see the report *Camino a la masacre*, published by the Center for Human Rights (CDHFBC 1998a). For a partly different version, see *White Paper on Acteal, Chiapas*, by the Federal Office of the Attorney General (Procuraduría General de la República 1998).

36. The Catholics were not allowed access to the church and their center until 1998.

37. The area includes both cultivable land and a large sandbank. The families had received money from Fideicomiso 95 to buy the land, including the right to the sandbank, as an ejido, and were registered as a Sociedad de Solidaridad Social, with the name "Campano Vitz—Campana del Cerro" (CDHFBC 1998a).

38. The road plans were initiated by the new president, Jacinto Arias, a native of Puebla. The Zapatista villagers held that only relatives of Arias would profit from the road since only they owned vehicles.

39. The Federal Election Institute, CONAI, and various NGOs had stated that the conditions for elections did not exist in Chiapas because of the militarization of the state, the presence of paramilitary groups, and the many conflicts in the communities. The elections were held notwithstanding, but in the conflict zone, 80 percent of the electorate chose to abstain.

40. The municipal president should not be confused with the Pedrano anthropologist Jacinto Arias.

41. According to the pro-Cardenista Sistema de Información Campesino (2007), the Zapatistas killed seventeen and injured another seventeen persons during 1996–97.

42. Reported by the electronic news service Melel Xojobal, November 18, 1997.

43. Personal communication by telephone, October 1997, with my host, Mariano Pérez Sántiz.

44. Corn and beans are the staple food, and normally, an adult Pedrano eats at least twelve tortillas a day.

45. Appeals were sent also to individuals who might be able to help, such as myself. A few support groups in Sweden were able to quickly raise some money that was sent, as groups in other countries probably did.

46. The commission consisted of thirty-two national and international delegates, and described the condition of the displaced in Chenalhó as alarming. Their report from December 3, 1997, is published in CDHFBC 1998a.

47. Alarm rose especially after a documentary by Ricardo Rocha was aired on the national television station Televisa, reporting on the refugee camps and the paramilitary activity in Chenalhó and other highland municipalities in Chiapas. The second part of Rocha's report was blocked by sources in the Interior Ministry, holding that it would be a "violation of National Security" to air the documentary (Paulson 1998). The documentary can be seen in a recut version on YouTube: www.youtube.com/watch?v=J5MLFdTBa9w (accessed February 26, 2012).

48. These diplaced people were said to be hosted principally in the municipal capital, Pechiquil, and C'anolal. Some, however, held that these PRI-leaning villagers were driven from their homes by the paramilitaries because they did not condone the use of violence.

49. The uniforms belonged to the public security forces stationed in Chenalhó and had been lent to the men by the commander of the group (Procuraduría General de la República 1998:80).

50. At this time there were five police bases in the region around Acteal, the closest in Majomut, and during the afternoon of the shooting, a police patrol investigating reports of a disturbance kept to the road, two hundred meters from the place of the massacre, hearing shooting, but reporting there were no incidents to report (CDHFBC 2009a). See CDHFB 1998b for testimony from the survivors.

51. Personal communication with Catholic Pedranos, October 2008. See also CDHFBC 2009b:64.

52. In April 2000 this aid amounted to a total of 3 million euros (newspaper *Sin Línea Diario*, cited in the electronic news service Melel Xojobal, April 10, 2000).

53. Because not all displaced families owned coffee fields, people in the camps decided that the coffee should be harvested and cleaned collectively and sold for shared use.

CHAPTER 8. MARTYRDOM AND THE CLAIM FOR RIGHTS

1. The debate gained new force with the tenth anniversary of the massacre in 2007; see, e.g., the articles by Águilar Camín (2007), and the response by the Fray Bartolomé de Las Casas Center for Human Rights (CDHFBC 2007b).

2. Mexican newspaper *Reforma*, cited in the electronic news service Melel Xojobal, January 16, 1998. The European Union eventually ratified the free trade treaty in 1999.

3. Procuraduría General de la República.

4. See also the website news posted by Amnesty International: www.amnesty.org/en/for-media/press-releases/mexico-new-investigation-acteal-massacre-essential-20090813 (August 13, 2009), accessed January 18, 2012.

5. Since Polhó is a Zapatista-controlled village, it is more restrictive toward visitors. Acteal provides an easy-access alternative for those interested in learning about indigenous struggle.

6. The observers are formally called "Brigadas Civiles de Observación" (Civil Observation Brigades, BriCO), and have been coordinated by the Fray Bartolomé de Las Casas Center for Human Rights since 1995 for indigenous communities in the whole conflict region that ask for them. Observers for Zapatista communities were organized primarily by the association Enlace Civil, also based in San Cristóbal.

7. See, e.g., the Christian Peacemaker Teams' website: www.cpt.org. See also Tavanti 2003:178–82.

8. On the ONIL stoves, see the Latino Medical Student Association at the

University of California, Irvine, *Newsletter* (Winter 2009), at shttp://www.ucilmsa .org/LMSA_Newsletter(Fall,Winter08).doc (accessed January 18, 2012). On the latter two projects, see Peace and Diversity Australia, www.peaceanddiversity.org .au/ (accessed January 18, 2012).

9. See www.globalexchange.org/tours/byCountry.html#16 (accessed January 18, 2012).

10. Margot Roosevelt, "Greetings from Zapatista Land," *Time*, September 3, 2001. The tour made a contribution of 800 pesos (90 USD) to the community.

11. Letter from coffee@highergroundstrading.com, March 12, 2009. See http: //highergroundstrading.com/fair-trade-tours/ (accessed January 18, 2012).

12. *El Universal*, cited in the electronic news service Melel Xojobal, August 11, 1999.

13. The annual prize is part of the activities of the French National Consultative Commission of Human Rights. Las Abejas shared the prize and 600,000 francs with five other associations from all over the world.

14. The sculpture was part of a series of ten planned by the artist, Jens Galschiot, to be erected in various parts of the world, each as a memorial "of a severe infringement against humanity." (Data from the artist's website: www.aidoh.dk, accessed January 19, 2012.)

15. Margot Roosevelt, "Greetings from Zapatista Land," *Time*, September 3, 2001.

16. E.g., in a communiqué from Las Abejas, September 22, 1999.

17. Las Abejas communiqué from December 27, 2007, in Schlittler Álvarez 2008:65.

18. Described by Schlittler Álvarez 2008:64, from the mass on the tenth anniversary of the massacre, December 22, 2007.

19. Speech by Bishop Felipe Arizmendi, reported by the electronic news service Melel Xojobal, 2000. My translation from Spanish.

20. Newsletters from Jesuit Pedro Arriaga, "Pascua tzotzil en Chenalhó," March 11, 2002; and "Ángeles y mujeres," April 12, 2002; the latter with attached text by Harriet Paterson titled "The Virgin of the Massacre: An Easter Pilgrimage. April 2, 2002."

21. Schlittler Álvarez 2008:63–65, and the website of Las Abejas, acteal.blog spot.com, under the entries for 2007 (accessed February 26, 2012).

22. I, too, was asked, of course, to come to the front for introduction. Since I had finally brought my dissertation about Las Abejas—delayed because of having my first child—I was also asked to give the book as an offering later during the mass.

23. Since January 22, 1998, the Las Abejas board sends out these communiqués on the 22nd of every month.

24. See, e.g., the video documentary *Acteal: Diez años de impunidad—y cuántos mas?* (2008), made by Las Abejas videographer José Alfredo Jiménez Pérez from

Yibeljoj (the version with English subtitles is called *Acteal; Ten Years of Impunity*): www.youtube.com/watch?v=9XjlT7ja20M (accessed February 26, 2012).

25. E.g., Las Abejas communiqué, June 9, CDHFBC 2009b:23.

26. Las Abejas has further demanded that the government disarm the paramilitaries and create safe conditions for the return of the displaced people; they returned to their villages in 2000 and 2001 (see chapter 9).

27. However, I believe many or most Catholic Pedranos do not perceive themselves as having rights in relation to family members and others. For example, a daughter does not refer to her "right" to protest her parents' demands that she marry someone she has not chosen herself.

28. The relevant United Nations conventions are the Geneva Convention Relative to the Protection of Civilian Persons in Time of War, of August 12, 1949; and Protocol Additional to the Geneva Conventions of 12 August 1949, and Relating to the Protection of Victims of Non-International Armed Conflicts (Protocol II), of June 8, 1977.

29. The signs were written in Spanish: "Sociedad Civil/Paz/Zona Neutral." In contrast to Chenalhó, this text and the white flags put on the houses in other municipalities—leftist mestizo friends told me—signaled that the inhabitants were (passive) supporters of the government.

30. Interview in Spanish with Sebastián Gómez, October 1995.

31. He is probably referring to the Inter-American Commission on Human Rights, which on several occasions has criticized the Mexican government for human rights violations in Chiapas.

32. Leader Antonio Gutiérrez addressing the meeting of Las Abejas (in Tzotzil), October 26, 1995.

33. Speed (2002:209–10) describes a similar usage among villagers in a Zapatista community in Chiapas, although she says these villagers referred to a general ideological position as being on the "side" of human rights.

34. E.g., field notes from Course in Human Rights, Yabteclum, April 19–20, 1996.

35. Las Abejas was formally given the right to speak by (technically) representing the International Work Group on Indigenous Affairs (IWGIA), which often uses its status as NGO observer in the UN to enable indigenous representatives to make statements. IWGIA also financed the travel costs for the three delegates; Vázquez was accompanied by one of the indigenous lay nuns working in Chenalhó and a former pastoral worker of the municipality, who also interpreted between Tzotzil and Spanish. (Vázquez read her address in Spanish, however.) I myself served as facilitator for the group during their stay.

36. These associations, among them the Comisión Mexicana de Defensa y Promoción de los Derechos Humanos, were petitioning the UN High Commissioner on Human Rights to investigate the situation of human rights in Mexico.

37. Reported by the electronic news service Melel Xojobal, August 18, 1998.

38. Ibid., May 27, 1999. *United Nations Press Release* (August 22, 2002): www .unhchr.ch/huricane/huricane.nsf/view01/E5977A496DE83196C1256C230 04B7825?opendocument (accessed February 25, 2012). *Noticieros Televisa* (August 23, 2002): www.esmas.com/noticierostelevisa/mexico/250797.html (accessed February 25, 2012).

39. *La Jornada*, cited in the electronic news service Melel Xojobal, July 22, 1999.

40. UN Document E/CN.4/2000/3/Add.3, November 25, 1999.

41. *La Jornada*, cited in the electronic news service Melel Xojobal, November 29, 1999. Representatives of the office of the UN High Commissioner on Human Rights met with Las Abejas also in 2003 and 2009. www.frayba.org.mx/ archivo/boletines/090817_declaracion_onu_acteal_onu.pdf (accessed February 25, 2012).

42. *La Jornada*, cited in the electronic news service Melel Xojobal, April 1, 2002.

43. SIPAZ (Servicio Internacional por la Paz) blog (November 10, 2009): http://sipazen.wordpress.com/2009/11/10/chiapas-more-prisoners-released-for-acteal-massacre-abejas-petition-the-iachr/ (accessed January 20, 2012). After the appeal in 2005, the commission had waited for the legal appeals in Mexico to take their course.

44. Las Abejas communiqué, January 22, 2006, my translation from Spanish.

45. The main exception concerns struggles for land and related forced displacement, for which the center offers legal support and public denunciations. However, these cases tend to be framed as the right of indigenous peoples to their territory, and not, for example, as the right of poor people to subsistence. (See, e.g., the center website, www.frayba.org.mx, and the publications under the "Reports" tab, then under the tag "conflicto agrario.")

46. Las Abejas communiqué, August 10, 2000, my translation from Spanish.

47. The San Andrés Peace Accords called for "a new relationship" between the state and the indigenous peoples. Core items were a constitutional guarantee of self-determination for indigenous peoples in Mexico, their right to a distinct culture and ethnic identity, and a collective right to the territory on which they live and its natural resources, in accordance with ILO Convention 169.

48. Sociedad Civil Las Abejas meeting in Chenalhó, October 26, 1995 (translation from Tzotzil).

49. See the official website of the project: www.proyectomesoamerica.org (accessed January 20, 2012).

50. See the official website of Instituto de Población y Ciudades Rurales of the state of Chiapas: www.ciudadesrurales.chiapas.gob.mx (accessed January 20, 2012).

51. The men, accused of being so-called "corta-cabezas," killing people for

money on behalf of mestizos, were from neighboring Tzotzil municipalities and had been caught when traveling through the village.

52. Extra prayer meeting in Yibeljoj, May 21, 1996.

53. Interview in Tzotzil with Marcela Vázquez Pérez, June 3, 1996.

54. Not all Catholics in Chenalhó agreed that this was the correct decision for the group in Acteal, and some told me on my return to the area in May 1998 that they thought those in Acteal should have fled.

55. Personal communication in Spanish with Las Abejas representative Diego Pérez Jiménez, September 16, 2000, in Stockholm, Sweden. Similar versions are found in various reports containing interviews with Las Abejas members. In the one-year commemoration of the massacre, a man played the role of Vázquez in the reenactment of the massacre and uttered similar words. The last, charged sentence appears in all the narratives I have seen.

CHAPTER 9. EXODUS? THE LIMITS OF CITIZENSHIP AND RIGHTS-BASED CLAIMS

1. Already by the time of my visit in May 1998, many displaced Catholics from Yibeljoj told me that support for the paramilitaries among PRI-loyal villagers had shrunk considerably after the massacre, and that the risk of returning was no longer great.

2. *La Jornada*, cited in the electronic news service Melel Xojobal, August 27, 2001.

3. The Zapatista autonomous municipality in Chenalhó, in contrast, refuses to participate in any negotiations with official governments. It has declared that no displaced members will return until the paramilitaries have been disarmed and safe conditions reestablished. Displaced Zapatistas continue to live in the camp in Polhó. However, there are also divisions within this Zapatista group, where individual families that could no longer endure living as displaced people have returned to their original villages (personal communication with Catholic Pedranos, October 2008).

4. Personal communication with Catholic Pedranos, October 2008.

5. Ibid.

6. Personal communication with Catholic Pedranos from both factions in separate conversations, October 2008. Two of them were close to the central leadership of each of the new Las Abejas associations.

7. Letter from one of the key persons in Asociación Civil Las Abejas, June 9, 2009.

8. E.g., communiqués from Organización de la Sociedad Civil "Las Abejas," Acteal, April 28, 2011, and November 28, 2011.

9. Most of them have migrated the last thirty years, changing San Cristó-

bal from a town of some thirty thousand inhabitants, of which almost all were mestizos, to a city of about two hundred thousand today, of which half are indigenous (Rus 2009).

10. Many, but not all, with this belief define themselves as Zapatista sympathizers. The interviews with indigenous colonia inhabitants were part of a research project led by me and financed by the Swedish International Development Agency, and were carried out by Pedrano collaborators during 2006–2009.

11. Interview in Tzotzil with Manuel Pérez Sántiz, August 10, 1995.

12. Numbers from "Bases de datos de la Encuesta sobre Migración en la Frontera Norte de México 1995, 1999–2009" (EMIF-NORTE), published by Consejo Nacional de Población (CONAPO) at: www.conapo.gob.mx/index.php?option=com_content&view=article&id=95&Itemid=262 (accessed February 26, 2012).

13. Ingresos por remesas familiares, distribución por entidad federativa, January–March 2003—October–December 2011, Banco Nacional de México: www.banxico.org.mx/SieInternet/consultarDirectorioInternetAction.do?acc ion=consultarCuadro&idCuadro=CE100&sector=1&locale=es (accessed February 26, 2012).

14. Studies about life for these Maya migrants are still emerging; see, e.g., Rus and Rus 2008; Eber 2011.

References

Águilar Camín, Héctor. 2007. "Regreso a Acteal I–III." *Nexos* 358 (October), 359 (November), and 360 (December).

Alfonseca, Juan. 2005. "El papel de las juntas y los comités de educación en la apropiación local de la escuela rural federal." *Memoria, conocimiento y utopía. Anuario de la Sociedad Mexicana de Historia de la Educación* 1 (January 2004–May 2005): 63–90.

Alvarez, Sonia E., Evelina Dagnino, and Arturo Escobar, eds. 1998. *Cultures of Politics, Politics of Cultures: Re-Visioning Latin American Social Movements.* Boulder, Colo.: Westview Press.

Amnesty International. 1997. *Amnesty International Report 1997.*

———. 2010. *Amnesty International Report 2010: The State of the World's Human Rights.*

Anaya Gallardo, Federico, et al. 2000. *Siempre cerca, siempre lejos: Las fuerzas armadas en México.* San Cristóbal de Las Casas, Mexico: Global Exchange / Centro de Investigaciones Económicas y Políticas de Acción Communitaria (CIEPAC) / Centro Nacional de Comunicación Social (CENCOS).

Appendini, Kirsten. 2001. "Land Regularization and Conflict Resolution: The Case of Mexico." Document prepared for Food and Agriculture Organization of the United Nations (FAO), Rural Development Division, Land Tenure Service.

Arendt, Hanna. 1968 [1951]. *The Origins of Totalitarianism.* New York: Harcourt Brace Jovanovich.

Arias Pérez, Jacinto. 1975. *El mundo numinoso de los mayas: Estructura y cambios contemporáneos.* Tuxtla Gutiérrez, Mexico: Gobierno del Estado de Chiapas, Instituto Chiapaneco de Cultura.

———. 1985. *San Pedro Chenalhó: Algo de su historia, cuentos y costumbres.* Tuxtla Gutiérrez, Mexico: Publicación Bilingüe de la Dirección de Fortalecimiento y Fomento a las Culturas de la Sub-Secretaría de Asuntos Indígenas.

————. 1994. "Movimientos indígenas contemporáneos del estado de Chiapas."
  In *El arreglo de los pueblos indios: La incansable tarea de reconstitución*, edited by
  Jacinto Arias Pérez. Tuxtla Gutiérrez: Secretaría de Educación Pública / Go-
  bierno del Estado de Chiapas, Instituto Chiapaneco de Cultura.

Aubry, Andrés, and Angélica Inda. 1997a. "El pueblo paramilitar de Los Chorros." *La Jornada*, December 28.

————. 1997b. "¿Quiénes son los 'paramilitares'?" *La Jornada*, December 23.

Balboa, Juan. 1997. "Soldados y policías 'buscan armas' y agreden a mujeres en
  Chenalhó." *La Jornada*, November 25.

Balboa, Juan, and Elio Henríquez. 1997. "Abstención de 80% en la zona de conflicto en Chiapas." *La Jornada*, July 8.

Barmeyer, Niels. 2003. "The Guerrilla Movement as a Project: An Assessment
  of Community Involvement in the EZLN." *Latin American Perspectives* 30(1):
  122–38.

————. 2008. "Taking on the State: Resistance, Education, and Other Challenges
  Facing the Zapatista Autonomy Project." *Identities* 15(5): 506–27.

Baronnet, Bruno. 2008. "Rebel Youth and Zapatista Autonomous Education."
  Latin American Perspectives 35(4): 112–24.

Barreiro, Alvaro. 1984. *Basic Ecclesial Communities: The Evangelization of the Poor.*
  Maryknoll, N.Y.: Orbis.

Basok, Tanya, and Susan Ilcan. 2006. "In the Name of Human Rights: Global
  Organizations and Participating Citizens." *Citizenship Studies* 10(3): 309–27.

Baxi, Upendra. 2002. *The Future of Human Rights.* New Delhi: Oxford University
  Press.

Bellinghausen, Herman. 1997. "En Chenalhó, presencia descarada de paramilitares." *La Jornada*, September 28.

————. 2004. "En Chiapas, la mayor concentración de tropas en el país, con-
  firma un estudio." *La Jornada*, January 12.

Benessaieh, Afef. 2004. "¿Civilizando la sociedad civil? La cooperación internacional en Chiapas durante los años noventa." In *Políticas de ciudadanía y sociedad civil en tiempos de globalización*, edited by Daniel Mato, 33–51. Caracas: Fac-
  ultad de Ciencas Económicas y Sociales, Universidad Central de Venezuela.

Benhabib, Seyla. 2004. *The Rights of Others: Aliens, Residents and Citizens.* Cambridge: Cambridge University Press.

Berryman, Phillip. 1987. *Liberation Theology: Essential Facts about the Revolutionary
  Movement in Latin America and Beyond.* London: I. B. Tuaris.

Bob, Clifford. 2005. *The Marketing of Rebellion: Insurgents, Media, and International
  Activism.* Cambridge: Cambridge University Press.

Boff, Leonardo, and Clodovis Boff. 1993. *Introducing Liberation Theology.* Maryknoll, N.Y.: Orbis.

Boltvinik, Julio, and Enrique Hernández Laos. 2000. *Pobreza y distribución del in-
  greso en México.* Mexico City: Siglo XXI Editores.

Bonner, Arthur. 1999. *We Will Not Be Stopped: Evangelical Persecution, Catholicism and Zapatistas in Chiapas, Mexico.* Boca Raton, Fla.: Universal Publishers.

Brysk, Alison. 2000. *From Tribal Village to Global Village: Indian Rights and International Relations in Latin America.* Stanford: Stanford University Press.

———. 2002. *Globalization and Human Rights.* Berkeley and Los Angeles: University of California Press.

Burguete Cal y Mayor, Araceli, ed. 2000. *Indigenous Autonomy in Mexico.* IWGIA [International Work Group for Indigenous Affairs] Document 94. Copenhagen: IWGIA.

Calnek, Edward E. 1962. "Highland Chiapas before the Spanish Conquest." PhD diss., University of Chicago.

———. 1970. Los pueblos indígenas de las tierras altas. In *Ensayos de antropología en la zona central de Chiapas,* edited by Normand McQuown and Julian Pitt-Rivers, 105–34. Mexico City: Instituto Nacional Indigenista / Secretaría de Educación Pública.

Cancian, Frank. 1992. *The Decline of Community in Zinacantán: Economy, Public Life and Social Stratification 1960–1987.* Stanford: Stanford University Press.

Carmack, Robert M. 1981. *The Quiché Mayas of Utatlán: The Evolution of a Highland Guatemala Kingdom.* Norman: University of Oklahoma Press.

Castells, Manuel. 1997. *The Power of Identity.* Vol. 2 of *The Information Age: Economy, Society and Culture.* Malden, Mass.: Blackwell.

CDHFBC (Centro de Derechos Humanos Fray Bartolomé de Las Casas). 1998a. *Camino a la masacre: Informe especial sobre Chenalhó.* San Cristóbal de Las Casas, Mexico: CDHFBC.

———. 1998b. *Esta es nuestra palabra: Testimonios de Acteal.* San Cristóbal de Las Casas, Mexico: CDHFBC.

———. 1999. "La guerra en Chiapas ¿Incidente en la historia?" *Informe Annual.* San Cristóbal de Las Casas, Mexico: CDHFBC.

———. 2000. *Masacre de Acteal: Actualización de información sobre los procesos penales y algo sobre la situación en Chenalhó.* San Cristóbal de Las Casas, Mexico: CDHFBC.

———. 2005. *La lucha interminable: Carpeta básica para talleres de derechos humanos.* 2nd ed. San Cristóbal de Las Casas, Mexico: CDHFBC.

———. 2007a. *Acteal a 10 años. Informe sobre la responsabilidad del estado méxicano en el caso Acteal.* San Cristóbal de Las Casas, Mexico: CDHFBC.

———. 2007b. "Carta a Héctor Aguilar Camín." *Nexos,* December 3.

———. 2009a. *Balance 2008.* San Cristóbal de Las Casas, Mexico: CDHFBC.

———. 2009b. *Por la verdad y la justicia: Acteal 11 años 5 meses y 17 días de impunidad: ¿Cuántos más?* San Cristóbal de Las Casas, Mexico: CDHFBC.

———. 2011. "Se cumplen dos años en que la Suprema Corte de Justicia de la Nación libera a los autores materiales de la masacre de Acteal." *Boletín* (CDHFBC) 15.

CENAMI (Centro Nacional de Ayuda a las Misiones Indígenas). 2000. *La iglesia autóctona. 40 años de servicio pastoral de Jtatic Samuel: "Del Concilio Ecuménico Vaticano II al tercer milenio."* Document in author's possession.

Chandler, David. 2004. "Building Global Civil Society 'From Below'?" *Millennium: Journal of International Studies* 33(2): 313–39.

Charters, Claire, Les Malezer, and Victoria Tauli-Corpuz, eds. 2011. *Indigenous Voices: The UN Declaration on the Rights of Indigenous Peoples.* Oxford, UK: Hart Publishing.

CIEPAC (Centro de Investigaciones Económicas y Políticas de Acción Comunitaria). 2002a. "Land Conflicts Intensify in Chiapas." *Chiapas Today Bulletin* 290 (May 15).

———. 2002b. "La coyuntura y el nuevo gobierno en Chiapas." *Boletín Chiapas al Día* 288 (April 30).

Cohen, Jean L. 1999. "Changing Paradigms of Citizenship and the Exclusiveness of the Demos." *International Sociology* 14(3): 245–68.

Collier, George A., and Elizabeth Lowery Quaratiello. 1999 [1994]. *Basta! Land and the Zapatista Rebellion in Chiapas.* Oakland, Calif.: Institute for Food and Development Policy.

Collier, George A., and Jan Rus. 2002. "Una generación de crisis en los Altos de Chiapas: Los casos de Chamula y Zinacantán, 1974–2000." In *Tierra, libertad y autonomía: Impactos regionales del zapatismo*, edited by Shannan Mattiace, R. Aída Hernández Castillo, and Jan Rus, 157–99. Mexico City: Centro de Investigaciones y Estudios Superiores de Antropología Social / International Work Group on Indigenous Affairs.

Collier, Jane F. 1973. *Law and Social Change in Zinacantan.* Stanford: Stanford University Press.

Collier, Jane F., and George A. Collier. 2005. "The Zapatista Rebellion in the Context of Globalization." *Journal of Peasant Studies* 32(3–4): 450–60.

Collier, Jane F., Bill Maurer, and Liliana Suárez-Navaz. 1995. "Sanctioned Identities: Legal Constructions of Modern Personhood." *Identities* 2(1–2): 1–29.

Comaroff, John L., and Jean Comaroff. 1997. "Postcolonial Politics and Discourses of Democracy in Southern Africa: An Anthropological Reflection on African Political Modernities." *Journal of Anthropological Research* 53(2): 123–46.

Couso, Javier, Alexandra Huneeus, and Rachel Sieder, eds. 2010. *Cultures of Legality: Judicialization and Political Activism in Latin America.* Cambridge: Cambridge University Press.

Cowan, Jane K., Marie-Bénédicte Dembour, and Richard A. Wilson, eds. 2001. *Culture and sRights: Anthropological Perspectives.* Cambridge: Cambridge University Press.

Dagnino, Evelina. 1998. "Culture, Citizenship, and Democracy: Changing Discourses and Practices of the Latin American Left." In *Cultures of Politics, Politics of Cultures*, edited by Sonia E. Alvarez, Evelina Dagnino, and Arturo Escobar. Boulder, Colo.: Westview Press.

———. 2003. "Citizenship in Latin America: An Introduction." *Latin American Perspectives* 30(2): 211–25.

———. 2007. "Dimensions of Citizenship in Contemporary Brazil." *Fordham Law Review* 75(5): 2469–82.

———. 2010. "Civil Society in Latin America: Participatory Citizens or Service Providers?" In *Power to the People? (Con-)Tested Civil Society in Search of Democracy*, edited by Heidi Moksnes and Mia Melin. Uppsala, Sweden: Uppsala University.

Diaz-Polanco, Héctor. 1997. *Indigenous Peoples in Latin America: The Quest for Self-Determination*. Boulder, Colo.: Westview Press.

———. 1998. *La rebelión zapatista y la autonomía*. Mexico City: Siglo XXI Editores.

Early, John D. 1983. "Ethnographic Implications of an Ethnohistorical Perspective of the Civil-Religious Hierarchy among the Highland Maya." *Ethnohistory* 30(4): 185–202.

———. 2006. *The Maya and Catholicism: An Encounter of Worldviews*. Gainesville: University Press of Florida.

———. 2012. *Maya and Catholic Cultures in Crisis*. Gainesville: University Press of Florida.

Eber, Christine. 1998. "Las mujeres y el movimiento por la democracia en San Pedro Chenalhó." In *La otra palabra*, edited by R. Aída Hernández Castillo, 84–105. Mexico City: Centro de Investigaciones y Estudios Superiores de Antropología Social.

———. 1999. "Seeking Our Own Food: Indigenous Women's Power and Autonomy in San Pedró Chenalhó, Chiapas, 1980–1998." *Latin American Perspectives* 26(3): 6–36.

———. 2000 [1995]. *Women and Alcohol in a Highland Maya Town: Water of Hope, Water of Sorrow*. Austin: University of Texas Press.

———. 2001a. "Buscando una nueva vida (Searching for a New Life): Liberation through Autonomy in San Pedro Chenalhó, 1970–1998." *Latin American Perspectives* 28(2): 45–72.

———. 2001b. "'Take My Water': Liberation through Prohibition in San Pedro Chenalhó, Chiapas." *Social Science and Medicine* 53(2): 251–62.

———. 2008. *Mujeres y alcohol en un municipio maya de los Altos de Chiapas: Agua de esperanza, agua de pesar*. Spanish ed. of *Women and Alcohol in a Highland Maya Town*, with new preface. Antigua, Guatemala: CIRMA / Plumsock Mesoamerican Studies.

———. 2011. *The Journey of a Tzotzil-Maya Woman: Pass Well over the Earth*. Austin: University of Texas Press.

Eber, Christine, and Brenda Rosenbaum. 1993. "'That We May Serve beneath

Your Hands and Feet': Women Weavers in Highland Chiapas, Mexico." In *Crafts in the World Market: The Impact of Global Exchange on Middle American Artisans*, edited by June Nash. Albany: State University of New York Press.

Eber, Christine, and Christine Kovic, eds. 2003. *Women of Chiapas: Making History in Times of Struggle and Hope.* New York: Routledge.

Eber, Christine, and Janet Tanski. 2001. "Obstacles Facing Women's Grass-roots Development Strategies in Mexico." *Review of Radical Political Economics* 33:441–60.

Eckstein, Susan, ed. 1989. *Power and Popular Protest: Latin American Social Movements.* Berkeley and Los Angeles: University of California Press.

Eckstein, Susan, and Timothy P. Wickham-Crowley. 2003. "Struggles for Justice in Latin America." In *What Justice? Whose Justice? Fighting for Fairness in Latin America,* edited by Susan Eckstein and Timothy P. Wickham-Crowley. Berkeley: University of California Press.

Edmonson, Munro S. 1993. The Mayan Faith. In *South and Meso-American Native Spirituality: From the Cult of the Feathered Serpent to the Theology of Liberation,* edited by Gary H. Gossen, 65–85. New York: Crossroad.

Eklund, Ronnie. 2008. "A Swedish Perspective on Laval." *Comparative Labor Law and Policy Journal* 29(4): 551–72.

Engler, Mark. 2000. "Toward the 'Rights of the Poor': Human Rights in Liberation Theology." *Journal of Religious Ethics* 28(3): 339–65.

Escobar, Arturo. 2004. "Beyond the Third World: Imperial Globality, Global Coloniality and Anti-Globalisation Social Movements." *Third World Quarterly* 25(1): 207–30.

Favre, Henri. 1984. *Cambio y continuidad entre los mayas de México: Contribución al estudio de la situación colonial en América Latina.* Mexico City: Instituto Nacional Indigenista.

Fazio, Carlos. 1994. *Samuel Ruiz: El caminante.* Mexico City: Espasa-Calpe.

Ferm, Deane William. 1991. *På de fattigas sida: Befrielseteologier i Asien, Afrika och Latinamerika.* Gothenburg, Sweden: Lindelöws förlag.

Ferreyra, Aleida, and Renata Segura. 2000. "Examining the Military in the Local Sphere: Colombia and Mexico." *Latin American Perspectives* 27(2): 18–35.

Figueroa Fuentes, Patricia, ed. 2000. *Rumbo a la calle—: El trabajo infantil, una estrategia de sobrevivencia.* San Cristóbal de Las Casas, Mexico: Caridad y Educación Integral, Melel Xojobal.

Fischer, Edward, and R. McKenna Brown, eds. 1996. *Mayan Cultural Activism in Guatemala.* Austin: University of Texas Press.

Forbis, Melissa M. 2006. "Autonomy and a Handful of Herbs: Contesting Gender and Ethnic Identities through Healing." In *Dissident Women,* edited by Shannon Speed, R. Aída Hernández Castillo, and Lynn M. Stephen. Austin: University of Texas Press.

Foweraker, Joe. 1990. "Popular movements and political change in Mexico." In

Popular Movements and Political Change in Mexico, edited by Joe Foweraker and Ann L. Craig, 3–20. Boulder, Colo.: L. Rienner.

Fox, Jonathan. 1997. "The Difficult Transition from Clientelism to Citizenship: Lessons from Mexico." *World Politics* 46(2): 151–84.

Fraser, Nancy. 2003. "Social Justice in Globalisation: Redistribution, Recognition, and Participation." *Eurozine*, pp. 1–10. http://eurozine.com/pdf/2003–01-24-fraser-en.pdf. Accessed December 17, 2011.

Freyermuth Enciso, Graciela. 2003a. "Juana's Story." In *Women of Chiapas*, edited by Christine Eber and Christine Kovic. New York: Routledge.

———. 2003b. *Las mujeres de humo. Morir en Chenalhó: Género, étnia y generación, factores constitutivos del riesgo durante la maternidad*. Mexico City: Centro de Investigaciones y Estudios Superiores de Antropología Social / Instituto de la Mujer / Porrúa.

Garza Caligaris, Anna María. 2002. *Género, interlegalidad y conflicto en San Pedro Chenalhó*. Mexico City: Programa de Investigaciones Multidisciplinarias sobre Mesoamérica y el Sureste, Universidad Nacional Autónoma de México–Instituto de Estudios Indígenas / Universidad Autónoma de Chiapas.

Gil Tébar, Pilar. 2003. "Irene: A Catholic Woman in Oxchuc." In *Women of Chiapas*, edited by Christine Eber and Christine Kovic. New York: Routledge.

Gledhill, John. 1997. "Languages of Rights and Struggles for Moral Relations: Exploring the Paradoxes of Popular Protest in Mexico." http://jg.socialsciences.manchester.ac.uk/Languages%20of%20Rights.pdf. Accessed December 18, 2011.

———. 2000 [1994]. *Power and Its Disguises: Perspectives on Politics*. London: Pluto Press.

———. 2003. "Rights and the Poor." In *Human Rights in a Global Perspective: Anthropological Studies of Rights, Claims and Entitlement*, edited by Richard Wilson and Jon P. Mitchell. New York: Routledge.

———. 2008 . "Introduction: Anthropological Perspectives on Indigenous Resurgence in Chiapas." *Identities* 15(5): 483–505.

Gómez Ramírez, Martín. 1991. *Oxchujk': Xlimoxna neel jme'tatik (Oxchuc: Ofrenda de los ancestros)*. Tuxtla Gutiérrez, Mexico: Gobierno del Estado de Chiapas, Instituto Chiapaneco de Cultura.

Goodale, Mark, and Sally Engle Merry, eds. 2007. *The Practice of Human Rights: Tracking Law Between the Global and the Local*. Cambridge: Cambridge University Press.

Gossen, Gary H. 1974. *Chamulas in the World of the Sun: Time and Space in a Maya Oral Tradition*. Cambridge, Mass.: Harvard University Press.

———. 1983. "The Other in Chamula Tzotzil Cosmology and History: Reflections of a Kansan in Chiapas." *Cultural Anthropology* 8(4): 443–75.

———. 1994. "From Olmecs to Zapatistas: A Once and Future History of Souls." *American Anthropologist*, n.s., 96(3): 553–70.

————. 1999. *Telling Maya Tales: Tzotzil Identities in Modern Mexico*. New York: Routledge.

Guiteras Holmes, Calixta. 1947. "Clanes y sistema de parentesco de Cancuc (Mexico)." *Acta Americana* 5(1–2): 1–17.

————. 1952. "Social Organization." In *Heritage of Conquest: The Ethnology of Middle America*, edited by Sol Tax, 97–118. Glencoe: Free Press.

————. 1961. *Perils of the Soul: The World View of a Tzotzil Indian*. [New York]: Free Press of Glencoe.

————. 1992. *Cancuc: Etnografía de un pueblo tzeltal de los Altos de Chiapas, 1944*. Tuxtla Gutiérrez, Mexico: Gobierno del Estado de Chiapas, Instituto Chiapaneco de Cultura.

Gutiérrez, Gustavo. 1996. *Essential Writings*. Maryknoll, N.Y.: Orbis.

Hale, Charles R. 2002. "Does Multiculturalism Menace? Governance, Cultural Rights and the Politics of Identity in Guatemala." *Journal of Latin American Studies* 34(3): 485–523.

————. 2005. "Neoliberal Multiculturalism: The Remaking of Cultural Rights and Racial Dominance in Central America." *Political and Legal Anthropological Review* 28(1): 10–28.

Harvey, Neil. 1998. *The Chiapas Rebellion: The Struggle for Land and Democracy*. Durham, N.C.: Duke University Press.

Hellman, Judith Adler. 1994. "Mexican Popular Movements, Clientelism, and the Process of Democratization." *Latin American Perspectives* 21(2): 124–42.

Henríquez, Elio. 2000. "18 mil indígenas protestan contra el Puebla-Panamá." *La Jornada*, August 17.

Hernández Castillo, R. Aída. 1994. "Identitades colectivas en los márgenes de la nación: Etnicidad y cambio religioso entre los mames de Chiapas." *Nueva Antropología* 13(45): 83–105.

————. 1995. "De la sierra a la selva: Identidades étnicas y religiosas en la frontera sur." In *Chiapas: Los rumbos de otra historia*, edited by Juan Pedro Viqueira and Mario Humberto Ruiz. Mexico City: Universidad Nacional Autónoma de México / Centro de Investigaciones y Estudios Superiores de Antropología Social / Centro de Estudios Mexicanos y Centroamericanos.

————, ed. 1998. *La otra palabra: Mujeres y violencia en Chiapas, antes y después de Acteal*. Mexico City: Centro de Investigaciones y Estudios Superiores de Antropología Social.

————. 2001. *Histories and Stories from Chiapas: Border Identities in Southern Mexico*. Austin: University of Texas Press.

————. 2003. "Between Civil Disobedience and Silent Rejection: Differing Responses by Mam Peasants to the Zapatista Rebellion." In *Mayan Lives, Mayan Utopias: The Indigenous Peoples of Chiapas and the Zapatista Rebellion*, edited by Jan Rus, R. Aída Hernández Castillo, and Shannan L. Mattiace. Lanham, Md.: Rowman and Littlefield.

————. 2006a. "The Indigenous Movement in Mexico: Between Electoral Politics and Local Resistance." *Latin American Perspectives* 33(2): 115–31.

————. 2006b. "Between Feminist Ethnocentricity and Ethnic Essentialism: The Zapatistas' Demands and the National Indigenous Women's Movement." In *Dissident Women*, edited by Shannon Speed, R. Aída Hernández Castillo, and Lynn M. Stephen. Austin: University of Texas Press.

Hewitt, W. E. 1991. *Base Christian Communities and Social Change in Brazil.* Lincoln: University of Nebraska Press.

Hidalgo, Onécimo. 1997. "El vuelo de Las Abejas." *La Jornada*, December 28.

Hill, Robert M., and John Monaghan. 1987. *Continuities in Highland Maya Social Organization: Ethnohistory in Sacapulas, Guatemala.* Philadelphia: University of Pennsylvania Press.

Hirschl, Ran. 2000. "'Negative' Rights vs. 'Positive' Entitlements: A Comparative Study of Judicial Interpretations of Rights in an Emerging Neo-Liberal Economic Order." *Human Rights Quarterly* 22:1060–98.

————. 2008. "The Judicialization of Mega-Politics and the Rise of Political Courts." *Annual Review of Political Science* 11:93–118.

Holston, James. 2008. *Insurgent Citizenship: Disjunctions of Democracy and Modernity in Brazil.* Princeton, N.J.: Princeton University Press.

Holzner, Claudio A. 2006. "Clientelism and Democracy in Mexico: The Role of Strong and Weak Networks." In *Latin American Social Movements: Globalization, Democratization, and Transnational Networks*, edited by Hank Johnston and Paul Almeida, 77–94. Lanham, Md.: Rowman and Littlefield.

Human Rights Watch. 2004. *Human Rights Overview: Mexico*, January 1.

Hunt, Eva, and June Nash. 1967. "Local and Territorial Units." In Social Anthropology, edited by R. Wauchope and Manning Nash, 253–82. Vol. 6 of *Handbook of Middle American Indians*. Austin: University of Texas Press.

Hurley vda. de Delgaty, Alfa, and Agustín Ruiz Sánchez. 1986. *Diccionario tzotzil de San Andrés con variaciones dialectales tzotzil-español/español tzotzil.* Vocabularios Indígenas 22. Mexico City: Instituto Lingüístico de Verano.

INEGI (Instituto Nacional de Estadística y Geografía). 1992. *XI Censo general de población y vivienda, 1990.* Aguascalientes, Mexico: INEGI.

————. 2005. *II Conteo de Población y Vivienda.* Mexico: INEGI, Subsecretaría de Desarrollo Social y Humano, Secretaría de Desarrollo Social.

Instituto Nacional para el Federalismo y el Desarrollo Municipal. 2003. *Enciclopedia de los municipios de México.* Mexico City: Instituto Nacional para el Federalismo y el Desarrollo Municipal, Gobierno del Estado de Chiapas

Ivison, Duncan, Paul Patton, and Will Sanders, eds. 2000. *Political Theory and the Rights of Indigenous Peoples.* Cambridge: Cambridge University Press.

Jacobson, David, and Galya B. Ruffer. 2003. "Courts across Borders: The Implications of Judicial Agency for Human Rights and Democracy." *Human Rights Quarterly* 25:74–92.

Jelin, Elizabeth. 1996. "Citizenship Revisited: Solidarity, Responsibility and Rights." In *Constructing Democracy: Human Rights, Citizenship and Society in Latin America*, edited by Elizabeth Jelin and Eric Hershberg, 101–19. Boulder, Colo.: Westview Press.

———. 2003. "Citizenship and Alterity: Tensions and Dilemmas." *Latin American Perspectives* 30(2): 309–25.

Jelin, Elizabeth, and Eric Hershberg, eds. 1996. *Constructing Democracy: Human Rights, Citizenship and Society in Latin America*. Boulder, Colo.: Westview Press.

Jolom Mayaetik, K'inal Antsetik, and Schweizerische Eidgenossenschaft. 2007. *Voces que tejen y bordan historias: Testimonios de las mujeres de Jolom Mayaetik*. San Cristóbal de Las Casas, Mexico: K'inal Antsetik.

Keck, Margaret E., and Kathryn Sikkink. 1998. *Activists beyond Borders: Advocacy Networks in International Politics*. Ithaca, N.Y.: Cornell University Press.

Kenney, Matthew. 2007. "Notes from San Pedro Chenalhó. Confronting Injustice in the Highlands of Chiapas." http://sampedrano.wordpress.com. Accessed December 18, 2011.

Khagram, Sanjeev, James V. Riker, and Kathryn Sikkink, eds. 2002. *Restructuring World Politics: Transnational Social Movements, Networks, and Norms*. Minneapolis: University of Minnesota Press.

Knight, Alan. 1991. "The Rise and Fall of Cardenismo, c. 1930–c. 1946." In *Mexico Since Independence*, edited by Leslie Bethel, 241–320. Cambridge: Cambridge University Press.

Köhler, Ulrich. 1990. *Zur Ethnographie der Tzotzil von Chenalhó*. Münster, Germany: Institut für Völkerkunde der Albert-Ludwigs-Universität Freiburg.

———. 1995 [1977]. *Chonbilal Ch'ulelal—Alma vendida: Elementos fundamentales de la cosmología y religión mesoamericanas en una oración en maya-tzotzil*. Mexico City: Universidad Nacional Autónoma de México.

Kovic, Christine. 2003a. "The Struggle for Liberation and Reconciliation in Chiapas: Las Abejas and the Path of Nonviolent Resistance." *Latin American Perspectives* 30(3): 58–79.

———. 2003b. "Demanding Their Dignity as Daughters of God: Catholic Women and Human Rights." In *Women of Chiapas*, edited by Christine Eber and Christine Kovic. New York: Routledge.

———. 2005. *Mayan Voices for Human Rights: Displaced Catholics in Highland Chiapas*. Austin: University of Texas Press.

———. 2008. "Rights of the Poor: Progressive Catholicism and Indigenous Resistance in Chiapas." In *Human Rights in the Maya Regionst*, edited by Pedro Pitarch, Shannon Speed, and Xóchitl Leyva -Solano. Durham, N.C.: Duke University Press.

Kovic, Christine, and Christine Eber. 2003. Introduction to *Women of Chiapas*, edited by Christine Eber and Christine Kovic. New York: Routledge.

Lancaster, Roger N. 1988. *Thanks to God and the Revolution: Popular Religion and Class Consciousness in the New Nicaragua.* New York: Columbia University Press.

Laughlin, Robert. 1969. "The Tzotzil." In Ethnology, Part 1, edited by Evon Z. Vogt, 152–94. Vol. 7 of *Handbook of Middle American Indians,* edited by Robert Wauchope. Austin: University of Texas Press.

Levine, Daniel H. 1992. *Popular Voices in Latin American Catholicism.* Princeton, N.J.: Princeton University Press.

Levine, Daniel H., and David Stoll. 1997. "Bridging the Gap between Empowerment and Power in Latin America." In *Transnational Religion and Fading States,* edited by Susanne Hoeber Rudolph and James Piscatori. Boulder, Colo. Westview Press.

Leyva-Solano, Xóchitl. 1995. "Catequistas, misioneros y tradiciones en Las Cañadas." In *Chiapas: Los rumbos de otra historia,* edited by Juan Pedro Viqueira and Mario Humberto Ruiz. Mexico City: Universidad Nacional Autónoma de México / Centro de Investigaciones y Estudios Superiores de Antropología Social / Centro de Estudios Mexicanos y Centroamericanos.

———. 2003. "Regional, Communal, and Organizational Transformations in Las Cañadas." In *Mayan Lives, Mayan Utopias: The Indigenous Peoples of Chiapas and the Zapatista Rebellion,* edited by Jan Rus, R. Aída Hernández Castillo, and Shannan L. Mattiace. Lanham, Md.: Rowman and Littlefield.

López-Montiel, Angel Gustavo. 2000. "The Military, Political Power, and Police Relations in Mexico City." *Latin American Perspectives* 27(2): 79–94.

Lundberg, Matthew D. 2004. "The Blood of the Martyrs is the Seed of Life: Liberation Theology, Martyrdom, and the Prophetic Dimension of Theology." *Koinonia* (Princeton Theological Seminary) 16:1–28.

Marshall, Thomas Humphrey. 1964. *Class, Citizenship and Social Development.* Garden City, N.Y.: Doubleday.

Marshall-Fratani, Ruth. 1998. Mediating the Global and the Local in Nigerian Pentecostalism. *The Journal of Religion in Africa* 28:278–315.

Mattiace, Shannan. 1997 "'¡Zapata vive!': The EZLN, Indigenous Politics, and the Autonomy Movement in Mexico." *Journal of Latin American Anthropology* 3(1): 32–71.

Megged, Amos. 1996. *Exporting the Catholic Reformation: Local Reformation in Early-Colonial Mexico.* New York: E. J. Brill.

Melel Xojobal. 1998–2011. *Sintesis informativa.* Electronic news service (San Cristóbal de Las Casas, Mexico). http://sintesisinformativa-melel.blogspot.com. Accessed February 27, 2012.

Mendez, J. B. 2002. "Gender and Citizenship in a Global Context: The Struggle for Maquila Workers' Rights in Nicaragua." *Identities* 9:7–38.

Merry, Sally Engle. 2006. *Human Rights and Gender Violence: Translating International Law into Local Justice.* Chicago. University of Chicago Press.

Modiano, Nancy. 1990 [1974]. *La educación indígena en los Altos de Chiapas.* Mexico City: Consejo Nacional para la Cultura y las Artes / Instituto Nacional Indigenista.

Moksnes, Heidi. 2000. "Por la paz y los derechos indios: De Chiapas hasta el corazón de México." *La Jornada*, December 10.

———. 2003. "Mayan Suffering, Mayan Rights: Faith and Citizenship among Catholic Tzotziles in Highland Chiapas, Mexico." PhD diss., University of Gothenburg, Sweden.

———. 2004a. "Militarized Democracies: The Neoliberal Mexican State and the Chiapas Uprising." *Social Analysis* 48(1): 116–25. Also published 2004 in *State, Sovereignty, War: Civil Violence in Emerging Global Realities*, edited by Bruce Kapferer. Series: Critical Interventions. A Forum for Social Analysis. New York: Berghahn.

———. 2004b. "Factionalism and Counterinsurgency in Chiapas: Contextualizing the Acteal Massacre." *European Review of Latin American and Caribbean Studies (Revista Europea de Estudios Latinoamericanos y del Caribe)* 75 (April): 109–17.

———. 2005. "Suffering for Justice in Chiapas: Religion and the Globalization of Ethnic Identity." *Journal of Peasant Studies* 32(3–4): 587–607. Also published 2006 in *Rural Chiapas Ten Years after the Zapatista Uprising*, edited by Sarah Washbrook. London: Routledge.

———. 2011. "Independence or Clientelism? Negotiating Indigenous Autonomy in the Urban Setting." *Stockholm Papers in Latin American Studies. Simposio Internacional Independencia y Dependencia en América Latina, 200 Años Después*. Stockholm: Institute of Latin American Studies. www.lai.su.se/splas/200%20 a%C3%B1os.pdf. Accessed February 27, 2012.

Morales Bermúdez, Jesús. 1992. "El Congreso Indígena de Chiapas: Un testimonio." In *Anuario 1991*, 242–370. Tuxtla Gutiérrez, Mexico: Instituto Chiapaneco de Cultura.

Morquecho Escamilla, Gaspar. 1992. "Los indios en un proceso de organización: La Organización Indígena de los Altos de Chiapas, ORIACH." Thesis for the Licenciatura degree, Universidad Autónoma de Chiapas.

Mulhare, Eileen M. 1996a. "Barrio Matters: Toward an Ethnology of Mesoamerican Customary Social Units." *Ethnology* 35(2): 93–106.

———. 1996b. "Preface." *Ethnology* 35(2): 79–80.

Naidoo, Kumi. 2010. "Boiling Point: Can Citizen Action Save the World?" *Development Dialogue* 54 (July).

Nash, June. 1970. *In the Eyes of the Ancestors: Belief and Behavior in a Mayan Community*. Prospect Heights, Ill.: Waveland Press.

———. 1993. "Maya Household Production in the World Market: The Potters of Amatenango del Valle, Chiapas, Mexico." In *Crafts in the World Market: The Impact of Global Exchange on Middle American Artisans*, edited by June Nash. Albany: State University of New York Press.

————. 1995. *The Explosion of Communities in Chiapas*. IWGIA [International Work Group for Foreign Affairs] Document 77. Copenhagen: IWGIA.

————. 2001. *Mayan Visions: The Quest for Autonomy in an Age of Globalization*. New York: Routledge.

Niezen, Ronald. 2000. "Recognizing Indigenism: Canadian Unity and the International Movement of Indigenous Peoples." *Comparative Studies in Society and History* 42(1): 119–48.

Nutini, Hugo G. 1996. Mesoamerican Community Organization: Preliminary Remarks. *Ethnology* 35(2): 81–92.

Ong, Aihwa. 2006. "Mutations in Citizenship." *Theory, Culture and Society* 23(2–3): 499–505.

Paoli, Maria Celia, and Vera da Silva Telles. 1998. "Social Rights: Conflicts and Negotiations in Contemporary Brazil." In *Cultures of Politics, Politics of Cultures*, edited by Sonia E. Alvarez, Evelina Dagnino, and Arturo Escobar. Boulder, Colo.: Westview Press.

Paulson, Joshua. 1998. *Zapatismo News Update: Special Report on the Massacre of Chenalho*. chiapas95@eco.utexas.edu (Chiapas95), a service of the Zapatista Front of National Liberation, January 22. Document in author's possession.

Peel, John D. Y. 1995. "For Who Hath Despised the Day of Small Things? Missionary Narratives and Historical Anthropology." *Comparative Studies in Society and History* 37(3): 581–607.

Peña, Guillermo de la. 2002. "Social Citizenship, Ethnic Minority Demands, Human Rights and Neoliberal Paradoxes: A Case Study in Western Mexico." In *Multiculturalism in Latin America: Indigenous Rights, Diversity and Democracy*, edited by Rachel Sieder, 129–56. New York: Palgrave Macmillan.

Pereira, Anthony W., and Diane E. Davis. 2000. "New Patterns of Militarized Violence and Coercion in the Americas." *Latin American Perspectives* 27(2): 3–17.

Pérez-Enríquez, María Isabel. 1994. *Expulsiones indígenas: Religión y migración en tres municipios de los Altos de Chiapas. Chenalhó, Larráinzar y Chamula*. Mexico City: Claves Latinoamericanas.

Pérez López, Enrique, and Sergio Ramírez Méndez. 1985. *Vida y tradición de San Pablo Chalchihuitán. Slo'il xmaxilik ti ¡Sampaloetike*. Tuxtla Gutiérrez, Mexico: Secretaría de Desarrollo Rural, Subsecretaría de Asuntos Indígenas, Dirección de Fortalecimiento y Fomento a las Culturas de Chiapas.

Pérez Pérez, Elías. 1992. "La escuela presbiteriana y la bilingüe en una comunidad tzotzil, Chimtic, Chiapas: Contrastes y continuidades." Thesis for the Licenciatura degree, Universidad Pedagógica Nacional (Mexico).

Petrich, Blanche. 1997. "La tragedia de los desplazados." *La Jornada*, December 14.

Pickard, Miguel. 2006. "Migration from a Chiapas Perspective." *CIEPAC* (Centro de Investigaciones Económicas y Políticas de Acción Comunitaria) *Bulletin*

519 (September 16). www.ciepac.org/boletines/chiapas_en.php?id=519. Accessed December 20, 2011.

Pineda, Luz Olivia. 1993. *Caciques culturales: El caso de los maestros bilingües en los Altos de Chiapas.*

———. 1995. "Maestros bilingües, burocracia y poder político en los Altos de Chiapas." In *Chiapas: Los rumbos de otra historia,* edited by Juan Pedro Viqueira and Mario Humberto Ruiz. Mexico City: Universidad Nacional Autónoma de México / Centro de Investigaciones y Estudios Superiores de Antropología Social / Centro de Estudios Mexicanos y Centroamericanos.

Pitarch, Pedro, Shannon Speed, and Xóchitl Leyva-Solano. 2008. *Human Rights in the Maya Region: Global Politics, Cultural Contentions, and Moral Engagements.* Durham, N.C.: Duke University Press.

Pozas Arciniega, Ricardo. 1987 [1977]. *Chamula.* Mexico City: Instituto Nacional Indigenista.

Procuraduría General de la República (Mexico). 1998. *White Paper on Acteal, Chiapas.* Mexico City: Procuraduría General de la República.

Ramírez Cuevas, Jesús. 1997. "Chiapas, mapa de la contrainsurgencia." *La Jornada,* November 23.

Robledo Hernández, Gabriela Patricia. 2003. "Protestantism and Family Dynamics in an Indigenous Community of Highland Chiapas." In *Women of Chiapas,* edited by Christine Eber and Christine Kovic. New York: Routledge.

Rocha Menocal, Alina. 2005. "Less Political and More Pro-Poor? The Evolution of Social Welfare Spending in Mexico in a Context of Democratisation and Decentralization." *Nord-Süd Aktuell* 3–4:346–59.

Rockwell, Elsie. 1994. "Schools of the Revolution: Enacting and Contesting State Forms in Tlaxcala, 1910–1930." In *Everyday Forms of State Formation: Revolution and the Negotiation of Rule in Modern Mexico,* edited by Gilbert M. Joseph and Daniel Nugent, 170–208. Durham, N.C.: Duke University Press.

Rosenbaum, Brenda. 1993. *With Our Heads Bowed: The Dynamics of Gender in a Maya Community.* Albany: Institute for Mesoamerican Studies, State University of New York.

Ross, John. 2007. "Ten Years after Acteal: New Massacres Loom in Mexico." *Counterpunch,* December 21.

Rostas, Susanna. 2003. "Women's Empowerment through Religious Change in Tenejapa." In *Women of Chiapas,* edited by Christine Eber and Christine Kovic. New York: Routledge.

Ruiz García, Samuel. 1993. *En esta hora de gracia. Carta pastoral.* Mexico City: Ediciones Dabar.

Ruiz Hernández, Margarito. 2000. "The Plural National Indigenous Assembly for Autonomy (ANIPA)." In *Indigenous Autonomy in Mexico,* edited by Araceli Burguete Cal y Mayor. IWGIA [International Work Group for Foreign Affairs] Document 94. Copenhagen: IWGIA.

Ruiz Mondragón, Ariel. 2003. "Desmitificar Chiapas. Bibliálogos: Entrevista con el historiador Juan Pedro Viqueira." *La Insignia* (Madrid). www.lainsignia. org/2003/marzo/cul_041.htm. Accessed December 20, 2011.

Rus, Diane, and Jan Rus. 2008. "The Migration of Indigenous Workers from Highland Chiapas to the United States, 2001–2005: The Case of San Juan Chamula." In *Migraciones en el sur de México y Centroamérica*, edited by Daniel Villafuerte Solís and María del Carmen García Águilar. Tuxtla Gutiérrez, Mexico: Universidad de Ciencias y Artes de Chiapas / Porrúa.

Rus, Jan. 1994. "The 'Comunidad Revolucionaria Institucional': The Subversion of Native Government in Highland Chiapas, 1936–1968." In *Everyday Forms of State Formation: Revolution and the Negotiation of Rule in Modern Mexico*, edited by Gilbert Joseph and Daniel Nugent, 265–300. Durham, N.C.: Duke University Press.

———. 1997. "Shared Destinies: Lineage and the Redefinition of Identity among the Tzotzils of Chiapas, Mexico." Paper presented at the annual meeting of the American Anthropological Association, Washington, D.C., November 20–24.

———. 2002. Afterword to *The Four Creations, An Epic Story of the Chiapas Maya*, by Gary H. Gossen. Norman: University of Oklahoma Press.

———. 2004. "Revoluciones contenidas: Los indígenas y la lucha por los Altos de Chiapas, 1910–1925 (Contained Revolutions: Indians and the Struggle for Control of Highland Chiapas, 1910–1925)." *Mesoamérica* 46:57–85.

———. 2009. "La nueva ciudad maya en el valle de Jovel: Urbanización acelerada, juventud indígena y comunidad en San Cristóbal de Las Casas." In *Chiapas después de la tormenta: Estudios en economía, sociedad y política*, edited by Marco Estrada Saavedra. Mexico City: Colegio de México / Comisión de Concordia y Pacificación (COCOPA).

———. 2010. "The End of the Plantations and the Transformation of Indigenous Society in Highland Chiapas, Mexico, 1974–2009." PhD diss., University of California, Riverside.

Rus, Jan, R. Aída Hernández Castillo, and Shannan L. Mattiace, eds. 2001. "The Indigenous Peoples of Chiapas and the State in the Time of Zapatismo: Remaking Culture, Renegotiating Power." *Latin American Perspectives* 28(2).

———, eds. 2003. *Mayan Lives, Mayan Utopias: The Indigenous Peoples of Chiapas and the Zapatista Rebellion*. Lanham, Md.: Rowman and Littlefield.

Rus, Jan, and Diego Vigil. 2007. "Rapid Urbanization and Migrant Indigenous Youth in San Cristóbal, Chiapas, Mexico." In *Gangs in the Global City*, edited by John Hagedorn. Urbana: University of Illinois Press.

Rus, Jan, and Robert Wasserstrom. 1980. "Civil-Religious Hierarchies in Central Chiapas: A Critical Perspective." *American Anthropologist* 7:446–78.

Sánchez Franco, Irene. 2004. "Las transformaciones de la diócesis de San Cristóbal de Las Casas." In *Anuario 2003*, 42–68. Tuxtla Gutiérrez, Chiapas: Centro de Estudios Superiores de México y Centroamérica, Universidad de Ciencias y Artes del Estado de Chiapas.

Sanders, Douglas E. 1977. *The Formation of the World Council of Indigenous Peoples.* IWGIA [International Work Group for Foreign Affairs] Document 29. Copenhagen: IWGIA.

Sassen, Saskia. 2003. "Economic Globalization and the Redrawing of Citizenship." In *Globalization, the State, and Violence*, edited by Jonathan Friedman, 67–86. Walnut Creek, Calif.: Altamira Press.

Scheper-Hughes, Nancy. 1992. *Death without Weeping: The Violence of Everyday Life in Brazil.* Berkeley and Los Angeles: University of California Press.

Schild, Veronica. 1998. "New Subjects of Rights? Women's Movements and the Construction of Citizenship in the 'New Democracies.'" In *Cultures of Politics, Politics of Cultures*, edited by Sonia E. Alvarez, Evelina Dagnino, and Arturo Escobar, 93–117. Boulder, Colo.: Westview Press.

Schlittler Álvarez, Jaime. 2008. "Etnogénesis y martirio: La masacre de Acteal y su relación con la construcción de la identidad de la sociedad civil Las Abejas." Thesis for the Licenciatura degree, Universidad Iberoamericana (Mexico).

Scotchmer, David G. 1986. Convergence of the Gods: Comparing Traditional Maya and Christian Maya Cosmologies. In *Symbol and Meaning beyond the Closed Community: Essays in Mesoamerican Ideas*, edited by Gary H. Gossen, 197–226. Institute for Mesoamerican Studies. Albany: State University of New York.

Scott, James C. 1985. *Weapons of the Weak: Everyday Forms of Peasant Resistance.* New Haven: Yale University Press.

———. 1990. *Domination and the Arts of Resistance: Hidden Transcripts.* New Haven: Yale University Press.

Shafir, Gershon, and Alison Brysk. 2006. "The Globalization of Rights: From Citizenship to Human Rights." *Citizenship Studies* 10(3): 275–87.

Shefner, Jon. 2008. *The Illusion of Civil Society: Democratization and Community Mobilization in Low Income Mexico.* University Park: Pennsylvania State University Press.

Sherman, William L. 1979. *Forced Native Labor in Sixteenth Century Central America.* Lincoln: University of Nebraska Press.

Sieder, Rachel, ed. 2002. *Multiculturalism in Latin America: Indigenous Rights, Diversity and Democracy.* New York: Palgrave Macmillan.

Sieder, Rachel, Line Schjolden, and Alan Angell, eds. 2005. *The Judicialization of Politics in Latin America.* New York: Palgrave Macmillan.

Sierra Guzmán, Jorge Luis. 2003. *El Enemigo Interno: Contrainsurgencia y fuerzas armadas en México.* Mexico City: Centro de Estudios Estratégicos de América del Norte / Universidad Iberoamericana / Plaza y Valdés.

Silverstein, Ken, and Alexander Cockburn. 1995. "Major U.S. Bank Urges Zapatista Wipe-Out: 'A Litmus Test for Mexico's Stability.'" *Counterpunch* 2, no. 3 (February 1).

SIPAZ (Servicio Internacional por la Paz). 2001. "The Mexican Army: A Key Factor in the Conflict in Chiapas," *SIPAZ Report* 6, no. 1 (February).

Sistema de Información Campesino. 2007. "Situación política en Chenalhó." *Nexos* 358 (October).

Siverts, Henning. 1965. *Oxchujk': En maya-stamme i Mexico.* Bergen, Norway: Universitetsforlaget.

Smith, Peter H. 1991. "Mexico Since 1946: Dynamics of an Authoritarian Regime." In *Mexico Since Independence,* edited by Leslie Bethel, 321–96. Cambridge: Cambridge University Press.

Sobrino, Jon. 2001. *Los mártires y la teología de la liberación.* http://servicioskoinonia.org/relat/162.htm. Originally published 1995 in *Sal Terrae* (October): 699–716.

Sociedad Bíblica de México. 1997. *Sch'ul C'op Jtotic Dios: Santa Biblia.* Mexico: Sociedad Bíblica de México.

Speed, Shannon. 2002. "Global Discourses on the Local Terrain: Human Rights and Indigenous Identity in Chiapas." *Cultural Dynamics* 14(2): 205–28

———. 2003. "Actions Speaks Louder than Words: Indigenous Women and Gendered Resistance in the Wake of Acteal." In *Women of Chiapas,* edited by Christine Eber and Christine Kovic. New York: Routledge.

———. 2008. *Rights in Rebellion: Indigenous Struggle and Human Rights in Chiapas.* Stanford: Stanford University Press.

Speed, Shannon, and Álvaro Reyes. 2005. "Rights, Resistance, and Radical Alternatives: The Red de Defensores Comunitarios and Zapatismo in Chiapas." *Humboldt Journal of Social Relations* 29(1): 47–82.

Speed, Shannon, and Xóchitl Leyva-Solano. 2008. "Global Discourses on the Local Terrain: Human Rights in Chiapas." In *Human Rights in the Maya Region,* edited by Pedro Pitarch, Shannon Speed, and Xóchitl Leyva-Solano. Durham, N.C.: Duke University Press.

Speed, Shannon, R. Aída Hernández Castillo, and Lynn M. Stephen, eds. 2006. *Dissident Women: Gender and Cultural Politics in Chiapas.* Austin: University of Texas Press.

Spronk, Susan, and Jeffery R. Webber. 2007. "Struggles Against Accumulation by Dispossession in Bolivia: The Political Economy of Natural Resource Contention." *Latin American Perspectives* 34(2): 31–47.

Stahler-Sholk, Richard. 2007. "Resisting Neoliberal Homogenization: The Zapatista Autonomy Movement." *Latin American Perspectives* 34(2): 48–63.

Stahler-Sholk, Richard, and Harry E. Vanden. 2011. "A Second Look at Latin American Social Movements: Globalizing Resistance to the Neoliberal Paradigm." *Latin American Perspectives* 38(1): 5–13.

Stahler-Sholk, Richard, Harry E. Vanden, and Glen David Kuecker. 2007. "Globalizing Resistance: The New Politics of Social Movements in Latin America." *Latin American Perspectives* 34(2): 5–16.

Stavenhagen, Rodolfo. 1992. *The Ethnic Question: Conflicts, Development, and Human Rights.* Tokyo: United Nations Press.

———. 2002. "Indigenous Peoples and the State in Latin America: An Ongoing Debate." In *Multiculturalism in Latin America: Indigenous Rights, Diversity and Democracy,* edited by Rachel Sieder, 24–44. New York: Palgrave Macmillan.

Stephen, Lynn M.. 1997. "Redefined Nationalism in Building a Movement for Indigenous Autonomy in Southern Mexico." *Journal of Latin American Anthropology* 3(1): 72–10.

———. 1999. "The First Anniversary of the Acteal Massacre: A Wake-up Call to the Militarization of Mexico." *Cultural Survival Quarterly* 23, no. 1 (Spring): 27–29. Electronic version available at www.culturalsurvival.org/publications/cultural-survival-quarterly/mexico/first-anniversary-acteal-massacre-chiapas. Accessed February 27, 2012.

———. 2006. "Indigenous Women's Activism in Oaxaca and Chiapas." In *Dissident Women,* edited by Shannon Speed, R. Aída Hernández Castillo, and Lynn M. Stephen. Austin: University of Texas Press.

Sullivan, Kathleen. 1992. "Protagonists of Change." *Cultural Survival Quarterly* 16, no. 4 (Winter): 38–40. Electronic version available at www.culturalsurvival.org/publications/cultural-survival-quarterly/mexico/protagonists-change. Accessed December 21, 2011.

Swords, Alicia C. S. 2007. "Neo-Zapatista Network Politics: Transforming Democracy and Development." *Latin American Perspectives* 34(2): 78–93.

Tavanti, Marco. 2003. *Las Abejas: Pacifist Resistance and Syncretic Identities in a Globalizing Chiapas.* New York: Routledge.

———. 2005. "Chiapas Civil Society Organizations: Cultural Resistance and Economic Alternatives through Fair Trade Cooperatives and International Networks." Paper presented at the 5th International Society for Third-Sector Research (ISTS) Regional Conference for Latin America and the Caribbean, "Sociedad Civil, Participación Ciudadana y Desarrollo, " Universidad Ricardo Palma, Lima, Peru. http://works.bepress.com/cgi/viewcontent.cgi?article=1021&context=marcotavanti. Accessed December 21, 2011.

Tax, Sol. 1937. "The Municipios of the Midwestern Highlands of Guatemala." *American Anthropology* 39(3): 423–44.

Tedlock, Barbara. 1992 [1982]. *Time and the Highland Maya.* Albuquerque: University of New Mexico Press.

Thomas, Norman D. 1979. "The Mesoamerican Barrio: A Reciprocity Model for Community Organization." In *From Tzintzuntzan to the "Image of the Limited Good": Essays in Honor of George M. Foster,* edited by M. Clark, R.V. Kemper, and C. Nelson, 45–58. Berkeley, Calif.: Kroeber Anthropological Society Papers.

Toledo Tello, Sonia, and Anna María Garza Caligaris. 2003. "Gender and Stereotypes in the Social Movements in Chiapas." In *Dissident Women,* edited by

Shannon Speed, R. Aída Hernández Castillo, and Lynn M. Stephen. Austin: University of Texas Press.

Torres Burguete, Jaime. 2000. "Actores y lucha por el poder en Chenalhó: Una visión desde adentro." *Memoria* (Centro de Estudios del Movimiento Obrero y Socialista [CEMOS], Mexico), no. 139.

Turner, Terence. 2003. "Class Projects, Social Consciousness, and the Contradictions of 'Globalization.'" In *Globalization, the State, and Violence*, edited by Jonathan Friedman, 35–66. Walnut Creek, Calif.: Altamira Press.

Van der Haar, Gemma. 2001. *Gaining Ground: Land Reform and the Constitution of Community in the Tojolabal Highlands of Chiapas, Mexico.* Latin American Research Series. Amsterdam: Rozenberg.

Viqueira, Juan Pedro. 1995. "Las causas de una rebelión india: Chiapas, 1712." In *Chiapas: Los rumbos de otra historia,* edited by Juan Pedro Viqueira and Mario Humberto Ruiz. Mexico City: Universidad Nacional Autónoma de México / Centro de Investigaciones y Estudios Superiores de Antropología Social / Centro de Estudios Mexicanos y Centroamericanos.

Viqueira, Juan Pedro, and Mario Humberto Ruiz, eds. 1995. *Chiapas: Los rumbos de otra historia.* Mexico City: Universidad Nacional Autónoma de México / Centro de Investigaciones y Estudios Superiores de Antropología Social / Centro de Estudios Mexicanos y Centroamericanos.

Vogt, Evon Z. 1969. *Zinacantán: A Maya Community in the Highlands of Chiapas.* Cambridge, Mass.: Harvard University Press.

———. 1976. *Tortillas for the Gods: A Symbolic Analysis of Zinacanteco Rituals.* Cambridge, Mass.: Harvard University Press.

Vos, Jan de. 1994. *Vivir en la frontera: La experiencia de los indios de Chiapas.* Mexico City: Centro de Investigaciones y Estudios Superiores en Antropología Social / Instituto Nacional Indigenista.

Warren, Kay B. 1978. *The Symbolism of Subordination: Indian Identity in a Guatemalan Town.* Austin: University of Texas Press.

Warren, Kay B., and Jean E. Jackson, eds. 2002. *Indigenous Movements, Self-Representation and the State in Latin America.* Austin: University of Texas Press.

Wasserstrom, Robert. 1983. *Class and Society in Central Chiapas.* Berkeley and Los Angeles: University of California Press.

Watanabe, John M. 1990. "From Saints to Shibboleths: Image, Structure, and Identity in Maya Religious Syncretism." *American Ethnology* 17(1): 131–50.

Webster, Douglas D. 1984. "Liberation Theology." In *Evangelical Dictionary of Theology,* edited by Walter A. Elwell. Grand Rapids, Mich.: Baker Academic. Reprinted online at http://mb-soft.com/believe/txn/liberati.htm. Accessed December 21, 2011.

Wilson, Richard. 1995. *Maya Resurgence in Guatemala: Q'eqchi' Experiences.* Norman: University of Oklahoma Press.

Wilson, Richard, and Jon P. Mitchell, eds. 2003. *Human Rights in Global Perspective: Anthropological Studies of Rights, Claims and Entitlements.* New York: Routledge.

Woodiwiss, Anthony. 2002. "Human Rights and the Challenge of Cosmopolitanism." *Theory, Culture and Society* 19(1–2): 139–55.

Yashar, Deborah. 2005. *Contesting Citizenship in Latin America: The Rise of Indigenous Movements and the Postliberal Challenge.* Cambridge: Cambridge University Press.

———. 2007. "Resistance and Identity Politics in an Age of Globalization." *Annals of the American Academy of Political and Social Science* 610:160–81.

Zunino, Mariela. 2010. "Integración para el despojo: el Proyecto Mesoamérica, o la nueva escalada de apropiación del territorio," pt. 1–3. *CIEPAC* (Centro de Investigaciones Económicas y Políticas de Acción Comunitaria) *Bulletin* 585 (June 21).

Index

CPSIA information can be obtained at www.ICGtesting.com
Printed in the USA
LVOW080121220912

299871LV00003B/1/P